# Transforming Mozambique
## The Politics of Privatization, 1975–2000

Many of the economic transformations in Africa have been as dramatic as those in Eastern Europe. Yet much of the comparative literature on transitions has overlooked African countries. This study of Mozambique's shift from a command to a market economy draws on a wealth of empirical material, including archival sources, interviews, political posters and corporate advertisements, to reveal that the state is a central actor in the reform process, despite the claims of neo-liberals and their critics. Alongside the state, social forces – from World Bank officials to rural smallholders – have also accelerated, thwarted, or shaped change in Mozambique. M. Anne Pitcher offers an intriguing analysis of the dynamic interaction between previous and emerging agents, ideas and institutions, to explain the erosion of socialism and the politics of privatization in a developing country. She demonstrates that Mozambique's present political economy is a heterogeneous blend of ideological and institutional continuities and ruptures.

M. ANNE PITCHER is Associate Professor of Political Science and the African Studies Co-ordinator for the Africana and Latin American Studies Program at Colgate University, Hamilton, New York. She is the author of *Politics in the Portuguese Empire: The State, Industry, and Cotton*, 1926–1974 (1993), and has published widely on African topics in edited collections and journals.

T0381712

# Transforming Mozambique

*The Politics of Privatization, 1975–2000*

## M. Anne Pitcher

*Colgate University, Hamilton, New York*

CAMBRIDGE
UNIVERSITY PRESS

CAMBRIDGE UNIVERSITY PRESS
Cambridge, New York, Melbourne, Madrid, Cape Town, Singapore, São Paulo

Cambridge University Press
The Edinburgh Building, Cambridge CB2 8RU, UK

Published in the United States of America by Cambridge University Press, New York

www.cambridge.org
Information on this title: www.cambridge.org/9780521820110

First published 2002
This digitally printed version 2008

A catalogue record for this publication is available from the British Library

ISBN 978-0-521-82011-0 hardback
ISBN 978-0-521-05268-9 paperback

In memory of my father, Charles Scholey Pitcher and my friend, Scott Kloeck-Jenson

# Contents

# Figures

# Preface

Little noticed amidst the fanfare surrounding regime changes in Eastern Europe, Latin America and Africa, the formerly socialist country of Mozambique has undergone a tumultuous transition to democracy and capitalism in the last ten years. Its privatization program has been called the most "successful" in Africa, while the peaceful completion of two national elections suggests that the chances for democratic consolidation are at least as good as, and probably much better than, many countries in the rest of Africa. The purpose of this book is to situate Mozambique's experiences within the comparative literature on the erosion of socialism and the transformation to a market economy. I focus on the politics of privatization in order to draw conclusions about the role of the state and social forces in structuring, challenging, supporting and undermining comprehensive change in transitional countries. I argue that although privatization has certainly altered the role of state institutions in Mozambique, the process and outcome of privatization have not eliminated state power, only redirected it. These findings challenge claims by supporters of neo-liberalism that transitions have been "revolutionary."

My initial approach to understanding Mozambique's transition from socialism to capitalism was to give a great deal of weight to international factors. When I first got interested in Mozambique in the 1980s, some of the more influential secondary literature placed the blame for the failure of socialism in Mozambique on South Africa's support for the counter-revolutionary movement, Renamo, and on policies of destabilization practiced by Western countries. Government pronouncements did not seem to disagree, and frequently blamed the South African backed "bandidos armados" for undermining the goals of the socialist and nationalist revolution. When I finally arrived in Mozambique in 1992, just before the signing of the accord that would end the seventeen-year conflict, my views only seemed to be confirmed. International "forces" were ubiquitous. Taxi drivers in the war-torn capital of Maputo demanded dollars and the lettering of the UN adorned every tenth car on the road. Employees of every nongovernmental organization from Oxfam to World Vision crammed the streets and gazed out of the open-air restaurants and cafes on the main boulevards of the capital.

The impact of the international context and the role of international actors in Mozambique have been important, but repeated fieldwork in Mozambique together with my study of transitions elsewhere have downgraded my assessment of their role from "determinative" to "influential." Since 1992, I have been to Mozambique four more times. On three of these occasions, I engaged in extensive fieldwork, worked in the archives, and conducted numerous interviews. Each of these methods has shaped in profound ways my analysis of Mozambique's transition from a country that was committed to socialism following independence to a country that has now adopted the principles of the market and the procedures of democracy.

My fieldwork has taken me from the factory floors of Maputo and Nampula City to the fields of Sofala, Zambezia, Nampula, and Cabo Delgado Provinces. Surveys and interviews with over a hundred rural inhabitants revealed the persistence of colonial practices and relations, and the endurance of rural distrust of institutions of power, not the ubiquity of international forces. In one village in Meconta District, Nampula, a simmering conflict over the price of cotton that pitted local and national state officials and company employees against rural producers recalled similar incidents from the colonial period. In another locality, frequent denunciations by smallholders of communal villages, state farms, party secretaries, and other Frelimo inventions reinforced the notion that not all of the blame for what had happened in Mozambique could be lain at the door of international interests, nor was assigning "blame" the most productive way of reflecting on what had happened to Mozambique. Most importantly, fieldwork revealed the ingenuity and the insecurity, the resistance and the resilience of rural peoples. While rural communities were internally differentiated, and some households were beset with conflict, local peoples had also devised individual and collective strategies to ignore, shape, or stop policies with which they disagreed. Where appropriate, I draw on extensive surveys and interviews with smallholders and local officials to present their responses to events since independence. Most of the household surveys (HS), group interviews, and individual interviews took place in the "cotton belt" of northern Mozambique. Cotton is one of the main exports of Mozambique and involves the participation of about a quarter of a million smallholders. The views of smallholders in cotton areas thus shed some light on the experiences of rural producers since independence. Also, I opted to examine provinces in northern Mozambique to balance the findings from the relatively more researched southern provinces.

I began in 1994 with a small pilot study of fifteen households in Montepuez District, Cabo Delgado. Based on those findings, I then devised a detailed survey consisting of both closed and open-ended questions. I administered these with the aid of Makua-Portuguese interpreters to over 100 households in Meconta, Monapo, and Mecuburi districts of Nampula Province during selected periods of fieldwork in 1994–95. Notably, all of the informants were either single, widowed, or divorced women, or couples. The inclusion of women in all surveys thus departed from the assumption in some of the recent work by agricultural economists on rural households in Mozambique that the man is the "head of household." By speaking with women alone or along with their husbands, I gained a more nuanced understanding of the skills and strategies they employed to survive the disruptions brought by natural disasters, war, and government policies. Part of the results and the methodological approach used in the surveys have previously been published in *African Studies Review* and the *Journal of Southern African Studies*. For enabling me to hear the stories of smallholders, I want to thank my translators from Portugese into Makua, the local language of much of the north; they were Lourenço Muarapaz, Guilherme Afonso, Juberto Moane, and João Lameiras. I appreciate greatly that those women and men with whom I spoke spent what little leisure time they had to share their experiences with me.

Rural challenges have not stopped with the peace accord. In some areas, rural peoples struggle to retain land that new investors claim, or they engage in conflicts with commercial operations over water and other resources. This was particularly the case in parts of Zambezia Province, where Scott Kloeck-Jenson and I conducted interviews with government officials, company directors, and rural peoples who had lost land following the "sale" of property to private investors by the Zambezia Company. We also carried out a survey in May of 1998 in the *localidade* (locality) of Mutange, Namacurra District, where we interviewed a small cross-section of residents to gain information on resource use and conflict in the area. The semi-structured survey of twenty-one households included six couples where we interviewed husbands and wives separately in order to gain insight into gendered understandings of resource rights and use. For the translation from Portuguese into Chuabo, we were very grateful to have the aid of Scott's long-term assistant, Raul Amade, and his cousin, Esperança. In the bibliography, I refer to all interviews and surveys in Zambezia as having been conducted with Scott Kloeck-Jenson. Part of the findings and the methodology of that research are published in Rachel Waterhouse and Carin Vijfhuizen, eds., *Estratégias das Mulheres, Proveito dos Homens: Género, Terra e Recursos Naturais em Diferentes Contextos Rurais em Moçambique*.

Study of archival material and secondary sources both preceded and followed my fieldwork. The Middlemas archives at Hoover Institution, Stanford University, consist of dozens of taped transcriptions by Keith Middlemas, Professor Emeritus of Sussex University. Professor Middlemas made these transcriptions from notes he took during interviews with Frelimo party members, state officials, diplomats, and company managers in Mozambique just after independence. They offer much insight into government and party deliberations regarding the decision to take over private companies, and they convey the reactions of company directors once nationalizations became a reality. They proved valuable in delineating the external pressures and internal constraints that the regime confronted during that critical period in the transition to socialism. Correspondence with Professor Middlemas clarified some of my questions about his interviews, and I am grateful to both the Hoover Institution and Professor Middlemas for making the material available to me.

Furthermore, resources at the Archivo Histórico de Moçambique (AHM) and the Centro de Estudos Africanos (CEA) in Maputo, Mozambique, strengthened and extended the research on colonial companies that I had collected at the Bibliotéca Nacional in Portugal during the 1980s. Through the use of newspapers, journals, telephone books, and government reports, I was able to trace what had happened to some of the former colonial companies in industry, commerce, banking, and agriculture after 1975. António Sopa, the staff at AHM and the librarians at CEA generously provided sources and suggestions to aid me with my work. In addition, a wonderful collection at the AHM of the iconography dating from the socialist period until the present offered a pictorial guide to how the government enacted socialism, what issues the regime considered the most important, and how it visually constructed these issues for the populace. I am thankful to those who worked with the collection, particularly Maria das Neves G. Cochofel, for showing me so much of the material they had gathered. Smaller collections of indexed newspaper articles at the Mediafax office and the Ministry of State Administration, and government reports at the Ministry of Agriculture, enhanced my understanding of why socialism eroded, how privatization was adopted, and who benefitted from this change. Copies of the newspaper articles that I collected from these latter institutions between 1994 and 1998 have been deposited at the CEA library. Moreover, my study of the impact of privatization would have been immeasurably more difficult had it not been for the superb investigative reporting skills of Carlos Cardoso, who founded and edited the on-line newspaper *Metical*. The assassination of this courageous and respected Mozambican journalist in November 2000 surely has dealt a serious blow to the struggle for press freedom.

Finally, interviews, conversations, and personal communications with government officials, bank directors, company managers, and representatives of non-governmental organizations from the World Bank to World Vision have enriched my analysis of the recent transformation to a market economy. With the generous support of a Fulbright grant from January to June, 1998, I conducted interviews with managers of some of the largest and oldest companies in the country, such as Grupo Entreposto and João Ferreira dos Santos, as well as with foreign investors. I interviewed directors from the oldest to the youngest banks in the country, and spoke at length with officials from the Ministry of Agriculture (national and district levels), the Ministry of Finances, the Ministry of Industry, Trade, and Tourism, and the Sugar, Cotton, and Cashew Institutes.

I talked with those national, provincial, and district government officials who were in charge of privatization in industry and agriculture.

Two major points emerged from the interviews – one about government and the other about the interaction of social forces with government institutions. The first point was the extent to which the Mozambican government "owned" the transformation. Implementing the process of privatization and enforcing the other strictures of structural adjustment required great participation by the state. State ministries, state units, state centers, state commissions, and state cabinets, organized the sale of state companies, prepared the dossiers, conducted the valuations, accepted bids, decided on the winners, and handed over the keys to companies. It was the state that confronted the problems of salaries in arrears, untrained personnel, and worker layoffs. And it was the state that monitored the new private operations, imposed taxes, and regulated firm behavior. The demands of the international financial institutions, Western donors, and a new constituency of private investors influenced the activity of government officials, but they did not determine it. These findings revealed to me that claims about the success of privatization have been quite superficial. They have narrowly noted that sales have taken place without looking at the role of government in the process or who the purchasers were.

Second, however, the interviews exposed the extent to which social groups, from smallholders to the private sector, "enfeebled," "excluded," and "empowered" the state – to paraphrase a claim made by Migdal, et al. – since independence. My work seeks to capture that dynamic of state-society interaction. I argue that it has not disappeared during the privatization process, not in Mozambique, and not in the rest of Africa. Some social groups have lost and others have gained from transformation, but throughout, their role has been integral to the story of how and why changes occurred the way that they did.

This study has been aided throughout by the previous work of scholars on Mozambique and the work of other scholars in the field, by the financial support of various institutions, and by the encouragement of my peers and my family. In Mozambique, I had stimulating conversations with other scholars such as Nina Bowen, Teresa Cruz e Silva, David Hedges, Arlindo Chilundo, Luis Covane, Natalina Monteiro, Paulo Mole, David Tschirley, Scott Kloeck-Jenson, Rachel Waterhouse, Ken Wilson, and those who came to the papers I presented at the Nucleus for the Study of Land and the CEA at Eduardo Mondlane University. To understand the rise of the private sector in Mozambique, I benefited enormously from conversations and interviews with Lisa Audet, Alan Harding, Louis Helling, Scott Jazynka, Américo Magaia, Raimundo Matule, António Machado, Egas Mussanhane, Arahni Sont and Fion de Vletter. Of the many government officials I interviewed or encountered, I also want to give special thanks to the director of the Cotton Institute, Erasmo Muhate, for his thoughtful comments and the unflagging support he has given me since 1994. He returned every phone call, followed up every query, responded to every email, and shared a great deal of information on cotton with me. More importantly, the integrity and dedication he brought to his work made a lasting impression on me. His example challenged the image of the rent-seeking, venal bureaucrat that has lately become so common in the literature on Africa.

Outside of Mozambique, the work of Peter Evans, Jean-Francois Bayart, Sara Berry, James Scott, and David Stark provided the theoretical signposts to guide me on my empirical journey and I owe a great intellectual debt to their work. Reading Scott's analysis of the Tanzanian and Russian experiments with collectivization in *Seeing Like a State* resonated so closely with the Mozambique experience that it was both horrifying and exciting to note the similarities. Bayart's masterful portrayal of the networks and alliances among African elites in *The State in Africa: The Politics of the Belly* helped me greatly to unravel the politics embedded in the privatization process of Mozambique, and the work of Evans convinced me how important the state was to this process. Finally, Berry and Scott reminded me that even those most marginalized from the political process find the means and the voice to negotiate or revise policies with which they disagree.

A Picker Fellowship, major grants from Colgate University in 1994 and 1995, and a Fulbright scholarship from the J. William Fulbright Scholarship Board provided financial support. The CEA under the direction of Dr. Teresa Cruz e Silva warmly served as the host institution for the Fulbright when I was in Mozambique in 1998. Harriet McGuire, the public affairs officer of the United States Information Service, which administered the Fulbright in Mozambique, unselfishly offered her assistance on all sorts of matters even after my departure. Furthermore, the following people and institutions – the joint Michigan State University/Ministry of Agriculture and Rural Development Project; Bill Messiter, formerly of Care-Mozambique; Nina Bowen and family; and the Land Tenure Center of the University of Wisconsin-Madison – supplied technical and logistical support for some of the fieldwork in northern Mozambique. The secretarial staff at Colgate University, particularly Cindy Terrier, gave valuable computer advice, while the reference librarians at Case Library were consistently helpful and accomodating. Ray Nardelli, Educational Technology Specialist of the Collaboration for Enhanced Learning at Colgate digitally reproduced the political poster and the company advertisements for the book's cover and for the illustrations in chapter 7. I would also like to thank António Sopa of the AHM and the companies who gave permission to reproduce the images used in the text. Two anonymous reviewers for Cambridge University Press also provided helpful comments. I am grateful to these organizations and individuals for aiding the completion of this work.

My colleagues, students, family and friends have shared their wisdom and listened to my ideas over the years. Conversations with Eric and Jessica

Allina-Pisano, Arlindo Chilundo, Kate Christen, Allen Isaacman, Liz MacGonagle, Carrie Manning, Mary Moran, Eric Morier-Genoud, Jeanne Penvenne, Kathie Sheldon, Rachel Stringfellow, and Sheri Young intellectually sustained me on my scholarly journey and I am very grateful. I especially want to thank my dear friend, Eric Morier-Genoud, who has supported my work and encouraged my ideas in countless ways. My husband, Martin Murray, has been generous with his praise, restrained in his criticisms, and, when all else fails, lavish in his attentions, and I am most appreciative.

Moments of great joy and sorrow have accompanied the research and the writing of this book. I want to end this preface with a dedication to two of the people who have been responsible for those moments. My husband and I welcomed our daughter, Alida Claeys Pitcher-Murray, into the world on 9 September 1997. From the minute of her arrival she has brought much happiness to her two brothers, Andrew and Jeremy, and to us. In January of 1998, the three of us left for Mozambique to begin my Fulbright grant, but *en route* I learned that my father had died and we had to return to the States. Nothing prepared me for the loss of someone who had been such a constant friend and mentor my whole life. My father was always there with a bit of humor or some astute observation to help me put things in perspective, and I greatly miss our friendship. He also had a wonderful gift for holding listeners spellbound as he wove a tale of sordid intrigue or great hilarity. I miss the inflections in his voice as he worked his way towards a dramatic denouement.

I encountered that mixture of humor and humanity also in my friend and colleague, Scott Kloeck-Jenson. When my family and I finally settled in Mozambique, Scott, his wife, Barbara, and their two kids, Noah and Zoe, warmly welcomed us into their home. As people often do when they are not in their "terra de natal," we bonded quickly and spent many evenings sharing funny and sorrowful stories about our families as well as our challenges in Africa. Scott and Barbara had both worked for the United States peace corps in Lesotho and had lived several years in Mozambique, and they were as comfortable in Africa as they would have been in the US. They navigated deliberately among the disparate communities in Maputo, from the ex-patriate American community to Maputo's street artists. I learned much by listening to them and by doing fieldwork with Scott in Zambezia Province in May 1998. In the summer of 1999 I returned to Mozambique briefly to finish up some interviews. Scott and Barbara and the kids were as welcoming as ever. They were also eagerly anticipating their return to the US when Scott's tenure as project director for the University of Wisconsin-Madison's Land Tenure Center Program concluded in January of 2000.

Sadly, only a week after my return to the States, I learned that the Kloeck-Jenson family had been killed in a car accident in South Africa. Many of their friends have mourned their deaths and given eloquent testimonies to their grace, their compassion, and their thoughtfulness. For myself, the image that I remember the most is the mischievous little twinkle Scott would get in his eyes when he had a story to spin. My father also got that twinkle and, in both men, it always foreshadowed a tale of great amusement but one from which the listeners were supposed to draw a moral lesson. It is with much appreciation and admiration for their storytelling gifts that I dedicate this book to the memories of my father, Charles Scholey Pitcher, and my friend and colleague, Scott Kloeck-Jenson.

The publisher has endeavored to ensure that the URLs for external websites referred to in this book are correct and active at the time of going to press. However, the publisher has no responsibility for the websites and can make no guarantee that a site will remain live or that the content is or will remain appropriate.

# Abbreviations and acronyms

| | |
|---|---|
| AC | aldeia comunal, communal village |
| ACIANA | Associação Comercial, Industrial e Agrícola de Nampula, Commercial, Industrial and Agricultural Association of Nampula |
| AICaju | Associação dos Industriais de Caju, Association of Cashew Industrialists |
| BCI | Banco Comercial e de Investimentos, Commercial and Investment Bank |
| BIM | Banco Internacional de Moçambique, International Bank of Mozambique |
| BNU | Banco Nacional Ultramarino, Overseas National Bank |
| BPD | Banco Popular de Desenvolvimento, People's Development Bank |
| *BR* | *Boletim da República, Bulletin of the Republic* |
| CAIL | Complexo Agro-Industrial do Limpopo, Limpopo Agro-Industrial Complex |
| CEA | Centro de Estudos Africanos, Center of African Studies |
| CEDIMO | Centro Nacional de Documentação e In formação de Moçambique, National Documentation and Information Center of Mozambique |
| CEP | Comissão Executora da Privatização, Executive Privatization Commission |
| CFM | Portos e Caminhos de Ferro de Moçambique, Ports and Railways of Mozambique |
| CIMPOR | Cimentos de Portugal, Cement of Portugal |
| CIRE | Comissão Interministerial para a Reestruturação Empresarial, Interministerial Commission for Enterprise Restructuring |
| CPI | Centro de Promoção de Investimento, Center for Investment Promotion |
| CUF | Companhia União Fabril, Union Manufacturing Company |
| EDM | Electricidade de Moçambique, Mozambique Electricity |

| | |
|---|---|
| E. E. | Empresa Estatal, State Enterprise |
| EMOCHÁ | Empresa Moçambicana de Chá, Mozambican Tea Company |
| ENACOMO | Empresa Nacional de Comercialização, National Trading Company |
| E. P. | Empresa Pública, Public Enterprise |
| Frelimo | Frente de Libertação de Moçambique, Mozambique Liberation Front |
| GAPRONA | Gabinete de Apoio a Produção da Província de Nampula, Office of Aid to Production in Nampula Province |
| GPIE | Gabinete de Promoção do Investimento Estrangeiro, Office for Foreign Investment Promotion |
| GREAP | Gabinete de Reestruturação de Empresas Agrárias e Pescas, Office for Restucturing Agricultural and Fishing Enterprises |
| GREICT | Gabinete de Reestruturação de Empresas da Indústria, Comércio e Turismo, Office for Restructuring Industry, Trade and Tourism Companies |
| Grupo AGT | Abdul Gani Tayob Group |
| IAM | Instituto de Algodão de Moçambique, Cotton Institute of Mozambique |
| IMPAR | Companhia de Seguros de Moçambique, Insurance Company of Mozambique |
| JFS | João Ferreira dos Santos |
| JVC | Joint-venture Company |
| LAM | Linhas Aéreas de Moçambique, Mozambique Airlines |
| LOMACO | Lonrho-Mozambique Company |
| MG | Moçambique Gestores, SARL, Mozambique Managers, Limited |
| MICTUR | Ministério da Indústria, Comércio e Turismo, Ministry of Industry, Trade and Tourism |
| MNR | Mozambique National Resistance |
| MPLA | Movimento Popular de Libertação de Angola, Popular Movement for the Liberation of Angola |
| NGO | Non-governmental organization |
| OMM | Organização da Mulher Moçambicana, Organization of Mozambican Women |
| OTM | Organização dos Trabalhadores de Moçambique, Organization of Mozambican Workers |
| PDP | Programa dos Distritos Prioritários, Priority District Program |
| PIDE | Portuguese Security Police |
| PRE | Programa de Reabilitação Económica, Economic Recovery Program |

| PRES | Programa de Reabilitação Económica e Social, Economic and Social Recovery Program |
| PROAGRI | Programa de Desenvolvimento Agrícola, Program for Agricultural Development |
| Renamo | Resistência Nacional Moçambicana, Mozambique National Resistance |
| SAAVM | Sociedade Algodoeira Africana Voluntária de Moçambique, African Voluntary Cotton Society of Mozambique |
| SAMO | Sociedade Algodoeira de Monapo, Monapo Cotton Company |
| SARL | Sociedade Anonima de Responsibilidade Limitada, Limited Liability Company |
| SCI | Sociedade de Controlo e Gestão de Participações Financeiras, SARL, Control and Management of Financial Participation Company, Limited |
| SDCM | Sociedade de Desenvolvimento do Corredor de Maputo, Maputo Corridor Development Company |
| SINTICIM | Sindicato Nacional dos Trabalhadores da Indústria de Construção Civil, Madeiras e Minas de Moçambique, National Union of Civil Construction, Timber and Mine Workers |
| SODAN | Sociedade de Desenvolvimento Algodoeiro de Namialo, Namialo Cotton Development Company |
| SPI | Sociedade de Participações de Investimentos, SARL, Investment Participation Company |
| STM | Sociedade Terminais de Moçambique, Mozambique Terminals Company |
| TDM | Telecomunicações de Moçambique, Mozambique Telecommunications |
| UEM | Universidade Eduardo Mondlane, Eduardo Mondlane University |
| UNIDO | United Nations Industrial Development Organization |
| UREA | Unidade para a Reestruturação das Empresas de Agricultura, Unit for the Restructuring of Agricultural Enterprises |
| USAID | United States Agency for International Development |
| UTRE | Unidade Técnica para a Reestruturação de Empresas, Technical Unit for Enterprise Restructuring |

# Glossary

| | |
|---|---|
| *aldeamentos* | strategic hamlets created during the colonial war by the colonial government |
| *blocos* | blocks of land especially designated for smallholder production after independence, which often corresponded to the concentrações designated during the colonial period. |
| *cabo* | chief's assistant |
| *cantineiros* | traders |
| *capataz* | overseer |
| *concentração* | designated blocks of land for smallholder production during the colonial period |
| conto | 1,000 Portugese escudos or 1,000 Mozambican meticais |
| *empresas estatais* | state enterprises |
| *empresas intervencionadas* | enterprises intervened in by the state but not officially nationalized |
| *empresas publicas* | public enterprises |
| escudo | Portuguese unit of currency; 1,000 escuados equal 1 conto |
| FICO | I am staying |
| *grupos dinamizadores* | dynamizing groups |
| *humu* | customary Makua lineage or land chief in northern Mozambique |
| *Lojas do Povo* | people's shops |
| *machamba* | field; pl. *machambas* |
| *mestiço* | person of mixed race in the colonial period |
| metical | Mozambican unit of currency; 1,000 meticais equal 1 conto |
| *muene* | customary Makua clan chief in northern Mozambique |
| *patrão* | boss |

xxii

| | |
|---|---|
| *portaria* | government directive |
| *privados* | private commercial farmers who farm over four hectares of land. In the cotton sector, the minimum amount of land devoted to cotton must be at least twenty hectares. |
| *regulo* | chief |
| *xibalo* | forced labor |

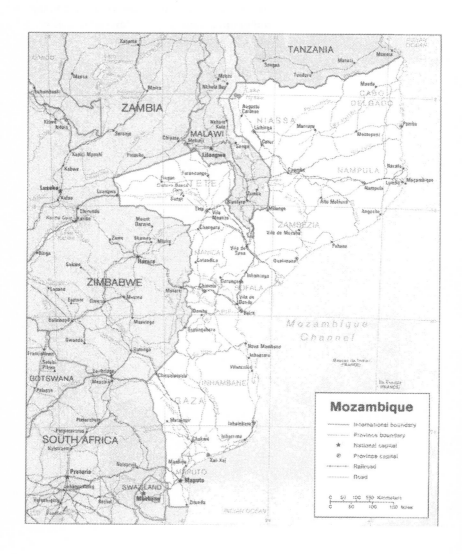

To avoid confusion, Mozambique's current administrative divisions are used when referring to places and locations in the text.

# Introduction

Visitors to Mozambique in the late 1970s needed few reminders that they were in a newly independent country, whose new leaders celebrated it as a "people's republic," a modernizing, nationalistic, and socialist state. Consciously crafted murals, brightly colored political posters, random graffiti, buttons, badges, and decals constantly informed even the most casual observers where the country had come from and where the new government wanted it to go. Sculptures depicted a valiant struggle against the colonial Portuguese and the triumphant victory by the Front for the Liberation of Mozambique (Frelimo) in 1975. Striking images illustrated the defense and consolidation of national independence under the leadership of the Frelimo one-party state. Bold slogans drawn on street pavements in the newly named capital of Maputo proclaimed the end of feudalism, colonialism, and backwardness, or celebrated the equality of women, the arrival of justice, and the construction of socialism. Phrases etched on the factory walls of state companies from Zambezia in the north to Maputo in the south exhorted workers to improve production; while colorful, state-commissioned posters implored rural peoples to breastfeed their babies, vaccinate their animals, give blood, educate their offspring, and harvest more cashew and cotton.

Just two decades later, however, the walls proclaiming socialist victory were whitewashed, the factory slogans had faded, and the murals had deteriorated. Private investors, both domestic and foreign, were visible in every economic sector from finance to fishing. Two national democratic elections had taken place in the 1990s that international observers had pronounced free and fair. A new visual imagery had emerged with an entirely different message. Now billboards entreated Mozambicans to "drink Coca-Cola!", or they honored a private company that had spent "100 years constructing a better Mozambique." Poster art encouraged Mozambicans to buy Colgate toothpaste, or smoke Palmars and GTs; to use OMO washing powder, fly LAM, or relax at the Hotel Cardoso. Company advertisements in the weekly magazine *Tempo* offered to fumigate houses and gardens against bugs, to provide a pleasant overland journey to Johannesburg, or to furnish comfortable parlors and offices. The faces of American film stars peering at shoppers from the back of second-hand t-shirts for sale in remote rural markets capped Mozambique's re-entry into the global capitalist economy.

Why has the discourse of the market supplanted the language of Marxism? Why have privatization and democratization replaced the state's socialist and nationalist agendas? Was extensive state intervention responsible for the collapse of the command economy and has the state's role now diminished, as neo-liberals prescribe? Do any continuities exist between the period of socialism and the period of capitalism and democracy that the changing iconography fails to capture? Or, as neo-liberals argue, are we witnessing a truly "revolutionary" change?

To address these questions, this study situates Mozambique's experience of institutional and ideological change since independence within the comparative literature on the creation, erosion, and transformation of command economies in the former Soviet Union and Eastern Europe. It also incorporates studies of economic and political change in Latin America and Africa to explain why the command economy failed in Mozambique, why the government adopted neo-liberal policies, and what the effects of restructuring have been. It examines the contradictions of state planning and the politics of economic management during the socialist phase, and it explores the ways in which political forces shaped the construction of a market economy during the 1990s.

Just as studies of regime change elsewhere have helped to illuminate particular aspects of Mozambique's experience, equally Mozambique offers a useful comparative case for the study of theoretical questions related to transitions. The book's diachronic approach relies on continual comparisons between regimes, policies, outcomes, and agents within Mozambique as it moves through time from the 1960s to the millennium, from the colonial period to independence to contemporary times. During that time period, Mozambique occupied several points on the spectrum of political economy. The country was capitalist and authoritarian during the colonial period; socialist and increasingly authoritarian following independence; authoritarian and increasingly capitalist from the mid-1980s until the early 1990s; and nominally democratic and capitalist after 1994. These phases invite comparisons with each other and with the experiences of other developing countries. They identify factors that explain the transition from one configuration to another and they reveal the changing roles of the state during each period. They expose the economic and political constraints and opportunities that have brought about the changes in institutional arrangements, and the political alliances and conflicts that have emerged as a consequence of those changes.

In addition, the ideological preferences and policy choices that the Mozambican government has made share common features with other countries in Africa as well as with countries in Eastern Europe. Like several other African states, it took a revolution in Mozambique to bring about the transition from colonialism to independence. In contrast to many of its immediate neighbors, however, a long period of domestic conflict plagued Mozambique after independence. Yet similar outcomes of political instability and great economic hardship in countries with and without internal conflicts encourages comparative analysis to discover the causal relationships that led to economic erosion.

Like other countries, Mozambique also has undergone a tumultuous and challenging transition to capitalism and Western-style democracy in recent years, but it has done so without experiencing a collapse of regime. In many ways, Mozambique has been the model patient envisioned in neo-liberal prescriptions. The government has jettisoned direct state management of factories and farms for greater reliance on the private sector, foreign investment, and World Bank loans. And, like their counterparts in Eastern Europe and the rest of Africa, government officials now trumpet liberal democracy rather than democratic centralism, while principles of the market rather than precepts of Marxism are more likely to be heard in the streets and shops of the capital, Maputo. In accordance with recent modifications in neo-liberal principles, the government attempts to practice "good governance," to capacity build, and even to foster "partnerships" with the private sector to pursue mutually beneficial goals. Its privatization program has been so comprehensive that international financial institutions have called it "the most successful in Africa" and "an example for others to follow."[1]

Scholars have debated vigorously the causes for such sweeping reforms. Neo-liberals have blamed the collapse of command economies on the unsuitability of state-centered models of development. They have attributed the low productivity and poor performance of parastatals to the rent-seeking behavior of political elites or the inefficiency of state managers. Their policy prescriptions have sought to push the state back out and allow the market and private individuals to bring economic growth.[2] Current neo-liberal formulas do stress the importance of "good governance" meaning "the exercise of political power to manage a nation's affairs,"[3] but the political power that neo-liberals envision these states exercising occurs in a highly circumscribed arena. States that practice "good governance" are administrative and technical managers, whose institutions perform tasks that the private sector cannot perform. When good governance prevails, states are effective and capable. They play by the rules, their institutions

---

[1] B. Baloi, "Privatizações são das mais bem sucedidas em Africa," *Domingo* (23 June 1996), p. 12; "Programa de privatizações em Moçambique é um exemplo," *Notícias* (3 June 1997).

[2] See especially, World Bank, *Adjustment in Africa: Reforms, Results and the Road Ahead* (New York: Oxford University Press, 1994); World Bank, *World Bank Development Report: From Plan to Market* (New York: Oxford University Press, 1996). Like B. Hibou, I treat the World Bank as an ideal-type and thus focus mainly on World Bank publications for my analysis of neo-liberal theory. See B. Hibou, "The Political Economy of the World Bank's Discourse: From Economic Catechism to Missionary Deeds (and Misdeeds)," *Les Etudes du CERI* (Centre d'études et de recherches internationales), 39 (March 1998), English translation (January 2000).

[3] World Bank, *Sub-Saharan Africa: From Crisis to Sustainable Growth, A Long-Term Perspective Study* (Washington, DC: World Bank, 1989), p. 60.

function properly, and they are responsive to public concerns and demands. They contribute to economic growth by extending the proper incentives to investors, enforcing property rights, maintaining order, and offering basic services such as education, health care, infrastructure, and environmental protection.

A "soft" variant of neo-liberalism makes allowance for the state to act **in partnership** with the private sector to provide pensions or to control pollution. Nevertheless, the emphasis remains on constructing a competitive, competent, and efficient environment for private enterprise. The states envisioned to carry out this process are greatly streamlined, democratic to be sure, but expected to be technical and neutral in their relations with different economic agents. Their roles are to encourage and to regulate but not to intervene.[4] They are nightwatchmen who objectively guard the goods and gains of private actors.[5]

The predominance of neo-liberal explanations and the widespread adoption of neo-liberal policies ironically serve to reinforce an alternative interpretation of the changes that have taken place over the last two decades. Several scholars of Mozambique treat the collapse of the socialist project there and its replacement by a free market economy as the predictable outcome of persistent and conscious efforts by the West to undermine Frelimo's revolutionary agenda and to re-subject the country to the demands of global capitalism. These scholars have argued repeatedly that external aggression by the former apartheid government of South Africa supported by the West derailed Frelimo's project and created the context for the ubiquitous influence that international financial institutions and donors now seem to enjoy. They offer a gloomy forecast of increasing marginalization and loss of sovereignty for countries like Mozambique, as the global integration of finance, markets, and trade relentlessly proceeds.[6]

The arguments of neo-liberals and their critics reflect to some degree the reality of transition in Mozambique. Certainly, South African aggression and the global ascendancy of neo-liberalism contributed to the collapse of the Frelimo project and hastened the process of economic liberalization and democratization, as many writers on Mozambique argue. Moreover, state companies did

---

[4] World Bank, *World Development Report, 1997: The State in a Changing World* (New York: Oxford University Press, 1997), pp. 3–9, 25–34.

[5] See the criticisms of governance by P. Evans, *Embedded Autonomy: States and Industrial Transformation* (Princeton, NJ: Princeton University Press, 1995), p. 25; C. de Alcántara, "Uses and Abuses of the Concept of Governance," *International Social Science Journal*, 155 (March 1998), pp. 105–13 and D. Moore, " 'Sail on, O Ship of State': Neo-Liberalism, Globalisation and the Governance of Africa," *Journal of Peasant Studies*, 27, 1 (October 1999), pp. 61–96.

[6] See for example J. Hanlon, *Mozambique: Who Calls the Shots?* (London: James Currey, 1991) and *Peace without Profit: How the IMF Blocks Rebuilding in Mozambique* (Oxford: James Currey, 1996); D. Plank, "Aid, Debt and the End of Sovereignty: Mozambique and Its Donors," *The Journal of Modern African Studies*, 31, 3 (1993), pp. 429–30; J. Saul, *Recolonization and Resistance in Southern Africa in the 1990s* (Trenton, NJ: Africa World Press, 1993); J. Mittelman, *The Globalization Syndrome: Transformation and Resistance* (Princeton, NJ: Princeton University Press, 2000), pp. 90–107.

accrue huge debts and operate inefficiently, as much of the neo-liberal literature claims. But understanding the trajectory of political and economic change in Mozambique since 1975 requires additional explanations. With regard to the collapse of the command economy, first I claim that the structural and institutional legacies of the colonial period affected several of the economic and political choices that the revolutionary government adopted just after independence. These legacies mitigated the impact of policies once they were implemented. Moreover, poorly designed, hastily enacted policies rooted in grandiose visions about the state's ability to transform society strangled the project almost from the beginning. In addition, the existence of social forces that contested and shaped every measure eroded the project over time. Indeed, the inability of the state to realize its "transformative vision" in the initial years of the revolution derived as much from the vigorous interaction of policies and their recipients on the ground as it did from the flawed principles on which policies were based.

As state erosion and domestic conflict supported by external actors increased in the 1980s, Mozambique adopted those measures typically associated with neo-liberalism. Yet my second claim is that the transition to a market economy in Mozambique has been a more complex and protracted endeavor than withdrawing state subsidies, selling state assets to the private sector, and shrinking the state. It has not been a matter of unleashing markets, as neo-liberals argue, nor has it been a case where the Mozambican state has relinquished all control to outside forces, as critics contend. Rather, the relationship that has emerged between the state and the market is one that participants have consciously negotiated and managed in a contested and unstable context. It is a political process with political consequences.[7] International actors as well as domestic social forces have shaped, thwarted, and reconfigured how privatization and market relations have taken place. Not only World Bank advisors, but also state elites and rural smallholders influence who benefits or who suffers from the process.

The active presence of multiple agents has meant that the process is not straightforward, but contentious; not predictable, but contradictory and uneven. The efforts of political elites to secure greater legitimacy, retain power, enhance state capabilities, and expand political influence have combined as well as clashed in the transition. Furthermore, the emergence of a private sector accompanied by deregulation and markets has exacerbated old tensions and introduced new cleavages in a rapidly changing social order, not only between workers and owners, but also between commerce and industry, and between different ethnic groups. The transition has reinforced and created tendencies toward factionalization and fragmentation, and these tendencies may weaken, not strengthen, the prospects for democratic consolidation.

---

[7] H. Feigenbaum and J. Henig, "The Political Underpinnings of Privatization," *World Politics*, 46, 2 (January 1994), pp. 185–207; H. Feigenbaum, J. Henig, and C. Hamnett, *Shrinking the State: The Political Underpinnings of Privatization* (Cambridge: Cambridge University Press, 1998).

Third, most supporters of the kind of "systemic privatization" or widespread ideological and institutional changes undertaken by Eastern European countries and by African countries like Mozambique anticipate and even welcome a reduction of the role of the state, and a reconfiguration of the political and economic elite. On the other hand, critics of neo-liberalism envision all sorts of dire consequences if this scenario is ever fully realized. But these outcomes cannot be assumed and they may not even be possible.[8] States are historical constructions, and the direction they adopt is influenced by the balance of social forces within and outside of their institutions. Certainly, privatization and the growth of markets **have** altered the roles of state institutions and produced new alliances and conflicts in society. In the case of Mozambique, the state no longer controls the commanding heights of the economy nor does it solely manage strategic state enterprises. But where the ruling party in power survives the transition, as it has in Mozambique, state institutions and party elites have taken advantage of restructuring to fashion new constituencies of supporters and to maintain some of the political and economic control they have exercised since independence in 1975. I call this process "transformative preservation" to draw attention to the continuing influence of the socialist period on the emerging market economy. The sale of state assets and the formation of new companies have extensively involved state institutions. State officials not only regulate but also facilitate private sector activities by granting tax incentives to a company in one instance or negotiating with smallholders to allocate land to a commercial operation in another. In many cases, government and party notables have become managers of new enterprises in agriculture or served as directors in new financial or industrial undertakings. These continuities in state power and state elites alongside the institutional ruptures introduced by privatization and democratization indicate that economic and political reforms have redirected the role of the state in the economy, but they have not led to its withdrawal as neo-liberals anticipated and critics feared. In spite of the adoption of neo-liberal rhetoric then, Mozambique's political economy appears to be somewhere between Marx and the market, between a centralized, state-driven economy and one largely run by the private sector.

Fourth and finally, the persistence of structural arrangements and social networks associated with the past caution us against interpreting the present in transitional countries as something wholly new. Rather, we should view economic and political change as a process of constant interaction between previous and emerging agents and organizational forces. Although the actors and institutions they analyze in Eastern European countries are obviously different, Stark

---

[8] D. Stark and L. Bruszt make a similar point in *Postsocialist Pathways: Transforming Politics and Property in East Central Europe* (New York: Cambridge University Press, 1998; repr. 1999), pp. 78–79.

and Bruszt capture the dynamic in Mozambique when they state: "we see social change not as transition from one order to another but as transformation – rearrangements, reconfigurations, and recombinations that yield new interweavings of the multiple social logics that are a modern society."[9] Thus, at the same time that the emergence of a market economy heralds a break with past economic and political practice, it may also serve to sustain a certain level of power and control that will depend very much on the historical legacies present in particular countries. My examination of these continuities and discontinuities, and the alliances, antinomies, and recombinations they produce in Mozambique, intends to contribute to the existing literature on post-socialism and on the politics of economic reform.[10]

### Theorizing transformation and explaining change in Mozambique

While studies of the transition to democratization and market-based economies in Eastern Europe and Latin America have proliferated, the work on transitions in Africa has been more limited and more circumscribed. Many studies examine the impact of structural adjustment, the techniques used for the sale or transfer of state assets, and the economic effects of privatization; far fewer studies

---

[9] Stark and Bruszt, *Postsocialist Pathways*, p. 7. I share Stark and Bruszt's concern about the meaning of the word "transition," but I think that neither "transition," nor "transformation" can be used without properly explaining what they refer to with regard to political and economic change. Since understanding those changes is the purpose of this book, I tend to use "transition" and "transformation" interchangeably in the text.

[10] On transitions in Eastern Europe, China and the former Soviet Union, see V. Nee and D. Stark with M. Selden, eds., *Remaking the Economic Institutions of Socialism: China and Eastern Europe* (Stanford, CA: Stanford University Press, 1989); J. Hausner, B. Jessop, and K. Nielsen, eds., *Strategic Choice and Path Dependency in Post-Socialism: Institutional Dynamics in the Transformation Process* (London: Edward Elgar, 1994); K. Verdery, *What Was Socialism and What Comes Next?* (Princeton, NJ: Princeton University Press, 1996); G. Grabher and D. Stark, eds., *Restructuring Networks in Postsocialism: Legacies, Linkages, and Localities* (New York: Oxford University Press, 1997); Stark and Bruszt, *Postsocialist Pathways*; V. Bunce, *Subversive Institutions: The Design and the Destruction of Socialism and the State* (New York: Cambridge University Press, 1999). For a comprehensive approach to the politics of privatization, H. Feigenbaum and J. Henig, "The Political Underpinnings of Privatization"; H. Feigenbaum, J. Henig, and C. Hamnett, *Shrinking the State*. Considerations of space do not permit a more thorough treatment of the relationship between democracy and economic reform, but see the review essays by B. Geddes, "The Politics of Economic Liberalization," *Latin American Research Review*, 30, 2 (1995), pp. 195–214 and J. Martz, "Review Essay: Economic Challenges and the Study of Democratization," *Studies in Comparative International Development*, 31, 1 (Spring 1996), pp. 96–120. For analyses of the debate over economic and political reform in Africa, see T. Callaghy, "Vision and Politics in the Transformation of the Global Political Economy: Lessons from the Second and Third Worlds" in R. Slater, B. Schutz, and S. Dorr, eds., *Global Transformation and the Third World* (Boulder, CO: Lynne Rienner, 1993), pp. 161–257; T. Callaghy and J. Ravenhill, eds., *Hemmed In: Responses to Africa's Economic Decline* (New York: Columbia University Press, 1993); H. Bienen and J. Herbst, "The Relationship between Political and Economic Reform," *Comparative Politics* (October 1996), pp. 23–42.

analyze the reasons for the adoption of sweeping economic policy changes, the political "winners" and "losers" from privatization, or the institutional effect of liberalization on the relationship between state and society.[11] In addition, most comparative studies on the erosion of socialism, emerging markets, and the process and impact of privatization have overlooked Mozambique.[12] This oversight has occurred despite the fact that Mozambique was once avowedly socialist and currently serves as the poster child for the "success" of neo-liberal prescriptions. Studies on the transition to democratization have treated Africa more generously, but of the dozen or so recent edited books on democratization in Africa, not a single one has a case study on Mozambique. Moreover, most of the literature on democratization in Africa has excluded in-depth study of the privatization process and the emergence of markets.[13]

Several reasons explain why studies of transformations have privileged countries of Eastern Europe and Latin America over those of Africa, and why the

[11] For the economic consequences of privatization and liberalization see C. Adam, W. Cavendish and P. Mistry, *Adjusting Privatization: Case Studies from Developing Countries* (Portsmouth, NH: Heinemann, 1992); W. van der Geest, ed., *Negotiating Structural Adjustment in Africa* (Portsmouth, NH: Heinemann, 1994); P. Bennell, "Privatization in Sub-Saharan Africa: Progress and Prospects during the 1990s," *World Development*, 25, 11 (1997), pp. 1785–803; O. White and A. Bhatia, *Privatization in Africa* (Washington, DC: World Bank, 1998); J. Paulson, ed., *African Economies in Transition*, Vol. 1: *The Changing Role of the State* (New York: St. Martin's Press, 1999); J. Paulson, ed., *African Economies in Transition*, Vol. 2: *The Reform Experience* (New York: St. Martin's Press, 1999); A. Ariyo and A. Jerome, "Privatization in Africa: An Appraisal," *World Development*, 27, 1 (1999), pp. 201–13. For the political aspects of privatization in Africa, see J. Herbst, "The Politics of Privatization in Africa" in E. Suleiman and J. Waterbury, eds., *The Political Economy of Public Sector Reform and Privatization* (Boulder, CO: Westview, 1990), pp. 234–54; J. Herbst, "The Structural Adjustment of Politics in Africa," *World Development*, 18 (1990), pp. 949–58; B. Grosh and R. Mukandala, *State-Owned Enterprises in Africa* (Boulder, CO: Lynne Rienner, 1994); J. Widner, ed., *Economic Change and Political Liberalization in Sub-Saharan Africa* (Baltimore, MD: Johns Hopkins University Press, 1994); R. Tangri, *The Politics of Patronage in Africa: Parastatals, Privatization, and Private Enterprise* (Trenton, NJ: Africa World Press, 1999).

[12] In addition to World Bank surveys, case studies of privatization in Mozambique are just emerging, see R. Tibana, "Structural Adjustment and the Manufacturing Industry in Mozambique" in Paulson, *African Economies*, Vol. 2, pp. 178–232; J. Alves, "Privatizing the State Enterprise Sector" in B. Ferraz and B. Munslow, eds., *Sustainable Development in Mozambique* (Trenton, NJ: Africa World Press, 2000), pp. 58–63; C. Cramer, "Privatisation and Adjustment in Mozambique: A 'Hospital Pass'?", *Journal of Southern African Studies*, 27, 1 (March 2001), pp. 79–103. The inclusion of Mozambique in comparative studies is more limited, but see White and Bhatia, *Privatization in Africa*; J. Paulson and M. Gavin, "The Changing Role of the State in Formerly Socialist Economies of Africa" in Paulson, ed., *African Economies*, Vol. 1, pp. 11–65; L. Pereira da Silva and A. Solimano, "The Transition and the Political Economy of African Socialist Countries at War (Angola and Mozambique)," pp. 9–67, and S. Jones, "Agriculture and Economic Reform in African Socialist Economies" in Paulson, ed., *African Economies*, Vol. 2, pp. 235–87.

[13] For case studies of the peace process and democratization in Mozambique, see B. Mazula, ed., *Mozambique: Elections, Democracy and Development* (Maputo: InterAfrica Group, 1996); and two new books that are too recent to have been incorporated into my work, C. Alden, *Mozambique and the Construction of the New African State: From Negotiation to Nation-Building* (Basingstoke: Palgrave, 2001) and C. Manning, *The Politics of Peace in Mozambique* (Westport: Praeger, forthcoming).

comparative work on Africa has ignored Mozambique. First, the African continent is not as politically and economically important to Western industrialized countries as Eastern Europe and Latin America. As a result, not as much public attention has been directed to the changes in Africa. Second, whereas countries such as Poland and the Czech Republic can be said to have undergone radical, even "revolutionary" transitions to democracy and capitalism, scholars perceive transitions in Africa, particularly those involving privatization and liberalization, as sluggish and incomplete. Even the World Bank, which tends not to call attention to failures, has lamented the slow nature of economic change in Africa.[14]

Despite its apparent "success" with privatization in contrast with other countries in Africa, Mozambique suffers from additional obstacles to inclusion in the comparative literature. Because it is a former colony of Portugal rather than of Britain or France, it has been treated as an "exception," even by those scholars who study it. Though few comparative analyses of Portuguese with French or British colonialism actually exist, scholars (particularly English-speaking scholars) have cast Portugal as a weaker, cheaper, and more coercive colonial power than Britain or France. Consequently, they have viewed the former Portuguese colonies as less developed and more different, historically and institutionally, than their Francophone and Anglophone contemporaries.[15] Not only does the case for Lusophone exceptionalism rest on thin ice, but it has deterred researchers from incorporating the Lusophone countries into comparative appraisals of colonialism, the rise and decline of socialism, and transitions to democracy and capitalism. Civil conflict in Mozambique until 1992 and the use of Portuguese as the official language equally have discouraged scholarly interest.

This book addresses the lacuna in the literature. It relies on archival material, government documents, newspaper accounts, and secondary literature to examine the economic legacy that new political actors confronted when Mozambique achieved independence in 1975. It analyzes the construction of the nationalistic,

---

[14] Bennell, "Privatization in Sub-Saharan Africa"; White and Bhatia, *Privatization in Africa*; E. Berg, "Privatisation in Sub-Saharan Africa: Results, Prospects and New Approaches" in Paulson, ed., *African Economies*, Vol. 1, pp. 229–89; E. Harsch, "Privatization shifts gears in Africa: More Concern for Public Acceptance and Development Impact But Problems Remain," *Africa Recovery*, 14, 1 (April 2000), pp. 8–11, 14–17.

[15] Perry Anderson has made the most theoretical case for Portuguese colonial exceptionalism, depicting it as "ultra-colonialism," that is, "the most extreme and the most primitive modality of colonialism. Forced labor in the Portuguese colonies is the most extreme form of exploitation existent anywhere in Africa.... But at the same time forced labor, the edifice and emblem of Portuguese colonialism, provides the clearest evidence of its retardation" (p. 99) in P. Anderson, "Portugal and the End of Ultra-Colonialism," Parts 1–3, *New Left Review*, 15–17 (1962). The theme of ultra-colonialism underpins several works on Mozambique; see for example A. Isaacman and B. Isaacman, *Mozambique: From Colonialism to Revolution, 1900–1982* (Boulder, CO: Westview Press, 1983), pp. 19–58 and Hanlon, *Mozambique: Who Calls the Shots?*, p. 9.

modernizing, and socialist ideological agenda of the new government, and the implementation of policies that both reflected and compromised that agenda. It then charts Mozambique's economic reorientation from a command economy to a capitalist one, and its political reconfiguration from a highly interventionist state with multiple roles to one whose roles are less visible but no less complex. Drawing upon interviews with national and local government officials, foreign and domestic investors, and representatives of non-governmental organizations, the study evaluates how the privatization process is structuring relations between state and business and assesses the impact of capital formation on the state's regulatory powers, policy-making capacity, and legitimacy. It examines who is investing, what types of investments foreigners and nationals are making, and the conflicts and coalitions that are emerging in industry and agriculture. Furthermore, it explores the visual and rhetorical effects of transformation by deconstructing government speeches and corporate advertisements. Finally, the work relies on several periods of fieldwork, household surveys, and interviews with smallholders, "traditional authorities," and government and company officials in Sofala, Zambezia, Nampula and Cabo Delgado Provinces during the years 1994–98 to gauge local level responses to, and influences on, the period of state intervention and that of liberalization and privatization.

My analysis blends the insights of comparative and historical institutional theory offered by Peter Evans and Theda Skocpol, the macro-historical approach of Barrington Moore, and the attention to states and social forces employed by James Scott, Jean-François Bayart, David Stark, Joel Migdal, and Sara Berry among others. It also builds on the work of Harvey Feigenbaum, Jeffrey Henig, and Chris Hamnett regarding the "political underpinnings" of privatization. The book weaves together four theoretical approaches to explain the complexity of state–market relations in transitional economies. First, it acknowledges that international trends and the transmission of global ideas and policies influence domestic policy decisions. It agrees that the international context may set the parameters for the choices that states make. Yet it also recognizes that international developments are themselves dynamic and changing, and that alone they cannot explain the causes and consequences of transition.[16]

Second, just as historical legacies shaped the nature of socialism, they have also molded the recent transitions to capitalism. As Barrington Moore so persuasively argued many years ago, developing countries share common problems, but "historical preconditions" from the existence of particular domestic institutions to the strength of certain classes can favor despotism or democracy, capitalism or communism.[17] Contemporary writers also trace the way

[16] M. Bratton and N. van de Walle, *Democratic Experiments in Africa: Regime Transitions in Comparative Perspective* (New York: Cambridge University Press, 1997), pp. 27–30.

[17] B. Moore, *The Social Origins of Dictatorship and Democracy: Lord and Peasant in the Making of the Modern World*, (Boston, MA: Beacon Press, 1966), chapter 7.

that historical preconditions influence existing political structures in Africa or are shaping the outcomes of reform in Eastern Europe, China, Vietnam, and elsewhere. These preconditions may act to prolong tyrannical practices and predatory acts. They may stifle emerging social groups or hinder new modes of thinking. Or, alternatively, they may recombine in new and different ways, exploring and developing innovative responses and adaptations to change.[18] To the extent that the outcome of reforms are path dependent – that is, derived from the historical specificity of the country in which they are implemented – due consideration must be given to the amalgamations and influences of earlier historical periods.

Third, the state occupies a central place in the analysis. As others have argued, I recognize that the state requires re-examination in Africa, but I challenge neo-liberal efforts to push the state back out and to force an analytical distinction between the economy and politics. I argue for the continued relevance of a comparative and historical institutional approach to the state as do Theda Skocpol, Peter Evans, Jean-François Bayart, Joel Migdal, and James Scott in works examining states from Brazil to Cameroon to the former Soviet Union.[19] I argue that the state has been just as influential in the development of capitalist forces as it was to the outcome of socialism. While the command economy has vanished, the new roles that the state has adopted and its political aspirations and objectives are integral to the features and functioning of the private sector. New theoretical conceptions need to make allowances for the continuous and contradictory, ambiguous yet pervasive, political and dynamic role of the state in a private economy.

Finally, any study of transition must recognize and evaluate the capacities and abilities of social agents – from old elites to rural smallholders – to affect the outcome of policy as Migdal, Scott, Bayart, and Berry have so painstakingly illustrated in their works. Social agents not only played a significant role eroding socialism; they also have modified, thwarted, hastened, and configured various aspects of the privatization process, influencing the trajectory of its development in transitional economies. Moreover, relations between social forces and the state can change and vary over time, over issues, within sectors, and among groups. States and social groups constantly negotiate and re-negotiate, resist and cooperate with each other. The dynamic this mutually constitutive interaction has set in place challenges neo-liberal projections about the role of the state

---

[18] C. Young, *The African Colonial State in Comparative Perspective* (New Haven, CT: Yale University Press, 1994); M. Mamdani, *Citizen and Subject: Contemporary Africa and the Legacy of Late Colonialism* (Princeton, NJ: Princeton University Press, 1996); Grabher and Stark, *Restructuring Networks*; I. Szelényi, *Privatizing the Land: Rural Political Economy in Post-Communist Societies* (London: Routledge, 1998); Stark and Bruszt, *Postsocialist Pathways*.

[19] See P. Evans, D. Rueschemeyer, and T. Skocpol, eds., *Bringing the State Back In* (Cambridge: Cambridge University Press, 1985). The work of other scholars mentioned in this and the following paragraph will be referred to in more detail below.

under capitalism and gives additional support to the argument that so-called capitalist development is as much a political undertaking as it is an economic one. Because each of these constructs is highly contested in the literature on Africa, I seek here to situate the Mozambican experience within the larger theoretical debates.

### International issues and actors

Like many countries in Africa, Mozambique's fortunes have always been intertwined with developments in other countries and regions. Existing written work records that Mozambican traders living along the country's extensive coastline were involved in elaborate commercial networks with Arab and Indian territories as early as the sixteenth century. The adherence to Islam by a large percentage of the Mozambican population, and the presence of a well-organized and established Indian community, attest to the influences on Africans in Mozambique of cultural contacts made through trade. A long-term pattern of migration for work on South Africa's mines and farms from the late nineteenth century, as well as migration across extremely porous and at times meaningless borders, strengthened Mozambique's connection with larger regional and international processes. Over 500 years of Portuguese influence – from commercial exchanges to a brutal period of colonial rule – have linked the country historically to developments in Europe and to Western structures of power and culture. Even after independence, Mozambique relied on the economic and political support of its ideological allies to weather the Cold War climate. Additionally, persistent interference from its hostile and powerful "neighbor" of South Africa contributed to instability in Mozambique after independence. More recently, the consolidation of the global capitalist economy following the downfall of the Soviet Union, the increased influence of international institutions such as the World Bank and the IMF, and the widespread implementation of privatization policies all indicate that regional and international factors have influenced political choices and economic outcomes in Mozambique.

Some of the scholarly claims about the impact of international actors on Mozambique, however, go beyond recognizing their influence to crediting them with primary responsibility for many of the country's tragedies since independence. While right-wing analysts after independence portrayed the country as a "'Soviet satellite'", controlled by Moscow,[20] some writers now cast Mozambique as the victim of orchestrated destabilization or as the object of a "conspiracy of interests" articulated by Western actors.[21] These claims suffer from several flaws. There is little attempt to classify different kinds

---

[20] Quoted by Isaacman and Isaacman, *Mozambique: From Colonialism to Revolution*, p. 171.
[21] Hanlon, *Mozambique: Who Calls the Shots?*, pp. 3–5. Plank sees the likely impact of Western aid and influence to be "neo-colonial vassalage," see Plank, "Aid, Debt and the End of Sovereignty",

of international influence and little recognition that the degree of influence of international factors may vary over time in conjunction with changes in the international system and/or changes in the relative strength of the country under examination. Ruth Collier has proposed that international influences can be one of three types. One type of international influence operates at the level of ideology, or as Collier puts it, "diffusion or contagion of models or ideas from abroad."[22] In the Mozambican case, Frelimo officials, like many other revolutionary movements that arose during the Cold War, were attracted to the ideology of Marxism-Leninism. Now, the government has embraced market and democratic principles, consistent with the tendencies of the global ideological order.[23]

The second international influence is "common, repeated, or parallel causation in a number of countries" by some outside actor or policy.[24] For Southern Africa, sustained pressure by South Africa against Mozambique and other independent countries in the 1970s and 1980s is an example of this type. South Africa's pressure was similar to the efforts that the US applied towards many Latin American countries, particularly those in Central America, during the 1970s and 1980s. It took the form of financial support for military operations, assassination attempts against leftist leaders (which apparently succeeded in the case of Samora Machel), trade embargoes, and other attempts to undermine Mozambique's political and economic stability in the hope of overthrowing what was perceived as a hostile regime. The last type of influence includes "features of the international system that present opportunities for or constraints in the behavior of individual countries."[25] For the study of Mozambique from the 1970s to the 1990s, these features include: the existence and then collapse of the bipolar system; the abandonment of a Keynesian approach by the world capitalist order; and the growth of an orthodox neo-utilitarian approach to political economy. What is *not* included among the international influences just mentioned are single, random events that may have hurt or helped Mozambique.

International features have shaped the context within which the Mozambican government has had to make decisions about economic policy and political transition. The changing dynamic of the international system – for example

p. 430. Mittelman in *The Globalization Syndrome* also argues that "with external debt more than one thousand times larger than its exports, Mozambique has lost whatever modicum of control it had over the development process. An ever-tightening web of conditionality constricts Mozambique's economic and political options" (p. 99), yet elsewhere he implies that "Mozambique" (the state? the people?) has the capacity to change this situation.

[22] R. Collier, "Combining Alternative Perspectives: Internal Trajectories versus External Influences as Explanations of Latin American Politics in the 1940s," *Comparative Politics*, 26, 1 (October 1993), p. 4.

[23] P. Evans, "The Eclipse of the State? Reflections on Stateness in an Era of Globalization," *World Politics*, 50 (October 1997), pp. 70–74.

[24] Collier, "Combining Alternative Perspectives," p. 4.

[25] Collier, "Combining Alternative Perspectives," p. 4.

the shift from a bipolar to unipolar system – has also interacted with relative changes in the authority and legitimacy of the Mozambican government to influence its ideological emphases, its policy choices, and its domestic priorities. While international processes and actors have affected the timing, direction, and intensity of outcomes in Mozambique and elsewhere in Africa, I argue that they have not determined those outcomes. Taken alone, they do not explain the wide diversity of institutional arrangements that presently exist in African countries following more than a decade of political and economic liberalization.[26] We have to demonstrate, rather than assume, the influence of these factors and place them in historical context. In Mozambique, there are times when they have exerted greater or lesser influence, and the government has taken them more or less seriously, but the history of the political economy of Mozambique should not be written as a narrative about a poor dependent country overrun by imperialism, globalism, capitalism, or any other "ism." The international perspective needs to be complemented by a focus on internal or domestic factors that may have influenced Frelimo's economic policy choices, outcomes, and changes in the years from 1975 to 2000. Domestic factors include the constraints and opportunities presented by the colonial legacy, the changing institutional and ideological construction of the state after independence and its manifestation in policy, and the role of social agents in challenging, modifying, shaping, and thwarting state policy.

### Historical legacies

I assume that states and social actors have relative autonomy. They have some room to maneuver and some choices they can exercise, but their interactions take place in a context that has been delineated by past experience. The legacy bestowed by the colonial period informed policy choices, state–society relations, and economic outcomes in Mozambique, and in other former colonies after independence, just as the socialist period influences those economies undergoing transformation now. By singling out the influence of particular moments from the past, I am "fracturing history"; that is, I am consciously bringing together a series of occurrences and practices for the purposes of comparison.[27] I privilege certain features of the colonial and socialist periods and trace their endurance or disappearance over time to make an argument about political continuities and discontinuities, and economic obstacles and advantages. To recognize that "the patterns of the past remain embedded in the present" as Crawford Young

---

[26] See also Collier, "Combining Alternative Perspectives," pp. 22–29; and Bratton and de Walle, *Democratic Experiments in Africa*, p. 30.

[27] T. Skocpol in A. Kohli, P. Evans, P. Katzenstein, A. Przeworski, S. Rudolph, J. Scott, and T. Skocpol, "The Role of Theory in Comparative Politics," *World Politics*, 48 (October 1995), pp. 43–44.

does,[28] however, is not to excuse the authoritarian actions of African rulers, nor is it to assume that political processes in Africa have remained static since independence.

The colonial period deserves attention because its legacy lives on in contemporary Mozambique. It continues in the stamped, lined paper that must be purchased and completed before a contract can be signed or a foreigner can get a visa. It lives on in the way that agrarian relations are structured, from the land that is allocated for growing particular crops to the designation *agricultor* for those who grow a hectare or more of cotton in the cotton belt. Agricultural exports such as cashew, tea, sugar, and cotton can be traced to the colonial period, and most textile, beverage, flour, beer, and cement factories were built not ten or twenty years ago under the Frelimo government, but thirty or forty years ago under the Portuguese. Mozambique's industrial and agricultural diversity as well as its bureaucratic red tape, its well-developed commercial relations as well as its inappropriate uses of land, are the products of choices made not by the present state, but by the previous one. Yet far too many of today's reports, studies, rapid rural appraisals, and participant observations by the hoards of foreign consultants hired at exorbitant rates by the World Bank and other international institutions give only cursory treatment to the colonial legacy. The current government gets blamed for some of the structurally entrenched inefficiencies that prevail; and policies get formulated on the basis of incorrect, superficial analyses of the obstacles that Mozambique faces. Researchers and consultants need to recognize that Mozambique's past furnishes the crucible in which present relationships get forged.

Lately, some scholarly work has gone to the other extreme by concluding from Mozambique's recent policies of privatization and structural adjustment that Mozambique is experiencing "recolonization."[29] Scholars cite the arrival of international investors like Lonrho and Anglo-American, who invested in Mozambique when it was a colony. They call attention to agricultural practices that bear a strong resemblance to practices during the colonial period. They note with some trepidation the domination of the banking sector by the Portuguese, many of whom represent the same banks that controlled the sector under colonialism. There are, of course, continuities with the past, as I have been so interested to point out. Some of them are (re)introductions of old practices and old power configurations, but in some cases, they really are continuities. That

---

[28] Young, *The African Colonial State*, p. 292.

[29] K. Hermele, *Mozambican Crossroads: Economics and Politics in the Era of Structural Adjustment* (Bergen, Christian Michelson Institute: 1990); Hanlon, *Mozambique Who Calls the Shots?*, introduction, chapter 22; O. Roesch, "Mozambique Unravels? The Retreat to Tradition," *Southern Africa Report* (May 1992), p. 30; Plank, "Aid, Debt and The End of Sovereignty," pp. 429–30; and J. Saul, *Recolonization and Resistance in Southern Africa in the 1990s* (Trenton, NJ: Africa World Press, 1993), Introduction and chapter 3; J. Hanlon, *Peace without Profit: How the IMF Blocks Rebuilding in Mozambique* (Portsmouth, NH: Heinemann, 1996).

is, they were never displaced by something new so that they are being (re)born again; instead, they have been maintained from the colonial period into the independence period. It seems important, then, to make a distinction between that which has continued from the past and that which is being **reintroduced** following a period in which it was excluded or eliminated. The distinction points to different strengths and motivations on the part of the post-independent state and the social agents that are influencing it now, or have influenced it in the past.

Moreover, there have been many innovations introduced since independence that the term "recolonization" obscures and even belittles. It seems to me that it **matters** that companies like Lonrho or Anglo-American have to confront a national and independent state rather than a colonial state; and it **matters** that the banking sector includes many Mozambicans, tied to the Frelimo party, as well as Portuguese who may, or may not have been around during the colonial period. In addition, the emphasis on the development of a national culture, a consciousness of the role of women and the rights of workers, and of course the conflict between Renamo and Frelimo, all arose after independence. They form part of a dynamic of rupture in Mozambique and one must acknowledge what factors gave rise to them, for they, in turn, will provide a legacy on which all future regimes will rest. Referring to the current period of privatization and of state restructuring as "recolonization" treats two periods in Mozambique's history as if they were equivalent and highly distorts both processes as a result. It equates a set of policy choices made by a national government in a particular global environment with over half a century (if we just talk about effective occupation) of rule by a colonial power in which Mozambique was directly subjugated to the political demands and economic interests of Portugal.

One may observe that the term "recolonization" enjoys a certain degree of currency in popular discourse and therefore to use it shows a sensitivity to the frustrations of the men and women; the young, the old and the infirm, who live on the streets and in the *cidades de caniço* (cane cities) composed of makeshift, handmade dwellings on the outskirts of most cities and district capitals (as opposed to the *cidade de cimento*, or cement buildings, in the city center). But this is not a sufficient reason to use it in scholarly analysis. First, there is the obvious point that scholarly analysis is often at odds with popular belief. Second, it should also be noted that the term "recolonization" is often publicly used under the most contradictory of circumstances. That is, the very same people who utter the term "recolonization" to reflect their disgust with structural adjustment also criticize the incompetence and corruption of state officials and policies for getting them into this dilemma in the first place. Additionally, in spite of their misfortunes, these individuals have also devised ingenious methods, which they honed during the colonial and post-colonial periods, of coping, surviving, and resisting policies that they dislike. In the countryside, for example, smallholders directly challenge the state with protests and illegal sales of crops over the borders. They refuse to sell their crops for low prices, they work in parallel markets, and they bribe and defy customs officials by smuggling goods into the country. They lobby the government and they cast their vote for the opposition during elections. They use non-governmental organizations to represent their views, and they seize on opportunities when they can. Current references to "recolonization" therefore might reflect legitimate frustrations, but the characterization is not analytically useful. It distorts the colonial period as well as the present one, and it does so by ignoring the role of the state and the role of social actors in shaping contemporary Mozambique.

### The role of the state

The conceptualization and practical experience of the state in Mozambique parallels that of other countries. Theoretically, the way that scholars have problematized the state in Mozambique suffers from the conceptual confusion that has characterized some of the work on the state in the rest of Africa. In practice, those who controlled the state after independence, like their counterparts elsewhere, expected it to play an extensive role in the economy. And similarly, the Mozambican state has adopted the recent prescriptions aimed at getting the state out of economic undertakings.

In the 1960s and 1970s, scholars of different political persuasions accepted the role of the state in the economy and the necessary connection between state intervention, modernization, and development. In the decade after widespread independence, scholars as well as government officials anticipated that states would promote growth and foster development, bring unity, and solidify the nation. For those who espoused modernization, states were expected to be the mechanism that would hasten economic and social development; they would be responsible for making their countries modern. They would bankroll large, technologically sophisticated industrial projects and mechanize agriculture.

By the 1980s, political and economic instability, retarded growth, slow development, and poor well-being in African countries prompted scholars to place the African state in the forefront of their attempts to discover what went wrong.[30] Much of the analysis was quite paradoxical. On the one hand, scholars observed that many institutions in African states were weak. States such as Angola, Somalia, and the former Zaire, but also those in Kenya and Zimbabwe, lacked the capacity to carry out their functions properly or they were unable to incorporate key social groups into the project of political and economic development. Some scholars attributed the cause of the poor performance of the

---

[30] For a discussion of the changing focus on the state, see V. Azarya, "Reordering State-Society Relations: Incorporation and Disengagement" in D. Rothchild and N. Chazan, eds., *The Precarious Balance: State and Society in Africa* (Boulder, CO: Westview Press, 1988), pp. 3–21.

post-independent state at least partially to the legacy of colonial rule. Colonial governments created institutions that were exploitative and/or ill-suited to the task of development and these were retained after independence. Or they pitted ethnic groups against each other such that in some countries, one ethnic group dominated political and economic power, whereas in the worst cases, civil conflicts arising from that history broke states apart. Furthermore, colonial governments did not properly train the generation of Africans who would occupy civil service jobs after independence.[31]

More economistic explanations offered by many dependency theorists suggested that state institutions were weak because of Africa's position in the world economy. Poor terms of trade for primary commodities and low levels of industrialization left African governments chronically short of funds to finance development projects. While the claims of dependency theory largely have been discredited, the advent of the global economy and fears about the effects of "globalization" have produced a variant on the dependency theme. According to current views, international financial flows and the rapidity of transport and communications further weaken the capacities of African states effectively to manage their economies. The increasing speed of financial transactions has undercut the ability of states to implement national economic strategies, while privatization nibbles away at their ability to control any income-generating resources.[32]

Ironically, scholars also have documented extensively how individuals and regimes, often within these very same "weak" states, have been remarkably capable and effective at using state institutions such as marketing boards to amass personal fortunes and to strengthen patron-client relationships or patronage networks. State officials have very efficiently redistributed resources to favored groups or used the power of the state to isolate and marginalize those who are out of favor. Scholars have devoted much attention to finding the right label for these seemingly intrusive regimes, calling them prebendal, neo-patrimonial, or personalist, but without resolving satisfactorily the paradox of how a state can be too weak to govern effectively and yet strong enough to channel resources, consistently and conspicuously, to a dominant ethnic or religious group.[33]

[31] C. Young, "The African Colonial State and its Political Legacy" in Rothchild and Chazan, eds., *The Precarious Balance*, pp. 25–65.

[32] J. Riddell, "Things Fall Apart Again: Structural Adjustment Programmes in Sub-Saharan Africa," *Journal of Modern African Studies*, 30, 1 (1992), pp. 53–68; L. Villalón and P. Huxtable, eds., *The African State at a Critical Juncture: Between Disintegration and Reconfiguration* (Boulder, CO: Lynne Rienner, 1998), see especially the alarmist note on which the book ends.

[33] See R. Joseph, "Class, State and Prebendal Politics in Nigeria," *Journal of Commonwealth and Comparative Studies*, 21, 3 (November 1983), pp. 21–38; R. Jackson and C. Rosberg, "Personal Rule: Theory and Practice in Africa" in P. Lewis, ed., *Africa: Dilemmas of Development and Change*, pp. 17–43; R. Bates, *Beyond the Miracle of the Market: The Political Economy of Agrarian Development in Kenya* (New York: Cambridge University Press, 1989), chapters 3 and 5.

Conceptions of the Mozambican state embody the paradox that is evident in descriptions of other African states. Theoretical analyses often cast the state as "weak," "soft," "underdeveloped," and "dependent" for its inability to pursue its stated goals or to avoid massive debt.[34] Yet paradoxically, the Mozambican state has also been seen as "interventionist," "authoritarian," and "coercive" for engaging in projects that belittled African customary practices, forcibly relocated people, or threatened the livelihoods of the peasantry.[35]

Neo-liberal prescriptions have helped to sustain the paradoxical portrayal of African states. On the one hand, since neo-liberals attribute the cause of poorly functioning economies to overly interventionist or "rent-seeking" states, they find solace in prescriptions that rest on the retreat of the state. The creation of "minimalist states" in Africa would appear to curb the appetites of Africa's strongmen by institutionally divorcing them from the means of accumulating wealth, thereby containing the power of the state. On the other hand, the advocacy of neo-liberalism by international financial institutions and its adoption by African countries reinforces those claims that African states continue to be undermined by forces beyond their boundaries. To those who argue that forces outside of the state generate the difficulties within African states, neo-liberalism is just another example of the hegemony exercised by the West.

The practical application of neo-liberal principles raises an issue of even greater concern. It has both encouraged and coincided with what Munro argues is a "marked tendency to de-privilege the state" in the analytical and historiographical literature.[36] In many respects, previous approaches to the state were too narrow (they focused only on the state) or too general (they did not account for the diversity found in Africa), initially too optimistic about the state's ability to transform society and then, later, too accusatory in their willingness to lay all the blame at the foot of the state. Scholars have turned their attention elsewhere, yet this appears to have occurred at the very moment when the African state is undergoing great institutional change and is subject to multiple economic and political pressures. It thus seems critical to re-examine the state, to resolve the paradoxes, and to explain the contradictions.

---

[34] C. Scott, "Socialism and the 'Soft State' in Africa: An Analysis of Angola and Mozambique," *Journal of Modern African Studies*, 26, 1 (1988), pp. 23–36; M. Ottaway, "Mozambique: From Symbolic Socialism to Symbolic Reform," *Journal of Modern African Studies*, 26, 2 (1988), pp. 211–26; M. Hall and T. Young, *Confronting Leviathan: Mozambique since Independence* (Athens, OH: Ohio University Press, 1997), chapter 4.

[35] B. Egero, *Mozambique: A Dream Undone* (Uppsala: Scandinavian Institute of African Studies, 1990), chapter 10; C. Geffray, *A Causa das Armas: Antropologia da guerra contemporanea em Moçambique*, trans. by A. Ferreira (Oporto: Edições Afrontamento, 1991) and M. Bowen, *The State Against the Peasantry: Rural Struggles in Colonial and Postcolonial Mozambique* (Charlottesville, VA: University of Virginia Press, 2000), introduction.

[36] W. Munro, "Power, Peasants and Political Development: Reconsidering State Construction in Africa," *Comparative Studies in Society and History*, 38, 1 (January 1996), pp. 112–48.

In spite of claims about "globalization" and the widespread adoption of neo-liberalism in Africa, the state has not disappeared. Like Munro, I argue that "the state is pivotal to the political future of African countries. Even in the most abject cases of political chaos in Africa, some institutional form of political and administrative organization exists, which calls itself, and is recognised as, the state."[37] Not only do people on the ground in South Africa and Mozambique acknowledge this, but so do non-governmental organizations and international financial institutions, the international court of justice, and international law. Moreover, Weiss has argued convincingly that globalization, which at any rate is probably overstated, was generated by states. She notes that many states actually initiated the current tendencies towards internationalization and that the degree to which internationalization continues will largely depend on the roles that national states adopt and the capacities that national states have.[38] This evidence hardly sounds like a eulogy for the demise of the national state. And finally, Hobsbawm has argued that the state remains the most effective mechanism for redistributing wealth in society.[39] It is likely to retain this role as wealth continues to accumulate in the hands of the few in spite of a new global preoccupation with eradicating poverty.

But if we must return to the state, how should we conceptualize it? Reconsidering "state construction" in Africa, Munro argues that "the character of states is ... determined both by political economy and by political argument. The former establishes the structural relations between accumulation and domination, but it is in the latter that relationships of domination and reproduction are finally fought out."[40] Although each of these components influences the other, for heuristic purposes we shall consider them separately for the moment. If we just look at the political economy side of the equation, Evans argues that what we should really be asking when we seek to uncover the character of states is not how much they are intervening, but what kind of intervention they are pursuing. He proposes a typology and a new vocabulary that offers a useful way of theorizing about state involvement in Africa, and in Mozambique particularly. He employs what he argues are "historically grounded ideal types" to characterize different state structures, relations between state and society, and the outcomes that state involvement in the economy helps to produce. Where states fall on the spectrum depends on what kinds of roles they play. At one end of the spectrum are predatory states. Predatory states are those that display the self-interested, rent-seeking behavior abhorred by the neo-liberals and by many of the citizens in those states. In predatory states, aggrandizing bureaucrats gobble up scarce national resources or implement policies that preserve

---

[37] Munro, "Power, Peasants and Political Development," p. 113.
[38] L. Weiss, *The Myth of the Powerless State* (Ithaca: Cornell University Press, 1998), pp. 204–8.
[39] E. Hobsbawm, "The Future of the State," *Development and Change*, 27 (1996), pp. 276–77.
[40] Munro, "Power, Peasants and Political Development," p. 122.

or enhance their power. In this scenario, the state works against society, bureaucrats lack rule-governed behavior, and the political economy suffers from extreme personalism and marketization.[41]

On the other end of the spectrum lay developmental states. Internal and external networks that link bureaucrats to each other and to other social forces work together in these states to foster development. At the same time, state institutions are still capable of formulating and implementing national objectives, and are not the "handmaidens" of powerful economic groups in society. Such "embedded autonomy" means that developmental states are able to maintain their institutional integrity at the same time that they are linked to the societies that they represent.[42] However, most developing countries, including Mozambique, cluster around the mid-point of the spectrum. Evans characterizes these as intermediary states because some of their state institutions are parasitical, while others are supportive. These states are inconsistent: they display the features of the two extremes of the spectrum, and they vacillate between the two over time and over space.[43] They are contradictory, and their behavior accounts for the paradoxical way the literature on African states has portrayed them. The roles they play are complex and require disaggregation.

To help us examine what states do and the ways that states might destructively as well as constructively perform certain roles, Evans has developed four rubrics to describe the kinds of state involvement that may occur. These roles may vary from sector to sector and may also be used in conjunction with each other in the same sector. When playing the role of "demiurge," the state is at its most interventionist, as Mozambique was from approximately 1977–83. Demiurge states distrust private capital and prefer instead to control most aspects of the economy from manufacturing to the provision of healthcare. Complementing the role of demiurge, but also analytically distinct from it, is the role of "custodian," where the state uses its capacity to restrict and regulate the activities of capital. Alternatively, when the state plays the "midwife" or practices "husbandry," as the Mozambican state now appears to be doing, it seeks to nurture and foster capital development. As midwife, the state helps to bring infant industries into being through incentives, tax breaks, or inducements to foreign investors to form links with nationals. When the state practices "husbandry," it protects and promotes existing companies.[44]

Through his comparative examination of the informatics industries in Korea, India, and Brazil, Evans usefully demonstrates that the roles played by states are historical products and can vary and evolve over time. However, what seems implicit but not explicit in his work are the power struggles or "political arguments" that influence and shape these roles and how well state institutions

[41] Evans, *Embedded Autonomy*, pp. 45–47.     [42] Evans, *Embedded Autonomy*, pp. 47–60.
[43] Evans, *Embedded Autonomy*, pp. 60–70.     [44] Evans, *Embedded Autonomy*, pp. 12–13, 77–81.

perform them. According to Munro, the "'moral calculus of state power'" is not simply an institutional question, it is also determined by the fashioning of an ideological message that enjoys or compels widespread support, and the acceptance, rejection, or mediation of state authority by social forces.[45] Ideology discursively expresses how the state intends to use its roles and what purpose the roles will serve. In the African context, however, the construction of a cohesive and legitimate ideological message has been complicated by the experience of the colonial period, where some interests sought to capture the state while others rejected and deplored it.[46] After independence, governments attempted to address this paradox by bringing together multiple and often contradictory rhetorics rooted in nationalism, modernization, populism, and socialism. In Mozambique, for example, although the Frelimo government adopted the language of Marxism-Leninism in 1977, it both complemented and contradicted that language by appealing to nationalism and modernization. It had complex reasons for combining all three, including attempts to legitimate the new state, to incorporate sectors of the society that the colonial regime had shunned, and to project a vision of Mozambique as a progressive, modern, and unified country. Unfortunately, the three strands coexisted uncomfortably in governmental rhetoric and eventually the differences among them played themselves out in government policy. As Munro argues for Africa generally, "state rhetorics of legitimation were fragmented and contradictory, rapidly becoming deeply mired in the tensions between sociopolitical incorporation and control in which the constitution and dissemination of knowledge took on deep political importance."[47] To understand why and how some states foundered and others did not, we have to consider how they interacted with social forces.

## Social forces

The different roles and ideologies that states adopt contribute to the creation of different relations between them and the various social actors they encounter. Equally, social forces help to shape, modify, reinforce, and thwart the roles of states over time. Lately, study of these social forces in Africa has exploded. The logic of neo-liberalism has shifted the focus to the market instead of the state, but also scholars have turned their attention to the study of agency rather than structure, to resistance from below rather than repression from above. The range of findings is enormous and the implications for conceptualizing

---

[45] Munro, "Power, Peasants and Political Development," pp. 122–24. The term, "moral calculus of power" cited by Munro comes from J. Lonsdale, "Political Accountability in African History" in P. Chabal, ed., *Political Domination in Africa: The Limits of State Power* (Cambridge: Cambridge University Press, 1986), p. 128.

[46] Munro citing Odhiambo in "Power, Peasants and Political Development," p. 134.

[47] Munro, "Power, Peasants and Political Development," p. 134.

the relations between state and society are great. Much of the work reveals examples of conflict as well as collaboration between social forces and states, and the use of "exit, voice, and loyalty" by different social actors to get what they want. Some scholars focus on the importance of "civil society", arguing that the existence of social organizations can help to bring about and sustain democratic and capable regimes.[48] Some expose the vibrancy of business associations and domestic capital and their importance for implementing and sustaining African forms of capitalism, while others examine how local communities and women's associations can be critical to governmental efforts to manage scarce resources. Scholarly work also considers the tenacity and resilience of the institution of chieftaincy in spite of enormous efforts by national governments to "modernize" by eliminating it. Equally, some have emphasized the importance of cultural practices, symbols, discourse, and the "invention of tradition," as mechanisms for mediating the exercise of power. Finally, much work examines the ways in which particular social groups, especially peasants, resisted and accommodated, exited from, or collaborated with colonial and post-colonial states to maintain access to land, to avoid or minimize incorporation into onerous state projects, or to gain power.[49]

---

[48] Following the rediscovery of "civil society" by political scientists, the literature has exploded, see especially N. Chazan, "Patterns of State-Society Incorporation and Disengagement in Africa" in Chazan and Rothchild, eds., *Precarious Balance*, pp.121–48; J. Harbeson, D. Rothchild, and N. Chazan, eds., *Civil Society and the State in Africa* (Boulder, CO: Lynne Rienner, 1994); G. Hyden, "Civil Society, Social Capital, and Development: Dissection of a Complex Discourse," *Studies in Comparative International Development*, 32, 1 (Spring 1997), pp. 3–30; P. Lewis, "Political Transition and the Dilemma of Civil Society in Africa" in P. Lewis, ed., *Africa: Dilemmas of Development and Change* (Boulder, CO: Westview, 1998), pp. 137–58.

For reasons that go beyond the scope of this chapter, I prefer the term "social forces" to "civil society." I find the discussion of civil society in Africa, particularly in the works above, too limited in its scope and too contingent on the development of democracy and capitalism. As a colleague of mine says, "Anyone who thinks civil society is undeveloped in Africa has obviously never witnessed a strike by market women." For a thorough and devastatingly critical evaluation of the use of "civil society" by scholars, as well as a more creative and sensitive application of the term to Africa, see J. and J. Comaroff, eds., *Civil Society and the Political Imagination in Africa: Critical Perspectives* (Chicago: University of Chicago Press, 1999). Their position is similar to that of Bayart, who also uses the term in a more nuanced fashion than the works above.

[49] On business associations and the role of domestic capital, see B. Berman and C. Leys, eds., *African Capitalists in African Development* (Boulder, CO: Lynne Rienner, 1994); and A. Spring and B. McDade, eds., *African Entrepreneurship: Theory and Reality* (Gainesville, FL: University Press of Florida, 1998). On chieftaincy, tradition and ethnicity see E. Hobsbawm and Ranger, eds., *The Invention of Tradition* (New York: Cambridge University Press, 1983); L. Vail, ed., *The Creation of Tribalism in Southern Africa* (Berkeley, CA: University of California Press, 1989); and E. van Nieuwaal and R. van Dijk, *African Chieftaincy in a New Socio-Political Landscape* (New Brunswick, NJ: Transaction Publishers, 1999).

A comprehensive essay on the growth of scholarship on the peasantry and its impact on our understanding of historical processes can be found in A. Isaacman, "Peasants and Rural Social Protest in Africa" in F. Cooper, A. Isaacman, F. Mallon, W. Roseberry and S. Stern, *Confronting Historical Paradigms: Peasants, Labor and the Capitalist World System in Africa and Latin*

While not all of the works have focused explicitly on the interaction of social agents with the state, they have important implications for reconceptualizing the roles of states in Africa. Their analysis shifts the portrayal of subjects as victims to subjects as actors, with the capacity to fashion, modify, and thwart the actions of states using historically specific cultural symbols, modes of organizing, and assertions of identity to do so. The focus on agency has lead to greater recognition and understanding of the role of domestic social actors such as urban capitalists or rural smallholders. Boone reinforces these analyses when she observes that

> despite the images and the partial reality of externally imposed rule and rulers, the forms of domination and economic exploitation that have emerged in contemporary Africa have been shaped in decisive ways by the societies that rulers seek to govern.[50]

Interactions between states and societies may be "mutually empowering," "mutually exclusive," or "mutually enfeebling," but both participants are affected by the experience.[51] For example, struggle and cooperation between the state and various social forces may act to change a state's role in one sector from demiurge to custodian. Such a change may signal the growing strength of capital **and** the willingness of the state to shift responsibility for the sector to other actors, perhaps enhancing the legitimacy of both participants in the process. Or, resistance by social groups to an ideological message with which they disagree may both undermine a state's capacity to perform particular roles and increase the position of that social group *vis-à-vis* other actors. Or, poorly conceived and poorly implemented policies may weaken both the state and the social groups to which its policies were initially addressed. As Migdal argues, "States are parts of societies. States may help mold, but they are also continually molded by, the societies within which they are embedded."[52]

In Mozambique, these social forces are many: capital, workers, and the peasantry; international advisors, multinational and national investors; whites, Indians, and Africans; urban youth and rural women. As in other African countries, social forces are highly disaggregated according to age, race, gender, social status, and wealth; across space from urban to rural areas, and from the north to the south of the country; and across historical time: pre-colonial prestige hierarchies compete and coexist with post-independent positions of

*America* (Madison, WI: University of Wisconsin Press, 1993), pp. 205–317; see also S. Berry, *No Condition is Permanent: The Social Dynamics of Agrarian Change in Sub-Saharan Africa* (Madison, WI: University of Wisconsin Press, 1993) for a very convincing account of how smallholders have mitigated the plans of colonial and post-colonial states.

[50] C. Boone, "States and ruling classes in postcolonial Africa: the enduring contradictions of power" in J. Migdal, A. Kohli, and V. Shue, eds., *State Power and Social Forces: Domination and Transformation in the Third World* (Cambridge: Cambridge University Press, 1994, repr. 1996), p. 109.

[51] Migdal, *et al.*, eds., *State Power and Social Forces*, pp. 23–30.

[52] Migdal, *et al.*, eds., *State Power and Social Forces*, p. 2.

power. Ethnic loyalties and issue-based grievances can also cut across these divisions constructing new alliances and identities. Such aggregation and differentiation reflect and influence the nature of the state as Bayart so lucidly illustrated for Africa generally.[53] Differences and alliances across time and space help to explain why one group of social actors may accept and legitimate the state while another group despises and rejects it. In the initial years of the Frelimo government, its socialist, nationalist, and modernist ideology and the policies derived from it appeared to be "mutually empowering" for urban, educated, African elites from the south from which the leadership was mainly derived. Moreover, support also came from a small working class concentrated in the industries around the southern capital of Maputo, and even smallholders, particularly those in the south who had some experience of wage-work and the "modern" ways of life that the Frelimo government was pushing. North of Maputo, the social landscape was different, and the interaction of state and social forces became "mutually enfeebling" and "mutually exclusive" over time. Except for isolated urban pockets constituting district and urban capitals in the provinces, smallholder and plantation forms of agricultural production had prevailed in the center and north of the country, and pre-colonial patterns of prestige and wealth survived alongside political positions introduced by the colonial and independent governments. Frelimo policies were initially blind to and dismissive of these complexities until passivity and resistance in the rural areas paralyzed state objectives. Although it is not at all certain that recent policy shifts will address the impasse, the government has been forced to woo new social constituencies and to change its economic approach partly because of the response by rural social actors in particular parts of the country.

Thus, these divergent features of the social landscape molded the state very differently after 1975. The divisions and combinations help to explain the differentiated responses to state projects and the extreme variations in policy outcomes, although they did not predetermine those outcomes. In some instances, the state struck political compromises in order to bolster its own legitimacy only to discover later that these compromises constrained economic development. At other times, the state enforced its political will and courted a great deal of social resistance in the process. Historical conditions helped to define the ways in which the Mozambican state interacted with the various social forces, but the state also made political and economic choices whose outcomes could not be predicted from the outset. The range in the relations between state and social actors, and the dynamic attached to those relations, explain why the state so often appears as a contradiction in Mozambique and, indeed, in the rest of Africa.[54]

---

[53] J-F. Bayart, *The State in Africa: The Politics of the Belly*, (New York: Longman, 1993).

[54] For the rest of Africa, these points are carefully demonstrated in Bayart, *The State in Africa* and Villalón and Huxtable, eds., *The African State at a Critical Juncture*, see especially Boone, " 'Empirical Statehood' and Reconfigurations of Political Order," pp. 129–41.

African countries today appear to have embarked upon a number of multiple, diverse, and complex reforms aimed at restructuring their economies. In some cases, governments have heartily embraced reforms, whereas in other cases governments have reluctantly adopted them. For some countries, the effects of the reforms have resulted in radical reorganization. Some countries now have market economies, private ownership, foreign investment, and democracy. In other nations, the effects are partial and piecemeal: governments have sold few state enterprises; official markets barely function. But whether these reforms were intended to appease the World Bank, or to make economies more efficient, or to create a radical break with commandist state ownership, everywhere they have been "political." They have involved historically constituted states battling, bullying, or appeasing manipulative elites or recalcitrant peasants in order to implement reforms. Their outcomes may be small or sweeping, but everywhere economic reforms bear the mark of the state's political engagement with social forces. Until prescriptions for restructuring Africa's economies acknowledge the politics of transformation, they will not provide reasonable solutions to Africa's ills.

# 1 The reconfiguration of the interventionist state after independence

The collapse of the Portuguese colonial regime in 1974 triggered rapid social and economic change in Mozambique. Supporters of the victorious revolutionary movement, Frelimo, held boisterous rallies welcoming the new freedoms that would come with independence. Meetings inside factories condemned capitalist exploiters and colonial collaborators. Gatherings in the countryside criticized the forced labor of yesterday and anticipated the cooperative projects of tomorrow. As might be imagined, the change of regime and the fears and expectations that accompanied it unsettled all normal economic activities, from the simplest financial transaction to the most complicated manufacturing tasks. Production in fields and factories slowed; orders went unfilled; and positions went vacant as business interests assessed their prospects of survival under a revolutionary regime and workers took to the streets to express their support for Frelimo. Not long thereafter, the new government began to intervene in the economy, first in the banking sector, and then in industry and agriculture. It nationalized rented property and proclaimed state ownership of all the land. It extended state intervention to health care, education, the practice of law, and the performance of funerals. By the early 1980s, state enterprises dominated almost every sector of the Mozambique economy.

Reflecting on the period just after independence, official sources often portrayed state intervention as an improvised response to economic breakdown, necessary to staunch sabotage and desertion by company owners and managers. I argue that more complex calculations explain both the structure, timing, and creation of the state sector. The decision to intervene or not in companies after the revolution partially derived from settler flight and sabotage, but also it was based on tactical evaluations about the government's ability and experience to run the economy at that point in time. Moreover, it greatly depended on the structure of the economy that the liberation movement had inherited from the colonial period. In addition, spontaneous worker takeovers and the determination of some capitalists to stay in Mozambique either accelerated or constrained intervention in the initial years. As the leadership of the new regime consolidated power, its ideological and theoretical preferences for a command economy surfaced. Extensive state intervention became one of the cornerstones of Frelimo ideology and central to its policy approach. While the government's commitment to socialism is often invoked to explain widespread state intervention, I argue that nationalist and modernist ideas also influenced the government's preferences for state-centered approaches. I illustrate the argument by examining the particular features of the colonial economy that Frelimo inherited; by discussing the timing, policy shifts, and eventual structure of the state sector; and by considering the multiple ideological influences on the formation of state power.

### Stratification and fluidity in the late colonial economy

The economy that Frelimo inherited at independence was a highly stratified one controlled by a rigidly authoritarian state. For most of the twentieth century, powerful colonial companies relying on the use of cheap African labor dominated the production of sugar, copra, cotton, cashew, and tea for export. Agricultural exports, together with revenue from the transit trade with South Africa and the migration of hundreds of thousands of African males to the South African gold mines, comprised the bulk of Mozambique's revenue. Foreign investors from the United Kingdom, South Africa, Switzerland, and Norway controlled many of the powerful agricultural undertakings that were in private hands. Companies such as Sena Sugar Estates, the Boror Company, or the Madal Company had operated in Mozambique since the turn of the twentieth century and dominated the production of export crops such as sugar, tea, and copra.

Subsidiaries of large, metropolitan, financial-industrial conglomerates also occupied the top of the economic hierarchy. The conglomerates had accumulated capital in Portugal during World War II and expanded their colonial investments following the war. The Champalimaud Group was one of the largest investors in Mozambique and had a monopoly on cement production throughout the colony. Other conglomerates such as Espírito Santo, the Português do Atlântico Group, and a group of interests centered around the Companhia União Fabril (CUF, Union Manufacturing Company) also had investments in sectors as diverse as cashew processing, banking, and tourism.[1]

---

[1] Considerations of length do not permit a fuller examination of the economic interests present in Mozambique at the end of colonialism but see L. Vail and L. White, *Capitalism and Colonialism in Mozambique: A Study of Quelimane District* (Minneapolis: University of Minnesota Press, 1980); G. Clarence-Smith, *The Third Portuguese Empire, 1825–1925: A Study in Economic Imperialism* (Manchester: Manchester University Press, 1985), chapter 6; D. Hedges and A. Rocha, "Moçambique durante o Apogeu do Colonialismo Portugues, 1945–1961: a Economia e a Estrutura Social" in D. Hedges, ed., *História de Moçambique: Moçambique no Auge do Colonialismo, 1930–1961*, Vol. 3 (Maputo: Departamento de História, Universidade Eduardo Mondlane [UEM], 1993), pp. 129–95; M. Pitcher, *Politics in the Portuguese Empire: The State, Industry and Cotton, 1926–1974* (Oxford: Oxford University Press, 1993), pp. 210–22; M. Newitt, *A History of Mozambique* (Bloomington, IN: Indiana University Press, 1995), chapter 17.

Furthermore, there was a group of companies that had their head offices and most of their capital in Mozambique and had amassed most of their profits locally. They used their profits to increase their investments inside Mozambique, or in a reversal of the logic of colonialism, they used their profits to expand into Portugal. Their founders were Portuguese or British, but the descendants of the original owners and personnel in managerial positions were born in Mozambique or had spent most of their lives there. During the early part of the twentieth century, legal restrictions on foreign investments and the relative weakness of metropolitan capital helped these companies to augment their concerns. They included powerful companies such as the Entreposto Group, a holding company that had subsidiaries in agriculture from the center to the north of the country (including one of the oldest companies in Mozambique, the Mozambique Company). The Entreposto Group also had interests in light industry and trade in the capital and in several northern provinces, and investments in tourism, insurance, and the Mozambique–Rhodesia pipeline. In the same category was the João Ferreira dos Santos Group with interests in cotton, rice, and sisal in northern Mozambique and holdings in light industry, finance, transport, and trade near the capital.[2]

Many of the powerful agricultural and agro-industrial companies also dominated the wholesale commerce of imports and exports. Companies such as the João Ferreira dos Santos Group (JFS), the Entreposto Group, and Boror Comercial, a subsidiary of the Boror Company, the largest copra producer in the country, imported items such as electrical materials, vehicles, and spare parts that were essential to the operation of their businesses. In turn, they exported cash crops often produced by African smallholders. Yet, large companies were not the only economic players involved in commerce at the time of independence. Portuguese settlers, *mestiços* (people of mixed race), Indians, and Africans also took part.

Although the scholarly literature largely has overlooked them, approximately 20,000 "Indians" originating from Goa (which Portugal also colonized) and the Indian sub-continent participated in the import-export trade and in retail trade in both the city and the countryside. Indian settlement in Mozambique dated at least from the seventeenth century and was linked to the vast commercial networks established between India and the East African coast.[3] By the late nineteenth and early twentieth centuries, second and third generation, Mozambican-born

---

[2] Mozambique, Banco de Moçambique, Direcção de documentação e estudos económicos, "Capitais dominantes nas principais empresas de Moçambique," *Estudos macroeconómicos e de conjuntura*, 1 (5 September 1977), pp. 83 and 89; "Group Entreposto – Expanding in Mozambique," *Focus on Mozambique*, pamphlet reprinted from *The International Review for Chief Executive Officers* (n.p.: Sterling Publications, 1994).

[3] On the early history of Indians in Mozambique see N. Alpers, *Ivory and Slaves in East Central Africa* (Berkeley: University of California Press, 1975); "Gujarat and the Trade of East Africa, c. 1500–1800," *International Journal of African Historical Studies*, IX, 1 (1976), pp. 22–44;

Indians had established fixed businesses throughout Mozambique.[4] By the late colonial period, companies such as Casa Damodar, Casa Gani, the Companhia Comercial Gordhandas Valabhdas, and others had regional importance in commerce in the north of the country. They purchased agricultural products such as copra or cashew from smallholders for export abroad and imported clothing, cooking utensils, and other consumer items for sale in the rural areas and towns. They operated along the coastal areas of Nampula around the ports of Nacala and Angoche, and on the island of Ilha de Moçambique, and within provinces such as Cabo Delgado, Nampula, and Zambezia. Indians also comprised many of the retail traders in the capital and in the smaller cities of Beira, Quelimane, and Nampula in the center and north of Mozambique.[5]

Alongside the Indians, thousands of Portuguese traders, or *cantineiros*, ran import-export businesses or operated retail establishments in the rural areas. Portuguese settlers monopolized most professional, administrative, managerial, and clerical positions in the urban areas, while a much smaller number of settlers benefitted from state-sponsored agricultural development schemes.[6] A small percentage of the African workforce also had wage-labor jobs in the urban areas while the bulk of rural, southern males migrated to the gold mines in South Africa. In the rest of the country, the majority of economically active, male and female Africans still derived their income from agriculture.[7]

Although private companies controlled key sectors of the economy, the colonial state intervened constantly to underwrite particular projects: to regulate

---

J. Leite, "Diáspora Indiana em Moçambique," *Economia Global e Gestão*, 2 (1996), pp. 67–108 and P. Machado, "'Without Scales and Balances': Indian Merchant Capital in Mozambique, *c.* 1770–1830," mimeo., 1997. The term "Indian" is somewhat of a misnomer since part of this group trace their origins to what is now Pakistan but because the term is widely used in Mozambique, I employ it here and throughout, dropping the quotation marks.

[4] Overseas Companies of Portugal, *Mozambique* (Lisbon: Overseas Companies of Portugal, 1961), pp. 9–10; K. Middlemas, *Cabora Bassa: Engineering and Politics in Southern Africa* (London: Weidenfeld and Nicolson, 1975), p. 260; "Ikbal Gafar nasceu para ser empresário," *Savana* (5 July 1996); J. Leite, "Diáspora Indiana," pp. 75–95.

[5] A. Castro, *O sistema colonial Português em África* (Lisbon: Editorial Caminho, 1980, 2nd edn.), p. 295; Mozambique, *Anuário da Província de Moçambique, 1972–1973*; "Ikbal Gafar nasceu"; J. Leite, "Diáspora Indiana," pp. 87–88; Sr. Biriba, director, Serviços Provinciais do Caju da Zambezia, Quelimane, Zambezia Province, interview, 20 May 1998 (conducted with Scott Kloeck-Jenson); Abdul Hamide Mahomede and Abdul Rasside Mahomede, owners, ARPEL, Quelimane, Zambezia Province, interview, 21 May 1998 (with Scott Kloeck-Jenson).

[6] J. Ribeiro-Torres, "Rural Development Schemes in Southern Moçambique," *South African Journal of African Affairs*, 3, 2 (1973), pp. 60–69; K. Middlemas, "Twentieth-Century White Society in Mozambique," *Tarikh*, 6, 2 (1979), pp. 35–45.

[7] See J. Penvenne, *African Workers and Colonial Racism: Mozambican Strategies and Struggles in Lourenço Marques, 1877–1962* (Portsmouth, NH: Heinemann, 1995) for a thorough study of African urban workers in the capital. Studies of male migration to the gold mines and its economic impact up to 1974 include R. First, *Black Gold: The Mozambican Miner, Proletarian and Peasant* (New York: St. Martin's Press, 1983) and L. Covane, *O Trabalho Migratório e A Agricultura no Sul de Moçambique (1920–1992)* (Maputo: Promedia, 2001). On agricultural work and livelihoods, I say much more below.

capital, to favor the powerful companies, to secure labor, to "discipline" the market. Through marketing boards, it supervised and regulated cotton, cereals, cashew, and sugar production. It controlled prices of major agricultural cash crops and subsidized production costs if world prices dropped. Through its control over the Banco Nacional Ultramarino (BNU), the central bank for the colony, it financed a huge network of colonial private and state companies from newspaper companies and insurance in the service sector to beer brewing, cashew processing, and cement production in the industrial sector to agricultural undertakings in sugar and cotton. It also supplied credit to the public sector for the construction of roads, ports, dams, and railways. Furthermore, through legislation, the colonial state taxed rural and urban Africans and, up to 1961, compelled them to seek work or to engage in public works projects under the hated *xibalo* (forced labor) system.[8] It mediated and negotiated among different economic interests, and, if the situation demanded it, the state could also be brutally repressive.

However, the economic stratification and political authoritarianism disguised a social order that was in flux by the 1970s. A lack of research on the late colonial period and the portrayal of Mozambique as a stagnant backwater by official Frelimo sources have obscured the changing economic and social dynamics within the colony prior to independence.[9] In the two preceding decades, the Portuguese state had become much more aggressively developmentalist, earmarking funds for large projects in the colonies and soliciting foreign investment. This was both a response to, but also coincident with, the formation of the European Community in the 1950s, the achievement of formal independence in much of the rest of Africa, and the presence of a growing resistance movement in the north of Mozambique. The injection of funds from the state and investors financed Mozambique's expanding industrialization near the southern capital of Maputo (formerly Lourenço Marques). Limited industrialization occurred near the second city of Beira and in Quelimane and Nampula as well. Between 1964–65 and 1972–73, the total number of registered businesses in Mozambique grew by 56 percent from 1,073 companies to 1,675 companies.[10] Many of the new businesses were financed by the same profitable foreign, metropolitan, and local interests that had long been entrenched in agriculture and agro-processing, but there were new foreign interests as well as investments by arriving Portuguese settlers. By the 1970s, Mozambique was the eighth most industrialized country

---

[8] Castro, *O sistema colonial*, pp. 40–41; Clarence-Smith, *The Third Portuguese Empire*, p. 212; Hedges and Rocha, "Moçambique durante o Apogeu," p. 172; C. Langa, "A actividade do Banco Nacional Ultramarino em Moçambique 1864–1974," Banco de Moçambique, Staff Paper no. 8 (June 1997), pp. 44–45.

[9] See *Mozambique Revolution*, especially no. 40 (September 1969), and the 1974 speech by Samora Machel to the Soviet Academy of Sciences in B. Munslow, ed., *Samora Machel: An African Revolutionary* (London: Zed Books, 1985), chapter 2.

[10] Mozambique, *Anuário da Província de Moçambique, 1972–1973*.

in Africa and had a rather diversified manufacturing base.[11] Metalworking, cement, and petroleum refining factories sprang up in a designated industrial zone near the capital. Mozambique had pesticide and fertilizer factories, chemical companies, and companies devoted to the construction of transport materials.

Though their lives were still greatly circumscribed, many Africans found new opportunities in the urban areas. A small number of mostly male Africans managed to become small shopkeepers, doctors, and lawyers, and to occupy lower level positions in public service.[12] They were joined by salaried Africans, who worked in industry, on the docks, in the public sector, or in trade. All together, of the 5½ million economically active Africans recorded in official statistics, approximately half a million participated in non-agricultural wage-labor jobs around the time of independence. The total included 100,000 skilled Mozambican males who worked in the mines of South Africa. Women comprised only approximately 15 percent of the total, but they were noticeable in the textile and cashew processing industries, in services, and in domestic work.[13] What the official figures did not capture, and what may have been considerable, was the income from informal production and trade by women of groundnuts, fruits, firewood, and beer.[14]

The bulk of the African workforce still participated in low-paying, labor intensive agricultural work for their subsistence and for their income. Yet changes were occurring in the family or smallholder sector, too. As southern males had done by migrating to the gold mines in South Africa for the better part of the twentieth century, northern males now began to combine wage work in the cities or work for settlers with crop production on their family farms and

---

[11] J. Torp, *Industrial Planning and Development in Mozambique: Some Preliminary Considerations*, Scandinavian Institute of African Studies, Research Report no. 50 (Uppsala: Scandinavian Institute of African Studies, 1979), p. 7.

[12] Until 1961, many urban Africans legally occupied the **assimilado** category – an insidious category granted to those Africans who adopted Portuguese language, culture, and habits. The category was abolished in 1961, though no doubt it was maintained in practice.

[13] Mozambique, *Recenseamento da População* (1980), tables 7 and 11A; L. Caballero, *The Mozambican Agricultural Sector- A (sic) Background Information*, Swedish University of Agricultural Sciences, International Rural Development Centre, Working Paper no. 138 (Uppsala: Swedish University of Agricultural Sciences, 1990), p. 22; K. Sheldon, "Sewing Clothes and Sorting Cashew Nuts: Factories, Families, and Women in Beira, Mozambique," *Women's Studies International Forum*, 14, 1/2 (1991), pp. 27–35; J. Penvenne, "Seeking the Factory for Women: Mozambican Urbanization in the Late Colonial Era," *Journal of Urban History*, 23, 3 (March 1997), pp. 342–79. As Penvenne notes on p. 353, it is very likely that the census undercounted urban women and the work they did.

[14] Informal work by women in the colonial period remains an underresearched area, yet photos by José dos Santos Rufino record trade by women as early as the 1920s. See J. dos Santos Rufino, *Albuns Fotográficos e Descritívos da Colónia de Moçambique*, Vol. 10 (n.p.: Hamburgo, Broschek & Co., 1929) and for the 1940s, see Penvenne, "Seeking the Factory," pp. 353–54; K. Sheldon also suggests it in "Machambas in the City: Urban Women and Agricultural Work in Mozambique," *Lusotopie* (1999), pp. 125–28.

informal trade.[15] Additionally, female farmers gained part of their income from the sale of cotton or cashews, or from making pots for sale in local markets. Some women also brewed beer to give to friends and family in exchange for extra labor. Monetary income from wage work, mining, or cash crops amounted to approximately 44 percent of the income of African farmers by the late 1960s, with the rest accounted for by the production of subsistence crops.[16]

The form and nature of the changes to the rural areas varied from region to region and community to community, but they reconfigured existing social and economic relations that the Portuguese administration had already greatly manipulated. On the one hand, pre-existing social patterns often determined who benefitted from economic opportunities. In some areas, for example, the beneficiaries of new schemes to promote "progressive farmers" were state-appointed "traditional authorities," known as *regulos* (chiefs), and their subordinates and relatives. Thus, social promotion schemes served to reinforce state-sponsored political and economic hierarchies in the rural areas.[17] Welding together more

---

[15] Here and throughout the book I use the terms "family sector" and "smallholders" interchangeably. They refer to agricultural production which is primarily engaged in by family members, though additional manual labor might be used during peak periods such as weeding and harvesting. As a relational category, usage of the term "family sector" has changed over time. During the colonial period, it was distinct from the private sector (companies and settlers), which used hired manual labor or mechanization or made contract farming arrangements to engage in agricultural production. Its usage continued under Frelimo to distinguish state enterprises, cooperatives, and collectives from production by African households. It continues today to differentiate production by smallholders from that of commercial companies and, in certain regions, from that of large farmers or *privados* (privates). See Mozambique, Ministério da Agricultura, Departamento de Estatística Agrária, "An [sic] Preliminary Analysis fo [sic] the Size of Land Holdings in the Family Sector in Mozambique Using Information from the 1993 Ministry of Agriculture Survey of the Family Sector" (May 1994), p. 7.

[16] See First, *Black Gold*, pp. 128–35 for the variety of activities engaged in by southern farming households, although she does not specify what women do. For specific references to women, see M. Taylor, "Spirits of Capitalism in Chokwe: Experiences of Work and Identity among Shangaan Peasants in Southern Mozambique," Ph.D. dissertation, Brandeis University (1998), pp. 142–46 and H. Gengenbach, "Where Women Make History: Pots, Stories, Tattoos, and Other Gendered Accounts of Community and Change in Magude District, Mozambique, *c.* 1800 to the Present," Ph.D. dissertation, University of Minnesota (1999), chapter 4 on pot-making by women. These accounts suggest that statistics such as those provided by Caballero probably overlooked a considerable informal trade in goods produced by women. See Caballero, *The Mozambique Agricultural Sector*, pp. 22 and 86.

[17] For examples of this phenomenon, see Ribeiro-Torres, "Rural Development Schemes," pp. 65–67; J. van den Berg, "A Peasant Form of Production: Wage-Dependent Agriculture in Southern Mozambique," *Canadian Journal of African Studies*, XXI, 3 (1987), p. 383; and A. Isaacman, *Cotton is the Mother of Poverty: Peasants, Work and Rural Struggle in Colonial Mozambique, 1938–1961* (Portsmouth, NH: Heinemann, 1996), chapter 8. The term "traditional authorities" is rather ambiguous as it may include state-appointed *regulos* or chiefs and their subordinates (*cabos*, etc.) and/or pre-colonial customary positions of authority, and/or post-colonial re-inventions of customary authority. Moreover, sometimes state-appointed traditonal authorities overlapped with customary positions of authority, and sometimes they did not. I clarify in the text the manner in which I am using the term and I drop the quotation marks.

firmly existing economic and political power did not always strengthen support for the Portuguese, however. Instead, it gave some state-appointed, traditional authorities a constituency through which they could mobilize their grievances against a regime they considered unfair and unjust. Although the regime parcelled out land and credit in the 1960s, simultaneously it blocked further accumulation by Africans, or appropriated land to distribute to Portuguese migrants, or enacted administrative reforms that disturbed existing customary boundaries. Some of those who had benefitted from social promotion schemes but suffered in other ways then convinced their communities to support Frelimo. Chiefly and/or customary support for the liberation struggle was not confined to Mozambique, moreover. Analysts of the liberation war in Zimbabwe also note the close connections between some chiefs or other holders of traditional power and the leaders of the struggle there.[18]

On the other hand, the economic and political changes equally fomented sharp social divisions. These divisions were twofold. First, some of the traditional authorities and their auxiliaries who had gained access to additional economic power had been implanted by the Portuguese. Their constituencies did not see them as legitimate and their added wealth sowed tension. Thus, some communities continued to be loyal to customary authorities that they themselves recognized, but who were unknown to the Portuguese and who were not necessarily beneficiaries of schemes sponsored by the colonial government. Disturbed by the favoritism of the colonial government to those whom these communities did not see as legitimate, these communities also entered into resistance against the colonial regime.[19]

Second, the emergence of a wealthier stratum of African farmers or traders (either as a result of their own guile or good fortune or because they benefitted from state-sanctioned cooperatives or provisions of credit and land) sometimes threatened state-appointed traditional and customary authorities and those who

---

[18] See D. Lan on the support of the *mhondoro* or spirit mediums in Dande district in *Guns and Rain: Guerrillas and Spirit Mediums in Zimbabwe* (London: James Currey, 1985); J. Alexander, "Things Fall Apart, The Centre Can Hold: Processes of Post-War Political Change in Zimbabwe's Rural Areas" in N. Bhebe and T. Ranger, eds., *Society in Zimbabwe's Liberation War* (Portsmouth, NH: Heinemann, 1996), pp. 185–86.

[19] In the late 1960s, the Portuguese engaged in strenuous attempts to discern who was legitimate and who was not: for Nampula (Mozambique District) and Cabo Delgado, see Arquivo Histórico de Moçambique (AHM), Secção Especial (SE), Portugal, Província de Moçambique, Serviços de Centralização e Coordenação de Informações (SCCI), "Prospecção das Forças Tradicionais-Distrito de Moçambique," by J. Branquinho (1969); and AHM, SE, Governo do Distrito de Cabo Delgado, SCCI, "Análise da Situação do Distrito desde 14 Setembro 1962 a' 31 Dezembro 1971." See also I. Lundin, "A pesquisa piloto sobre a Autoridade/Poder Tradicional em Moçambique-Uma somatório comentado e analisado" in I. Lundin and F. Machava, eds., *Autoridade e Poder Tradicional*, Vol. 1 (Maputo: Ministério da Administração Estatal, Núcleo de desenvolvimento administrativo, 1995), p. 20 and J. Guamba, "Reforma das orgãos locais," II Seminário sobre a reforma dos orgãos locais e o papel da autoridade tradicional, Ministério da Administração Estatal, Maputo (19–23 April 1993), p. 24.

had not benefitted from the schemes. This new group of "progressive farmers" or wealthier smallholders criticized "traditional" authority, relied on civil rather than customary law to get married or to seek title to land, and went to administrative authorities rather than chiefs or their subordinates to solve problems.[20] They produced for formal markets, hired labor, and lobbied for greater security of individual land tenure. They often held religious beliefs and values that were different from those of chiefs or the rest of their social group. For example, in southern Mozambique, capital accumulation by "progressive" farmers in Gaza Province differentiated them from traditional authorities in the area. Moreover, chiefs and their subordinates frowned on the adoption of Christianity and other beliefs by wealthier smallholders.[21] In the north, rifts occurred even within chiefly lineages. On the Mueda plateau in Cabo Delgado, young members of the Makonde ethnic group dominated two successive cooperative movements, the Sociedade Algodoeira Africana Voluntária de Moçambique (SAAVM, the African Voluntary Cotton Society of Mozambique) and Machamba 25. According to Adam, "The leaders of SAAVM and Machamba 25 were strictly related to the leading families of the seat of the chieftaincy in Mueda. They were cousins, children, or parents of assistant heads and heads of the regulado of Mueda."[22] Yet the involvement in other activities and accumulation of wealth by relatives threatened the *regulo* himself, because these actions undermined his ability to control the supply of labor.[23] Moreover, other rural Africans viewed members of the cooperative with suspicion. They referred to cooperative members as "whites" or "black-whites" because they had attained better economic positions than the average rural African household. They had access to more resources and land, and their interests diverged from those of others.[24] A similar phenomenon occurred in the southern part of the country too, where smallholders referred to beneficiaries of the settlement schemes as "whites in their moneypockets." The label had two meanings: Africans in the schemes had money like whites did. Second, in their pockets they might be white, but otherwise they were black, even if they were acting superior, like whites did.[25]

---

[20] AHM, Fundo do Governo Geral (GG), Portugal, Província de Moçambique, Comissão de Estudos de Planos de Fomento, Grupo de Trabalho da Promoção Social, "Promoção da população rural integrada nas regedorias" (1962), p. 12.

[21] O. Roesch, "Socialism and Rural Development in Mozambique: The Case of Aldeia Comunal 24 de Julho," Ph.D. dissertation, University of Toronto (1986), pp. 80–81 and Taylor, "Spirits of Capitalism," p. 132.

[22] Y. Adam, "Mueda, 1917–1990: resistência, colonialismo, libertação e desenvolvimento," *Arquivo*, 14 (October 1993), p. 23.

[23] D. Hedges and A. Chilundo, "A contestação da situação colonial, 1945–1961" in Hedges, ed., *História de Moçamibique*, p. 237; H. West, " 'This Neighbor is Not My Uncle!': Changing Relations of Power and Authority on the Mueda Plateau," *Journal of Southern African Studies*, 24, 1 (March 1998), p. 151.

[24] Adam, "Mueda," p. 23.   [25] Taylor, "Spirits of Capitalism," pp. 133–34.

By the late 1960s, then, disparities appeared between districts and provinces in the country that had been prioritized by the government and those that the government had not favored; between the more developed south and the less developed north; between areas that were productive and those that were not; between communities that had benefitted from the Portuguese and those that had not; between individuals who had accumulated some capital and those who had not. Cross-cutting cleavages arose between the wealthy and the poor, the young and the old, men and women, more "modern" versus more "traditional" people, rural versus urban residents. Splits as well as alliances emerged between the majority of rural Africans and a "progressive" minority, and between those who wielded political power and those who recently had gained economic power. Economic changes and policy shifts, and the strategies of resistance and accommodation that rural people adopted to mediate their impact, had reshaped and in some cases destabilized rural communities. The Portuguese confronted a volatile rural situation which they worsened through repression. The government continued to promote growth but also to repress rural resistance through the formation of *aldeamentos* (strategic hamlets), control over internal movement, and imprisonment of alleged subversives, including imprisonment of traditional authorities.[26] Imprisonment and the formation of *aldeamentos* only heightened rural distrust of the Portuguese.

For its part, the Frelimo movement took advantage of the rural tensions to incorporate and recruit dissatisfied peoples into the movement. Those who had taken advantage of colonial reforms and then found their aspirations blocked by favoritism or protectionism to Portuguese settlers were attracted to Frelimo. They were joined by those who had been repressed by, or had economic grievances against, the Portuguese.[27] Traditional authorities who lacked legitimacy sometimes sought out the revolutionary movement in order to gain respect. Equally, Frelimo tried to recruit, sometimes forcibly, prestigious local leaders because they commanded authority and could bring more members into the movement.[28] The tensions that these groups brought with them would later provoke conflicts within Frelimo, the resolution of which would shape decisively by 1975 the kind of movement it would be. Moreover, the fragmentation and disintegration of customary and traditional institutions prior to the end of

[26] J. Coelho, "Protected Villages and Communal Villages in the Mozambican Province of Tete (1968–1982)," Ph.D. dissertation, Department of Social and Economic Studies, University of Bradford (1993), chapters 5–7, and AHM, SE, Cabo Delgado, "Análise," n.p.

[27] The most notorious example, of course, was Nkavandame and his supporters alongside many impoverished Makondes, but there were others also. See Coelho, "Protected Villages," chapter 7, *Mozambique Revolution*, and M. Pitcher, "Disruption Without Transformation: Agrarian Relations and Livelihoods in Nampula Province, Mozambique 1975–1995," *Journal of Southern African Studies*, 24, 1 (March 1998), pp. 123–24.

[28] AHM, SE, SCCI, "Prospecção," p. 171 and AHM, SE, Cabo Delgado, "Análise," p. 6 and p. 31; H. West, "'This Neighbor'", pp. 151–52.

colonialism have not been given the attention they deserve in more recent debates about traditional authorities in Mozambique, yet their implications for interpreting Frelimo's later experience in the rural areas are significant. That many rural communities were quite disturbed before independence suggests that Frelimo's challenge was not necessarily to destroy an existing framework but to bring a measure of security to places that were already in great disarray.

## A tactical transition

Given the shifting allegiances and dynamic economic changes occurring within Mozambique, it is doubtful how much longer the Portuguese could have controlled the situation; but at any rate, changes in the metropole dramatically altered Mozambique's political future. Following a coup in Portugal in April of 1974, a new government in Portugal reached an agreement with Frelimo to end the war in Mozambique. Frelimo formed a government, followed by formal independence in June of 1975. Almost immediately upon taking power, Frelimo signalled that it would rely on the state to address the economic crisis resulting from the abrupt change of government and to confront the legacy left by colonialism. Even before official independence, the Transitional Government passed a measure in February of 1975 that sanctioned state intervention into businesses on the following grounds: threats of dismissal of workers, the halting or reduction of production, the destruction of equipment, decapitalization or disinvestment, and abandonment. The measure considered a company abandoned if it had not been working normally for more than ninety days and, in those cases, the government nationalized the company, transferring *de facto* but not always *de jure* ownership to the state.[29] In those cases where the government did not take legal possession, state intervention took various forms. Following an inquiry into a company's shortcomings or abuses, the government sometimes replaced the entire management with an administrative commission to manage the company, suspended one or more of the managers, obtained finances to run the company, or made any other corrections necessary to keep the company functioning. In industry, the government often established production councils or dynamizing groups. Composed of workers and Frelimo members, these organizations worked alongside, or instead of, an administrative commission in order to keep a company in operation. In those companies where the government established administrative commissions or production councils, the companies legally remained under private ownership. Yet the Office of

---

[29] Decreto-lei 16/75 (13 February 1975), *Boletim Oficial de Moçambique*, I Série. The state did not always take out legal titles to the properties over which it assumed control. It relied instead on a constitutional provision that the state owned all the land to support its claim. See J. Bruce, "Options for State Farm Divestiture and the Creation of Secure Tenure," Land Tenure Center, University of Wisconsin-Madison (28 December 1989).

Control over Industrial and Commercial Production in the Ministry of Industry and Trade made all decisions governing their production.[30]

Explanations of the immediate post-independence period consistently emphasized the improvisational character of this early state intervention into the economy. Analysts and government reports presented intervention as an expedient but reluctant response to capital flight, absenteeism, and sabotage, and they were almost apologetic about the measure. Rather than the planned implementation of some ideological blueprint, state intervention was a response to economic breakdown and a measure to maintain production. Reluctantly, the government intervened when it became clear that owners were deliberately going into debt, sending capital out of the country, smashing up machinery, or not repairing equipment.[31]

Much evidence supports the argument that the government was reactive rather than proactive, tactical rather than ideological in the first two years after independence. The argument merits consideration because doing so shows how the colonial legacy, not ideology, initially influenced the pattern of state intervention. Moreover, it reveals some of the compromises that were made during the early years. These compromises would later shape the trajectory of the command economy and the transition to a free market one. However, Frelimo's early caution and pragmatism should not obscure a stronger tendency within the movement and one that was obvious to many in 1975. The Frelimo movement was anti-capitalist and statist and would become decidedly so once it consolidated power. We examine both of these tendencies in some detail.

The rate of settler departure in the initial years after independence lends credence to claims that government measures were reactive rather than revolutionary. Most of the quarter of a million settlers had left Mozambique by 1976. Because they controlled key sectors of the economy, their exodus caused substantial negative economic effects.[32] Almost anyone connected to the former colonial government left and, because the previous government had many economic investments, the impact was considerable and far-reaching.

---

[30] Mozambique, Ministerio da Indústria e Comercio, Gabinete de Controlo de Produção Industrial e Comercial, "Recomendações Gerais as Comissões Administrativas," 1976; J. Hanlon, *Mozambique: The Revolution Under Fire*, (London: Zed Books, 1984), pp. 47–48 notes that enterprises were shifted from one legal category to the other, as in the case of Companhia do Buzi.

[31] See Mozambique, "Programa de emergencia" (September 1976), pp. 5–6; L. Caballero, T. Thomsen, and A. Andreasson, *Mozambique – Food and Agriculture Sector*, Rural Development Studies no. 16 (Uppsala: Swedish University of Agriculture, 1985), p. 39; Hanlon, *The Revolution Under Fire*, p. 76, and M. Wuyts, *Money and Planning for Socialist Transition: The Mozambican Experience* (Brookfield, VT: Gower Publishing, 1989), p. 41.

[32] D. Wield, "Mozambique – Late Colonialism and Early Problems of Transition" in G. White, R. Murray, and C. White, eds., *Revolutionary Socialist Development in the Third World* (Lexington: University Press of Kentucky, 1983), p. 85.

Government employees left jobs with the railways and road transport sector, at the ports, the dams, and the national bank. The former government had controlled all of these sectors. The government-run, marketing boards in charge of supervising the cotton or sugar or cereals trade lost most of their administrators, and the research and testing components of the agriculture ministry lost scientists and technicians. In the private sector, foreign owners deserted construction companies near the capital and sizeable tea plantations in the center of the country. For example, the owners of Monteiro e Giro, a group of tea plantations in Zambezia province, abandoned it immediately at independence and the state intervened to maintain production. Initially, at least, individuals of Portuguese or Indian ancestry and colonial companies also deserted extensive wholesale trade networks as well as local retail trade operations that conducted business in the countryside. In Maputo and Beira, many owners of clothing and footwear businesses, funeral parlors, papermills, stationary shops, and jewelry stores fled across the border to South Africa and Rhodesia or journeyed back to Portugal.

Moreover, some company owners and managers destroyed valuable infrastructure and equipment, or transported it out of the country prior to their departure. Every visitor to Maputo hears the story about how the Portuguese owners of a waterfront hotel blocked its elevator shafts with cement before they fled the country. In Zambezia, government officials reported that managers of private companies smuggled sums of money out of the country, failed to pay workers their salaries or paid them late, and destroyed company machinery.[33] For example, the managers of the Boror Company smuggled copra out of the country on a boat going down the river near Quelimane. Before they left, the owners sabotaged equipment, destroyed documents, neglected to pay employees, and depleted the company's capital, a situation which prompted the government to intervene in 1976.[34]

The nature of the transition, together with the fact that Portugal had also experienced a revolution, likely prompted many people either to make trouble for the new regime or to go. Because of insecurity or racism, many settlers were unwilling to make a commitment to a largely black, independent, government in Mozambique. Many had ingrained prejudices that prevented them from hearing the more conciliatory overtures of the Frelimo government towards the Portuguese people (in contrast to the harsh criticisms Frelimo reserved for colonial officials). Some of the settlers made inflammatory remarks about imagined Frelimo atrocities, or tried to form movements to undermine the new government. Much of the support for the short-lived, settler-based,

---

[33] Mozambique, "Relatório da Província da Zambezia ao III Conselho Agrário Nacional" (June 1978), p. 2.

[34] Vail and White, *Capitalism and Colonialism*, p. 1; N. Afonso, "Boror: criar novas relações de produção," *Tempo*, 385 (19 February 1978), p. 54.

counter-revolutionary movement, FICO (I am staying) came from this quarter.[35] As the Portugese security police (PIDE) had done before it, FICO portrayed Frelimo supporters as white-hating, black nationalists who were prepared to murder whites once they got into power. One of the means that supporters of FICO used to spread their message was to attack whites who were suspected of backing Frelimo.[36] Undoubtedly, such messages and actions had the effect of scaring off investors, whether or not they actually feared a Frelimo government.

Embroiled in its own governmental reorganization, Portugal also abandoned settlers in Mozambique as well as in Angola, offering little in the way of moral or political pressure on the new regimes in these countries to negotiate with settlers on a case by case basis. In addition, the new government in Lisbon had already nationalized many of the national and colonial assets of powerful Portuguese companies such as CUF, Espírito Santo, and Champalimaud, leaving them with no stake in the former colonies. Such actions caused settlers to doubt the willingness of the Portuguese government to defend their interests against a potentially expansionist Frelimo government. According to one informant, Portugal gave very little support to Portuguese capitalists and would not negotiate with the Mozambican government on their behalf. This response may have caused those who were less powerful, such as the owners of small and medium businesses, to flee. However, for those who fled to Portugal, the reception was not much more favorable. One informant recalled that radical supporters of the Portuguese government stoned settlers' cars that had been shipped from Maputo to Lisbon.[37] At any rate, Portugal was experiencing its own economic reorganization and political instability and this undoubtedly contributed to the insecurity of settlers.

Even with widespread abandonment and sabotage, the degree of state intervention and nationalization in the first two and a half years after Frelimo assumed leadership was selective and limited, evidence which further supports official claims that the measure was expedient. Out of a total of approximately 1,675 companies existing throughout the country at the time of independence, the state was only involved in approximately 319 companies in key sectors of the economy by 1977, the year the government officially proclaimed its adherence to Marxism-Leninism.[38] Of the top 100 companies in Mozambique, the government only actively intervened in or nationalized approximately 25 percent.[39]

---

[35] See K. Middlemas, "Twentieth-Century White Society", pp. 43–44 and *Cabora Bassa*, pp. 335–36.

[36] Middlemas, *Cabora Bassa*, p. 328.

[37] António Galamba, former director, Banco Standard Totta de Moçambique, Maputo, interview, 9 April 1998.

[38] Wield, "Mozambique – Late Colonialism," p. 89 and Wuyts, *Money and Planning*, p. 43.

[39] British-Portuguese Chamber of Commerce, "As maiores empresas de Moçambique" (1970), mimeo.

Except for the takeover of tea companies in Zambezia, establishing a state presence in the economy was an urban phenomenon rather than a rural one. Most of the companies that the government intervened in were small (under twenty workers) and medium (between twenty and a hundred workers) industrial and commercial companies, and they did not require specific expertise to operate them. Without legally nationalizing the companies, the government appointed administrative commissions composed of state officials who took strategic company decisions regarding the purchase of raw materials, production targets, and employment. For example, the state established administrative commissions in seven out of thirteen cashew processing factories. It also intervened in the majority of civil construction and public works factories, and non-electrical machinery. It was involved in about one-quarter to one-third of electrical material construction, metalworking, and transport material factories. In the sector of mineral extraction, the government only intervened in one company and that was an investment in Mozambique by a Rhodesian subsidiary of Lonrho, a large multinational. Since Rhodesia was subject to UN sanctions at the time, the takeover was understandable. Most of the industries and even many of the agro-processing factories were located in Maputo.[40]

With a few exceptions, large and small producers of tobacco, sugar, copra, cashews, and sisal saw no state intervention in management or the nationalization of assets immediately after independence. Tea was the only sector with any significant capital in which the government intervened and it had been dominated by small and medium settlers who had left the country. Out of eighteen tea plantations (all of which were located in Zambezia Province), the government established administrative commissions in half of them and controlled about 43 percent of the total capital in the sector.[41] Otherwise, the government intervened mostly to take over abandoned small settler farms rather than large agricultural companies. For example, around twenty-five fruit and vegetable farms in the district of Maputo had come under the control of the Ministry of Agriculture by 1976. On those farms, the government established dynamizing groups made up of party activists and former workers to manage the farm. Administrative commissions and cabinets regulated output.[42]

The pattern and pace of state intervention lend support to claims regarding the government's improvisational nature in this early period. Leaving aside for the moment the question of whether the government was inclined or not to

[40] Mozambique, Banco de Moçambique (BM), "Capitais dominantes"; Torp, "Industrial Planning," p. 17.

[41] BM, "Capitais dominantes" and Mozambique, Ministério da Agricultura, Direcção Provincial de Agricultura da Zambézia, "Relatório a 2a Reunião do Conselho Agrário Nacional" (25–30 April 1977), n.p.

[42] "Criar novas condições para o maximo aproveitamento da produção," Tempo, 316 (24 October 1976), pp. 48–54.

abolish the private sector, from an institutional perspective, the government was not equipped to engage in massive takeovers just after the revolution. As an indication of its inexperience, the government repeatedly restructured national and provincial state institutions.[43] It was disorganized and its goals were unclear. Politically, the government neither had the legitimacy nor the administrative personnel to intervene into or to nationalize every company in the country.

Lacking personnel and experience, the Frelimo government took over what had been left behind, and also built upon and continued a colonial legacy of state intervention. The new government assumed all assets formerly belonging to the colonial state, even prior to official independence on 25 June 1975. As these assets were already part of the public domain under the former regime, "nationalization" was essentially a technical exercise. These included the ports, railways and a share of the Cahora Bassa Dam. Notably, the assets assumed by the new government included BNU, the colonial state bank. BNU became the Banco de Moçambique (Mozambique Bank), the national bank for the new country. At the same time, the government took over two credit institutions previously funded by the colonial government. By 1977, the three financial institutions together accounted for almost 60 percent of the deposits in the country. With regard to credit, the Banco de Moçambique controlled about 71 percent of the credit in the country.[44]

The transfer of assets from the colonial state to the independent one meant that the new government gained majority or minority shares in all those companies in which these financial institutions or the colonial state had investments. BNU's investments had been considerable, but the Búzi Company was the only large company in which the new government gained a majority share. Historically, BNU had invested in this sugar, cotton, and copra growing company in Sofala province. Like BNU, the Banco de Moçambique nominated members of the board but retained the management that existed prior to independence.

The nationalization of BNU also gave the government minority shares in several limited companies. The government gained a share of the Zambezia Company, which produced cotton, copra, and tea during the colonial period. The rest of its minority shares were in industries that had been founded near the end of the colonial period. Some of these were in agro-industrial processing, such as sugar, edible oils, and cashew, or in industries such as beer, civil construction, metallurgy, bicycle production, furniture, cement, and coal. With the exception of beer factories, where the Banco de Moçambique retained a minority share in all nine companies, generally the bank had a share in only one or two companies in each sector and did not participate in management. Most of the companies

---

[43] Mozambique, Ministério da Agricultura, "Reunião do sector estatal agrário," Maputo (13 February 1979).
[44] Mozambique, *Boletim Oficial de Moçambique*, I Série (59), 2o Suplemento (17 May 1975), Decreto 2/75 and Lei Orgânica do Banco de Moçambique.

were located in Maputo.[45] By simply nationalizing what was public before, the independent state gained a foothold in some of the productive sectors in the country but did not yet declare them "state enterprises."

Because the government lacked the capacity to intervene in every company, it did not have the power and the interest to confront those companies that were determined to stay in Mozambique. Those that remained subsequently shaped certain aspects of the command economy, participated in its erosion, and influenced the transition to a free market economy. The continued existence of a private sector, particularly one dominated by large agricultural companies, rather glaringly exposed the limitations of the anti-capitalist rhetoric that had been employed during the liberation struggle. As early as 1964, *Mozambique Revolution*, the mouthpiece of the movement wrote "FREE NATION means the elimination of all the concessionary monopolies dealing in cotton, sugar, sisal, tea, which only benefit one person or a small number of people."[46] Yet initially these companies were neither nationalized nor brought under state management. Some were **never** nationalized. The Mozambique Company, one of the oldest concessionary companies in the country, and its parent company, the Entreposto Group, remained after the revolution and have continued to operate in Mozambique to this day. Moreover, two other companies with long histories in the country, João Ferreira dos Santos and the Madal Group, remained in private hands with few losses of their assets. They, too, have continued to function. Even companies such as Sena Sugar Estates, Indústria de Caju Mocita, Companhia de Culturas de Angoche, and others that the movement claimed were outposts of foreign imperialists were not nationalized or intervened in immediately, though later, circumstances would force the government's hand. In fact, in the case of Anglo-American, which owned Mocita, the government expressed great willingness in having the company stay and wanted to know what guarantees the company needed.[47]

Official justifications for taking over companies and the pattern of governmental intervention suggest a pragmatic response to settler abandonment and economic breakdown in the initial years after independence. In addition, a lack of capacity and inexperience made the government cautious and counselled it to work with those companies that wished to stay. The government may also have feared the ramifications of nationalizing the assets of foreigners. Thus, what was or was not abandoned, together with those assets inherited from the colonial legacy of extensive state control, helped to shape the pattern of state intervention in the first few years.

[45] Mozambique, BM, "Capitais dominantes."
[46] "What Do We Want?", *Mozambique Revolution*, 2 (January 1964), p. 4.
[47] Hoover Institution, Stanford University, Keith Middlemas Collection (HI/SU/KMC), tapes 21–23, M 19, interview N. Heffer (Anglo-American Corporation representative in Mozambique), November–December 1976, interview by Keith Middlemas.

## Re-configuring the interventionist state

After 1977, the government largely abandoned the caution and pragmatism of the earlier years. Instead, state intervention became the cornerstone of Frelimo's ideological and policy approaches. It served as the basis upon which Frelimo would seek to reorder the power structure and transform social and spatial relations in Mozambique. By 1982, only 27 percent of firms in industry, commerce and agriculture remained private; the rest had become state enterprises (*empresas estatais*) or continued to be "intervened" in (*empresas intervencionadas*).[48] With a few notable exceptions, the state controlled most strategic sectors in the economy, large as well as small companies, in the north and south of the country. To explain this outcome, it is critical to recognize that a divergent approach was gathering pace alongside the apparent pragmatism of the early years.[49] The approach was decidedly revolutionary and statist. Spontaneous worker and peasant takeovers intensified it, and rhetoric that criticized and threatened the private sector reinforced it. These events offer compelling evidence that settlers and companies may have been harassed and forced into leaving Mozambique and that the government had every intention of adopting a dominant role in the economy from the outset; it was not just responding reluctantly to the exodus of settlers. Indeed, by 1977, the crystallization of Frelimo's ideology around an anti-capitalist, statist message and its growing political strength signalled the country's considerable movement toward a command economy.

The anti-capitalist and statist character of Frelimo had deepened considerably following a crisis in the movement in 1968–69. The crisis resulted in the death of Eduardo Mondlane and eventually established Samora Machel as the new leader. It erupted around the expulsion of Lazaro Nkavandame, who had been an early supporter of the liberation movement. By the late sixties he was a member of the Central Committee and the Provincial Secretary of Cabo Delgado in charge of trade.[50] A "progressive" Makonde farmer and trader, Nkavandame and his supporters advocated an anti-colonialist position that celebrated Mozambique's ethnic diversity and, at least in the rural areas, promoted peasant production and trade. Yet he and his associates benefitted disproportionately from two cotton cooperatives that they had formed in the late 1950s and from his control over production on the Mueda plateau during the 1960s. His noticeable capital accumulation prompted the locals to call him a "white" because of his wealth and led to skepticism about the egalitarian intentions of the revolutionary movement. As one resident later reflected on the actions of Nkavandame, "We discovered that Frelimo had a master."[51] Official

---

[48] Hanlon, *Revolution Under Fire*, p. 76.
[49] J. Mosca, *A Experiencia Socialista em Moçambique (1975–1986)* (Lisbon: Instituto Piaget, 1999), pp. 72–73.
[50] "Editorial," *Mozambique Revolution*, 38 (March–April, 1969), p. 2.
[51] Adam, "Mueda," pp. 34–35.

explanations of his actions later given by the Frelimo leadership pointed to the divisive, exploitative potential behind his position. "Africanizing" trade and production would only change the color of the exploiter not the exploitation itself; ethnic diversity would quickly become ethnic difference, undermining the national unity that would be so crucial to post-independence reconstruction. These fears were used to justify his removal, the purge of this strand from the party, and the adoption of an explicitly anti-capitalist, modernist, and nationalistic line.[52]

Consistent with the adoption of an anti-capitalist position, official representations after the 1968–69 crisis emphasized the emergence in the liberated areas of forms of production rooted in cooperative and collective peasant farming. Some of these forms of production built upon mutual aid societies and cooperatives that had existed during the colonial period. The former provided support for local peoples during times of need, while the latter marketed the cash crops of smallholders. As they became transformed into collectives and cooperatives in the liberated zones, Frelimo documents contrasted the more noble functions and purposes of the new organizations with the exploitative actions of large companies.[53] However, collective production was limited and circumscribed. Some collective production took place to supply schools, health clinics, and the army in the liberated zones, but individual smallholder production predominated. After 1968, those cooperatives that existed were for the purpose of marketing goods in Tanzania; they were not devoted to production.[54]

More in evidence during the liberation struggle were state-centered approaches to production. Their existence suggests that state intervention after independence was more premeditated than official sources have claimed. After Samora Machel became the head of Frelimo in 1968, the Department of Defense assumed control over agricultural production for the revolutionary movement. The Frelimo Central Committee employed a centralized and hierarchical approach to food and cash crop production not simply because it considered the method a necessity for the revolution but because the Central Committee deemed it "a factor of social and ideological transformation," a central plank in a movement that was heading in an increasingly socialist and statist direction.[55]

[52] "Press Statement on Lázaro Kavandame," *Mozambique Revolution*, 38 (March–April, 1969), p. 10–11.
[53] Frelimo-Mozambique Liberation Front, "Documents of the Second Congress of FRELIMO-Mozambique Liberation Front," Niassa, Mozambique (July 1968), p. 11.
[54] Y. Adam, "Mueda," p. 36; L. de Brito, "Une relecture nécessaire: la genese du parti-Etat Frelimo," *Politique Africaine*, 29 (March 1988), p. 25 and L. de Brito, "Le Frelimo et la construction de L'etat national au Mozambique: le sens de la référence au marxisme (1962–1983)," Ph.D. dissertation, Université de Paris VIII-Vincennes (1991), p. 127.
[55] A. Casal, "Discurso socialista e camponeses africanos: legitimação política-ideológica da socialização rural em Moçambique (FRELIMO, 1965–1984)," *Revista Internacional de Estudos Africanos*, 14–15 (January–December 1991), p. 43.

It defined a key role for the Department of Production, Commerce and Cooperatives, the Political Commissariat, and its provincial political-military bodies in planning and directing production and rationalizing labor to make it more efficient. In other words, Frelimo officials envisioned an embryonic revolutionary state as the mechanism that could best organize the economy. In addition, the movement devoted more attention to organizing and controlling collective production in the liberated zones than to cooperative or smallholder production.[56] Finally, the movement began to detail the assets and ownership of the largest companies in industry, mineral prospecting, and agriculture and vowed to drive out the "foreign invaders" once it got into power.[57] Even before independence, Frelimo's rhetoric and practice privileged state-centered approaches to the economy, and directly or indirectly threatened private companies and smallholder farmers.

The anti-capitalist, statist rhetoric only intensified as the revolution wore on. In a speech in February 1974 before the April coup in Portugal, Machel defined capitalist production, whether by monopoly companies or by "small settlers," as exploitative and parasitical. He proposed as alternatives collective or cooperative production mobilized by the Frelimo party. He also advocated that the movement dominate internal and external trade.[58] Although individual traders continued to exist within the country, the government achieved control over wholesale trade from 1976 by creating ENACOMO (Empresa Nacional de Comercialização, National Trading Company), a state company responsible for commerce within and without the country. Its purpose was to acquire goods and equipment for the state sector and to act as an importer and exporter. It had warehouses, loading equipment and trucks, and sold goods to the *Lojas do Povo* (People's shops), stores created by the government to price and sell goods at the local level.[59]

By September 1974, Frelimo had become the transitional government. Certainly, the highly charged environment surrounding the transition was not conducive to the retention of the remaining settlers. But where there existed a will to stay, spontaneous worker strikes and takeovers weakened it. Threatening language, anti-capitalist speeches, arbitrary arrests, and expulsion orders issued by the Frelimo government undermined the rest of it, particularly in Maputo, and particularly in industry. According to Middlemas, many of the large companies and banks would have stayed "so long as guarantees

[56] "Editorial," *Mozambique Revolution*, 32 (December 1967–January 1968), p. 2; Casal, "Discurso socialista," pp. 45–46.
[57] See *Mozambique Revolution*, 40 (September 1969), p. 65.
[58] B. Munslow, ed., *Samora Machel: An African Revolutionary* (London: Zed Books, 1985), chapter 2.
[59] Mozambique, *Boletim da República*, I Série, Decreto 23/76 (3 June 1976) and Decreto 24/76 (17 June 1976).

against nationalisation were made," but these Frelimo could not consistently provide.[60]

President Machel's investiture speech left little doubt as to what the movement thought of capitalists. Discussing the colonial period, he asked:

Who ruled? The rulers were those who served the interests of a handful of big exploiters. Years of rule enabled them to accumulate fortunes through the abuse of power, by theft, large sums given in exchange for favors granted to the companies, rewards for ceding the country's resources and even for selling human beings.[61]

Early legislation on state intervention and nationalization of land, rented property, medical and other services supported Machel's statements. Huge salary increases for workers and the takeover of the central bank also accompanied these measures and frightened many companies, small businesses and settlers. Verbal and physical harassment hastened their departure. Those who remember the initial years after independence recall with trepidation what was known as the 24/20 order. To receive a 24/20 meant that you were given 24 hours to leave the country with 20 kilos of luggage maximum. One Portuguese man who has lived in Mozambique all his life and been connected to private business interests stated that, after Frelimo took power, people whose only sin was that they owned businesses were arrested and threatened with immediate expulsion. In order that they would not leave the country completely empty-handed, those under arrest would "upgrade" their situation to a 24/20 order by selling their possessions to the police or by declaring what property they owned during the colonial period. Having declared their assets and transferred some of their material goods over to the police, former businessmen would quickly pack their bags.[62]

For those who had already left, the State Intervention Act hampered their return. It stated that any owner who was out of the country for more than ninety days would have his company taken over by the state. Such a policy forced a decision on those who were more inclined to take a "wait and see" attitude in the months following formal independence. Further, those who failed to take out Mozambican citizenship also found they were unwelcome.[63] These hardly sound like "defensive measures," adopted during a moment of crisis. Instead, they are steps in the process of bringing about the

[60] Middlemas, "Twentieth-Century White Society," p. 42.

[61] Samora Machel, "Frelimo's Tasks in the Struggle Ahead," *Mozambique: Revolution or Reaction?* (Oakland: LSM Information Center, 1975), p. 7.

[62] The order originated when Armando Guebuza was Minister of the Interior and earned him the nickname *Vinte-quatro/Vinte* (24/20), see W. Finnegan, *A Complicated War: The Harrowing of Mozambique* (Berkeley: University of California Press, 1992), p. 191. The source for the application of the order to businessmen wishes to remain confidential.

[63] Hall and Young, *Confronting Leviathan*, p. 50; K. Middlemas, "Twentieth-Century White Society," p. 44.

"destruction of the private sector" as one government document bluntly stated in 1976.[64]

Events on the ground also threatened and played into Frelimo's interventionist inclinations. Given its inability to manage the pace of change in the early years, the government relied on local initiatives to carry out proposals for communal villages, collectives, and cooperatives, but local efforts often did not correspond to the intentions of the party in a number of ways. First, even where the government recognized the practicality of retaining the private sector in the short term, local supporters became more radical than the leadership by engaging in spontaneous takeovers in the name of the Revolution. Whether motivated by anti-capitalist rhetoric or encouraged by legitimate grievances, workers stalled production or occupied factories spontaneously. These actions prompted the government to step in. *Grupos dinamizadores* (dynamizing groups) sometimes initiated and directed these actions. Dynamizing groups were either started by members of the party or they formed spontaneously in urban neighborhoods, rural villages, and work places during the transition. Their purpose was to explain the party line, carry out basic governmental functions, prevent the destruction of local businesses and factories, and maintain production. Yet some dynamizing groups operated without direct supervision from the national government or the party to encourage slowdowns and stoppages, or to demand better working conditions. For example, just after the transition at a factory that produced motors, a member of the dynamizing group motivated a group of workers to organize a slowdown in order to increase their wages. Suddenly, the factory went from producing 150 motors a week to only 25 motors.[65]

Moreover, a representative of Anglo-American reported in 1976 that its cashew factory was at a standstill due to a clash between the local dynamizing group and the company directors.[66] Foreign supporters of Frelimo also reported that dynamizing groups were acting too spontaneously and were not serving the roles that the national party intended for them.[67] These observations and incidents help to explain why Anglo-American representatives identified "lack of discipline" as one of the main problems facing Mozambique and expressed great concern about the "indiscipline" of the dynamizing groups. In subsequent years, the national government acted to resume production and to curb "indiscipline" in the factories by reworking the party line. It drew a link between maintaining production and being a good Frelimo supporter.[68] Collectively, the incidents illustrate the government's initial inability to control the

---

[64] Mozambique, "Programa de emergencia" (1976), mimeo.
[65] "Trabalhadores criam melhoria do trabalho," *Notícias* (9 August 1976).
[66] HI/SU/KMC, interview of Neville Parkin, tapes 21–23, M17, November–December 1976.
[67] HI/SU/KMC, interview of Franny Ginwallah, member of the African National Congress, South Africa, tapes 21–23, M14, January 1976.
[68] Mozambique, "Programa de emergencia," (September 1976), p. 75.

pace of change in the critical years of the transition, a situation that invariably encouraged some investors to leave and invited more centralized solutions.

Second, local actors in factories and on farms took advantage of change to act in their own self-interest and against the stated goals of the revolution or the pragmatic appeals of the government. These social forces – which in the rural areas often included "progressive" African farmers, wage laborers, and/or individuals formerly tied to the colonial government – formed cooperatives on abandoned settler land for the benefit of a select group of people. Management structures and salary differentials often replicated hierarchical colonial patterns. Moreover, beneficiaries of the cooperatives often were those who had occupied more privileged positions in the colonial period. Reports from Gaza, for example, stated that members of a cooperative there included relatives and family members at the expense of others, and that district government offices aided the cooperative members more than non-cooperative members. In Zambezia Province, a cooperative president turned out to be a former *capataz* (overseer), who had worked for a settler.[69] In industry, reports claimed that reactionary forces insinuated themselves into administrative commissions and dynamizing groups. They continued patterns established during the colonial period by pursuing their self-interest at the expense of the nation.[70] Such practices motivated government officials to intervene more effectively to reach their desired goals.

Third, there were cases where the party's interest in creating a communal village or collective production meshed well with popular interest in change, but these were still insufficient to resolve all of the difficulties that arose in the post-independence period. For example, rural producers on the Aldeia Comunal 24 de Julho just outside Xai-Xai in Gaza willingly responded to Frelimo's call to organize into communal villages. Residents themselves chose the site where the communal village was to be built and spent only three weeks constructing the new village. In this case, voluntary reorganization fulfilled the government's agenda, without much more than verbal encouragement from the party leadership. Interaction and communication with the leadership was good and even the provincial governor participated in building the village. However, problems lay just beneath the surface. The government had to replace two first secretaries of the dynamizing group for having characteristics that were inconsistent with Frelimo's message. One had been a member of the colonial, para-military, police force and the other was fervently religious.[71]

Local enthusiasm also initially compensated for a lack of organizational capacity and for poorly conceived plans regarding collective production and the construction of the early state farms. Again in Gaza, residents of the AC

---

[69] Mozambique, Ministério das Finanças, "Relatório sobre a situação actual do desenvolvimento agricola e propostas de alteração a política de crédito," Maputo (September 1978), pp. 32–35.

[70] Mozambique, MIC, GCPIC, "Recomendações gerais."

[71] Roesch, "Socialism and Rural Development," pp. 94–99.

24 de Julho tried to run an agricultural cooperative and a fishing cooperative, while residents of the communal village AC A Voz da Frelimo at Goine helped restart the production of bananas on a former plantation that had become a state farm. As former wage laborers on the plantation, local residents knew how to grow bananas even though the party member sent to manage the state farm had no experience with banana production.[72] Moreover, in Netia, Nampula, where peasants had produced cotton for cash in the colonial period, residents responded quite enthusiastically to the policy of collective production. By 1976, approximately 1,500 families worked on about 400 collective farms and 90 People's and Party farms created either from old *concentrações* (blocks of land designated during the colonial period) or from former settler farms around Netia. At Eripele, 80 families decided to engage in collective production of cotton. GAPRONA (Gabinete de apoio a produção da provincia de Nampula, the Office of Aid to Production in Nampula Province) – the state supplier of goods and services at that time – gave them nineteen tractors to clear and prepare land.[73] Yet in each case, shortages of seeds, tools, or consumer goods, administrative and transport difficulties, and poor planning exposed the limits of central state power just after the revolution.

The chaos after independence thus drove the state to intervene in the economy in order to continue production but equally, the government contributed to the disturbances through its use of anti-capitalist rhetoric and actions. Government directives inspired workers and peasants to occupy factories and farmlands and, if the leadership appeared to be moving too slowly, to take the initiative into their own hands. In other cases, individuals subverted the message for personal gain and quickly forgot the goals of the revolution. Unable to control the actions of either its zealous supporters or those interested in self-enrichment, the state opted to rely increasingly on more direct forms of intervention. Furthermore, where the interests of the movement were able to depend on the enthusiasm of local residents, the leadership still confronted challenges that it had not anticipated and did not have ready answers for. By 1977, all of these issues had pushed the movement much more clearly in favor of a strong, centralized state and the adoption of an ideology to justify it.

### Frelimo's fusion of nationalism, modernism, and socialism to justify the interventionist state

From 1977, Frelimo refined its ideological message in order to gain legitimacy, and in order to consolidate political power for the purpose of controlling events on the ground. Following Verdery, I use the term "ideology" to connote not

---

[72] Roesch, "Socialism and Rural Development," p. 108.

[73] UEM, Centro de Estudos Africanos (CEA), "A transformação da agricultura familiar na Província de Nampula," CEA Relatório no. 80/3 (1980, repr. 1986), p. 75; K. Habermeier, "Cotton: From Concentrations to Collective Production," *Mozambican Studies*, 2 (1981), pp. 41–43.

only a set of beliefs, but also "the systemically structured processes and the experienced social relations through which human subjectivities are constituted and through which humans act upon the world."[74] Like Verdery, I argue that it is more appropriate to recognize several "ideologies" rather than one ideology because Frelimo sought to implement several core ideas in the period after 1977. These ideas were socialism, nationalism, and modernism. Although they were frequently woven together in complex and interesting ways, for analytical purposes, I examine separately each of the strands in order to draw some conclusions about the types of policies that the government adopted. Recognizing the existence and use of these strands helps us to understand the contradictory nature of state intervention into the economy and the compromises that the state made with private capital, smallholders, and other social forces.

I examine first the commitment to socialism. It began to take shape around the crisis of 1968, but documents from the Third Frelimo Party Congress of 1977 presented most fully the new government's justification for its actions as well as its ambitions for the future. References to the "leading role of the state in the economy," "the socialisation of the countryside," the "transformation of social relations in production," and the "building of a socialist society" inundated Congress documents, underpinning the commitment to Marxism-Leninism announced during the Congress. The historical analysis depicted the oppression of Mozambique by Portuguese colonialism, its exploitation by monopoly capitalism, and the existence of widespread class conflict – typical features of a socialist historical interpretation. Declarations regarding the extension of state control over property, the creation of state enterprises, and the need for central planning of the economy by the state identified the efforts that Frelimo already had taken to advance socialism in the country.[75] Expressions of goals and objectives revealed the intention to continue the socialist struggle in the future with the state as the cornerstone. In the years immediately following the Third Congress, official government reports, legislation, and speeches repeated the analyses, assertions, goals, and intentions of the Congress, often quoting directly Congress documents as proof that they were following the party line. The 1980 Constitution clarified and codified many of the principles advanced at the Congress.

The rhetoric of Marxism-Leninism used throughout the Third Congress documents leaves little doubt as to Frelimo's intention to create socialism, but it was socialism of a particular and problematic kind. Repeated references to the role of the state and the almost endless list of tasks to which the state would devote

---

[74] K. Verdery, *National Ideology*, p. 9.

[75] Frelimo Party, "Economic and Social Directives," Third Congress of Frelimo (3–7 February 1977), reprint by Centro Nacional de Documentação e Informação de Moçambique (CEDIMO), Documento Informativo no. 6, Série E (1 June 1978) and "Central Committee Report," Third Congress of Frelimo (3–7 February 1977), CEDIMO, Documento Informativo no. 7, Série E (6 June 1978).

itself revealed the authoritarian and Stalinist character of Frelimo's socialism, an ideological preference that was later reflected in its policies, as subsequent analyses have borne out.[76] To make matters worse, the economic analysis that underpinned the ideological project was at times quite superficial, contradictory, unrealistic, and just plain wrong. The documents hastily summarized the economic history of colonialism in Mozambique: the beginning of the Central Committee Report and the Economic and Social Directives devoted barely two pages to the oppressive history and the economic conflict it engendered. Moreover, the documents presented only the shallowest account of the class struggle that was supposed to have brought about the revolution.[77]

Contradictions and confusion proliferated throughout the documents. One page referred to workers as the "leading force for the building of a socialist society" yet the same page later claimed that the peasantry was the "principal force of the Revolution."[78] Sections on development claimed that "communal villages are the fundamental lever for liberating the people in the rural areas," but later passages informed readers that "state enterprises are the indispensable instrument for the planned, harmonious, secure and independent development." The documents earmarked industry as a "dynamising factor for economic development" but determined that heavy industry was the "decisive factor for economic development." Whether readers (and presumably listeners) were to equate or differentiate *leading* and *principal, fundamental* and *indispensable, dynamising* and *decisive*, the documents left unclear. Furthermore, the analysis completely misrepresented the livelihoods of rural people. It stated that under colonialism, "the peasant was relegated to subsistence production,"[79] even though other sections of the report noted on the one hand that the colonial government forced peasants to sell crops at low prices, and on the other hand that peasants in the liberated areas were able to increase production for sale.[80] The extraction of a surplus, either forcibly during the colonial period or voluntarily under Frelimo tutelage, did not suggest that subsistence characterized the lives of peasants. Rather they produced for their own consumption as well as for the market or the revolutionary cause. Unfortunately, government officials have perpetuated this misunderstanding about the nature of production in the countryside nearly

---

[76] M. Cahen, "Check on Socialism in Mozambique – What Check? What Socialism?", *Review of African Political Economy*, 57 (1993), p. 48; L. de Brito, "Le Frelimo et la construction," pp. 190–92; J. Cravinho, "Modernizing Mozambique: Frelimo Ideology and the Frelimo State," Ph.D. dissertation , Oxford University (1995), chapter 2, no page numbers, thesis sent on diskette to author; J. Alexander, "The Local State in Post-War Mozambique: Political Practice and Ideas about Authority," *Africa*, 67, 1 (1997), pp. 2–4.

[77] Frelimo Party, "Economic and Social Directives" and "Central Committee Report"; Hall and Young, *Confronting Leviathan*, pp. 62–68 reinforce these points, but collapse competing discourses under the umbrella of Marxism.

[78] References in this paragraph are from Frelimo Party, "Central Committee Report."

[79] Frelimo Party, "Central Committee Report," p. 28.

[80] Frelimo Party, "Economic and Social Directives," see "1. Introductory Notes."

until the present day.[81] Furthermore, the Third Congress documents accorded an important role to state enterprises and barely mentioned the private sector. They stated simply that the remaining private companies must strictly follow the orders of the state. In spite of the fact that in 1977 the peasantry was still responsible for the majority of production and private enterprises still existed, state enterprises were to take the lead. In industry, the documents prioritized heavy industry, even though Mozambique had neither the cash nor the expertise to build and maintain it.

Socialist principles may have been *primus inter pares*, but they were not the only strand in Frelimo's philosophy. The second major ideological strand was nationalism.[82] Frelimo shared with the leaders of other African nations the challenge of building a sovereign nation-state from a former dependent colony. Frelimo's immediate task on taking power was to eliminate the vestiges of colonialism and deepen the process of "imagining" Mozambique as an independent nation, a process that had started with the revolution. Just after Frelimo formed the transitional government in September 1974, Samora Machel argued: "As regards the State and its institutions, it is first necessary to decolonize, and secondly, to build the appropriate structures for People's Democratic Power." Regarding the former task, Machel traced its components:

To decolonize the State means essentially to dismantle the political, administrative, cultural, financial, economic, educational, juridical and other systems which, as an integral part of the colonial State, were solely designed to impose foreign domination and the will of the exploiters on the masses.[83]

Beyond the decolonization of the structures and institutions inherited from colonialism, the new government strove to create a national identity by referring to a shared history of oppression, designating a common language (that it happened to be the language of the colonizers, Portuguese, was conveniently overlooked), and employing the symbols of a flag and a national anthem to unify Mozambique. It also quite consciously ignored and denounced those features that might divide the country, such as kinship ties, tribal, ethnic, and racial differences. Aware that institutions alone could not imbue a sense of nationalism, however, the new government also promoted a decolonization of the mind, a process that would both reclaim an imagined national past and create a better future. Machel exhorted his listeners to "reconquer our Mozambican personality, to bring about the resurgence of our culture and to create a new

---

[81] On Frelimo's dualistic view of the economy see B. O'Laughlin, "Through a Divided Glass: Dualism, Class and the Agrarian Question in Mozambique," *Journal of Peasant Studies*, 23, 4 (July 1996), pp. 1–39. The argument for continuity of inimical colonial and post-colonial policies towards the peasantry is developed by Bowen, *The State Against the Peasantry*.

[82] See also de Brito, "Le Frelimo et la construction," pp. 194–200 and pp. 244–93.

[83] Machel, *Revolution or Reaction*, p. 12.

mentality, a new society."[84] The elements of the new society would include free and available education, improved living conditions, the liberation of women, and reform of the legal system. These are features associated with a socialist state, but at the same time, they are often on the list of promises made by the nationalistic leaders of newly independent nations.

The struggle against colonial rule, the quest for national sovereignty, and the creation of a distinctly Mozambican society were recurrent themes in the Third Congress documents. They criticized the "foreign domination" that existed before and Mozambique's "dependence on external factors" as a result of colonialism. They aspired to have a "sovereign state" and they advocated the formation of national defence and security forces. They intended to develop Mozambican society and promote Mozambique's culture and personality; they studiously avoided analysis of the ethnic, linguistic, and cultural diversity of Mozambicans. These were as much nationalist as they were socialist aspirations, and articulated elsewhere on the continent by African leaders with very different ideological orientations than the leaders of Frelimo. Yet the government never constructed the nationalism of a Joseph Mobutu or a Hastings Banda. The tensions that arose in Mozambique took on a very different hue from those that arose in Zaire or Malawi. The historical trajectory of the independence struggle in Mozambique and the socioeconomic backgrounds of Frelimo leaders help to explain the different ideological choices and their effects.

Modernism constituted the third element in the set of ideologies promoted by the Frelimo government.[85] But it was a modernism that was closer to the ideas of Parsons and Huntington than those of Marx, and it was a modernism to which the Portuguese also had been attracted. Like Marx, Huntington, and Parsons, the Frelimo party admired and praised the attributes of modernity, but Frelimo's view lacked Marx's critical understanding of the instability, class conflict, and violence brought by modernization.[86] Instead, Frelimo's message bore closer affinity to the political and cultural assumptions of the structural-functionalists and modernization theorists of the 1960s and 1970s, even though the message rejected their central economic tenets, such as a reliance on the market and the utility of competition. Modernization theorists argued that in order for a society to develop, it had to overcome the hidebound customs and traditions of "tribal" life and embrace the features of modern, industrialized societies. Parsons' formulation of pattern variables captured the differences

---

[84] Machel, *Revolution or Reaction*, p. 14.

[85] Cravinho, "Modernizing Mozambique," chapter 3, is particularly concerned to emphasize the modernizing elements of Frelimo's ideology and approach. I agree with him but will argue below that, in spite of the compatibility of nationalism, modernism and socialism, there were also serious contradictions in theory and in practice.

[86] On Marx's analysis of modernization, see D. Harvey, *The Condition of Postmodernity: An Enquiry into the Origins of Cultural Change* (Cambridge, MA: Blackwell, 1990, repr. 1994), chapter 5.

between the "value orientations" of traditional and modern societies and identified the social changes necessary for development to occur. In modern societies, rationality replaced the irrationality of simple societies; the impersonal, bureaucratic connections of the modern system supplanted the personalistic, collective ties of the tribal community; and universal values superseded attachments to particularistic beliefs.[87] A single, national entity with clearly demarcated yet complex functions characterized the modern polity, as Huntington argued, and distinguished it greatly from the dispersed, particularistic communities linked by ethnicity and kinship.[88] Similarly, modern man, the subject who would operate in this modern world, was rational and scientific, not superstitious and obscurantist. He planned ahead, was ambitious, valued technical skills, and did not dwell on the past. He was informed and committed to work, and respected women's rights.[89]

In Mozambique, the influence of modernism was evident in the choice of development goals, the exhortation to jettison traditional values, and the reverence for rational and scientific thought. It derived from the urban and Protestant backgrounds of many of the top leaders, as well as their experiences living in industrialized countries. Again, the Third Congress served as a guide to the modernist leanings of the government; Machel's speeches were also suffused with modernist assumptions. Congress documents denounced repeatedly the obscurantism of traditional practices, oppressive feudal structures, and cultural backwardness. They worshipped the benefits of scientific investigation, scientific knowledge, sophisticated technology, and the "New Man, free for all time from ignorance and obscurantism, from superstition and prejudice."[90] Machel's speeches envisioned a transformation that would exchange the village for the city, the farm for the factory, the tribe for the nation.[91] Repeatedly, it was expected that the state would formulate and direct the process of transformation.

These three strands have a certain compatibility among them that helps to explain why they fused together so well in the message articulated by the government. All three ideologies make normative claims about the outcomes of their objectives. They contain within them assumptions that societies will be positively transformed if their objectives are realized. The concepts of rationality, of progress, and of centralization find a certain resonance in all of them. In addition, all three explicitly accept the nation-state as the most appropriate

[87] T. Parsons, *The Social System* (Glencoe, IL: The Free Press, 1951), chapter 5.
[88] S. Huntington, *Political Order in Changing Societies* (New Haven: Yale University Press, 1968), pp. 8–12.
[89] A. Inkeles and D. Smith, *Becoming Modern: Individual Change in Six Developing Countries* (Cambridge, MA: Harvard University Press, 1974), pp. 34–35, pp. 278–88.
[90] Frelimo Party, *Central Committee Report*, p. 35.
[91] Machel, "Independencia implica benefícios para as massas exploradas" (3 February 1976). Cravinho, "Modernizing Mozambique" also notes modernist assumptions infused the poetry written by party notables, see chapter 3.

form of political organization. "Tribes" are divisive, backward, and reactionary. Nation-states are unified, modern, and progressive. They have modern bureaucracies; they intervene.

Socialism and modernism occupy a great deal of common ground, even if the 1960s variant of modernization differs from socialism on the role of the market and the competitive man who participates in it.[92] Socialist man and modern man are rational and scientific (a woman may have rights under socialism and modernization, but she is not referred to as a New Woman or Modern Woman in either theory). They make plans and execute them; they do not live for the moment nor let superstition cloud their judgment. Socialist societies and modern polities have skilled workers, technology, educated citizens, and a bureaucratic state. Their mode of organization is thought to be superior to that of feudal or backward societies. Furthermore, socialism has proved readily adaptable to nationalistic aspirations, in spite of its internationalist leanings. Both discourses also value collective projects and the concept of unity. In addition, modernism accepts that the nation-state is a vast improvement on simpler, more decentralized forms of organization and allows for the state to play an activist role in society. The presence of these common ideas and assumptions reinforced each other in the ideology conceived by Frelimo. When Frelimo later refashioned its ideology to incorporate capitalist values, several of these ideas would remain, stripped of their socialist associations.

Yet the different ideological strands also contradicted each other, challenging the internal consistency of Frelimo's message. Marxism-Leninism might be progressive and support the exploited, but it was also borrowed from abroad; it was not homegrown and national. Mia Couto, a well-known Mozambican writer, perceptively exposed this contradiction in one of his short stories, "The secret love of Deolinda," in which an unmarried woman helps to support her family by shelling cashews in a Maputo factory. One day she returns home wearing a picture of Marx on her lapel that she has been given at work. Seeing the picture, her father accuses her of having an affair with a white foreigner and makes her take it off. Although she puts the picture away, Deolinda kisses it every night before she goes to bed.[93] Symbolically, the misunderstanding of Marx by both Deolinda and her father illustrate the difficulty of combining nationalism and socialism. Nationalism explicitly disdains and distrusts anything foreign. By definition, the Mozambican government had imported Marxism from abroad. It proposed a foreign theory as a solution or as salvation for the beleaguered country.

Socialist and modernist ideas also encountered contradictions on the ground. The Frelimo movement drew some of its support from "progressive" farmers

---

[92] Inkeles and Smith, *Becoming Modern*, pp. 299–300.
[93] M. Couto, *Everyman is a Race*, trans. by David Brookshaw (Portsmouth, NH: Heinemann, 1994), pp. 110–13.

who had seen their efforts to acquire land and wealth stymied by discriminatory Portuguese policies. Since some of the "progressive" farmers lived in the south where Frelimo had no physical base, it was important during the struggle that Frelimo fashion a message that appealed to them. Some of these farmers had "modern" ideas regarding marriage practices, conflict resolution, and agricultural production. They were often educated and they were drawn to messages that promised to restructure and modernize rural relations. But they were also potential adversaries because they wanted to accumulate capital and employ labor. The contradictory treatment of this modernist-capitalist group by the government would surface repeatedly after Frelimo got into power.

If we examine how Mozambique was to be "imagined" as a nation, we find another contradiction, that between nationalism and modernism. In the construction of the nation, it is possible that being Mozambican could have entailed a respect for the customary beliefs and practices that were so prevalent throughout the country, whether these consisted of participation in ancestor worship or a reliance on kinship networks. It is possible that where the Frelimo government deemed these practices exploitative or obscurantist, it could have discouraged them and slowly phased them out, or allowed them to continue in some altered state at a symbolic level. Yet modernist and socialist elements in Frelimo's ideology denounced these beliefs and practices as "traditional" and prohibited them. Since Socialist Man and Modern Man had not yet been created, the ideology was in effect denouncing many values held by the country's inhabitants, particularly those in the rural areas, without being able at the moment to replace them with anything meaningful.

What exacerbated the contradictions among the strands was that each also contained within it pairs of opposing tendencies that constructed Mozambique as a divided, almost dualistic society.[94] Discursively the opposing tendencies revived the bifurcation between the civil and the customary that had been disintegrating during the late colonial period. After 1977, one was either progressive or reactionary, Mozambican or foreign, modern or traditional. When the initial euphoria over the victory of Frelimo dissipated, many people encountered difficulties consistently identifying with all of the "positive traits" in the new society: socialist, Mozambican, and modern. The framing of the post-independence discourse in this manner thus both unified and alienated sections of Mozambican society. In some areas of the country, the resulting tensions later gave the counter-revolutionary movement, Resistência Nacional Moçambicana (Renamo, Mozambique National Resistance), the opportunity to take advantage of ambivalent, even hostile feelings that some people had towards the new

---

[94] O'Laughlin, "Through a Divided Glass" has examined the ramifications of this approach for rural areas; Sidaway and Power have noted that Frelimo's conception of urban areas, which would appear to be emblematic of modernity, also suffered from contradictions, see J. Sidaway and M. Power, "Sociospatial Transformations in the 'Postsocialist' Periphery: The Case of Maputo, Mozambique," *Environment and Planning A*, 27, 4 (1995), p. 1471, note 23.

regime. In southern and urban areas of the country, it was much easier to wear the Mozambican, socialist, modern image articulated by the regime because people had already been exposed to and assumed part of that identity through migrant labor, through movement from rural to urban areas, through education, and through support for the liberation movement. In many rural areas of the north, colonial-capitalism had not succeeded as completely in transforming agrarian relations, yet at the same time, the insecurity generated by late colonial economic demands had reinforced certain customary patterns of production and exchange. Modernist thought in particular challenged a social order built around customary practices and kinship networks. Many poorer rural peoples respected this order because it brought some measure of security to a very tenuous existence. The early enthusiasm of rural peoples for the Frelimo project suggested they were willing to exchange that fragile existence for a secure one, but they needed guarantees. What people received when the command economy was at its height was condemnation.

### The state as cornerstone of the Frelimo project

Alongside the crystallization of the ideological message, state control over the economy deepened and expanded. Citing the decisions taken at the Third Congress, the government began to intervene in companies that it designated as "strategic" or vital for the economy. To be strategic, a company had to employ many workers, be a major supplier of goods to urban areas, or make a significant contribution to the country's balance of payments through exports.[95] These criteria included most areas of the economy from oil refining to beverages, tea, tobacco, and fishing. Further, the passage of Decree-law 18/77 gave the state considerable powers to intervene in existing private companies if, in its determination, economic sabotage had taken place. Arguing that the "State ought to discipline private activity" and singling out in particular those companies that had practiced "economic sabotage," the decree allowed for the nationalization *without compensation* of all of those enterprises that at the time of the law had administrative commissions. The creation of state enterprises from these companies was through a *portaria* (government directive) submitted jointly by the Ministry of Development and Economic Planning, the Ministry of Finances, and the ministry under whose jurisdiction the company fell. These same ministries worked with the administrative commissions until the companies officially became state enterprises. During the transformation, the government along with the commissions would decide to consolidate or abolish companies according to what was best from a technical and financial

---

[95] "Planificação no Gúrué", *Tempo*, 400 (4 June 1978), pp. 17–18.

point of view. The ministry responsible for overseeing the state enterprise then appointed the management of the new state enterprise.[96]

Finally, the government consolidated the legal transformation of intervened enterprises into state enterprises. It passed legislation designating any socio-economic unit created by the state for the purpose of material improvement of the country as an *empresa estatal* (state enterprise) and the letters "E.E." followed the company name. The government selected their management and approved their annual plans. Representatives of the Frelimo party participated in the management councils and workers' assemblies. They also helped to select workers who were adjuncts to the general manager. State enterprises could borrow money from state credit and banking institutions and were expected to issue annual reports to these same institutions.[97]

Following the decrees, the government incorporated or consolidated former private companies under its authority. The creation of a state enterprise from one or more private companies depended on the particular characteristics of each sector or each company. Nevertheless, some general patterns can be discerned. In services of national importance such as banking, trade, customs transactions, or insurance, the government's preference was to centralize all services into one organization, transfer the assets from all the private companies to the state company, and then abolish most of the private companies. In banking, the government abolished all of the private banks except for Banco Standard Totta de Moçambique (BSTM), which was allowed to remain private and would be the bank for all foreign transactions. Otherwise, the private banks were required to cease all transactions by 1 January 1978 and to transfer their deposits to the national bank, Banco de Moçambique, or the new development bank, the BPD (Banco Popular do Desenvolvimento, People's Development Bank).[98]

The Banco de Moçambique had multiple roles. It accepted personal deposits, loaned money to the government, set interest rates, controlled the money supply, regulated foreign exchange, and supervised the dispersion of credit. It also acted as a commercial bank by granting short-term loans for the purchase of producer-grown export crops such as cotton, cashew, sugar, tea, copra, and sisal. In addition, it allocated funds to individuals and private companies in accordance with government economic objectives.[99] At the same time, the government combined the two credit institutions it had taken over in 1975 into the BPD. Its primary duty was to offer medium- and long-term credit to state and cooperative,

[96] Mozambique, *Boletim da República (BR)*, I Série, Decreto-Lei 18/77 (28 April 1977).
[97] Mozambique, *BR*, I Série Decreto-Lei 17/77 (28 April 1977).
[98] "Reestruturação do sector bancário," Lei 5/77 (December 1977) reprint by CEDIMO, Documento Informativo no. 3, Série A (3 March 1978).
[99] Mozambique, *Boletim Oficial de Moçambique*, Decree 2/75 and Lei Orgânica do Banco de Moçambique, and Mozambique, Ministério das Finanças, "Relatório sobre a situação actual," p. 58.

rather than individual, projects in agriculture.[100] For these activities, the bank received 1 billion escudos (the old Portuguese unit of currency, later replaced by the metical) subscribed by the state.

In agriculture and industry, the size of the company and the sector's importance to exports or to urban consumers guided the decisions of the Ministry of Agriculture and the Ministry of Industry and Trade respectively. In industry, if the product manufactured was for national distribution and consumption, or if the companies in the sector employed many workers, the government grouped individual companies under the direction of a single administration. For example, the government combined fourteen electronics companies in the state enterprise, ELECTROMOC, E.E., while six companies made up the state enterprise for metalworking, ECOME, E.E. In some cases, the transformation of a private company into a state enterprise was in name only. For example, in the colonial period the Companhia de Cimentos de Moçambique, which had a monopoly on cement production in Mozambique, had factories in the provinces of Nampula, Sofala, and Maputo. When the government nationalized the company, its basic structure remained the same – three units of production grouped into a single company – but the Ministry of Industry and Trade managed it.

In agriculture, the state targeted for nationalization or intervention those crops and companies that contributed to the country's exports or had some national significance. Those former colonial companies that had specialized in the production of particular crops such as tea or cotton tended to be organized by sector, with individual companies grouped under a single administration responsible to the Ministry of Agriculture. For example, the state brought together most of the former tea plantations in EMOCHÁ, E.E. after 1977, which was one of the earliest state enterprises in agriculture. The new state enterprise not only included companies such as Monteiro e Giro, which had an administrative commission just after independence, but also those tea plantations in which the state had not previously intervened at all.[101] By 1981, EMOCHÁ was responsible for running nineteen separate units of production; only two companies remained outside of the state enterprise framework for tea.

Most of the tea plantations were located in one province, so it could be argued that having a single management centralized decision-making and was more efficient. Cotton production, on the other hand, was scattered throughout the country and depended on close contact with thousands of smallholders who produced it for sale to the ginneries. Yet, as in tea, all former private cotton companies eventually became units of production within a single state

---

[100] Mozambique, Ministério das Finanças, "Servir os Interesses das Largas Massas é o Objectivo da Reestruturação da Banca," reprint by CEDIMO; "A Reestruturação da Banca da Moçambique," Documento Informativo, no. 3, Série A, (1 March 1978), p. 3 and see Lei 6/77, *BR*, I Série (31 December 1977).

[101] n.a., "Vai ser criada empresa estatal do chá," *Tempo*, 360 (28 August 1977).

enterprise. When this structure proved cumbersome, the government created a Secretary of State for Cotton (which in turn became the Cotton Institute). The secretary oversaw cotton production through provincial level delegations that supervised cotton state enterprises.

In addition to the large specialized companies, there were large, medium, and small companies that grew a variety of crops. Those large companies that had produced diverse agricultural crops and raised livestock during the colonial period frequently remained structurally in tact after independence. If the state decided to intervene in or nationalize them, it ran them as autonomous entities. For example, even though they also produced tea, the Zambezia Company and the Companhia Agricola do Boror remained outside of the domain of EMOCHÁ, the state company for tea. In the colonial period, these two companies also had produced copra and livestock, and it would have been difficult to include these activities in the state tea enterprise. Technically, the Zambezia Company remained private because the government only held a minority share in the company. In reality, the other shareholders disappeared leaving the state to manage tea, livestock, and copra production.[102] Regarding the small and medium agricultural companies targeted by state intervention or nationalization, the approach varied again. If their production was for local rather than national consumption (for example, cattle raising in Zambezia or chicken hatcheries in Inhambane), a department within the provincial government or local cooperatives administered the companies individually.[103]

Intervention after 1977 may have been more methodical, but it contained inconsistencies. Private companies continued to exist and began to form relationships with the government. Their existence once again reveals the contradictions in the legitimating discourse and the limitations and pragmatism of Frelimo's approach. In banking, for example, Frelimo allowed one bank, Banco Standard Totta de Moçambique (BSTM), to remain and the bank operates in Mozambique today. Several reasons explain its survival. The first has to do with the capital base of BSTM in comparison with the other private banks in Mozambique at the time of the revolution. While the majority of the banks were branches of metropolitan banks located in Portugal, BSTM was the only shareowning bank in Mozambique.[104] At the time of independence, 15 percent of the shares belonged to interests based in Mozambique and thus domestic interests comprised part of the bank's capital (which was the largest of any company in the country). The more national character of BSTM may have influenced

---

[102] João Manuel Sousa Ribeiro, director-general, Companhia da Zambezia, Quelimane, Zambezia Province, interview, 21 May 1998 (with Scott Kloeck-Jenson).

[103] Direcção Provincial de Agricultura, Quelimane, Zambezia Province, email communication, June 1998.

[104] Mozambique, BM, "Capitais dominantes," p. 63 and Simon Bell, senior economist, World Bank, Maputo, interview, 18 February 1998.

the government to look favorably upon it. Second, while approximately 40 percent of its capital was Portuguese, 30 percent of it was British, and 10 percent was South African (with 5 percent belonging to Standard Bank of South Africa and 5 percent belonging to Anglo-American). According to one source, "Reports from Maputo state that the South African government gave a clear warning that if any South African businesses were nationalised then it would cut off all economic links with Mozambique."[105] Since Mozambique continued to rely on South Africa for revenue in the areas of transit trade and migrant labor, the government took the South African warning seriously. BSTM was not nationalized.

Third, several BSTM personnel were committed to staying. The former director of BSTM, António Galamba, noted that whereas many other bank directors had left the country, his determination to remain in Mozambique in spite of taunts and harassment helped to protect the bank from closure.[106] And lastly, most of the other banks were wholly Portuguese and were branches of oligopolistic, industrial-financial conglomerates that dominated the Portuguese economy. In Mozambique, these metropolitan offshoots, such as Banco Pinto e Sotto Maior and Banco de Fomento Nacional, had made bad investments in a number of companies, even before the end of the colonial period. As a result, the banks were in debt, could not pay their depositors, and had failed for all intents and purposes. To complicate matters, the Portuguese government had nationalized the assets of the industrial-financial conglomerates in Portugal following the revolution and was not maintaining either the banks or the companies in which the banks had invested in Mozambique. Forced to intervene with loans and technical support to maintain such companies as MARAGRA in sugar, Quimica Geral, MOBEIRA (a flour mill in Beira), and the Companhia de Cimentos de Moçambique, the Mozambican government chided the Portuguese government for its negligence in a series of conversations between the two governments in 1977–78. By 1978, when Portugal began to reverse its policy of nationalization and return banks and companies to the private sector, the government there expected Mozambique to pay compensation to the owners of the companies it had intervened in and to pay the depositors of the failed banks.[107] The Mozambican government responded by closing or combining all the banks, transferring their deposits to the Banco de Moçambique, nationalizing the companies, and refusing to pay compensation. It spared BSTM.

[105] EIU, Quarterly Economic Review of Tanzania and Mozambique, 2nd Quarter (London: Economist Intelligence Unit, 1979), p. 14.

[106] António Galamba, former director of Banco Standard Totta de Moçambique, Maputo, interview, 9 April 1998.

[107] Moçambique-Portugal, "Conversações no ambito da reestruturação da Banca em Moçambique," CEDIMO, no date.

Similar stories can be repeated in other sectors of the economy, yet much of the historiography on the early independence period has ignored those companies that remained after the revolution. Huge agricultural companies such as Madal, JFS, and Entreposto hung onto most of their pre-independence activities, which included cotton, copra, tea, and tobacco production. Later, these companies would expand into new fields. In each sector of industry, from electronics to beverages, several small and medium private companies survived the steady expansion of the state into the economy, tolerated by a government that in the end had neither the capacity nor the will to extend its reach into every factory and every field in the country. New investments even trickled in. MABOR, the international tire manufacturer, formed a joint-venture with the Mozambican government after independence, and the government also signed contracts with private and state companies in Portugal to give technical assistance and sell equipment to various Mozambican projects.[108]

There are several reasons why these private companies remained. Some of the large companies contained non-Portuguese capital. At the beginning, Frelimo hesitated to intervene in companies with British or South African capital. For example, initially the government did not take over the British concern, Sena Sugar Estates, and it did not confiscate the assets of the South African company, Anglo-American. As they did for BSTM, the threats of the South African government initially protected the holdings of Anglo-American. Equally, Anglo-American's directors wanted to stay. Just after independence, several of them unequivocally expressed their interest in remaining in Mozambique and accepted early on that they would have to work with a socialist government. They saw great potential in Mozambique and had no desire to leave – at least in the short term.[109] Furthermore, the government never intervened in or nationalized most of the assets of the Madal Group, a major producer of copra in Zambezia. One director of Madal surmised that because a Norwegian was the major shareholder in Madal by the 1970s and Norway was a major supporter of the Frelimo government after independence, Frelimo left Madal alone.[110]

In addition, some of the companies remained because they had much of their capital in Mozambique and would risk losing all of it if they left. For example, most of the capital of the Entreposto, Madal, and JFS groups was in Mozambique and had been for most of the twentieth century. These were huge, diverse enterprises, not smaller subsidiaries of large conglomerates in Portugal. The Frelimo state also valued their expertise, and this equally figured

---

[108] N. Janet and A. Pacheco, "Capital estrangeiro sobre regime de excepção," *Expresso* (12 September 1981), pp. 16–17.

[109] HI/SU/KMC, Heffer interview.

[110] Nigel Pollard, managing director, Madal Company, Maputo, interview, 2 March 1998.

in the options that each company weighed with regard to staying or leaving. As Vicente Cruz, the administrator for the Entreposto Group observed:

"I didn't follow it too closely, but we arrived at the point where we figured that we would be handing everything over to the state. There were negotiations but the Mozambican state itself asked if Entreposto would maintain its territory. Only the coal mines and all the property activity were nationalized, but that was common everywhere."[111]

José Luís Ferreira dos Santos, one of the present owners of JFS, which was founded in 1897, stated also:

"There was hardship, it was thought that everything would be lost. With the revolution, no one knew what would happen the next day. But that didn't mean we were going to give up: no one ever said such a word."[112]

Some of the few remaining small and medium companies and many Indian traders made similar calculations. For example, João Dionísio, a trader and flower grower, had 9,000 Portuguese contos in Mozambique at independence. As this was a substantial amount of money for him and he risked losing it, he decided to stay.[113]

Finally, in some sense those companies that stayed were national companies, not simply because their capital was invested in Mozambique but because of a long history in the country. Some of the directors and owners of these companies had been born in Mozambique, they identified with Mozambique, and considered the companies Mozambican. Apparently, the nationalistic part of Frelimo also agreed. Again, as José Lúis Ferreira dos Santos explains the longevity of JFS:

"Many people believe that we had contacts with Frelimo and that's why we survived. I deny that! The company survived owing to a conjuncture of factors. It had a good name, associated with my grandfather, with very strong roots in the country. The Mozambicans believed in that name. Our grandfather was constantly called to settle conflicts, arbitrate disputes. The firm is more than a hundred years old, but it is still known as "João"! And my parents steadfastly decided not to leave Mozambique. Both were absolutely determined to carry out their objectives. Of course the fact that the company was large and very diversified helped: some activities disappeared, while others were new, and others grew..."[114]

The medium-sized entrepreneur, João Dionísio, reiterates the sentiments of the larger businesses while emphasizing the dilemma of his identity:

"In Portugal I am Mozambican and here I am Portuguese.... I didn't hesitate in staying. To survive the nationalizations and the revolution wasn't easy but to leave could be confused with cowardice and that wasn't on. I love Africa. I have everything here."[115]

[111] "Vicente Jorge Cruz, economia em português," *Expresso*, 1344 (1 August 1998).
[112] "Primos Ferreira dos Santos: ir à compras 'ao João,'" *Expresso*, 1344 (1 August 1998).
[113] "João Dionísio, sair podia ser cobardia," *Expresso*, 1344 (1 August 1998).
[114] "Primos."    [115] "João Dionísio."

One company, Casa Gani, owned by an Indian family, actually made money selling suitcases to departing settlers during the transition. According to one of its owners, "'I never sold as much as on that occasion [independence]. Suitcases that had been in the warehouse for two years, I sold in only two months.'"[116] The tolerance of a residual private sector alongside the construction of socialism demonstrates that the government would bend the rules if doing so served its interest, or if it lacked capacity in a particular sector or region. Indeed, local compromises, ideological contradictions, practical considerations, and the limits of power and expertise frequently reshaped Frelimo policy and over time, would contribute to its eventual undoing.

This creative interplay between an ideological agenda and practical considerations receded into the shadows as the ideology became more systematically formulated and the Frelimo party gained power in the late 1970s. For those private companies that remained, the government adopted a very "hands on" approach. The government did not legally nationalize many of the share-owning companies, but it did intervene directly in their management. Although the legal differences between a state enterprise and an "intervened" company may have been distinct, in practice, the government ran "intervened" companies such as the Companhia Industrial de Matola and the Companhia de Boror very much like state enterprises. They had administrative commissions appointed by the ministry responsible for them and were subject to the same import, export, and credit controls as state enterprises. Moreover, the government expected those private companies that were not subject to intervention to submit annual work plans, objectives, and accounts, to accept state representatives, and to sell and buy from the state. They had to make deposits in banks of the government's choosing and to seek permission if they increased, moved, or decreased capital. The government did allow private companies to export their profits if by doing so they did not disrupt the financial health of the company and if the profits were made in a legal and normal way.[117] In the event that the government decided to nationalize a private company for a reason besides "economic sabotage," it promised to pay compensation. But it is unlikely that this ever happened. The government did welcome new investments by the private sector, but companies needed authorization from the National Planning Commission. The government reserved the right to participate in any companies whose start-up was financed from abroad. It did not draw up a code of investments for new investors, however, and according to the governor of the Banco de Moçambique, authorization depended very much on whether "the business fits our interest, that it squares with our plan."[118]

The government continued to extend its control over private companies and to pass legislation governing the behavior of the state sector until the

---

[116] "Ikbal Gafar nasceu."    [117] Decreto-Lei 18/77.
[118] Janet and Pacheco, "Capital estrangeiro," p. 17.

mid-1980s. The priority accorded to intervention and nationalization suggests that the Frelimo government clearly wanted to control the most productive aspects of the economy. At the peak of intervention and nationalization, the state sector included some 600 firms, many of which were created from the amalgamation of several former colonial companies. With the formal tasks of state intervention and nationalization nearly complete by the end of the 1970s, the movement turned to the transformation of Mozambique.

# 2 Demiurge ascending: high modernism and the making of Mozambique

> Let us leave for those at the top the intricate charts.
> How ingenious are the reports of those state enterprises
> happily in deficit either because of drought
> or because it said in the newspaper there was too much rain
> or because of the sun or because the tractor had lost a screw
> or perhaps because the traffic police had not fined Vasco da Gama
> for traffic offenses on the Calcutta spice run.
>
> José Cravereinha, "The Tasty 'Tanjarines' of Inhambane"[1]

It was a misfortune that Mozambique achieved its independence at a time of great economic and political instability, globally as well as regionally. These circumstances increased the risks associated with extensive state intervention into the economy, and intensified the negative political and economic consequences that confronted the regime when state farms, communal villages, and central planning largely failed. But many who try to explain the failure argue that Frelimo might have succeeded were it not for all of these external factors. Alternative explanations swing the pendulum to the other extreme: they argue that the principles and policies of state intervention were deeply flawed and they could never have succeeded regardless of the external factors.

The argument that the project of state intervention collapsed because of external factors usually takes the following form. It concedes that Frelimo's economic policies were not entirely workable nor always socially just in their consequences, but of greater significance was that the environment in which Frelimo launched the policies was unstable and unlucky. Exogenous factors – the climate, oil prices, sanctions against Rhodesia, South African aggression, and the Cold War – were largely to blame for the failure of socialism.[2] A derivation of this theme is to be found in the writings of those who look at the

---

[1] J. Cravereinha, "The Tasty 'Tanjarines' of Inhambane," in *The Penguin Book of Southern African Verse*, S. Gray, ed. (New York: Viking Penguin, 1989), pp. 355–60.

[2] Hanlon, *Mozambique: The Revolution Under Fire* and *Mozambique: Who Calls the Shots?*, Part 1; J. Saul, *Recolonization and Resistance*; Saul offers a more balanced analysis in an earlier work, see J. Saul, ed., *A Difficult Road: The Transition to Socialism in Mozambique* (New York: Monthly Review Press, 1985).

growth figures for the late 1970s and argue that Frelimo almost succeeded.[3] These views are based on a kind of wishful thinking: if only there had not been a flood in 1977 and a drought in 1982; if only Mozambique had not had to bear sanctions against Rhodesia; if only South Africa had not financed external aggression against Mozambique. Then maybe a centrally planned and state directed economy would have worked.

Other analyses focus on Frelimo principles and policies as causes for the party-state's failures. Some argue that Frelimo principles were not socialist enough or not democratic enough; implementation was increasingly authoritarian and Stalinist; the policies contained an anti-peasant and anti-countryside bias, or their focus was too urban or too southern.[4] On the left, Michel Cahen has launched the most totalizing criticism of Frelimo's socialism. He argues that no Marxist state nor socialist economy was ever created; that, in fact, the Stalinist model was used in support of a national project. Stalinist Marxism was not an end in itself, but rather a discursive and political means by which a "universalistic elite" sought to construct a nation where one had not existed before.[5]

On the right, the World Bank and other adherents of neo-liberal positions downplay exogenous factors and squarely place the blame on Frelimo's socialist and state-centered approach. These arguments make passing references to the destruction caused by Renamo's protracted war against Frelimo until 1992, or to the floods, or to drought, but on the whole the approach concentrates on the unsuitability of a state-centered, or "dirigiste," model of development.[6] These views derive from more general neo-liberal claims that the state is an ineffective player in the economy. It does not provide the right incentives, and its interference leads to rent-seeking, corruption, and low morale. State enterprises do not care about profits and therefore do not efficiently distribute resources, and they over employ labor. In short, relying on the state is a bad formula for economic recovery, much less growth.[7]

[3] Mozambique, National Planning Commission, "Economic Report," Maputo, mimeo, January 1984.

[4] M. Cahen, *Mozambique: La Revolution Implosée*; "La crise du nationalisme," pp. 2–13; L. de Brito, "Une relecture nécessaire," pp. 15–27; C. Geffray and M. Pedersen, "Nampula en guerre," pp. 28–39 in *Politique Africaine*, 29 (March 1988). See also Geffray, *A Causa das Armas*; Cahen, "Check on Socialism," pp. 46–59 and G. Clarence-Smith, "The Roots of the Mozambican Counter-Revolution," *Southern African Review of Books*, 2, 4 (April/May 1989), pp. 7–10.

[5] Cahen, "Check on Socialism."

[6] World Bank, Southern Africa Department, Macro, Industry and Finance Division, "Mozambique: Impediments to Industrial Sector Recovery," mimeo. (15 February 1995); World Bank and the Government of Mozambique, "Mozambique: Evaluating the Impact and Effectiveness of the Enterprise Restructuring Program," Confidential Preliminary Discussion Draft, mimeo. (22 July 1996); L. Landau, *Rebuilding the Mozambique Economy: Assessment of a Development Partnership*, Country Assistance Review, World Bank (Washington, DC: World Bank, 1998).

[7] World Bank, *Sub-Saharan Africa*, chapters 2 and 3.

These explanations are inadequate. The "if only there had not been a flood or a drought" approach is quite romantic. If a country cannot succeed or even partially realize many of its economic objectives because there is a drought or oil prices go up or the number of migrant laborers get cut, then there seems to be little point in formulating economic policies at all. Whether we are talking about Botswana or Mozambique, there will always be factors that hinder or disrupt or modify the implementation of policies; they are an unavoidable component of policy making. These factors need to be seen as common challenges to the realization of policy objectives and analyzed as such, not treated as if they had the power to undermine an entire political and economic program.

Of course, there are circumstances which are extraordinary and atypical. Not every country has to execute its policy agenda in the midst of a growing counter-revolution, as Mozambique had to do. If one looks at newspaper articles, government speeches, or scholarly writings, however, most of them hardly mention the war before 1983. It seems sensible then to isolate the period between 1977 and 1983 and to examine the principles and policy effects, before attacks were systematic, before the counter-revolutionary movement, Renamo, constituted a significant threat, and before the impact of the war was widespread. If factors such as drought, high oil prices, or loss of transport revenue (or on the positive side, aid from the United Nations, the Scandinavian and Eastern bloc countries, and the supply of cheap oil from the Soviet Union) are treated as part of the package that comes with running a country, and therefore influential but not decisive, we need some other way to explain poor economic results and rural dissatisfaction, constant structural alterations and procedural changes. All of these fuelled the momentum for the intensification of the war after 1983 and all of them, added together, attest to a policy failure of quite profound proportions by 1983–84.

Those arguments that contend the project failed because it was not socialist enough or was too socialist only partially improve our understanding of the period. Both of these views rightly challenge us to consider the suitability of the model that Frelimo chose, and they question the capacity of the Mozambican state to carry out the project of transformation that it imagined. Yet, implicit in the criticism that Frelimo was not socialist enough is an ideal-type model of socialism that no country can be said to have approximated or ever will approximate. Regarding the contrasting view, that the principles of socialism are flawed, it is often articulated in a polemical way and lacks historical specificity. Both seem to ignore, moreover, the complexity of Frelimo's ideology and the enormity of the task facing the newly independent country.

Local level studies avoid the normative abyss by examining the actual implementation of policies in particular parts of the country. For example, they might explore the negative or distorted impact of communal villagization in the southern part of Mozambique, or examine the failure of cotton state farms in the north, or discuss the mixed impact of Frelimo's denunciation of "traditional authorities." Their strength is not only that they focus on particular state policies in detailed and concrete ways, but also that they present the recipients of these policies as agents in their own right who work actively to negotiate, moderate, hijack, or thwart the effects of state policies. I mean to combine government reports and secondary sources conducted on the local level with my own field-work and research to construct a new conceptual framework for understanding the period from 1977 to 1983. I argue that the nearly disastrous outcome of state policies derived as much from the vigorous, sometimes explosive interaction of policies and their recipients on the ground as it did from the inappropriateness of the "transformative vision" that Frelimo designed for Mozambique and the kind of state it constructed to implement the vision. International conditions at the time played influential, but not determinate roles. Rather, the colonial legacy, a complex ideology, an expansionist state, poorly implemented poli-cies, and social forces that contested and shaped every measure account for the eventual outcome.

### From "how much" to "what kind" of state

What we need to know is: what informed the political and economic strategy adopted by Frelimo and why did it achieve such poor results? Why, when the flaws of the approach became quite apparent, was the Frelimo government either unwilling or unable to ameliorate their effects prior to 1983? To answer these questions, we have to remember Frelimo's ideological starting point, to examine the institutions the government tried to construct, and to evaluate the kinds of policies it tried to implement. We have to consider not only the international environment but also the colonial legacy. And finally, we have to explore the ways in which different social agents, such as private companies and rural producers, interacted with and responded to state policies.

I agree with Cahen that the choice of Marxism was a particularly rigid one. Struggles within the party appear to have precluded choices that in retrospect now look more appropriate for a developing, largely agrarian country. But in positing Marxism-Leninism as the umbrella under which a more penetrating dis-course of nationalism took place, Cahen has collapsed different discourses that existed with different temporalities and derived from different material origins. What seems to explain the difficulties of the post-independent Mozambican state is not that Marxism-Leninism served as the umbrella for all of these other universalizing, authoritarian goals, but that it had to compete ideologically and practically with the goals of nationalism and modernism. Socialism was not yet dominant because the production relations it entailed did not yet exist. Thus, alongside a discourse censuring exploiters and praising the dignity of workers, there existed a parallel modernist discourse denouncing "backwardness" and applauding rational man, and a nationalist discourse condemning "tribalism" and emphasizing unity. Since this same discursive blending seems to occur often in many so-called "socialist" countries, it suggests that socialist principles are unable to become the dominant ideology in the way that capitalism has, probably because a socialist mode of production has never fully been established. "Whether by caprice or by the perverse regularity of history," write Brus and Laski,

> one of the main common features of the countries of 'real socialism' is that they started their transition to socialism under conditions of immaturity in orthodox Marxist (and Schumpeterian) terms. Hence the overriding objective of the victorious revolution was to eliminate the retardation, economically as well as socially and culturally.[8]

The implementation of the "transformative vision" embodied in the ideology of the Third Congress hinged on an interventionist state and the complicity of the state's subjects. In Mozambique, as in other countries where governments adopted "real socialism," the task was not to construct a superior and more efficient form of social organization on the back of a fully mature, capitalist system as the theory anticipated, but rather to use state ownership of the means of production to drag the society out of backwardness. The explanation for relying on the state to accomplish these goals was not only that it was more just in contrast to the colonial system that preceded it, but also that it was the fastest, most rational, and most capable actor in the society. Under the direction of the state, Mozambicans would achieve food self-sufficiency, acquire advanced methods of production, enhance their scientific knowledge, and free themselves from dependence on others through industrialization. To realize these goals, the state had to be capable of meeting three demands. First, it had to create institutions capable of handling the additional roles required of a highly interventionist state. Second, existing and new institutions had to be capable of shouldering Frelimo's ideological contradictions and inconsistencies as they became manifest in policy. Third, state institutions had to be flexible enough to adapt as challenges changed over time and to treat different sectors and actors on a case-by-case basis.

To analyze the dynamic of state intervention and to conceptualize some of the institutional demands required of the state in Mozambique, the comparative institutional approach developed by Peter Evans provides a useful framework. Evans seeks to characterize states by placing them on a continuum in accordance with the role that the state plays in achieving particular developmental outcomes. At one extreme lie predatory states such as the former Zaire that prey

---

[8] W. Brus and K. Laski, *From Marx to the Market: Socialism in Search of an Economic System* (Oxford: Clarendon Press, 1989), p. 22. In their terminology, "real socialism" refers to those countries that claimed to be socialist as of 1989, as opposed to "genuine socialism" or the theoretical portrayal of socialism according to Marx and Schumpeter.

on their societies, amassing individual fortunes for state officials at the expense of development. At the other extreme are states such as those in Japan and Taiwan that primarily undertake the responsibility of developing their countries by engaging directly in production, protecting particular sectors and subsidizing others. Through their efforts, they help to facilitate sectoral growth and development.[9]

John Saul has characterized Mozambique as a "left-developmental dictatorship."[10] The label refers both to the developmental objectives behind policies and to the manner in which those policies were promoted. The difficulty with Saul's characterization is that part of the label refers to the intentions behind policies (which are always hard to judge) rather than the roles that the state adopted and what outcome they achieved. If we include outcomes, Mozambique seems to fit better Evans' characterization of an "intermediary state." "Intermediary" states are neither predatory nor developmental but combinations of the features that characterize the two extremes: "the balance [between predatory and developmental approaches] varies over time and from organization to organization within the state," and the outcomes of these approaches also vacillate between the extremes.[11] From the north to the south, in industry and in agriculture, the Mozambican state adopted roles and achieved outcomes that placed it squarely in line with other intermediary states.

Evans offers four rubrics to capture the different roles that intermediary states may play in the developmental projects of their countries. Although he specifically applies the categories to industry, they can also be applied to the state's role in the economy generally. In support of his approach, he argues that,

traditional ways of labeling the state roles make it too easy to slip back into the comfortable feeling that the parameters of state involvement are known and we need only worry about 'how much.' New words are flags, recurring reminders that the question should be 'what kind.'[12]

Many scholarly characterizations of the Mozambican state and the colonial state that preceded it illustrate the problem with a "how much" approach. Scholars characterize the state as "weak" for failing to achieve its economic objectives, and for its inability to organize production or to manage a state farm efficiently.[13] Yet depictions of its coercive approach to communal villages, the brutal and insensitive forced removal of urban people during Operation Production, and its harsh treatment of "traditional authorities" imply a "strong" state.[14] We disaggregate these contradictions if we shift the focus on state intervention

---

[9] Evans, *Embedded Autonomy*, pp. 43–60.
[10] Saul, *Recolonization and Resistance*, pp. 71–74.
[11] Evans, *Embedded Autonomy*, p. 60.     [12] Evans, *Embedded Autonomy*, p. 13.
[13] Scott, "Socialism and the 'Soft State'"; Ottaway, "Mozambique: From Symbolic Socialism"; Hall and Young, *Confronting Leviathan*, chapter 4.
[14] Egero, *Mozambique*, chapter 10; Geffray, *A Causa das Armas*; Bowen, *The State Against the Peasantry*.

from "how much" to "what kind." Evans suggests that we conceive of the roles that states play in the economic arena as that of "custodian" and "demiurge," and as practitioners of "midwifery" and "husbandry."

In its role as custodian, the state formulates, applies, and enforces rules for the developmental project. In the realm of production, these rules can be inspirational; they can stimulate existing businesses to invest in new equipment, new markets, or new technology. Or they can be regulatory – establishing a fixed minimum producer price for a company's purchase of an agricultural crop – or even punitive, punishing those who dump goods on the parallel market or avoid paying customs duties. Depending on the sector or an individual company's behavior, the same rule might be punitive for one sector or business while it protects and encourages another. As custodian, the state plays a rather conservative role; its job is to regulate, not to transform.[15]

Playing the demiurge involves the state much more directly in the production process and has much greater potential to be transformative in its outcome. As demiurge, the state initiates and develops a sector or business, competing with or even prohibiting private competition. In the most extreme cases, the state may expand its role to include all or most aspects of the economy, including healthcare, commerce, and education in addition to more typical state undertakings such as public utilities or public transportation. Although the most expansionist forms of the demiurge role might suggest an adherence to a socialist ideology, the numerous examples of African states of all ideological hues that have adopted strongly interventionist roles demonstrate that the desire directly to control key sectors of the economy spans the ideological spectrum.[16] In the case of Mozambique, the nationalist, socialist, modernist strategy to which the Frelimo leadership had committed itself was conducive to an expansionary role. There, the state was responsible for planning most economic activities – from the supply of inputs to factories to the provision of consumer goods to the rural areas. It directed most investment towards the public sector. It prioritized the growth of heavy industry, favored the creation of giant agricultural projects, sought to control commercial networks, and reorganize the countryside. It criticized "obscurantism," abolished traditional authorities, and prohibited rainmaking ceremonies, polygyny, and other customary practices. It emphasized the virtues and values of "modern man," who, through rational and scientific thought, was to form the foundation of the new country.[17]

The multitude of negative outcomes now associated with the role of demiurge indicate that it contains some structural flaws from the outset. Since it is often

---

[15] Evans, *Embedded Autonomy*, p. 78.

[16] Without devaluing ideological differences, Young has drawn attention to the convergence of policies and their outcomes in different African states, see Young, *Ideology and Development in Africa*.

[17] Frelimo Central Committee, "Central Committee Report," chapter 4.

ideologically grounded in a distrust of private capital, the demiurge role tends to be expansionary. It hauls in other sectors of the economy beyond those to which it might have initially restricted itself. Such expansion may test the limits of the state's capacity, or rather its ability to reasonably carry out stated policy objectives. Second, organizational preferences may drive expansion so that state firms begin moving into other sectors. As Evans states,"From inside the state apparatus, temptations of institutional aggrandizement may be hard to distinguish from possibilities for promoting transformation."[18] These flaws surface repeatedly in the case of the Mozambican state.

The roles of custodian and demiurge personify an uneasy, even hostile relationship between the state and capital. In these two roles, the connection between the state and capital is strained, even broken. By contrast, when the state acts as midwife or practices husbandry, the relationship with capital is potentially more cooperative and supportive. As midwife, the state aids and assists the creation of capital enterprises. As the term implies, it nurtures infant capital along, or facilitates links between transnational and national capital, but its role is secondary not primary. It brings capital into existence. Once capital is established, the state can continue to promote and protect it through various techniques that fall under the rubric of husbandry. It can engage in tasks that capital might not otherwise undertake or simply encourage existing private enterprises to expand or strengthen their investments.[19] The early disdain of the Mozambican government for private capital precluded the development of these latter two roles. Nevertheless, at those points where the Mozambican state overstepped its reach, private companies filled the void.

Having adopted a clearly expansionist position, the government then proceeded to construct the command economy in a difficult international environment and in an historical context with which its policies were incompatible. Internationally, the Cold War environment prompted Western countries to isolate Mozambique diplomatically. After first attempting to work with Mozambique, South Africa began to direct trade away from the port of Maputo and to reduce the numbers of migrants. These actions were consistent with P. W. Botha's adoption of the doctrine of "total strategy" after becoming prime minister of the apartheid government in 1978.[20] Moreover, the global economy may be more recognizable now but Mozambique felt the effects of its power keenly even in the late 1970s. Most capitalist countries spurned Mozambique. They refused to extend to it the grants and aid that they offered to other newly independent countries. As a result, the government relied on those countries that were sympathetic to its aims. While many Nordic countries offered their support, Bulgaria, Romania, and the Soviet Union also contributed finance,

---

[18] Evans, *Embedded Autonomy*, p. 80.     [19] Evans, *Embedded Autonomy*, p. 81.
[20] M. Murray, *South Africa: Time of Agony, Time of Destiny* (London: Verso Press, 1987), chapter 1.

expertise, and their managerial styles to various projects in Mozambique. The input of these countries invariably affected the substance and direction of policies. Added to its financial woes, the government had to contend with rising oil prices and the impact of its decision to pass sanctions against Rhodesia. All of these factors exacerbated the challenges faced by the new government, but they did not create them.

The colonial legacy also conditioned the eventual effects of new policies in several ways. First, the contrasts between the cities of Maputo and Beira and the rest of the country reflected the uneven development of capital and the preferences of investors for more urban areas. After independence, it was not easy to connect the new language of liberation emanating from Maputo to life in the farthest northern village or district. In economic matters, it was not easy to exercise oversight of state projects and personnel in the north from the capital in the south. Structural and technological differences also divided large colonial companies from medium and small settler farms which, in turn, were different from smallholder farms. All of these demanded different management techniques. Second, independence had disrupted the wholesale and retail trades. Oligopolistic firms had dominated the wholesale trade, while hundreds of Indians, Portuguese, and Africans had undertaken retail trade across the length and breadth of the country. Third, the colonial state had supported low wages, disciplined labor, offered subsidies, and granted tax incentives. Previous production arrangements vitally depended on these measures, yet the new state either could not or would not maintain all of the institutional arrangements it had inherited from the colonial period.

Fourth, at independence, Mozambique was an agricultural country with the majority of its population living in the countryside. Rural Mozambicans constructed their living from a variety of sources: wage work on plantations and mines; agricultural production for subsistence and for sale; the manufacture of crafts; and the commerce of food, alcohol, second-hand clothes, soap, and other items of personal use. Rural to rural and rural to urban migration were common but infrastructure and communications were poor. Customary practices, especially in the northern reaches of the country, continued to structure life for many. Kinship and patron–client relations acted as shields against economic misfortune, although these relations fluctuated with the degree of influence of the cash economy, the types and methods of production, the arrival of religious messages and groups, and the degree of exposure to colonial norms and institutions.

For post-independence policies to be acceptable in the rural areas, they had to be cognizant of the intricacies and insecurities of rural life. Often they were not. The self-sufficient peasant living by his (in spite of gender awareness the peasant was still seen as male) own subsistence, providing just for his family, was a romantic fiction, yet it informed most policy debates around the rural areas. At other times, the government assumed that smallholders could just pick up and move with relative ease to the proposed communal villages and state farms. Overall, the new government displayed a surprising lack of awareness of the intricate and fragile blending of land use, wage work, and labor exchange that was the local producer's response to the uncertainties of rural life. In time, rural peoples did what they have done so often in Africa. To mitigate uncertainty, they manipulated, modified, resisted, and thwarted, state policies. When combined with the other challenges faced by the Frelimo leadership, the dynamic interaction that occurred between rural peoples and the state, whether it was compromise or resistance, apathy or sabotage, also blunted the project of transformation.

### Envisioning the commanding heights

In the period from 1977 to 1983, the Mozambican state attempted to be a custodian and a demiurge, rather than a practitioner of midwifery and husbandry. By the late 1970s, the state controlled most of the leading sectors of the economy in agriculture as well as industry. In socialist parlance it occupied "the commanding heights" and, in true modernist fashion, what the state intended to do was embodied in the Plan, the fulfillment of which was obligatory. According to Machel,

"The victory of Socialism is a victory of science, it is prepared and organized scientifically. The Plan is the instrument of scientific organization of this victory."[21]

But the science of plotting Mozambique's socio-economic future must have been quite unreliable because the plans and their objectives changed frequently. There were many plans, formulated and reformulated, alternately expanding and contracting as objectives were met and unmet. The plans had temporal and spatial dimensions: multiple institutions existed to formulate and enact them for every conceivable time frame and locale, from the neighborhood to the nation. There were annual plans, prospective indicative long-term plans, and also district, provincial, and national plans. The National Planning Commission made annual plans for the country. Provincial governors and district administrators made plans for the respective geographic areas under their jurisdiction. Ministers of agriculture or industry or finance formulated plans for their sectors; units and cabinets and directorates within these ministries devised plans for their subsector or area of specialization. On the shop floor or the state farm, factory managers and directors, production councils, and production brigades also had their plans.

---

[21] President Samora Machel, quoted in "A batalha do plano," *A Voz da Revolução* 73 (June 1981), p. 32.

The objectives of the plans veered sharply from the utopian to the mundane. The most ambitious contained the state's futuristic vision of a socially engineered urban and rural landscape. These plans demanded that their recipients forego some pleasure or renounce some belief in exchange for material and mental improvement that would appear at some future date if the plan were faithfully executed. Other late twentieth-century states with a penchant for grand schemes share these features. James Scott, drawing on the work of David Harvey, labels the practice "high modernism":

The temporal emphasis of high modernism is almost exclusively on the future.... To the degree that the future is known and achievable – a belief that the faith in progress encourages – the less future benefits are discounted for uncertainty. The practical effect is to convince most high modernists that the certainty of a better future justifies the many short-term sacrifices required to get there.[22]

In Mozambique, the Political and Organizational Offensive, a ten-year plan for the period 1980–90, epitomized high modernism. This plan demanded that its recipients reject the wrong ideas and assimilate "correct ideas, correct methods" to fulfill it. It embodied the state's aspirations to transform social relations by restructuring production in the countryside through collective farms, state farms, and cooperatives. It promised to overcome the negative effects of dispersed living through the relocation of people to communal villages and outlined greater participation for workers in the factories. It offered rough blueprints for the creation of large-scale, irrigated, highly mechanized, agricultural projects such as the Vale do Limpopo, the Vale de Incomati, and the 400,000 hectare scheme in Cabo Delgado and Niassa so typically associated with a high modern state. To express these goals to a largely non-literate population, the architects of the offensive designed dramatic posters featuring men, women, and children boldly engaging in production tasks. It was to be a decade of "radical transformation," a decade of "Victory over Underdevelopment."[23]

Of course, the plans and policies served other purposes. If successful, they would legitimate politically the Frelimo party, consolidate the central role of state institutions in the economy, and entrench the power of the elites in the party and the government. If realized, the country would also prosper economically. Moreover, if the plans contained a high modern vision, many also contained more pragmatic concerns such as methods to increase exports and the replacement of imports by crops or products found within Mozambique. The more technical plans established quotas for the production and trade of

---

[22] Scott, *Seeing Like a State*, p. 95 and see Harvey, *The Condition of Postmodernity*, chapter 2.
[23] President Machel began tracing the direction of that plan in late 1979, see Machel, "Coordenemos as nossas forças para a realização das metas," *Notícias* (5 August 1979); for additional elaborations of the plan see "A batalha do plano envolve-nos a todos vamos ganhá-la conhecendo as suas metas," Resolução de VIII Sessão do Comité Central, reprinted in *Notícias* (20 December 1980); "A batalha do plano".

every conceivable item in Mozambique from medicine to matches, detailed the state's budget for the coming year, or assessed the availability of credit.

Actual implementation was meant to follow the principles of democratic centralism, an approach that placed the central state at the apex of a chain of commands that would then be systematically implemented through all layers of society. The central state not only controlled the purse strings for all the projects but also it was the major decision-maker. As explained by the Third Frelimo Congress and embodied in the constitution of 1980, the practice of democratic centralism entailed that lower bodies were subordinated to the decisions of higher ones and the decisions of lower bodies could be overruled by higher bodies.[24] Over time, the very hierarchical nature of this approach became reflected in the discourse used to encourage it. Perhaps because of the escalating war, or perhaps because it harkened back to the revolutionary struggle where Frelimo had proved itself more capable, the discourse of state intervention became couched in terms of military methaphors: a "prolonged war," an "economic struggle." Like the chain of command in an army, plans at the local level obeyed plans at the national level. Government leaders referred to efforts to increase output, eliminate sabotage, and eradicate "worker indiscipline" as "offensives" or "campaigns." Government speeches described groups of workers as "squads" and "brigades," production as a "battle," the elimination of sabotage as "a war on the enemy within," and success as "victory."[25] The Soviet Union and Tanzania had employed a similar language; Mozambique must have taken note.[26]

The language, the objectives, and the method of implementation of plans left no doubt whatsoever about the state's intention to assume the commanding role of demiurge, and its desire (but not its ability) to be a "developmental" state. To the extent that the state assumed other roles, these often reinforced the demiurge role. In its capacity as custodian, for example, the government controlled and ridiculed the activities of the private sector. Officials of private companies and banks, when referring to the years of state intervention and nationalization, speak as if they were mired in quicksand. Except in unavoidable circumstances, the government did not encourage or support entrepreneurial behavior. According to a representative of the Entreposto Group,

It wasn't easy. One could not do business the same way as before, one could not engage in normal business activity. All sorts of conditions were attached to imports of primary materials and equipment. Everything was so centralized.[27]

---

[24] Frelimo, "Statutes," Third Congress of Frelimo (3–7 February 1977), chapter 3, article 13 and Mozambique, *The Constitution of the People's Republic of Mozambique* (Maputo: Minerva Central, 1980), Part III, chapter 1, articles 37 and 38.

[25] Machel, "Verificação e penalização," *Tempo*, no. 547 (5 April 1981), p. 19; L. de Brito, "Une relecture nécessaire"; J. Alexander, "The Local State," p. 3.

[26] Scott, *Seeing Like a State*, pp. 148–49, p. 234.

[27] Odette Nunes, financial director, Entreposto Group, Maputo, interview, 8 April 1998.

Echoing the response of the Entreposto representative, one of the owners of
JFS said, "Many times commercial and industrial activity was at a standstill.
It was like a ghost office: there was no light, no telephone...few people."[28]
The remaining private bank also found that obstacles were placed in the way
of doing business. According to one of its representatives, "The Banco de
Moçambique controlled all of the large accounts, while Standard Totta was
only able to finance Indians and some of the small Portuguese who remained in
Mozambique."[29]

The heavy emphasis on the demiurge and custodial roles did not leave much
room for the practice of midwifery or husbandry nor was the government particularly interested in these. Initially, it avoided, even shunned the nurturing,
cooperative relationships with capital that midwifery and husbandry imply.
Nevertheless, economic necessity and geographical considerations forced the
government to rely on the private sector and the smallholder sector at various junctures, an occurrence that most of the literature, with the exception of
Cahen, has largely overlooked. While Cahen interprets the continuation of a private sector as another indication that Frelimo was not really socialist, it should
be pointed out that most socialist societies tolerate a small private sector out of
sheer necessity.[30] In Mozambique, concessions to the private sector were hardly
generous but they were critical, and they would influence later developments.
They consisted sometimes in simply turning a blind eye to the continued functioning of large private companies such as JFS, Entreposto, and Madal, smaller
trading operations run by Indians, and smallholders. Large companies remained
active in sugar, copra, sisal, and cotton production; and in cashew, sugar, and copra processing. They produced as little as seven percent of marketed food crops
to as much as fifty percent of the copra supply.[31] Madal's accounts, for example, indicated that the company continued its huge cattle and copra operations
in Zambezia Province despite nationwide salary increases that cut into profits
and difficulties acquiring new machinery that hindered production. Madal consistently made profits from these undertakings at least until the war began to
disrupt operations from the mid-1980s.[32]

Beyond tolerating the activities of private capital, state concessions to the
private sector also became manifest in small, uncoordinated compromises.
Nationally, President Machel stated that private companies ought to be helped
by the state and financial organizations so they could fulfill their tasks. He even
asserted that " 'private activity has an important role to play in straightening out
our country'."[33] Moreover, just two years after nationalizing all of the banks

[28] "Primos."      [29] Galamba, interview.

[30] Cahen, *Mozambique: La Révolution Implosée*, pp. 137–67.

[31] Cabellero, *The Mozambican Agricultural Sector*, pp. 33–55.

[32] Sociedade agrícola do Madal, SARL, *Relatório* (1979–87).

[33] S. Machel, quoted by J. Hanlon, "Mozambique to Revive Role of Private Sector," *Washington
Post* (20 March 1980).

in Mozambique, the government employed the financial services of a private American bank, Equator Bank, in 1979. Most major Western financial institutions had shunned Mozambique and it was desperate for credit. Equator Bank specialized in granting lines of credit to so-called "high risk" countries. Equator offered lines of credit to Mozambique's central bank so that in turn, the central bank could finance its state companies and extend credit to state and private companies selling export crops on the international market.[34] In addition, the government began to woo foreign investment with offers of incentives if they invested in Mozambique, and it formed a joint-venture with JFS to produce bicycles.[35] It bestowed honors on two private factories that met their production targets, and it welcomed several new joint-ventures in fishing and textiles respectively.[36]

At the provincial level, compromises with the private sector and with smallholders were also common simply because the government could not manage to run everything. Very early on, for example, district officials in one northern province supplied transportation to two private companies.[37] Moreover, smallholder production of food and cash crops continued in many areas. In rural commerce, although the government established a state marketing board, it also negotiated marketing arrangements with private traders at the provincial level. According to the Law of Private Commerce, the government allowed private traders to operate as long as they observed government-set prices and adhered to the dictates of the state. At this time, there were approximately 4,000 private traders still in operation.[38] Private traders began to handle parts of the retail cashew trade as early as 1982. They bought cashews, one of Mozambique's largest export earners, from rural producers, particularly in Zambezia and Nampula Provinces.[39] These compromises and concessions to private capital and smallholders made little difference to the overall direction of policy up to 1983, but they figured prominently in the direction that policy took in the mid-1980s. They also determined who benefitted from policy changes during the 1990s. Many of the companies with whom the state made arrangements in the early 1980s subsequently emerged as powerful economic and political agents in the privatization process. For the period from 1977–83, however, the demiurge was clearly in the ascendancy.

---

[34] Lisa Audet, vice-president and representative, Equator Bank, Maputo, interview, 3 March 1998.
[35] "Fábrica de Bicicletas de Moçambique aproveitar capacidade instalada," *Notícias* (8 February 1978).
[36] "Mozambique attracting foreign investment," *New African* (August 1980), p. 80.
[37] Mozambique, Ministério da Agricultura, Direcção Nacional de Organização da Produção Colectiva, Gabinete de apoio a produção da província de Nampula (GAPRONA), Reunião do sector estatal agrário (13 February 1979), p. 7.
[38] On private traders, see Tarp, "Agrarian Transformation in Mozambique," mimeo., n.d., pp. 14–15; Caballero, *The Mozambican Agricultural Sector*, p. 36 and p. 50.
[39] Mahomede and Mahomede, interview; Biriba, interview.

## The industrial demiurge

The state's vision for industry drew on the themes that the party had already developed for the society as a whole – the notion of transformation and modernization. Industry would be the crucible where a worker's socialist identity would be forged and it would be one of the bases for development. In accordance with the high modern approach that informed the substance of Frelimo policy, the emphasis in industry would be on big projects. In its ten-year plan for 1980 to 1990, the government projected an investment of 1 billion US dollars for agricultural and industrial projects. In industry, these included proposals for an aluminum plant, an iron and steel industry, pulp and paper mills, and additional cement factories and textile mills.[40] These may have been factories that Mozambique needed, but the government also desired heavy industry because of its symbolic value: it considered modern those countries that had aluminum plants and iron and steel industries.

For the state to engineer this transformation and to manage those factories that already existed required institutions. These changed frequently in the early years, but by 1979–80, an elaborate, hierarchical structure had been established for all sectors of the economy and the society. State intervention into industry was the responsibility of the Ministry of Industry and Energy in coordination with the National Planning Commission. Industry was divided into ten branches of activity, such as metalworking, textiles, and hotel and tourism, etc. The ministry formulated annual and monthly production plans for all the branches. Management units appointed by the ministry for each branch of activity then formulated production quotas for each state enterprise or for each factory that had been "intervened in" but had not been officially nationalized. All of the factories in which the state was involved had management teams that the ministry appointed. These worked closely with the management units that were in charge of each branch of industrial activity. At the factory level, the management was almost identical in function to the management of a private company. It was expected to draw up budgets, do the accounts, promote personnel, maintain the equipment and, above all, to produce.[41]

Underestimating the importance of creating socialist managerial styles, the government devoted much more attention to finding the appropriate organizational structures for workers rather than management. In particular, the government was interested in a structure that would further socialism but also

[40] J. Kronholz, "Mozambique Woos Foreign Investment but Keeps Socialism," *Wall Street Journal* (30 December 1980); C. Castel-Branco, "Problemas estruturais de industrialização" in C. Castel-Branco, ed., *Moçambique: Perspectivas Económicas* (Maputo: Imprensa Universitária, 1994), p. 100.

[41] Decreto-Lei 17/77, *BR*, I Série (28 April 1977); "Os dez ramos de actividade," *Tempo*, 524 (26 October 1980), pp. 26–27.

increase production. On the factory floor, the government initially expected local Frelimo activists or dynamizing groups to organize workers. National and regional party activists coordinated the strategy of the dynamizing groups, but the groups drew their membership from the local population with an emphasis on the "lower income strata of the population in order to avoid becoming dominated by local traders, state functionaries, or the intelligentsia – groups which tended to be more literate and articulate."[42] In theory, the principle of democratic centralism should have ensured that dynamizing groups carried out the wishes of the leadership on the factory floor. In practice the central state lacked the capacity to control members and their actions. In some instances, members were neither from the "lower income strata" nor were they disciplined practitioners of the party line. For example, in a steel factory that employed 400 workers in 1977, several members of the dynamizing group were believed to have worked with the Portuguese security forces during the colonial period. Meanwhile the nineteen-year-old secretary of the group paraded around the factory like a demagogue, berating the workers to become more disciplined.[43]

Confronted with the poor performance of dynamizing groups, the government complemented them with production councils. When production councils exhibited similar problems to those of the dynamizing groups, the government created another institution, the factory committee. It was designed to correct the difficulties with production in those state companies that had more than one unit of production. Factory committees consisted of the secretary and the assistant secretary of each production unit brought together to negotiate with the management on behalf of all workers. By 1981, the most important factories had a party cell and a factory committee, in addition to production councils and dynamizing groups for each shop floor.[44]

What were the outcomes of attempts to build a socialist and modern industry in independent Mozambique by 1983? There were accomplishments and failures, and they justify the characterization of the Mozambican state as an "intermediary" one. The government did complete a few of its industrial projects, such as the construction of two textile mills, a fish processing complex, and a tire factory (a joint-venture with a private company). For workers in some existing and new plants, conditions were probably better than during the colonial period. Government commitment to employment and to improving the treatment of workers meant that more factory jobs became available and that levels of exploitation – so notorious during the colonial period – declined. There is also very little evidence of widespread rent-seeking, thus neo-liberals have

[42] Wield, "Mozambique – Late Colonialism," p. 88 and Wuyts, *Money and Planning*, p. 89.
[43] P. Sketchley and F. Lappé, *Casting New Molds: First Steps Toward Worker Control in a Mozambique Steel Factory* (San Francisco: Institute for Food and Development Policy, 1980), pp. 26–27.
[44] "Iniciada a criação de Comités de Fábrica," *Tempo*, 547 (5 April 1981), pp.16–17.

*Demiurge*

...l its occurrence in state enterprises. In Mozambique, wage
...lies on transport, housing, and food allowed wage packets
...probably exa...n the past, and the regular payment of salaries provided
increases, a...many workers. The provision of free health care, greater
to go fur...h, and on-site creches also contributed to an improved work
added...cashew factories, for example, government supporters and
acce...h as the Organização das Mulheres Moçambicanas (OMM,
...Mozambican Women) made a conscientious and sustained ef-
...ow poorly treated women had been during the colonial period,
...working conditions for women after independence.[46] These
...may help to explain why urban workers have tended to maintain
...or the Frelimo government for more than two decades.
...rial output was three-quarters of pre-independence levels by 1981
...of pre-independence levels by 1985. It might actually have been
...not the Ministry of Industry and Energy been able to keep such a close
...individual plants. Ironically, in this respect, the uneven spatial clustering
...industrial units around urban areas during the colonial period aided state
intervention after independence. Because 66 percent of Mozambique's industry
was either in Maputo (50 percent) or Beira (16 percent), the government was
more able directly to supervise production than it would have been if factories
had been scattered all over the country. For example, government officials made
surprise visits to factories in Maputo to root out indiscipline by workers or to
expose disorganized and dirty working conditions. Following a visit by the
Minister of Industry and Energy, António Branco, to several factories around
Maputo, the weekly magazine, *Tempo*, reprinted photos of section chiefs found
sleeping on the job during the night shift.[47]

Even with the constant attention of the Ministry of Industry and Energy, the
government did not realize fully its objectives for industrial "transformation."
Industry was no more modern in 1983 than it had been in 1975. Owing to lack of
experience and funds, the government had to shelve most of its grand schemes,
such as an aluminum plant and an iron and steel industry. Unfortunately, the
bulk of investment had gone to these grand projects, so there was little left for
investment in already existing capacity.[48] Existing plant and plant machinery
began to deteriorate rather dramatically. While some factories surpassed their

[45] "Fábrica de refeições de Maputo apta a produzir 2,500 pratos diários," *Notícias* (31 May 1978);
B. Tomé, "Indústria do caju rompe com a dependencias tecnológica," *Tempo*, 445 (22 April 1979), pp. 23–25; "Caju de Moçambique – heroínas do trabalho," *Tempo*, 493 (23 March 1980), pp. 15–17.
[46] "Caju de Moçambique"; K. Sheldon, "Working Women in Beira, Mozambique," Ph.D. dissertation, University of California, Los Angeles (1988).
[47] "Em Maputo: Aprofundar a Ofensiva nas empresas estratégicas," *Tempo*, 547 (5 April 1981), pp. 14–15.
[48] Castel-Branco, "Problemas estruturais," pp. 104–8.

quotas, most failed to meet production targets. They lacked ra
not repair broken machinery, and experienced numerous prod

Several interrelated features of industrial production during 's, could
to explain the mixed results in industry. First, the highly stratifi 's, 49
inherited from the colonial period affected production after indep,
so many scholars have acknowledged. Under colonialism, Portugu
occupied most of the skilled occupations. Their departure after inde
left shortages of skilled labor in factories such as textiles, paper, mor
metalworking. Some factories never recovered from the transition. S
even the close proximity of the ministry to the industrial plants over wi
had supervision could not eliminate the systemic difficulties associated
planning every aspect of the production process. The "planning paradox"
sociated with command economies has a number of features to it. Since it .
impossible to take into account every single factor that goes into formulating
production targets for hundreds or thousands of goods, plans are inconsistent
almost by definition.[50] If we just look at the calculation of price, which is only
one component of the intricate planning process, we get an idea of the enormity
of the planning task. In the Soviet Union, the government had to determine 8
million prices.[51] If the Mozambican government had to calculate just 1 percent
of that figure, or 80,000 prices, that posed an enormous challenge. In addition,
the government based the plans on the assumption that it could control each and
every stage in the production process. In fact production is made up of "inter-
dependent stochastic processes" that require a certain degree of flexibility from
those involved. Rigid planning often could not accommodate this variability.[52]
In practice, the obligatory quotas were almost never met in Mozambique nor
in any other socialist country.

Third, failure to meet production quotas meant that shortages began to occur in the areas of food and beverages, clothing, plastics, bicycles, and soap.
These shortages may have contributed to low morale or worker "indiscipline"
in factories – an occurrence that Samora Machel frequently alluded to and that
state-owned enterprises in other countries also experienced.[53] The government
then searched for other means to address poor relations in factories and to

[49] "Na fosforeira de Moçambique trabalhadores analisam problemas da empresa," Notícias (14 June 1978); Texmoque-Textil de Moçambique, SARL, Relatório, 1980; Textáfrica, Relatório, 1980; "Texteis-Melhorar a organização das empresas para garantir as metas do PEC/81," Tempo, 550 (26 April 1981), pp. 7–9; C. Muianga, "Agro-Alfa 2 Produção comprometida," Tempo, 711 (27 May 1984), pp. 5–6; A. Elias, "Falta de fósforos é dor de cabeça," Tempo, 736 (18 November 1984), pp. 10–11; F. Ribas, "Cerveja e refrigerantes: Só bebe quem tem vasilhame," Tempo, 740 (16 December 1984), pp. 8–12.

[50] Brus and Laski, From Marx to the Market, pp. 41–43.

[51] Y. Aharoni, The Evolution and Management of State-Owned Enterprises (Cambridge, MA: Ballinger Publishing, 1986), p. 47.

[52] Brus and Laski, From Marx to the Market, pp. 41–43.

[53] Aharoni, The Evolution, pp. 47–48 on conflicts with SOEs.

improve production targets. These means consisted of frequent reorganization of production ("workers' committees," "production councils," "factory committees," etc.), a reliance on prizes for "good workers," and punishment and castigation of bad workers. However, resorting to these methods compromised the presuppositions and objectives of the model because the government had to give in to market-like mechanisms such as rewards or prizes for good performance, or it had to resort to various forms of force. Use of these mechanisms suggest that the more pressing goal of meeting production targets compromised the state's claim to be a superior form of social organization.

Finally, and perhaps the greatest problem, was that manufacturing depended on agriculture to supply approximately 50 percent of its raw materials.[54] Since the government also was applying its transformative vision to agriculture, the ensuing disruption affected planning targets and actual industrial output. Agriculture, more than industry, brutally exposed the flaws in the high modern approach.

### The vision for agriculture

The proposals for agriculture were grandiose and ambitious in their design and were also decidedly more difficult to implement than in industry. They depended on great state capacity and the availability of huge resources, neither of which Mozambique had. Unlike industry, which by its physical nature had already "collected" workers, locating groups of them in one space, agricultural patterns were more varied and more unruly. They defied the vision of an orderly, scientifically engineered project controlled by the state. Agrarian relations varied from south to north, within provinces, and even within districts. Rural producers were differentiated according to income, land size, status, age, and gender. They put together every conceivable combination of production in order to gain a living. In addition to varied production methods, actual households might be crowded together in the *aldeamentos* left over from the colonial period or they might be dispersed over hundreds of kilometers, in accordance with their cultural preferences or production needs.

What the state proposed for these multiple existences in the countryside was nothing short of "transformative," a term that President Samora Machel would employ again and again when referring to the plan for agriculture. The state attempted to refashion spatially and politically the social and productive relations of rural people by sweeping them into communal villages and centralizing their production strategies. The strategy theoretically involved, as Scott has observed of Tanzanian collectivization, "a disorientation and then a reorientation": first the movement of people from one space to another, and then a

---

[54] Torp, *Industrial Planning*, p. 36.

reconfiguration of the space in which they lived and produced.[55] All over the country, orderly, linear villages would bring together rural peoples in specially demarcated spaces, replacing the dispersed and chaotic patterns that apparently described living habits throughout Mozambique. Alongside communal villages would arise a new productive sphere characterized by efficiently run cooperatives and mechanized state farms. The end result would be complete structural rationalization, which, if realized, would bring a totalizing conformity to the countryside. Conformity also served nationalistic goals: making everything the same helped to achieve national unity.

The objectives were nationalistic, socialist, and high modern, romantic and political. New patterns of living and production would liberate the peasant from backwardness and feudal ways of thinking. *Aldeais comunais* (communal villages) would provide badly needed healthcare, education, and services and of course, governmental and party oversight, thereby leading to the "improvement" of rural lives. Because they were located in a central location, smallholders would have better access to services and inputs.[56] Simultaneously, whether producers previously had worked on isolated plots or had been wage laborers formerly coerced to work on plantations, the new patterns of production intended to re-engineer agrarian relations, distilling, refining, and simplifying them from the multiple patterns that had prevailed in the colonial period. Production would become more efficient, output would therefore increase, living standards would improve, and thus the peasant would be liberated from the exploitative relations of the past. Politically, the purpose was to extend state and party control over the countryside, and to eliminate challenges from customary elites such as chiefs and their advisors, and any others who might have collaborated with the colonial government. Grouping rural peoples in designated, smaller spaces would facilitate that control. Rationalization would enable the government to monitor and control the actions of rural inhabitants. Restructuring would allow the replacement of the values and institutions of the past with ideas and structures of the ruling party.

### The agricultural demiurge

As with industry, the state took the leading role in reorganizing living habits and agricultural production, as well as trade to, through, and within the countryside. By 1983, after much institutional reorganization, departments and directorates within the Ministry of Agriculture took primary responsibility for the rural areas, not only state farms and cooperatives, but also communal villages and individual households. For the marketing of agricultural tools, consumer goods, and food crops, the state organized a marketing network called Agricom after

---

[55] Scott, *Seeing like a State*, p. 235.
[56] For an interesting discussion of Frelimo's urban bias, see Cravinho, "Modernizing Mozambique," chapter 3, no. 4.

1981. Agricom was under the control of the Ministry of Domestic Commerce.[57] In addition, the government replicated at the provincial level those institutions that monitored communal villages, aided state farms, and fostered cooperatives. These answered to the provincial governors and respective national ministries.[58]

To bring about a transformation in rural social relations, the principle of democratic centralism prevailed with a clear chain of command flowing from ministers in Maputo down to local party activists and government officials. The government organized rural areas at the lowest level into *bairros* (or small wards), *bairros* into *aldeias* (villages), *aldeias* into *circulos* (circles), and *circulos* into *localidades* (localities), or if they were more populated, then they were organized into administrative posts. The government then grouped administrative posts and localities into districts, districts into provinces, and provinces into the country of Mozambique. Like a military unit, the national minister and the national departments gave orders to the provincial director and his departments, and he then gave them to the district director and his respective departments. In turn, *chefes de postos* (heads of posts) or presidents of localities would receive and implement their orders and in turn, would instruct village and ward heads. Parallelling these governmental structures and often sharing the same personnel were party units as well as party organizations. Thus at the local level might be found party secretaries and dynamizing groups followed by district and provincial party headquarters and their respective officials. Party organizations at each level included the Organization of Mozambican Women, the Organization of Mozambican Youth, the Organization of Mozambican Workers (OTM), the Organization of Mozambican Professors, and popular militia groups.[59]

A scientific logic informed the spatial design and the visual aesthetic of the communal villages, but pre-existing colonial structures and the rural strategy then being followed by Mozambique's neighbor to the north, Tanzania, equally influenced the shape of the villages. Like the Tanzanian villagization schemes with which they shared an ideological affinity, Mozambique's communal villages sought to improve the lives of rural peoples by easing their access to services. The ideal communal village would house somewhere between 250 and 1,000 families and would contain government and party offices, a police station, military personnel, a health post, a school, a people's shop, storage facilities for agricultural production or consumer goods, and some local, low-tech industries such as a craft-making shop or flour mill.[60] Like the Portuguese *aldeamentos*

---

[57] J. Cravinho, "Frelimo and the Politics of Agricultural Marketing in Mozambique," *Journal of Southern African Studies*, 24, 1 (March 1998), pp. 93–113.

[58] Caballero, *et al.*, *Mozambique – Food and Agriculture Sector*, see appendices.

[59] F. Martinez, *O povo Macua e a sua cultura* (Lisbon: Ministério da Educação, Instituto de Investigação Científica Tropical, 1989), p. 31.

[60] Sources disagree on the exact number, see Casal, "Discurso socialista," p. 55; Tarp, "Agrarian Transformation," p. 8; Coelho, "Protected Villages," p. 335 and de Brito, "Le Frelimo," p. 251.

onto which many of the communal villages (especially in the north) literally were grafted, they adopted a square or rectangular pattern sliced through the center by two intersecting avenues. The most important village organizations such as the government and the party headquarters clustered around the central intersection. Village housing was then to be neatly arranged in straight rows along each wing of the main intersection.[61] A modified version was simply to arrange houses in neat rows on either side of a main thoroughfare.

A rearrangement of productive activities was to parallel the switch to communal villages. Rural inhabitants might be allotted a small parcel on which to grow their food crops but most production would take place on collective plots, pre-cooperatives (and once fully transformed, in cooperatives), and especially state farms. Huge state farms constituted the centerpiece of intervention in the agricultural sector. The government planned approximately eight large-scale projects that were to receive 75 percent of the funding for the state sector. The plans included farms devoted to cash and food crop production. They targeted almost every province in the country from north to south, and depended mostly on the financing of the Soviet Union and Eastern European countries. They were to be highly mechanized and use modern technology. They were expected to employ 10 percent of the workforce and to provide the bulk of the country's meat, milk, and eggs by 1990. The government also intended for them to be responsible for the production and sale of some of the country's most important export crops such as cotton, tea, and sugar.[62]

Smaller, state farms engaged in more specialized tasks such as cotton or sugar production, or chicken hatcheries. Those state farms that specialized in producing crops for export were often under the direction of a Secretary of State for Cotton, Cashew, or Sugar. Highly centralized planning and distribution characterized most of them. Some of these state farms, such as the State Enterprise for Cotton in Cabo Delgado coexisted over a period of time within a larger agricultural project such as Cabo Delgado's 400,000 hectare scheme and were subject to overlapping supervision by two or more state bodies, one responsible for the scheme and the other responsible for cotton. Others, such as the State Enterprise for Cotton in Nampula or the sugar complex at Buzi near Beira, were managed as single crop state farms, but they often covered an entire province.

Although the government never properly articulated what the relationship between state farms and local inhabitants was to be, the hope was that cooperative

---

[61] Martinez, *O povo Macua*, p. 30, fig. 9.

[62] See G. Myers and H. West, "Land Tenure Security and State Farm Divestiture in Mozambique: Case Studies in Nhamatanda, Manica, and Montepuez Districts," LTC Research Paper 110, Land Tenure Center, University of Wisconsin-Madison (January 1993), p. 56 on the 400,000 hectare scheme in Cabo Delgado and in Gaza, see Provincia de Gaza, Unidade de Produção do Baixo Limpopo, "Relatório da U.P. B.L. por ocasião da I reunião nacional do sector estatal agrário," Macuse, Zambezia (12 February 1979).

production by local peasants would form the basis of state farm output. It was to take place on land belonging to former settlers or on former *concentrações*, areas of land that the Portuguese had specially demarcated for more intensive cash crop production by Africans during the colonial period. Also, the state would designate additional *blocos* (blocks) near the newly formed communal villages for cooperative production. This approach to production differed little from the old *concentração* scheme used by the Portuguese and shared many similarities with the approach used by Tanzania.[63] Through centralization, the allocation of designated plots, and the provision of machinery for collective use, family sector producers would be more able to provide for their own subsistence, and they would be able to channel output to the state farm for processing, packaging and eventual distribution to the urban areas or abroad. Ultimately, the intention was that there would be one and a half million cooperative members cultivating 1.4 million hectares by 1985; by 1990, the government expected to incorporate fully all of the family sector into cooperatives, which would boost membership to 5 million participants and the total area to 7 million hectares.[64]

## Flawed principles, mistaken practices, unforeseen responses

The kind of transformation that the Frelimo party envisioned for the countryside was impracticable in principle and disruptive in practice. What the state proposed was to reorganize approximately 9 million rural people into villages, reconstruct their housing, provide for their services, and rearrange their production. Other countries in Africa have adopted more modest approaches and yet achieved poor outcomes; Mozambique was no different. By the early 1980s, communal villages only included about 20 percent of the total rural population. The majority of the villages and the population included in them were in Cabo Delgado, where Frelimo began its liberation campaign and the Portuguese responded with *aldeamentos*. After Cabo Delgado, Gaza, Nampula, and Manica had the greatest amounts of villagization, while Zambezia, one of the most populous provinces in Mozambique, had the fewest number of villages. Only 2 percent of its population was affected. In addition, only 30 percent of communal villages had consumer cooperatives by 1982. Producer cooperatives also fell far short of the anticipated 1.5 million people that were supposed to be in them by 1985.[65]

Given the small percentage of the population affected, communal villagization and cooperative production hardly seemed catastrophic, but these results

---

[63] Coelho, "Protected Villages," p. 350.

[64] Caballero, *et al.*, *Mozambique – Food and Agriculture Sector*, p. 64.

[65] Frelimo Party, *Out of Underdevelopment to Socialism*, Report of the Central Committee, Fourth Congress (Maputo: Frelimo Party, 1983), p. 20, 28; Coelho, "Protected Villages," p. 345 and pp. 352–56.

were indicative of greater economic difficulties. Notably, state intervention in the economy was in serious trouble by the early 1980s. The challenges of nature such as bad weather and poor soil partially explained the poor output, but human errors accounted for most of it. At a meeting in 1981 to review the year's agricultural results, the Ministry of Agriculture chronicled a plethora of flaws: mismanagement, corruption, labor shortages, indiscipline, poor roads, lack of spare parts or transport, shortages of consumer goods, delays of inputs, of harvests, and of sales. From Zambezia to Sofala, in cashew as well as timber, plans had not been fulfilled in any province or any sector. Administrative foul-ups were numerous. Most of the large state agricultural projects had faltered and already were undergoing significant reorganization. Because the state projects showed such appalling results, smallholders were returning to their own farms. "Members of the cooperatives," one government official remarked, "are feeding and clothing themselves from their family fields because that's where they work longer."[66]

Output was abysmal. Except for tea, Mozambique's export crops of cotton, sugar, cashews, copra, and sisal, which were tied to the state sector through control over production, processing, or trade, all dropped following independence. Cashews had been one of Mozambique's major export earners in the 1970s, but production began to drop just before independence and continued to fall thereafter. By 1980, the government had become so concerned at the decrease of cashews that it began a national cashew campaign to mobilize smallholders to improve their care and harvesting of trees. It commissioned posters to exhort smallholders to increase production, and it offered prizes to honor the peasant, locality, district and province that produced the most cashews.[67] Yet cashew production at least for official markets continued to deteriorate in the 1980s. The output of 85,000 tons in 1985 was almost half what it had been in 1975; by 1997, with output at 43,000 tons, it was half again what it had been in 1985.[68]

For the smallholder or family sector, state intervention brought a decline in total marketed agricultural production and jeopardized home consumption. With the majority of credit going to the state sector, smallholders received little support. Without funding, family sector production, which included two of the country's greatest export crops, cotton and cashews, as well as most of the domestically traded food crops of maize, cassava, rice, and peanuts,

---

[66] Mozambique, Ministério de Agricultura, "Reunião do Conselho Consultivo Alargado" (April 1981), p. 4, and see the rest of the document for the flaws in agriculture.

[67] "Comercialização de Caju," *Notícias* (21 November 1980); "Emulação socialista na campanha de comercialização de castanha de Caju," *Notícias* (25 November 1980).

[68] See J. Leite, "A guerra do caju e as relações Moçambique-India na epoca pós-colonial," Documentos de Trabalho no. 57, CEsA (Lisbon 1999), table 1 for the offical statistics on cashew production between 1970 and 1997.

declined. Smallholders lacked the resources to invest in tools, apply pesticides and fertilizers, and properly care for cashew trees or cotton bushes. Despite the changes, the family sector and private companies continued to contribute around 22 percent and 26 percent respectively to marketed production.[69]

The seemingly uniform aesthetic embodied in the plans for agriculture concealed a glaring contradiction in Frelimo's approach to rural producers at the level of the national leadership. On the one hand, official documents referred to peasants as "subsistence" producers – as if they were not migrating, or did not want to migrate to mines and plantations, and as if they did not have, or did not want to gain, cash incomes from crop sales.[70] This view persisted at the national planning level despite the fact that the Center of African Studies at Eduardo Mondlane University in the capital had documented elaborate patterns of male rural migration to tea plantations in Zambezia, detailed the livelihoods of worker-peasants in southern Mozambique, and traced extensively the work patterns and marketing practices of smallholders in the north of the country.[71]

On the other hand, at the core of the transformative strategy was the assumption that rural producers could simply relocate, reorganize, and reorient their livelihoods like workers changing jobs. Machel's assertion that communal villages would be "cities of the countryside" rather naively presumed that producers were highly mobile and eminently adaptable.[72] Like workers who could take their spinning skills from one textile factory to another, rural producers could carry anywhere their experiential knowledge of soil acidity, water retention, rainfall patterns, and tree pruning.

Accompanying this contradictory view of rural people was an idea that the state knew best. The design of the strategy adopted for the rural areas was dismissive of local knowledge and devalued the contribution that rural people could make to development. Instead, because the state had access to "scientific" knowledge, it was the state that would formulate plans, set quotas, choose suitable growing areas, and determine the optimal growing period. In Mozambique, government officials, like their counterparts in countries as

---

[69] Ministério das Finanças, "Relatório sobre a situação," pp. 51–52; A. Casal, "A Crise da produção familiar e as aldeias comunais em Moçambique," *Revista Internacional de Estudos Africanos*, 8–9 (January–December 1988), p. 163; B. O'Laughlin, "Past and Present Options: Land Reform in Mozambique," *Review of African Political Economy*, 22, 63 (1995), pp. 102–4.

[70] Mozambique, "Relatório da Província da Zambézia ao III Conselho Agrário Nacional" (June 1978), mimeo., p. 3; O'Laughlin, "Through a Divided Glass," pp. 15–17.

[71] See for example, UEM, CEA, "A Transformação" and "A Actuação do estado ao nível do distrito: o caso de Lugela," CEA Relatório 81/9 (Maputo, 1980–81); UEM, CEA, "Plantações de Chá e Economia Camponesa: Informação Basica para um Plano Director da Zona Gurúe-Socone, Alta Zambézia," Projecto da Emochá: Relatório (A), 1982 and "O Papel Dinamizador da Emochá na Transformação Socialista da Alta Zambézia," Projecto da Emochá: Relatório (B), 1982; First, *Black Gold*. These form part of a large number of reports produced by the CEA at this time.

[72] Machel, "Independencia implica," p. 5, and see also the persistence of this vision in Machel, "Coordenemos as nossas forças."

ideologically different as Nigeria and Tanzania, saw producers as backward and inefficient. Only by herding them into villages or state farms would production increase and the life of the farmer improve.[73]

Beyond its conception, serious flaws in the implementation of the new agrarian strategy further undermined its effectiveness and limited its capacity to transform the countryside. Central weaknesses beset the implementation of the scheme for transformation from the start. In fact, agriculture was **not** like industry and the government was **not** prepared for all the variation. As early as 1978, some government officials were so concerned with the disastrous results that they tried to shift the focus away from state farms, but they were unsuccessful. They could not get the backing of the entire leadership to make the shift. The belief that a modern, highly mechanized, and concentrated approach to agriculture was the correct option was too strong. Also, both the Soviet and East European donors on whom the Mozambican government relied and state farm directors had a vested interest in the production methods associated with state enterprises.[74] The leadership thus persisted with the approach in the face of obvious drawbacks.

The explanations for the difficulties can be divided into two groups – those problems that affected all newly independent African states to a greater or lesser degree, and those that were specific to the command approach that Mozambique pursued. The first category included the structural shortcomings left by the colonial period as well as the usual weaknesses and understandable mistakes of a newly independent and inexperienced government. Like many other countries, Mozambique lacked educated, skilled labor as a result of discriminatory educational policies towards Africans during the colonial period. With the departure of settlers following independence, companies lost qualified personnel who could manage production or maintain equipment. Colonial planners also located industry, infrastructure, and communications around the capital and selected urban areas. Such regional and national disparities did not facilitate a centralized approach to agriculture run from the capital. In this respect, the north suffered more than the south of the country. It lacked infrastructure such as warehouses and agricultural machinery. The communication of plans, quotas, and instructions from Maputo to remote cotton areas in Zambezia or Nampula was difficult if not impossible. Poor roads and too few traders undermined the timely arrival of necessary inputs for agriculture and thwarted the distribution of harvested crops to factories for processing and eventual export.

---

[73] G. Williams, "Taking the Part of Peasants: Rural Development in Nigeria and Tanzania" in P. Gutkind and I. Wallerstein, eds., *Political Economy of Contemporary Africa* (London: Sage, 1976), p. 153.

[74] J. Barker, "Gaps in the Debates about Agriculture in Senegal, Tanzania and Mozambique," *World Development*, 13, 1 (1985) pp. 69–70.

Such legacies meant that colonial practices and institutions sometimes got replicated the farther away from the capital that one got, simply for lack of a better, fully formed alternative. The situation in Nampula Province offers an insightful example of the degree to which the colonial period continued to shape the plans and the relations of production after independence. The Ministry of Agriculture created nine state farms in Nampula. These state farms specialized in export sectors such as tobacco and cotton, or in products destined for urban areas such as timber, chicken hatcheries, and fruit. The Ministry of Industry assumed control over processing facilities for cashews, which were another major agricultural export from Nampula.[75] Interestingly, the government did not establish state farms in crops grown for domestic consumption, presumably because these crops did not bring a financial return or confer a political benefit in the way that export crops and products to urban areas did.

The goals behind the state farms that were established may have differed from those of former private colonial companies, but the two shared several features. First, processing facilities for both were highly concentrated. Throughout colonial Mozambique, large private monopolies had dominated the export sectors of sugar, tea, tobacco, cotton, and sisal. For example, from the 1930s to the 1960s, one colonial company controlled the purchase, processing, and export of all cotton grown in Nampula.[76] After independence, the government continued to concentrate the processing of exports such as cotton and tobacco, making one state farm in each sector responsible for all of the production in Nampula. Second, while the state farms relied partially on direct state production and collective production to grow and harvest export crops, they also relied heavily on the family sector, as in the colonial period. In Monapo, Meconta and Mecuburi, three districts of Nampula Province, many of these smallholders continued to clear, seed, weed, and harvest cotton as before, and to carry their cotton to designated markets.[77] For some smallholders, only a change in name differentiated what they did in the colonial period from what they did in the post-colonial period. In Corrane, Meconta District, for example, individual production on specially designated blocks of land that the Portuguese had called *concentrações* became "collective" production on *blocos* (blocks). Otherwise, little changed except for the persons who profited from their production.[78] In cashew and cotton, many smallholders in Nampula Province continued to interact with a centralized economic unit where processing facilities were concentrated and handled

[75] Mozambique, Ministério de Agrícultura, Direcção de Economia Agrária, Sector de Análise de Unidades Económicas (SAUE), "Dossier das Empresas Estatais Agrárias da Província de Nampula," Maputo (January 1988).

[76] Pitcher, *Politics in the Portuguese Empire*, pp. 118–19.

[77] Group Interview (GI), rural producers, Monapo District, Nampula Province (May 1994); Household surveys (HS), Monapo District, Nampula Province (May 1994); Mecuburi District (June 1995); Meconta District, Nampula Province (June 1995).

[78] Household surveys, Corrane, Meconta District (June 1995).

by a single organization. As in the 1950s, the price for cotton continued to be set by the state. Beyond producing cash crops along lines that resembled the past, smallholders continued to produce food crops for their subsistence and for sale on individual *machambas* (fields) that they had either inherited from their families or that they had simply cleared.[79] Yet production took place in an insecure, disrupted environment that contained many of the burdens but lacked some of the guarantees of the colonial period. As one producer from Nampula remarked, "Under Samora Machel, even before the war, there was nothing in the shops, we had to wear sacks, there were no clothes, nothing."[80]

As a new government, Frelimo also made mistakes and lacked experience. It overestimated the enthusiasm of rural peoples for its schemes and underestimated the challenges of restructuring settlement and production. It placed too much faith in party and bureaucratic discipline and people's loyalty. When these failed to increase productivity or lower costs, the government tended to favor punishment over incentives as a tactic to foster cooperation or increase output. It spent too much money, and there were few accounting procedures in place to find out where the money went. As one report stated: "At the level of the state enterprise there is not the least effort, much less economic concern, with trying to recoup the state's expenses or at least to obtain self-sufficiency."[81]

Equally, in its allocation of credit, the government appeared to replicate the skewed patterns of the colonial period. As in the past, Maputo and Gaza received the bulk of the credit while Nampula and lastly Inhambane received very little. In a damning criticism, the Ministry of Finances charged: "In this sense, the distribution of credit is identical to the colonial period. Credit is concentrated in the same districts and the same crops as in the colonial period."[82] As these occurrences appear to be widespread among African countries of all ideological hues, they cannot solely be attributed to state intervention. Rather, they may be a product of inexperience, a certain degree of path dependency that shapes the process from the moment of independence, and/or the rent-seeking behavior of individuals within the government.

Outcomes in many cases were similar to, or worse than, results in the colonial period. We must examine a second order of complications to understand why. These second-order complications arose specifically as a result of extensive state intervention in the economy in the guise of settlement schemes, collectivization, state farms, and state-controlled trade. Here, the lack of state capacity to realize the stated objectives, the ensuing disorientation of rural producers that

---

[79] GI, rural producers, Monapo; HS, Monapo District, Nampula Province (May 1994); Mecuburi District (June 1995); Meconta District, Nampula Province.

[80] *Regulo* no. 4, Netia Administrative Post, Monapo District, Nampula Province, interview, 21 May 1994.

[81] Mozambique, Ministry of Agriculture, "Reunião," p. 9.

[82] Ministério das Finanças, "Relatório sobre a situação," p. 60.

occurred when the objectives were not realized, and ultimately, rural manipulation and resistance combined to explain outcomes that deviated from the state's expectations. In the role of demiurge, the state had to have the administrative and financial ability to realize its visions. Administratively, the government needed to create institutions with the appropriate capacity for managing the agricultural sector, from the allocation of credit to the provision of tools to the export of processed and packaged cash crops. Yet delays in the provision of tools and other inputs, a shortage of consumer goods at state-run shops, and schemes that fell short of the ideal-type clearly illustrated that the government lacked the capability to intervene successfully in every aspect of agrarian production and distribution. Frequent institutional changes within the Ministry of Agriculture right down to the provincial level and the re-dimensioning of large projects and state farms reinforce the point that the government was overextended.

Moreover, the realization of such an ambitious project as transforming relations of production in agriculture required enormous financial resources and the competence to manage them. Once again, Mozambique did not have these. Certainly, it could be argued that high oil prices, dwindling revenue from services with South Africa, migrants remittances, and sanctions against Rhodesia until 1980 undercut the state's efforts to finance properly the state sector. But they do not explain why the state did not then decide to temper its ambition with practicality, and they do not explain the gross mismanagement of funds once they were in the hands of the state sector.

On the ground, the government introduced state farms and collective production without regard for the complex and precarious existence of rural producers and rural laborers. Officials failed to consider the importance of space to smallholders. What Scott has noted about rural life in Tanzania was equally true for rural Mozambicans: "The existing economic activity and physical movement of the Tanzanian rural population were the consequences of a mind-bogglingly complex, delicate, and pliable set of adaptations to their diverse social and material environment."[83] No amount of planning could capture in significant detail the diverse patterns that prevailed. In Mozambique, as in Tanzania, state farms and collectives disrupted historical patterns of production and the ability to rely on local "place specific" knowledge to maintain or increase output.[84] In Nampula and Cabo Delgado, for example, the formation of communal villages and collectives severed smallholders' symbolic connections to particular pieces of land and separated them from cashew trees they had long cultivated, without offering a viable replacement.[85] Implementation was often unresponsive

[83] Scott, *Seeing Like a State*, p. 246.     [84] Scott, *Seeing Like a State*, p. 251.
[85] Geffray and Pedersen, "Nampula en guerre"; H. West, "Sorcery of Construction and Sorcery of Ruin: Power and Ambivalence on the Mueda Plateau, Mozambique (1882–1994)", Ph.D. dissertation, University of Wisconsin-Madison (1997), chapter 4.

to regional, productive, cultural, and historical differences in the country but completely sensitive to the centralization of power in the hands of the state.

In addition, the schemes lacked temporal considerations. They disregarded the fine but absolutely critical balance between subsistence production and cash income. They did not consider how labor time might be divided between working for the state farm and working for one's own subsistence. They failed to recognize regional variations in the pattern of production and to distinguish, for example, between the different demands on labor time made by smallholder versus plantation forms of production. Furthermore, the government enforced schemes without sufficient knowledge of how producers divided time among household duties, and without realizing how gender, age, status, and ethnicity influenced labor activities.[86]

The enormity of the state's task also meant that reorientation never arrived in some parts of the country. Rather, deprivation and neglect characterized these areas. Zambezia Province, for example, had the lowest percentage of rural peoples in communal villages of any province in the country by 1982.[87] Ironically, parts of this province in the center of the country might have been quite receptive to the idea of village formation, due to a long history of male migration to large plantations. If communal villages had been located close to former plantations, provided with services, and accompanied by fields for food production, migrants and their families may have been attracted to the convenience that the new arrangement offered. As it was, for those thousands in Zambezia who never saw a communal village, the injustices were still acute: neglect undercut their ability to produce or to work. They lost wage-labor jobs and had no consumer goods. Most markets for crops disappeared, crop prices stagnated, and roads deteriorated.[88] Additionally, in contrast to the pervasive denunciations of exploitation by state officials, the continued existence of powerful companies like Madal must have struck many as the worst kind of hypocrisy.

### Disruption without transformation and the rural response to instability

To transform the rural areas was really a two-step process: it involved destruction and creation. To construct a new society, the old one had to die, but transformation was incomplete. The policies fashioned and implemented for agriculture certainly introduced a new dynamic of power and production into

---

[86] O'Laughlin, "Through a Divided Glass," pp. 17–28; for specific examples from Gaza Province, see L. Harris, "Agricultural Co-operatives and Development Policy in Mozambique," *Journal of Peasant Studies*, 7 (April 1980), p. 343; and for Nampula Province see Pitcher, "Disruption Without Transformation," pp. 124–27.

[87] Coelho, "Protected Villages," p. 345.

[88] Vail and White, *Capitalism and Colonialism*, chapter 9.

rural life, but they were disruptive rather than transformative, "intrusive rather than hegemonic."[89] Their impact illustrates quite vividly Berry's claim that state policies do not simply succeed or fail in a vacuum; it is the interaction between the state and rural agents that helps to determine their outcome. Most often these interactions should be seen as a series of "inconclusive encounters."[90] In Mozambique, state policies and the response to them sometimes rearranged existing methods of production and sometimes disturbed prior political allegiances, but they did not revolutionize agrarian relations. To revise Scott, the government disoriented rural populations without being able to reorient them because rural peoples were **not** the "prostrate" objects that the state presumed them to be.[91] State disruption bred insecurity in the rural areas, contributed to the appalling drops in production, and prompted a reliance on a multitude of strategies to ensure survival.

No wonder then that, over time, those affected also shaped and eventually undermined villagization, cooperative and state farm production as they did in Tanzania, or they protested government neglect. In some parts of the country, producers, traders, and even some private companies took the form of engaging with the state, taking advantage of state incapacity to strike compromises with state officials. These compromises modified the impact of government efforts and contributed to a continuity with the colonial period. Private traders struck deals to purchase cashew or deliver consumer goods, and companies such as Madal and Entreposto managed to find a niche for themselves in the largely command economy. Chiefs and other "traditional" notables continued in positions that they had occupied before. They simply ignored or avoided the dictates of the state, or they took opportunistic advantage of situations where the state was floundering.[92] For example, there was a chief in the district of Mecuburi in the north of the country who was also a Frelimo secretary, and in at least five zones of Mecuburi District, there has been a history of collaboration between the Frelimo secretary and "traditional" authorities.[93] Rich and middle farmers who had gained positions of status and wealth during the colonial period managed to hang onto them after independence by controlling cooperatives with state compliance or becoming village presidents and secretaries.[94] They

---

[89] Berry, *No Condition*, p. 48.     [90] See Berry, *No Condition*, chapter 3.

[91] Scott, *Seeing Like a State*, pp. 88–89. I find rather curious Scott's claim that among other elements, high modernist plans originate in "weakened or prostrate civil society that lacks the capacity to resist these plans." Surely, his own work has demonstrated above all that "civil society" is not prostrate, it is only presumed to be.

[92] Alexander, "The Local State"; Pitcher, "Disruption Without Transformation"; West, "Sorcery of Construction," pp. 240–42.

[93] Cooperação Suisse, "'Uma vida boa': perspectivas locais de desenvolvimento em Nametil, Mecubúri," MóZ-44, Mecubúri District, Nampula Province (April 1997), p. 29.

[94] Harris, "Agricultural Co-operatives," p. 342; Pitcher, "Disruption Without Transformation," pp. 136–37; Bowen, *The State Against the Peasantry*, chapter 6.

manipulated the contradictions in Frelimo's own ideology by emphasizing their modern attributes over their capitalist leanings.

Rural producers also subverted or modified policies through disengagement. They drifted back to former homesteads and lands. They withdrew labor from state farms and cooperatives and worked their own plots instead. In the northern province of Nampula, for example, residents challenged villagization by avoiding it if possible and returning clandestinely to their lands. In Monapo District, some local people constructed houses in a communal village in the administrative post of Netia but then returned to their own *machambas*, unwilling to leave their cashew trees.[95] In Mecuburi District, one resident deliberately moved away in order to avoid the communal village. As an alternative, he occupied unclaimed land that was beyond the jurisdiction of the village authorities.[96]

Collective production equally deteriorated as producers voted with their feet and avoided it. For example, some of the original producers associated with one scheme in the north claimed they were not paid on time after the first harvest, so they quit. Many also withdrew from the scheme because there was no guarantee of receiving inputs from the state and thus the risks of continuing production were too high. Some women chose to privilege their own food security by working at home, instead of taking the risks involved in collective production. Some men hedged their bets and joined the scheme but continued to sow cotton at home. Many of them were thus absent at crucial work periods on the collective farms.[97] While collectively some of these efforts can hardly be termed "resistance," they nevertheless undermined government attempts to remake Mozambique.

Furthermore, Frelimo's denunciations of customary practices and leaders led to the alienation of people rather than their incorporation into the new state project.[98] Former *regulos* and their supporters both subverted and sabotaged official policies. They subtly undercut the state's legitimacy by referring to villages and rivers by their old names rather than by the new names the government had decreed for them. Local inhabitants often defied or ignored the authority of village presidents, party secretaries, and other representatives of state power by supporting instead *regulos* or other former holders of customary or colonial positions of power. When villagization and collective production created insecurity, local peoples perceived the actions of Frelimo officials as "illegitimate." Residents in some parts of the country then turned to customary leaders

---

[95] GI, Rural producers, Monapo and Mecuburi Districts; *Regulos* no. 3 and no. 4, Netia Administrative Post, Monapo District, Nampula Province, interviews, 21 May 1994.

[96] HS, no. 15, Mecuburi.

[97] Habermeier, "Cotton," p. 52 and UEM, "A Transformação," pp. 59–60, 77–78.

[98] On the contradictions and compromises that resulted from this policy in Manica, see Jocelyn Alexander, "Land and Political Authority in Post-War Mozambique: A View from Manica Province," Land Tenure Center, University of Wisconsin-Madison, 1994.

rather than Frelimo officials for aid.[99] Despite the ambiguities that attended the position of *regulo* in the colonial period (and continue to do so), they and the lineage networks they belonged to became the means through which many smallholders mediated their experience of Frelimo policies.[100] Inhabitants also continued to practice customs they considered valuable, in defiance of a regime that denounced them as "feudal." According to a *regulo* in Mecuburi District, Nampula, "The secretary of Frelimo had power but people continued to engage clandestinely in customary practices, like initiation rites."[101]

Local compromises, as well as the challenges to official policy, should be viewed as the outcomes of multiple strategies by inhabitants to cope with instability. Rural peoples relied on all available economic, political, and social mechanisms to reduce uncertainty – from informal markets to lineage networks to cooperation with the state, if that would work. These mechanisms might be pursued in conjunction with one another. That is, producers might hedge their bets by participating in collective production *and* producing on their own fields or a producer might adopt a single strategy such as withdrawal. These multiple responses to insecurity help to explain how *regulos* and other traditional notables in central and northern parts of the country were able to maintain or resume power during these years. Furthermore, they help to explain rural sympathy for, if not outright participation in, Renamo. Collectively, these strategies weakened the transformative project in the rural areas.

## Summary

Grandiose principles, socialist to be sure, but rooted in high modern visions of what could be accomplished in a poor country, greatly contributed to the deleterious impact of industrial and agricultural policies from 1977 to 1983. In addition, the lack of funds, inexperience, honest mistakes, the overly hasty resettlement of large numbers of people, and the disruption of customary economic and political practices explain the government's inability to achieve certain policy goals, even before the war began seriously to affect parts of the country. Some of these difficulties reasonably would have beset any newly independent country, but also many of them originated in high expectations about the possibilities of state intervention. Even had the principles been realizable and the state capable, the responses of workers and rural producers conditioned and

---

[99] Hence *humus* (customary land chiefs) as well as *cabos* (colonial adjuncts to *regulos*) attracted support, see Geffray and Pedersen, "Sobre a guerra," Mozambique, MAE, "Algumas considerações," p. 28; HS, Monapo and Mecuburi Districts; GI, *Regulos*, Monapo District.

[100] Today, the ambiguity of the position *regulo* is manifest in the interchangeable use of the term *muene* and *regulo* in some communities, while in other localities the two positions remain distinct. On the need to create the traditional, see Ranger in Hobsbawm and Ranger, *The Invention of Tradition*.

[101] *Regulo* no. 1, Mecuburi District, interview.

thwarted government efforts to engineer socially the industrial and agricultural transformation of Mozambique.

While the outcome does not reveal a "predatory" state, neither does it suggest that the state was "developmental." Instead it was an "intermediary" state that realized some objectives with regard to institutional reorganization and improvements in particular social indicators, but fell short in other areas. Over time, the flaws of design and their implementation on the ground so consumed the state that the vision got lost, distorted, and derailed. From the allocation of credit to the organization of work, government practices and ensuing social responses replicated colonial patterns in some instances, or disrupted relations in other cases. Little transformation occurred. By the 1980s, the government refined its utopian projections for the economy to just one single-minded goal – increasing production. As the decade progressed, the state not only adopted more authoritarian measures to reach its objective, but also expanded the number of compromises it had with capital, with workers, and with rural actors. These contradictory measures heralded the beginning of the state's institutional erosion.

# 3　State sector erosion and the turn to the market

"The state must involve itself with large development projects and the major social sectors of education, health, housing, and justice. . . . the state should not sell matches."

President Samora Machel[1]

"How can we want to manage hotels like the Polana and the Dom Carlos . . . when we don't even know how to manage our own kitchens?"

President Samora Machel[2]

Two periods of economic and political reform have characterized the years since 1983 in Mozambique. The erosion of the state sector constituted the first period from approximately 1983 to 1990, while the transition to private ownership and a market economy after 1990 define the second period. In his study of regime change in transitional countries, Róna-Tas argues that what differentiates the two periods is the source of the change. In the first period, "self-interested individuals pursuing private gain" initiate state sector erosion from below. In the second period, the state generates the transition to capitalism from above primarily "through decisive legislative action with the explicit purpose of creating a market economy."[3] I adopt Róna-Tas' approach to explain changes in Mozambique's political economy after 1983. The division into two periods is explanatory: it reveals more clearly the sequencing of the reform measures, and it exposes the social pressures that both prompted and frustrated the reforms.

The emphasis in this chapter on social pressures and reform sequencing differs markedly from explanations of events in the 1980s offered by government officials and some scholars. Several of these sources have continued to blame "exogenous" factors, such as the civil war or the weather, for Mozambique's economic crisis in the 1980s and pressure from the West for the decision to

[1] Samora Machel quoted by J. Hanlon, "Mozambique to Revive Role of Private Sector," *The Washington Post* (20 March 1980).
[2] Samora Machel quoted by X. de Figueiredo, "Economia moçambicana mudará após o congresso da Frelimo," *Diário de Notícias* (23 April 1983).
[3] A. Róna-Tas, "The First Shall Be Last? Entrepreneurship and Communist Cadres in the Transition from Socialism," *American Journal of Sociology*, 100, 1 (July 1994), p. 47.

adopt market principles. Although my argument acknowledges South African aggression, or the influence of the World Bank, or regime transitions in other socialist countries as influential factors affecting Mozambique's reforms, it finds that the types and timing of reforms can best be explained by examining the discontents at the bottom, the powerholders at the top, and select groups organized around particular interests within Mozambican society.

Theoretical support for my argument derives from the extensive literature that has addressed transitions especially in Eastern Europe, but also in Latin America and parts of Asia. Some scholars narrowly focus on the technical aspects of restructuring former state enterprises; others explore the class forces that contributed to transition as well as the elements in society that have benefitted or suffered from regime change. Both of these approaches have helped to disaggregate the continuities and changes in Mozambique during the last couple of decades. By contrast, the research on transition in Africa has been more limited. Scholars have directed much attention to democratization, but fewer studies have examined privatization in those countries previously dominated by an extensive state sector. Part of the reason may be that shifts in Africa are less likely than shifts in Eastern Europe to affect economic and political stability in developed countries and therefore they have attracted less attention from scholars. The reason also may lie in the partial and incomplete nature of many of the transitions in Africa in comparison with many of the dramatic changes in Eastern Europe. In some instances, political and economic change in Africa has been reluctant and halting. One-party rule remains and governments have pledged to undertake economic reforms only to avoid them in practice. In other cases, including Mozambique, substantial economic policy shifts have occurred and multi-party elections have taken place, but without unseating the existing regime. The ability of these regimes to stay in power while undertaking substantial reform contrasts sharply with the collapse of regimes in Eastern Europe. The longevity and flexibility of some of these regimes provide fruitful ground for cross-national research. By comparing Mozambique's experience with that of other countries, I highlight several of the parallels and the contrasts in the transition to market economies in Africa.

### State sector erosion: 1983–1990

In his study of regime transitions, Róna-Tas distinguishes between the erosion of a socialist economy and the transition to a capitalist one. During the erosion phase, the state struggles against the deterioration of those activities under its control, granting only a limited range of operation to the private sector for pragmatic purposes. The government allows the private sector to participate in commercial activities in a restricted manner but, as the phase proceeds, "some restrictions on the private sector are lifted or are enforced less vigorously."[4] The relaxation of controls in turn encourages the entry of additional private actors, yet the state continues to dominate strategic sectors of the economy in finance, agriculture, and industry. Moreover, financial, labor and land legislation that is inimical to the private sector remains in place.

Róna-Tas draws on the experiences of Eastern European countries to explain the erosion phase and the subsequent transition to a market economy, but much of the Mozambican experience also illustrates his claims. By the early 1980s, the country had entered a severe economic crisis. The state sector suffered huge financial losses, in industry as well as agriculture. By the mid-1980s, principal agricultural exports of cotton, sugar, and cashew nuts had plummeted: only shrimp exports increased and then stabilized at around $34 million a year during the period ("$" refers to US dollars throughout). Owing to decreases in the value and volume of exports accompanied by huge increases in imports, Mozambique had a severe balance of payments crisis. The government received emergency food aid from a diverse assortment of countries to cover the country's minimum food requirements and made strenuous efforts both to reschedule its debt and to seek additional assistance. Many industries had collapsed and state farms were unproductive.[5]

After 1983, many sources tended to attribute Mozambique's economic decline to the effect of the growing counterrevolutionary movement Renamo. When viewed in contrast to the discourse voiced prior to 1983 regarding Mozambique's economic difficulties, the degree of agreement in government reports or news articles about the causes of economic decline is quite striking. Previously, as we have discussed, government officials, reports, and newspaper articles cited numerous factors to explain poor output or decreases in production. Workers lacked discipline, managers needed skills, materials did not arrive on time, or the government favored state companies in the allocation of credit – there were abundant explanations, even if some were less important than others. After 1983, the pluralism of the earlier discourse largely vanished. Government reports as well as works by scholars sympathetic to Frelimo largely blamed Renamo not only for the hardships that the country was undergoing during the 1980s but also for the government's past failures to accomplish its goals.[6] And if the reader remained unconvinced, journalists and government reports

---

[4] Róna-Tas, "The First Shall Be Last?," p. 48.

[5] Mozambique, "Strategy and Program for Economic Rehabilitation, 1987–1990," report prepared by the Government of Mozambique for the meeting of the consultative group for Mozambique, Paris (July 1987), Maputo (June 1987).

[6] Hanlon, *Mozambique: The Revolution Under Fire* and *Mozambique: Who Calls the Shots?*, Part 1; J. Saul, *Recolonization and Resistance*; W. Minter, *Apartheid's Contras: An Inquiry into the Roots of War in Angola and Mozambique* (Atlantic Highlands, NJ: Zed Press, 1994). This is not to say that these works ignored some of the failings of the Frelimo government; it is really a question of where the emphasis lay, and it lay squarely with the impact of the war.

submitted evidence of the drought from 1982 to 1984, and the floods of late 1984 to assuage any lingering doubts.[7] For example, in a report prepared by the Mozambican government for a meeting by the Consultative Group for Mozambique in 1987, three pages detailed the contemporary "exogenous constraints" that were responsible for Mozambique's decline. These included South Africa's efforts to destabilize Mozambique through support for Renamo and the application of sanctions against the colonial regime in Rhodesia prior to 1980. The report cited increases in the price of petroleum, droughts, floods, and cyclones to complete the dismal picture. By contrast the report devoted just three paragraphs to flaws in the government's management of the economy.[8] Government officials rarely discussed openly the lessons that might have been learned from the 1977 to 1983 period, while the war was the lens through which they viewed most incidents after 1983.

Certainly, statistics reveal a staggering degree of destruction caused by the war over the course of the decade. Renamo probably exacted around $5 1/2 billion in damage over a five-year period in the 1980s.[9] It targeted not only schools and hospitals, but tea, cotton, and sugar processing facilities; not only government buildings but infrastructure such as roads, bridges and railways. By 1984, 489 schools and 102 health clinics had already been destroyed.[10] In all, destabilization cost the lives of approximately 1 million people and wreaked $15 billion worth of damage.[11] Approximately 1.6 million people fled to neighboring countries and the war internally displaced around 3.7 million Mozambicans.[12] Rural flight drastically affected food and cash crop production, and decreased the income that Mozambique received from agricultural and other exports. Only fishing remained practically unaffected by the war, as Renamo apparently had no boats and Frelimo forces protected most coastal areas relatively well. In addition, Renamo activities destroyed 900 rural trading shops that had begun to re-establish in rural areas and sent rural traders fleeing to the relative security of district capitals or larger cities. In the five provinces of Cabo Delgado, Nampula, Zambezia, Tete, and Niassa, the relaxation of controls on private trading had increased the number of traders to nearly 3,000 by 1982, but Renamo attacks precipitated a sharp

---

[7]  See for example P. Fauvet, "Mozambique's Vulnerability," *Africa News* (5 March 1984), pp. 5–11 or P. Gregson, "Economia de Moçambique totalmente paralisada," *A Tarde* (11 April 1985). Even Cahen, not known to mince words, noted that he did not wish to "play the game of the enemy" by being overly critical in the mid-1980s. See Cahen, "Check on Socialism," p. 47.

[8]  Mozambique, "Strategy and Program," pp. 6–9.

[9]  S. Askin, "Economic About-turn in War-torn Mozambique," *Weekly Mail* (14–20 October 1988).

[10]  M. Holman, "Why Machel is Wooing the West," *Financial Times* (24 April 1984).

[11]  Hanlon, *Mozambique: Who Calls the Shots?*, pp. 40–42.

[12]  H. Andersson, *Mozambique: A War against the People* (New York: St. Martin's Press, 1992), p. 107 and Sidaway and Power, "Sociospatial Transformations," p. 1466.

decline. By the 1990s, approximately 2,000 rural traders existed in the entire country.[13]

Moreover, the existence of approximately 3.7 million internal refugees by 1987 dramatically increased Mozambique's reliance on expensive food imports to feed those populations destabilized by the war. Before independence, marketed production of rice and maize had averaged between 150,000 and 200,000 tons a year. These figures dropped to between 40,000 and 75,000 tons on average up to 1988. In some years, food aid constituted 90 percent of the national grain supply. Droughts followed by floods in selected parts of the country only compounded the insecurity arising from Renamo actions.[14]

Yet other catalysts, such as a lack of state capacity and widespread rural discontent, contributed to the economic crisis **and** to Renamo's heightened presence. These factors drove the government's reform choices after 1983, even if government rhetoric focused frequently on the "armed bandits." As one government official revealed in a moment of candor, "The war has made things worse, but if there were peace tomorrow we would still have these economic problems."[15] Other government officials intermittently voiced the same concerns over the course of the decade. Thus, many of the policy choices after 1983 addressed a much broader set of economic and political issues and actors than those simply generated by the war.

With the state under threat from several directions, the Frelimo government sought to crush its enemies and strengthen its alliances at home and abroad. These efforts entailed approaches that often worked at cross-purposes. The government aimed to isolate and disable Renamo through threats and alarmist propaganda as well as through peace accords and high-level meetings with South Africa, Renamo's major supporter. After the Nkomati Accord of 1984 forced Renamo to rely increasingly on means of support within Mozambique,[16] the Mozambican government responded by strengthening links with sympathetic neighboring countries and socialist states in Eastern Europe. At the same time, it began assiduously courting the West and Western financial institutions. President Machel and then President Chissano visited Washington DC for talks with American government officials, and equally they increased relations with

---

[13] T. Bager, V. Tickner, and L. Sitoi, "Rehabilitation of the Retail Trading Network involved in Agricultural Marketing in the Five Northern Provinces of Mozambique," mimeo. (February 1989), p. 8; Addison and MacDonald, "Rural Livelihoods," p. 5.

[14] P. Vallely, "Mozambique: Will War Wreck Mozambique's IMF recovery?", *Facts and Reports* (Amsterdam) (13 March 1987); Caballero, *The Mozambican Agricultural Sector*, p. 45; Ministry of Planning and Finance, Poverty Alleviation Unit, "Rural Livelihoods and Poverty in Mozambique," background document for the "Poverty Reduction Strategy for Mozambique" by A. Addison and I. MacDonald (February 1995), mimeo. p. 3.

[15] G. Alagiah, "Mozambique: Siege Survival Tactics," *South* (May 1987).

[16] A. Vines, " 'No Democracy Without Money': The Road to Peace in Mozambique (1982–1992)," Catholic Institute for International Relations briefing paper (April 1994), pp. 5–6.

Portugal and other countries in Western Europe. Meetings with Western and South African businessmen climbed up the government agenda in tandem with increased talk about the "free market" and "restructuring."[17]

Domestically, the state adopted a paradoxical approach because it confronted heterogeneous social forces. It mixed liberalization with authoritarianism; it was at once accommodating and coercive, conciliatory and inflexible. In one part of the country, it sought local compromises and employed *ad hoc* measures to rule. In another region, it was unyielding, authoritarian, and militaristic. It continued to follow a socialist, high-modern master plan to realize its objectives. At one moment, it responded to pressures from below by relaxing restrictions on trade, working together with private companies, or allocating land to smallholders. Otherwise, it reinforced state participation in industry or increased its presence in the countryside.

The outcome of these measures exhibited the contradictions of the approaches, their mixed reception on the ground, and the insecurities of a country at war. Renamo attacks often mitigated the impact of the more conciliatory reforms and reinforced the state's reliance on coercive mechanisms. Relying on coercion generated increased hostility in the countryside which further undermined the state's legitimacy. Where the more conciliatory reforms actually helped to revitalize the private sector, its re-emergence eroded the state's ideological and social foundation over time. Ultimately, the effects of a repressive authoritarianism coupled with an intractable war brought about the conditions for a transition to a market economy and a nominally liberal democracy.

### Refining state intervention in industry and services

In industry, the government adopted measures to reduce or withdraw credit from those state companies that were not performing well, and it encouraged companies under its guidance to realize a profit.[18] Within existing state companies, the government decentralized management. It created provincial level managers for those firms that had previously been under the direction of central government, and in other cases it gave local company directors greater responsibility for day-to-day decisions. Noting that it was necessary "to cut the umbilical cord between the Ministries and the state companies," Mario Machungo, occupying the newly created post of prime minister, implored managers in 1987 "to act like dynamic economic agents": to organize the labor force, provide suitable

---

[17] P. Van Slambrouck, "Mozambique Tones Down Marxist Rhetoric, Turns 'Practical' on Economy," *Christian Science Monitor*, 28 April 1983; "Moçambique: A hora da economia de mercado," *Africa Journal* (Lisbon), 19 September 1984; R. Davies, *South African Strategy Towards Mozambique in the Post-Nkomati Period: A Critical analysis of Effects and Implications*, Research Report no. 73 (Uppsala: Scandinavian Institute of African Studies, 1985), pp. 35–38.

[18] "Moçambique liberaliza a economia," *Primeiro do Janeiro* (12 May 1985) and M. Machungo, speech, reprinted in "Programa de reabilitação económica," *Notícias* (20 June 1987).

working conditions, make their own financial decisions, and use their inputs appropriately.[19] Reform efforts also addressed workers. The government made salary levels more flexible and more reflective of high or low output. It admonished managers to eliminate unproductive labor and to reward those who worked hard with bonuses and prizes.[20] For example, workers in the Companhia Industrial de Matola, a grain mill and biscuit factory outside Maputo, received bicycles, clothing, radios, watches, and food for meeting their production quotas. The government also awarded the company the title of "vanguard enterprise" for the city of Maputo in 1985.[21]

Furthermore, while not relinquishing its role as demiurge, the state sought strategic alliances with capitalist countries and foreign investors through concessionary arrangements or joint-ventures. Officials solicited bids in the US for oil exploration off the coast and lobbied India to supply alumina for a proposed plant in the south that would use energy from the Cahora Bassa Dam.[22] They invited external finance and donations to support the restoration of the country's major, coast-to-inland transport corridors such as that from Maputo to South Africa, Beira to Zimbabwe, and Nacala to Malawi. The European Community as well as individual countries within it, the Scandinavian countries, the United States, and Canada, all pledged investments to these larger projects by 1986.[23] Equally, the Mozambican government welcomed foreign participation in projects to rehabilitate the ports and railways, the road system, telecommunications, and urban sewage treatment.[24] In particular, South Africa's largest freight handling company, Rennies, as well as Anglo-American, invested in transport operations and terminals at the port of Maputo from the mid-1980s.[25]

Moreover, the government began to form joint-ventures with private investors in selected industries. For example, it signed a contract with a Portuguese company in 1987 to rehabilitate Textáfrica in Sofala Province, central Mozambique. It was one of the largest textile companies in the country, yet its output had dropped drastically owing to shortages of cotton coming from the countryside, worker absenteeism, obsolete or broken equipment, and, possibly, deliberate sabotage by employees.[26] The government gave the Portuguese company the

---

[19] Machungo, speech, *Notícias*.

[20] "Moçambique liberaliza," *Primeiro do Janeiro* and Machungo speech, *Notícias*.

[21] "Os melhores recebem prémios na CIM," *Notícias* (15 August 1983); L. Jossias, "Partido e Estado saúdam direcção e trabalhadores da CIM," *Notícias* (23 July 1985).

[22] R. Murray, "RSVP, Says Maputo at Last," *African Business* (March 1983) and n.a., "Mozambique to Process India's Alumina," *African Business* (May 1982).

[23] "Moçambique: uma economia desarticulada," *Comércio do Porto* (6 November 1986).

[24] "Mozambique to Process India's Alumina," *African Business* (May 1982); "Projectos," *Semanário Económico* (Lisbon) (15 May 1987).

[25] R. Davies, *South African Strategy*, pp. 41–42.

[26] "Emma: sobreviver na esteira de dificuldades," *Diário de Moçambique* (*DM*) (16 March 1987). Manning argues that employees of Textáfrica formed a nucleus of support for Renamo during the war, see Manning, "Constructing Opposition," p. 186. Loyalty to Renamo may have resulted

responsibility to restructure the management of Textáfrica, to restore and replace machinery, and to improve the quality of the textiles produced.[27]

The pursuit of joint-ventures also extended to contracts with Eastern European countries. In 1987, the Mozambican government reached an agreement with a Bulgarian state firm to takeover the management of another state textile company in Maputo. The Mozambican government hoped to increase productivity, attain better quality, introduce new machinery, and improve worker–management relations. Much of this was accomplished. The Bulgarian firm rationalized pay scales and reorganized the work day. It sent workers for specialized training in Bulgaria, and repaired or replaced old and broken machinery. To improve morale, the company agreed to provide free medical care on-site for workers and to subsidize 30 percent of the cost of meals. It improved hygiene and working conditions. These changes succeeded in improving output and the company realized a marked increase in profits by 1988.[28]

Finally, the state attempted to create a more conducive economic environment in order to appeal to, and retain, private companies. Vowing to hang on to strategic sectors, the state first sought to return much of the retail trade followed by light industry in the secondary sector to the private sector.[29] The government created an institution in 1984 within the Ministry of Planning with the specific mandate to attract foreign investment. It revived the Mozambique trade fair, FACIM, to promote Mozambique's products to the outside world and to exhibit foreign goods. At the 1984 fair, Portugal, South Africa, and twenty-three other countries displayed their products in FACIM.[30]

The emergence of new guidelines governing private sector activity signalled a loosening of restrictions and a limited reliance on market principles. A foreign investment law passed in 1984 stated that foreign companies could invest in areas that would increase exports or substitute for imports, thereby improving the balance of payments, and they could invest in areas that would use domestic labor or develop the economy.[31] The government also issued specific guidelines governing tax benefits and incentive packages for national investors.[32] Subsequent laws further defined the rules governing investment proposals, authorization, employment, taxation and finance, and profits. Measures such as the liberalization of many fixed prices, a more flexible approach to

in the factory's production difficulties and may have been precisely why the government shifted the responsibility to some other entity.

[27] F. Henrique, " 'Textil' de Chimoio nova dinamica de gestão," *Notícias* (7 October 1987).

[28] Frelimo, Comité Central, Departamento de Política Económica, "Envio de materiais elaborados para uma palestra proferida no seminário sobre 'Problemas e tarefas para a organização e gestão das empresas da indústria e da construção'," 51/cc/DPE/89 (25 May 1989).

[29] "Investimento estrangeiro vai ser regulamentado," *Primeiro do Janeiro* (Porto) (21 July 1982).

[30] "Portugal cria novo seguro de crédito?", *Expresso* (25 August 1984).

[31] *Boletim da República (BR)*, Lei no. 4/84, I Série, 18 August 1984, capitulo II, artigo 3.

[32] *BR*, Decreto 7/87 and Decreto 8/87, III Série, 30 January 1987.

salary levels, and the freedom of private companies to import and export goods directly signalled the government's willingness to encourage private sector growth.[33] The structural adjustment packages of 1987 and 1989 reaffirmed the state's interest in accommodating the private sector and fostering limited market activity.

Foreign as well as national private companies responded positively, but cautiously, to the changes. Business organizations and private companies in South Africa began to identify opportunities in sectors such as fishing, shipping, trade, and tourism. Mozambique initiated serious negotiations with several large US and South African companies regarding investment in fertilizer plants, titanium prospecting, freight handling, and iron and steel production.[34] In addition, Portuguese investment started to return.[35] Within Mozambique, the Entreposto Group, a company that had remained following the revolution, signed a contract with the Ministry of Agriculture to supply spare parts and repair farm machinery on state farms. In a short period of time, it was doing twice the business it had done at the time of independence, and decided to expand its operations. It had also trained a considerable number of mechanics and had saved the government approximately $3 million by repairing old machinery instead of replacing it with expensive imports.[36] At MABOR General, a Mozambican affiliate of General Tire, the American tire company, managers were ecstatic in 1988 when the company made a profit for the first time in nearly ten years. They owed the turnaround to the liberalization of prices and the devaluation of the metical which had lifted the price of tires. Whereas previously tires could be purchased for "'the same price as ten kilos of lettuce'," now, the management argued, "'a truck tyre's meticais price matches its $250 value'."[37]

### Reducing the demiurge in agriculture and rural trade

As in industry, the government tried to improve and modify state intervention in agriculture. Following the Fourth Frelimo Party Congress of 1983, it exhorted state companies to make a profit and to cut costs. It revised accounting procedures and kept stricter control over budgets. It offered prizes to workers, or threatened penalties if output did not increase. The government decentralized several state farms and gave local management greater autonomy to make decisions about inputs, the workforce, production, and planning.

---

[33] n.a., "Maputo liberaliza economia e incentiva sector privado," *Jornal de Notícias* (Oporto) (12 May 1985).
[34] Davies, *South African Strategy*, pp. 38–44; Askin, "Economic About-turn."
[35] L. Ribeiro, "'Iniciativa privada é reconhecida pelo partido e pelo Governo'," *O Tempo* (Lisbon) (11 February 1988).
[36] "Mozambique's Farm Machinery Graveyards," *African Business* (November 1983).
[37] Askin, "Economic About-turn."

As in industry, the government solicited international agencies and foreign countries, especially from the West, to finance the rehabilitation of state farms. France, for example, pledged 200,000 contos to purchase new equipment for Boror Company, a large copra company in Zambezia Province that the state had taken over from its French and Swiss owners about a year after independence.[38] Another French non-governmental organization supplied fifteen million meticais of goods such as clothes and soap to Agricom, the state supplier of agricultural goods and services. These items were to aid in the purchase of corn and other agricultural crops from the family sector in northern Mozambique.[39]

Redistribution of land and joint-ventures with the private sector also comprised the government's agenda. On several occasions, large private companies pursued direct negotiations with national government officials to receive attractive deals. For example, by 1987, the government had redistributed three-quarters of CAIL (Complexo Agro-Industrial do Limpopo, Limpopo Agro-Industrial Complex), a large state farm in Gaza Province. Although local small-holders received portions of the state farm, they were not the only beneficiaries of its partition, in spite of promises to aid the "family sector" made at the Fourth Frelimo Party Congress. Instead, several large private companies and a new category of "private farmers" received about 36 percent of the distributed land area. Regarding the large companies, the Ministry of Agriculture directly negotiated two joint-ventures named LOMACO and SEMOC between private companies and the government. These were the largest single recipients of CAIL's restructuring. They received approximately 5,100 hectares in total.[40] The private share of LOMACO came from Lonrho, a British multinational with extensive investments all over Africa. After the revolution, Lonrho had retained its investment in the Beira oil pipeline, despite government intervention. Sensing the tide turning in the 1980s, Lonrho's energetic director, Tiny Rowland, then began a controlled expansion of the multinational. He courted Machel and served as a mediator in the conflict with Renamo. During the 1984 drought, the company also contributed to the relief effort in Mozambique by delivering 1,000 tons of seedcorn from its fields in Kenya.[41] The persuasive diplomacy and timely gifts brought handsome dividends for the company. The government gave Lonrho the right to manage, and profit from, 2,500 hectares of CAIL and invited it to participate in other ventures.[42]

[38] "Zambezia: Reabilitação da Boror em defesa do maior palmar mundial," *DM* (4 July 1985).

[39] "Agricom recebe apoio para fazer comercialização," *Notícias* (7 October 1986).

[40] C. Tanner, G. Myers, R. Oad, J. Eliseu, E. Macamo, "State Farm Divestiture in Mozambique: Property Disputes and Issues Affecting New Land Access Policy – The Case of Chokwe, Gaza Province," University of Wisconsin-Madison Land Tenure Center report prepared for USAID-Maputo and the Government of the Republic of Mozambique, Ministry of Agriculture (May 1992), pp. 33–34.

[41] "Lonrho oferece sementes de milho," *Tempo*, 700 (11 March 84), pp.11–12.

[42] "Revolutionary Marxism Puts Its Money on Capitalism," *The Guardian* (9 May 1984). It was rumored in 1984 that Lonrho would receive 10,000 hectares of CAIL; by 1985–86, that figure

On those state farms that specialized in the major export crops, the government continued to intervene in their production through separate secretaries of state or institutes designated for each crop, such as the secretary of state for sugar or cotton. These agencies were responsible for overseeing seed testing and development; the distribution of seeds, insecticides, and fertilizers to state farms and/or smallholders; and the purchase and processing of harvested crops. While these remained heavily involved in the overall planning of production, national government officials responded to pressures from private companies and agreed to establish joint-ventures with them. Once again, it tended to privilege large national and foreign companies for partnerships. The national government granted to them all the tax incentives and import-export rights that had been approved in the investment legislation. Following precipitous drops in exports of sugar, for example, the government signed a contract with the British sugar firm, Tate and Lyle, as early as 1983 in order to renovate five sugar processing factories. The contract allowed Tate and Lyle to import directly the materials and machinery required to complete the renovation. It did not have to import through the state company in charge of imports.[43] In cotton, too, although the government would not approve legal contracts until the early 1990s, it pursued a joint-venture with Lonrho. Two national companies that had survived intervention and nationalization, Entreposto Group and João Ferreira dos Santos, followed suit.[44] The government allocated to each company specified "zones of influence" in the northern provinces of Nampula and Cabo Delgado where they could engage in cotton production. It granted to companies the right to produce cotton directly or to secure contract farming arrangements with smallholders in their zone. Although many government employees remained on the payroll of these companies, the government allowed the companies much discretion in the planning, management, and organization of the production, ginning, and sale of cotton.[45]

The government also negotiated arrangements locally with smaller private companies and private farmers for production and trade in other export sectors and in food crops. As the process got underway, the government introduced a distinction between "private farmers" and the "family sector" and began to privilege "private farmers" accordingly, giving them more land and more technical support, much as the Portuguese had aided colonial settlers and the more progressive African farmers during the colonial period. Under the Frelimo government, the distinction was based on a number of somewhat inconsistent

had been reduced to 2,500 hectares. See M. Bowen, "Socialist Transitions: Policy Reforms and Peasant Producers in Mozambique" in T. Bassett and D. Crumney, eds., *Land in African Agrarian Systems* (Madison, WI: University of Wisconsin Press, 1993), p. 335 and Tanner, *et al.*, "State Farm Divestiture," p. 33.

[43] "Reconversão da Indústria Açucareira Nacional," *DM* (26 July 1983).

[44] Interview, JFS, *Expresso*; T. Nougueira, "Projecto Montepuez: Algodão vai cobrir (de novo) os campos," *Tempo*, 1058 (20 January 1991), pp. 10–15.

[45] I discuss the cotton scheme more fully in chapter 6.

criteria that varied from region to region in the country, but the single most important criterion appears to have been the "capacity to farm" – that is, whether an individual or household had the means to farm a piece of land were he/she to receive it.[46] In the redistribution of the CAIL state farm at Chokwe in Gaza, for example, the government classified smallholders or family sector producers as those farmers with an average of two hectares, while *privados* or privates often had over four hectares of land, access to oxen, plows, or tractors (either through renting or owning them) and they employed wage labor. Notably, many of those who were in charge of the redistribution process at the local level as well as those who were allowed to take advantage of the redistribution had been "progressive farmers" during the colonial period, and thus were viewed as having the potential to be "productive" again. They included Mozambicans, but also a small percentage of Portuguese settlers who had remained after the revolution. They contracted individually with the government regarding the kinds and amounts of crops to be grown, and were required to sell a percentage of their output to the state. Approximately 740 of these "private farmers" received 8,560 hectares during the redistribution of the CAIL state land.[47] In Zambezia province to the north, private farmers also received parcels of state land, although it is not clear what criteria was used to identify them.[48]

Moreover, private trade for some agricultural goods began to take shape. Private trade had already rebounded to a certain extent in the early 1980s, working in the niches where the state marketing agency was ineffective. In some parts of the country, the role of private traders during the 1980s was extensive and critical. As the war disabled parts of the state trading network, travelling Indian traders filled the space. Using private security forces that sometimes included as many as sixty men, Indian traders fanned out across the rural hinterland in Zambezia, Nampula, and Cabo Delgado to purchase food and cash crops and to deliver consumer goods such as second-hand clothing, cooking oil, and soap to smallholders. One Indian trader who operated between Cabo Delgado and Nampula Province during the war years noted that for several years he was the only outsider that villagers in remote areas saw.[49] In Zambezia Province also, the state company for cashews subcontracted a private company in 1982 to purchase cashews from smallholders on its behalf. The government granted the company a monopsony to purchase all of the cashews grown in the province. It supplied the company with clothes and other goods to give to producers in exchange for raw cashews. The private company then sold the raw cashews to the state cashew company, which either processed them inside the

---

[46] Tanner, *et al.*, "State Farm Divestiture," p. 27, p. 33.

[47] Bowen, "Socialist Transitions," p. 334; Tanner, *et al.*, "State Farm Divestiture," pp. 28–29, 33; Taylor, "Spirits of Capitalism," pp. 170–74.

[48] "A hora da economia de mercado," *Africa Journal* (Lisbon) (19 September 1984).

[49] Sr Salimo and Sr Tayoob, traders, Nampula Province, conversation, 7 May 1994.

country or exported the raw nuts abroad. By 1984, the state permitted several of the remaining private cashew processing companies to export their own output without going through state channels.[50]

Smallholders did not go unnoticed in the reforms. When it was not blaming Renamo, the government attributed the decreases in food production, and much of the rural discontent, to smallholder dissatisfaction with government policies. Beginning with the Fourth Frelimo Congress, government officials began to give more emphasis to the family sector, acknowledging the contribution it had made to food and cash crop production. Officials channelled consumer goods to the rural areas in return for food or export crops. Under the Economic Recovery Program (PRE), the government also increased prices of major agricultural crops, or dropped fixed prices all together in an attempt to stimulate output. It allowed family sector producers to market a part of their crop as long as they sold a part of it to the state.[51] Moreover, implicit in many of the arrangements that the government negotiated with commercial companies was the understanding that these companies would engage in contract-farming arrangements with smallholders. The large companies were to purchase the crops from smallholders and then process and sell them. Both the government and the large companies expected that smallholders would supply either wage labor or produce maize, cotton, or cashews in a manner quite similar to that of the colonial period. To meet the objectives of this revised agrarian strategy, the government redistributed state farm land to smallholders in particular areas, or allowed producers to abandon collective farming and resume production on individual fields. As early as 1982, it allocated to smallholder families in Maputo District one hectare each of land that was not being used by the state farms in Manhiça valley.[52] Throughout the 1980s, smallholders all over the country began to receive small parcels as a result of the re-dimensioning of state farms following production difficulties. Smallholders near the Chokwe irrigation scheme in Gaza Province benefitted from the parcelization of land by Frelimo party officials between 1983 and 1987. Smallholders received around 19,100 hectares of land under the new policy, but as we noted above they received far smaller parcels on a per household basis than those considered "private farmers."[53] In Zambezia, Nampula, and Cabo Delgado Provinces to the north, smallholders also reclaimed or requested land from state farms for subsistence and cash crop production.[54]

Finally, the government developed a more comprehensive orientation to the rural areas by implementing the Priority District Program (PDP). The PDP

---

[50] Biriba, interview; Mahomede and Mahomede, interview.    [51] "A hora da economia."

[52] M. Matusse, "Em curso: recuperação e aproveitamento do Vale da Manhiça," *DM* (7 December 1982).

[53] Tanner, *et al.*, "State Farm Divestiture," p. 33.

[54] Fieldwork, Montepuez District, Cabo Delgado Province, April–May 1994; Nampula Province, April–June 1994, June–July 1995; Namacurra District, Zambezia Province, May, 1998.

identified four investment areas that were considered commercially viable rather than spreading scarce financial resources equally across the country. It sought to channel resources to priority districts within Mozambique where "economic, military, and climatic situations presented the best opportunity for positive results."[55] It targeted, in particular, districts that could contribute significantly to increases in the trade of important food crops or to improved foreign exchange through increased exports. But above all, it demonstrated a clear intent to reduce state intervention and to introduce a market-driven system based on private traders, private companies, and the family sector.

In the midst of war, what effects did these reforms have? First, while the state's efforts brought some increases in output and won support from private traders, progressive farmers, and commercial companies, it also gave rise to increased pressures to reform by the private sector. Over time, the reform measures gathered a momentum of their own. Like other governments, the Mozambican government discovered that a "controlled opening" to the private sector only unleashed additional demands to further restructure the economy. These demands coincided with the collapse of the Soviet Union and the growth in importance of neo-liberal doctrines abroad, offering strong inducements to the besieged state to embark on a transition to capitalism.

Second, the reform measures were ineffective, or brought as many hardships as they did benefits. Even with exhortations to operate more efficiently, the reorganization of work methods, or the use of incentives, companies failed to meet quotas or to operate their machinery fully. For example, the Companhia Industrial de Matola, which had awarded prizes to its workers, consistently failed to produce at capacity.[56] Heavily dependent on imports, the national matchmaking factory near Maputo frequently halted production when inputs failed to arrive in a timely manner.[57] Domestic shortages of bottles and dyes delayed the manufacture of beer and paint.[58] After 1987, structural adjustment opened the door even wider to parallel markets and corruption as new and existing actors sought to take advantage of pent-up demand and shortages generated by the war. Faced with competition from South African goods, steep price rises, or floods of goods from donors, many state firms in sectors as diverse as agricultural toolmaking and paint found they could not afford to purchase inputs or compete effectively. Many deteriorated or stopped working all together.[59] In

---

[55] Bowen, "Socialist Transitions," p. 329. For the implementation of the PDP in Nampula, see Pitcher, "Disruption Without Transformation."

[56] F. Couto, "Moçambique: O 'Grau Zero' da Economia," *Notícias* (3 September 1985).

[57] Elias, "Falta de fósforos."

[58] F. Ribas, "Cerveja e refrigerantes"; R. Uaene, "Indústria de Tintas: Das cinco fábricas apenas tres sobrevivem," *Tempo*, 765 (9 June 1985), pp. 20–23.

[59] A. Luís, "Agro-Alfa: Produção sem mercado," *Tempo*, 988 (17 September 1989), pp. 12–15; A. Luís, "Indústria de Tintas: O reverso da boa vontade," *Tempo*, 1002 (24 December 1989), pp. 18–21.

sugar processing, for example, the only remaining private firm was responsible for almost three-quarters of the total exports of sugar from Mozambique in 1985.[60] Some private firms that were dependent on supplies from state firms also collapsed.

Furthermore, while legal and illegal imports inundated clothing shops or market stalls, the average Mozambican could not afford to purchase them. Members of the urban working class, to whom Frelimo had directed so much of its rhetoric and so many of its programs, found that they could not meet the higher costs of housing, food, and healthcare with their stagnant wages. Over a two-year period, for example, food prices climbed 300 to 600 percent.[61] Confronted with civil unrest and strikes, the government incorporated a social component into the structural adjustment package in 1989 to ameliorate its effects, changing the name to the Economic and Social Recovery Program (PRES). These additions included a commitment to alleviating poverty through promoting employment, improving mechanisms for providing essential services, especially in the areas of health, education, and water, and guaranteeing at least a minimum income to the poorest in society. At the same time, the PRES reiterated the government's interest in reducing the deficit, restoring commercial networks, increasing exports, prioritizing the private and family sectors, and raising productivity to achieve self-sufficiency.[62] Yet these measures had little overall effect on the conditions of urban workers. To protest their frustration with low wages, high prices, and the withdrawal of subsidies, workers from Nampula to Maputo, in cashew processing, metal working, and tire making plants, on the railroads and the roadways, in the hospitals and in housing went on strike during 1990. These occurrences would be repeated throughout the decade.[63]

Given the importance of smallholders to Mozambique's economy, the reform efforts directed at them also appear rather meager. Credit schemes that could have supported the re-growth of smallholder production either did not exist, or, with the approval of donors, they targetted the private farmer sector. Producers continued to experience a shortage of agricultural tools or could not acquire them owing to their high prices. The criteria for redistributing land and securing title to it was vague or varied from district to district, and smallholders lacked the resources and information that would have allowed them to take advantage of changes to land policy. In some cases, conflicts emerged

---

[60] Cabellero, "The Mozambican Agricultural Sector," p. 38.

[61] A. Gumende (journalist, Mozambique Information Agency) quoted by the *New Internationalist*, 192 (February 1989), p. 15 in a special issue on Mozambique.

[62] Mozambique, GPIE-Office for Foreign Investment Promotion, *Investor's Guide to Mozambique* (Maputo: GPIE, 1992), pp. 27–28.

[63] R. Uaene, "Greve precisa de regras," *Tempo*, 1006 (21 January 1990), pp. 18–21; R. Uaene, "As greves vem da barriga," *Tempo*, 1007 (28 January 1990), pp. 6–12; F. Manuel, "Cometal Mometal: a greve do diálogo adiado," *Tempo*, 1035 (12 August 1990), pp. 8–11; A. Luís, "Greves: quando não há justiça," *Tempo*, 1095 (13 October 1991), pp. 13–17.

between smallholders, private farmers, and the new joint-ventures.[64] Finally, PDP schemes also favored more productive districts in the country and their priorities were biased against marginalized economic zones, which by definition, contained mostly smallholders. Policy shifts in agriculture, then, did not advantage smallholders. Instead, they contributed to increasing socio-economic and regional differentiation and to the uncertainty of tenure that had characterized the late colonial period. Large companies concentrated in export sectors and made contract-farming arrangements with smallholders. Private or "progressive farmers" moved into niches such as vegetable or maize production. Indian traders resumed control over rural trading networks, though the war hampered their expansion.[65]

In aggregate, the reforms both reflected and intensified fragmentation and dissension within the state. The factionalization occurred at the very time when Frelimo was attempting institutionally to disengage the party from the state and when it was fighting a war. By 1989, at least three loosely organized factions existed within the party and the country. These factions were fluid, shifting and overlapping on a range of issues, which contributed to a lack of direction but also to a certain flexibility regarding policy. First, while most political actors recognized the need for reform, there remained a group who sought a modification but not an abandonment of socialist principles and state intervention. It accepted some reductions in government interference or greater attention to increased efficiency and productivity in state companies, but it was skeptical of market principles and viewed private sector growth as inimical to its interests.[66] It remained committed to socialism and to the central role of the state in production and exchange. The group included several prominent government officials at the national level, many provincial party and state officials, and members of the OMM and the OTM. The party had cut loose the latter two organizations from the state when the one-party state restructured. In addition, the group had the support of urban workers and residents. They had seen prices rise when the state withdrew subsidies on basic consumer items, or they had lost jobs due to the collapse of companies, and they had to shoulder new charges for healthcare and education. By the early 1990s, this group would see its fortunes wane.

The second group favored substantial reform of the state sector, supported emerging markets, and endorsed a greater role for the private sector. Supporters of this group thought the state sector should be streamlined and restructured, but maintained, while they desired controlled private sector growth and a reliance on the market. Yet this group was internally differentiated and constantly

---

[64] Tanner, *et al.*, "State Farm Divestiture," pp. 27–37 and Taylor, "Spirits of Capitalism," p. 180.

[65] Wuyts, *Money and Planning*, pp. 143–47; J. Carrilho, "Acesso e uso de terra para a agricultura," 2o Seminário sobre o Estudo do Sector Agrário (Second Seminar on the Study of the Agrarian Sector), Maputo (16–20 April, 1990), mimeo., pp. 18–19.

[66] J. Santa Rita, "Frelimo Faces a Turbulent Congress," *The Daily News* (24 July 1989), p. 9.

shifting during the 1980s. Disagreement within and among ministries often erupted over the substance and pace of reforms and their intended beneficiaries. A series of exchanges between the prime minister and the Ministry of Agriculture illustrated some of the tensions. Following the passage of structural adjustment, the Ministry of Agriculture carried out a detailed study of state enterprises to determine whether they should be dismantled, privatized, or remain in the state sector. In a report to the prime minister, the Ministry of Agriculture argued that approximately half of the state enterprises in agriculture be restructured and gave the criteria behind its choices. Further, it recommended that many of the agricultural activities currently undertaken by state companies be shifted to smallholders.[67] In response, the prime minister expressed greater confidence than the Ministry in the ability of the state sector to reform itself, desired a slower pace of state sector reform, and made no reference at all to the potential role of smallholders.[68] The Ministry of Agriculture snapped back a reply, calling attention to the money lost by state enterprises, their bloated management structures, and inefficient production. In a vigorous defense of smallholders, ministry officials stated, "In our opinion, there is absolutely no economic rationality in the existence of state enterprises ... which dedicate themselves to crops which the peasants do and can do better ... with a simple production organization."[69]

The exchanges reveal the lack of clarity in policy that the state still displayed by the late 1980s, and they expose the range of interests that participated in the debate. The decision to privatize by 1990 resolved some of the conflict over restructuring, but the role of smallholders in the Mozambican economy continued to be problematic. Although the "agrarian populist" faction in the Ministry of Agriculture and other ministries achieved some victories for smallholders, these were limited. During the 1990s, privatization policies, reinforced by international trends, favored the growth of large, private companies, thereby demonstrating a continuity of policy that stemmed all the way back to the colonial period.

Finally, a growing perspective within government, within the country, and among some Western donors wished to further neo-liberal reforms. The third

---

[67] Mozambique, Ministerio da Agricultura, Direcção de Economia Agrária, Sector de Analise de Unidades Económicas (SAUE), "Reorganization of the Agrarian Managerial Sector" (1988). English translation in G. Myers, H. West, and J. Eliseu, "Appendices to Land Tenure Security and State Farm Divestiture in Mozambique: Case Studies in Nhamatanda, Manica and Montepuez Districts," Land Tenure Center, University of Wisconsin-Madison, Research Paper no. 110 (January 1993), appendix 7.

[68] "Reorganization of the Agrarian State Sector: Observations and Orientations from the Prime Minister, 1989" (25 May 1989) in Myers, et al., "Appendices," appendix 9.

[69] "Reorganization of the Agrarian State Sector: Comments and Suggestions by DEA/SAUE on the Prime Minister's Orientations and Observations of May 24th, 1989" (1 June 1989) in Myers, et al., "Appendices," appendix 10, p. 154.

group consisted of those who heartily welcomed the new emphasis on emerging markets and investment. The group now demanded "a formal recognition of the 'marriage' between the politician and the businessman."[70] The group included state officials, particularly in the Ministry of Finances and the Ministry of Industry and Trade, who formulated and implemented some of the policy changes such as structural adjustment and the withdrawal of restrictions on private sector activity. The small domestic private sector, foreign businesses interested in investment, and Western powers committed to propagating market principles and privatization provided the bulk of support for this position. Although the group played a restricted role during the 1980s, its amalgamation with elements of the second group led to a dominant role in policy making by the mid-1990s.

### State pathologies and official coercion

If the intentional and unintentional effects of reforms and elite fragmentation hastened the erosion of socialism, a "militarised authoritarianism"[71] and a range of "standard bureaucratic pathologies"[72] equally played their part. Renewed attempts to create order, control populations, force production, and monitor internal movement were predictable but rather poor responses to an escalating war waged largely in the rural areas, and to the spectrum of public apathy and anger that followed in the wake of Frelimo's policy failures. While the use of coercive tactics was a response to Renamo, paradoxically, coercion also aided Renamo's increasing organization and strength during the 1980s, just as repressive policies by the Portuguese during the colonial period played into the hands of Frelimo. There are several explanations for the source and degree of Renamo's increase in organization and strength. Its continued reliance on external sources, particularly South Africa, for military supplies and logistical aid seems beyond dispute. Equally, however, the evidence points to increased efforts by Renamo to build a highly centralized military organization and to attract domestic support. After the Nkomati Accord between South Africa and Mozambique in 1984, it began using its Portuguese name and acronym of Renamo (Resistência Nacional Moçambicana) rather than the English abbreviation of MNR (Mozambican National Resistance) it had used previously, to signal that it had moved inside Mozambique and was Mozambican. In contrast to government portrayals of Renamo as "armed bandits," Vines argues that after Nkomati, Renamo had refashioned itself militarily to function without the constant backing of South Africa, to operate more effectively within Mozambique (with the help of South African radio equipment), and to establish local bases.

---

[70] Rita, "Frelimo Faces," p. 9.     [71] Alexander, "The Local State," p. 8.
[72] Scott, *Seeing Like a State*, p. 243.

It had a hierarchical, military command structure with well-coordinated and planned offensive maneuvers and good communications.[73] The organization also recruited a "political and administrative core" of officials from Sofala, Zambezia, Tete, and Manica Provinces and established health and education structures. It had political representatives abroad, and created rather ineffective "political commissars" and political delegates (in some cases "reinforced" by its leader Dhlakama's handpicked loyalists) at the district and local level. It also attracted clandestine urban support that included businessmen, factory workers, and railway employees in several provincial and district capitals.[74]

Moreover, the movement began to adjust its military strategy to suit domestic conditions and contingencies. Recent scholarship has documented the varied tactics and approaches to the conflict adopted by Renamo and Frelimo forces within and among provinces in Mozambique. It has detailed the specific historical, cultural, political, and socio-economic conditions that contributed to the support of, or neutrality with regard to, Renamo. Where support for Frelimo remained strong, for example in the southern part of Mozambique, Renamo's tactics aimed to reduce morale through sabotage and torture because it could not gain a critical mass of support. In the center and north of the country, however, Renamo incorporated ideological appeals and political persuasion into its violent repertoire, achieving varying levels of success in gaining local adherents or, at least, assuring neutrality.[75] These findings indicate that while Renamo probably could not have been sustained without South African aid, nevertheless, the opposition did attempt to establish local bases of support and authority, often using a similar mixture of coercion and incentives as that used by the colonial and Frelimo governments.

---

[73] A. Vines, *Renamo: Terrorism in Mozambique* (Bloomington, IN: Indiana University Press, 1991), pp. 30, 80–87.

[74] Manning, "Constructing Opposition," p. 168, pp. 176–86.

[75] Geffray's examination of domestic sources of discontent against Frelimo and the local basis of support for Renamo in Erati district, Nampula Province generated a great deal of controversy, but also inspired more extensive research on which my claims in this paragraph are based. See O. Roesch, "Renamo and the Peasantry in Southern Mozambique: A View from Gaza Province," *Canadian Journal of African Studies*, 26, 3 (1992), pp. 462–85; Vines, *Renamo*; K. Wilson, "Cults of Violence and Counter-Violence in Mozambique," *Journal of Southern African Studies*, 18, 3 (1992); M. Chingono, *The State, Violence and Development* (Aldershot: Avebury, 1996); Alexander, "The Local State"; Hall, and Young, *Confronting Leviathan*, chapter 7; C. Nordstrom, *A Different Kind of War Story* (Philadelphia, PA: University of Pennsylvania Press, 1997), chapter 3; and articles by J. McGregor, C. Manning, and M. Pitcher in the special issue on Mozambique, *Journal of Southern African Studies*, 24, 1 (March 1998). For criticisms of Geffray, see B. O'Laughlin, "Interpretations Matter: Evaluating the War in Mozambique," *Southern Africa Report*, 7, 3 (January, 1992) and "A Base Social da Guerra em Moçambique," *Estudos Moçambicanos*, 10 (1992), pp. 107–42; P. Fry, "Between Two Terrors," *Times Literary Supplement* (9–15 November 1992), p. 1202; Saul, *Recolonization and Resistance*; A. Dinerman, "In Search of Mozambique: The Imaginings of Christian Geffray in *La Cause des Armes au Mozambique. Anthropologie d'une Guerre Civile*", *Journal of Southern African Studies*, 20, 4 (December 1994), pp. 569–86.

Determined to protect itself and convinced of its own propaganda about the external basis of Renamo, the state became more authoritarian and more intransigent. Peppered with words such as "armed bandits," "plans," and "offensives," government pronouncements were the most visible signs of a renewed commitment to defending the socialist, high modern template that had been in place since 1977. The government reiterated the virtues of conforming to plans, warning that "it constitutes a patriotic duty of all citizens" to fulfill the plan and the budget.[76] The government also relaunched in 1985 the political and organizational offensive it had first launched in 1980–81, but this time, it was more blatantly militaristic. The government vowed to liquidate totally the "armed bandits," whom, they argued, were "criminals paid by the old colonial and capitalist bosses" whose objective was to "recolonize Mozambique."[77] Equally, it promised to "combat with severity indifference, passivity, disorganization, theft, sabotage, corruption, and illegal marketing in the State apparatus and in economic and social units."[78] Newspapers and journals continued to print vitriolic articles about the evils of capitalism. Even after the passage of the PRE, the minister of trade, Aranda da Silva, still claimed that "we do not see this as a contradiction of our socialist goals," and other government officials declared that they had not abandoned Marxism.[79] As late as 1989, Frelimo party officials invited prominent foreign socialists and communists such as Joe Slovo, the secretary-general of the South African Communist Party; Miguel Martinez, of the Communist Party in Chile; Mario de Andrade, a founding member of the MPLA (Movimento Popular de Libertação de Angola, Popular Movement for the Liberation of Angola) in Angola; and left-wing activists from Brazil to Yemen to attend their meetings and to view their factories.

Matching the bellicose language and the defense of socialism, the state incorporated military tactics into its repertoire. In Manica Province, where Renamo probably was established earlier than in other provinces because Manica shared a border with the former Rhodesia, most party-state officials carried weapons, participated in and formed military units from the late 1970s. In addition to protecting and defending local populations, officials used military discourse and authoritarian tactics to demand loyalty and silence critics.[80] The government increased security of major roadways, cities, and towns and augmented its military presence in those rural areas that were most economically productive.[81] It

---

76   L. David, "Realizar o plano é dever patriótico," *Tempo*, 708 (6 May 1984), pp. 16–18.

77   Mozambique, Council of Ministers, "Relançar a Ofensiva Política e Organizacional para resolução das nossas dificuldades actuais," text reprinted in *Tempo*, 756 (7 April 1985), pp. 21–24 at p. 23.

78   *Ibid.*, p. 21.

79   Alagiah, "Seige Survival Tactics" and Askin, "Economic About-turn."

80   Alexander, "The Local State," p. 4.

81   Alagiah, "Seige Survival Tactics"; for a demonstration of the overlap between security measures and the PDP, see Pitcher, "Disruption Without Transformation," pp. 131–32.

restricted internal movement and enlarged its surveillance. Those who traversed the country were required to carry a special pass that stated the purpose of their movement and that it had been authorised by a district or provincial official.[82]

Increased communal villagization in designated areas complemented the military strategy. But rather than comprising the building blocks of a more socially just society, as before, communal villages came to represent military fortresses and state compulsion. With their productive function shorn away and their transformative purpose forgotten, they became holding pens for a bewildered and hungry population. In Manica Province, for example, the government constructed villages after 1981 to house displaced people and refugees under military protection. And although the war arrived later and proceeded more erratically in Nampula Province than in Manica, the government engaged in forced communal villagization as the 1980s proceeded.[83] In one administrative post, sixteen additional communal villages were constructed in 1983 and 1984, bringing the total number of villages in the area to forty-one. Most of these communal villages exceeded the guidelines regarding the optimum population to be included, and residents reported that they had been forcibly moved to them.[84] The overcrowding and late formation of some villages appear to have been due to compulsion rather than to voluntary resettlement and arose from security concerns rather than a desire to transform rural life.

In addition to compelling where and how people lived, the government also tried to force production. After President Machel criticized urban overcrowding and goods shortages in the cities in a 1982 speech, local officials in Nampula city responded by detaining and deporting anyone who could not prove residency or employment in the city.[85] A year later, a much broader national measure, "Operation Production" (Operação Produção), followed. It represented the height of "bureaucratic pathology" where the government was determined to show that it still had a monopoly on power, illustrated through the realization of its stated objectives, which in this case was the rounding up of society's "undesirables and parasites." The "operation" was designed to identify allegedly unemployed and/or itinerant persons in urban areas and relocate them for work in rural areas. In principle the program was meant to be voluntary, but in practice, government representatives used coercive tactics to corral and resettle suspected loafers and wanderers and those unlucky enough to be without employment.[86] The government resettled some Mozambicans, who were rounded up in Maputo, in the center of the country where they were placed

---

[82] Hanlon, *Mozambique: The Revolution Under Fire*, p. 262.
[83] Alexander, "The Local State," p. 7; Geffray and Pedersen, "Nampula en guerre," pp. 39–40.
[84] Pitcher, "Disruption Without Transformation," p. 130.
[85] Egero, *Mozambique: A Dream Undone*, p. 188.
[86] H. Matusse, "Operação Produção: Evacuados vão receber familiares," *Tempo*, 678 (9 October 1983), pp. 22–24; Egero, *Mozambique: A Dream Undone*, p. 188.

in jobs at a rural sugar processing factory.[87] The operation placed others as far away as Cabo Delgado and Niassa Provinces in the north. The government expected them to take up farming even though many had no rural experience. They lacked the intricate understanding of local soils and climatic conditions necessary to be good farmers.[88]

Where smallholders were already established, local government officials sometimes adopted draconian measures to increase production. In the mid-1980s, the governor of Nampula, the Provincial Frelimo Party Committee, and the Provincial Assembly journeyed around Nampula advising smallholders of proper work habits and commanding them to work. According to the governor, "to produce cotton and cashew nuts is not a favor, it is an order of the State. The Governor cannot request a favor, he gives an order for everyone to produce cotton, clean cashew trees, and collect cashews to sell in order to receive *capulanas* and soap."[89] To realize these orders, the governor returned to several approaches that had been used in the colonial period. First, he appointed *capatazes* (overseers) to demarcate plots for smallholders and to supervise production. Second, he informed administrators that they should help both state and private companies to recruit labor. Third, he issued cards to each producer, on which to inscribe the total hectarage of cotton planted or the number of cashew trees tended, the amounts harvested, and the monetary value of the crop once it was sold. After the sale, producers could then use the amounts stated on the card to purchase consumer goods. Fourth, the governor prohibited travel during the agricultural campaign, except for an emergency. He argued that it would prejudice production if people were travelling around the province. Finally, he stated that he would have the militias seize anyone who was found not to be working.[90]

Nor were the larger private enterprises free from interference, despite all the government initiatives aimed at attracting and fostering them. Government institutions still intervened heavily in the economy and government officials were very involved in where private investment should be located, what it should produce, and where it would sell its goods. Foreign investors still had to work closely with state firms to purchase particular raw materials or other necessary inputs, and the state bank still constituted the main source of credit for national companies.[91]

[87] J. Cossa, "Produzir açucár com ou sem dificuldades," *DM*, 15 June 1984.
[88] Fieldwork, Montepuez District, Cabo Delgado Province, April–May 1994.
[89] S. Moyana, "Produzir algodão e castanha de caju não é favor é ordem do Estado," *Tempo*, 836 (19 October 1986), p. 13.
[90] Moyana, "Produzir algodão."
[91] "Foreign Investment in Mozambique: Legal Basis, and Company Law," *Financial Gazette* (Harare) (16 October 1987); "Investment in Mozambique: Finance and Trade, Investment, Land, Taxes," *Financial Gazette* (Harare) (23 October 1987).

The government's "militaristic authoritarianism" had its payoffs: the Mozambican army confined Renamo's activities to the rural hinterland and the movement failed to capture any major cities in the 1980s. The government remained in power, no doubt aided by the use of threats, punishment, and surveillance. Yet, as the war intensified, the government faced swelling discontent over communal villages and collective production. As Alexander writes:

Communal village inhabitants perceived the villages as intended solely to increase security and control, and then only variably to good effect. In all cases, the villages were portrayed as bearing a range of other costs, including increased social conflict, losses in production and the spread of disease.[92]

In Nampula, too, residents in overcrowded and inadequately supplied villages began to face the prospect of hunger as Renamo attacks increased. To ease conditions, Frelimo officials not only encouraged the division of some communal villages into smaller units but also allowed some residents to return to their former homes and land. They turned a blind eye to the complete abandonment of some villages and, in other instances, they tolerated the creation of "false villages" where fictitious, makeshift houses stood, too small for even an adult to stand within and without beds, or windows, or even a granary.[93] At best, these concessions brought neutrality; they did not win support for the government.

Operation Production also had negative results, as can be imagined. Those whom the government had forcibly removed from Maputo were sent to work in jobs for which they had no experience or which were demanding and dangerous. In one case, officials sent victims of Operation Production to work at a sugar factory in the center of the country where food was inadequate, conditions poor, and medical assistance irregular. Not surprisingly, these and other victims managed to escape the scheme and return to the city.[94] Others who had been removed had to be returned to their place of origin when their removal was found to be unjust. Furthermore, Operation Production inadvertently spurred the growth of small, clandestine businesses as people struggled to show they had work in order to avoid relocation. Their growth also eroded the command economy.[95]

In addition, the government's security efforts were selective and reinforced regional economic imbalances. They favored areas with economic potential while ignoring those that were less viable. Protection thus overlapped with

---

[92] Alexander, "The Local State," p. 7.

[93] Geffray, *A Causa das Armas*, pp. 125–30; for responses to communal villages on the Mueda Plateau, Frelimo's apparent stronghold in Cabo Delgado, see West, "Sorcery of Construction and Sorcery of Ruin," chapter 4.

[94] Cossa, "Produzir açucár."

[95] C. Muianga, "Funcionamento ilegal e um risco para a saúde pública," *Tempo*, 751 (3 March 1985), pp. 15–17.

the favoritism towards more productive areas exhibited by the Priority District Program. Obviously, the military's presence or absence also affected Renamo's ability to attract support or to control designated territories.[96]

Ultimately, the war provided the backdrop against which reforms and intransigence, concessions and coercion took place. The war turned mistakes of judgment or inexperience into enormous catastrophes and mitigated the full implementation of policy adjustments. The government had to divert its attention to security concerns and lost the capacity and resources to reverse many of its errors or pursue its reforms. Attempts to reorient agricultural production or to improve industrial output had to be shelved while the government devoted half of the budget to defence spending. The war diverted funds away from education and health and scared off private investors.[97] Those private companies that were already in operation faced large expenses financing their own militias. By 1987, the external debt was $3.2 billion and the West was providing food aid, medical supplies, and other necessary goods. From south to north, those Mozambicans fleeing the skirmishes and attacks in rural areas migrated across the border, or crowded into protected cities or makeshift rural camps. They threatened the fragile legitimacy that Frelimo enjoyed with urban populations, and exacerbated struggles for land and jobs in rural areas.[98]

Faced with intermittent but destructive conflicts in nearly all the provinces of Mozambique, the government sought to negotiate. For its part, Renamo's inability to capture or hold additional territory, combined with a drought, produced a stalemate by the early 1990s. With neither side able to secure outright victory, both parties wanted to end the war. The moment of transition had arrived.

### The transition to a market economy and liberal democracy, 1990–2000

Róna-Tas claims that the transition to capitalism begins when the state constructs institutions appropriate to the private sector and adopts policies that enact a market economy. Whereas a small surviving private sector may wring begrudging concessions from a reluctant state during the erosion phase, during transition, the state is more proactive. It sets the rules and government officials may use political power to secure economic benefits for themselves.[99] Elites

---

[96] For the impact in Nampula, see Pitcher, "Disruption Without Transformation."

[97] "Maputo liberaliza economia e incentiva sector privado," *Jornal de Notícias* (12 May 1985); G. Graham, "Donors Pledge $700 m in Aid to Mozambique," *Financial Times* (13 July 1987); Abrahamsson and Nilsson, *Mozambique: The Troubled Transition*, p. 120.

[98] Mozambique, Ministerio da Agricultura, Direcção de Economia Agrária, Departamento de Projectos, "Contribuição para o estudo da vulnerabilidade social das familias camponesas (aspectos metodologicos)" by V. Pankhova, 1990; Taylor, "Spirits of Capitalism," p. 234; fieldwork, Zambezia Province, May 1998 (with Scott Kloeck-Jenson).

[99] Róna-Tas, "The First Shall Be Last?", p. 47.

are thus able to "survive" and participate in the new private economy, even if, as has been the case in Eastern Europe, they lose political power.

Two years before the peace accord was even signed, Mozambique's 1990 constitution delivered the clearest indication of a change of policy. The constitution omitted any mention of socialism; the closest reference to the earlier orientation expressed the desire to create "a socially just society."[100] The section on workers' rights accorded them basic protection under the constitution and granted them the right to strike, but the constitution neither privileged workers nor claimed to be a workers' state. In economic matters, agriculture continued to constitute the "base of national development" while industry was the "driving factor in the national economy" (articles 39 and 40), but the state exchanged its demiurge role of direct intervention for one that was more custodial. It pledged to regulate and promote economic growth and national development, and it recognized the contribution of foreign and national investors to the process (articles 42–45). It expected to practice midwifery and husbandry by encouraging private agents to develop their potential, be they the family sector, national entrepreneurs, or small businesses (articles 42–44). Although the constitution recognized state property and the state continued to own the land, it also allowed cooperative, mixed, and private property (article 41).

Additional legislation and the creation of new institutions connected to the private sector and the growth of the market put the constitutional principles into practice. From 1991, laws and decree-laws stipulated the procedures for valuing and selling state enterprises, and defined the conditions for private purchase. They established credit institutions and created funds to help small business and/or national investors. They stated the regulations on taxation, repatriation of profits, the employment of foreigners, the procedures for imports and exports. The creation or modification of organizations accompanied the legislation. At the national level, centers and commissions attracted foreign and national investment. Several government bodies evaluated and sold small industrial and agricultural state enterprises, while the purpose of one government unit was to evaluate, negotiate, and sell large state enterprises. Organizations at the provincial level handled the privatization of state enterprises that had local importance.

In tandem with economic restructuring, changes to the political system also took place. In 1992, the Frelimo government and Renamo signed a peace accord ending seventeen years of war in Mozambique. As a condition of the peace accord in 1992, the country moved to a multi-party system and held democratic elections in 1994. The Frelimo party received a majority of votes and repeated its victory in the second national elections in 1999, though by a smaller margin. The Frelimo party has continued to control the presidency and a majority of the seats

---

[100] Mozambique, *Constituição*, Maputo, 1990, article 6.

in parliament. In stark contrast to the discredited leaders and broken regimes associated with the transitions in Eastern Europe, then, the Mozambican state has survived monumental political and economic changes. Like one-party states in Vietnam and China, the Frelimo government in Mozambique has reformed, but remained in power. Although the weakness of the main opposition, Renamo, helps to explain why Frelimo did not collapse, I argue that their survival can also be attributed to their political experience. Their ability to juggle contradictory social pressures and the ordeal of a long period of civil conflict have taught them a certain flexibility, such that they were more able than most East European states to adjust to the changes brought by the transition.

To be sure, the nature of political and economic power has altered. The government no longer controls the commanding heights of the economy. It does not set exchange rates, nor subsidize consumer items, nor engage in detailed planning. It has disentangled the party from the state and undercut substantially the power of party secretaries at the local level, re-recognizing formally many "traditional authorities" in the process. It has decentralized political power and some aspects of the budgetary process. Regular elections and the shift to multi-party politics have introduced new forms of accountability and new pressures into the political system, all of which have changed substantially the kind of power the state exercises. But elections have also brought legitimacy to the Frelimo government and, ironically, the economic transition has preserved the state, even while it has transformed it.

To understand these developments requires examination of the single most important and controversial component of economic transitions: privatization. Privatization has a double meaning in the literature. First, it refers specifically to the transfer of ownership or control over assets from the state to the private sector and the encouragement of private instead of public sector investment in new or existing projects in the formal economy. This definition focuses narrowly on the various methods that states may use to privatize, such as the total or partial sale of assets, the use of management or leasing contracts, the contracting out of services to the private sector, public or private share offerings, and worker buy-outs. Second, privatization refers to a more general process of market creation, price liberalization, and other incentives that intend to aid or attract private capital formation. Without these mechanisms, the simple transfer of assets or control to the private sector probably would not be realized.[101]

In Mozambique, both the specific and the general processes have been discernible since the mid-1980s, but both have solidified since the peace accord in 1992. To date, the Mozambican government has sold around 1,000 small, medium, and large state companies in all sectors of the economy, including

---

[101] R. Young, "Privatisation in Africa," *Review of African Political Economy*, 51 (July 1991), pp. 50–51; C. Vuylsteke, *Techniques of Privatization of State-Owned Enterprises*, Vol. 1, World Bank Technical Paper no. 88 (Washington, DC: World Bank, 1988), pp. 8–9.

trade, industry, energy, construction, water, agriculture, and transportation. The majority of these companies are small and medium companies located in the industrial zone around the capital of Maputo, and the government has sold the majority of them in their entirety to national investors.[102] For those large or strategic enterprises in industry and agriculture that have been privatized, the government has created joint-ventures, with the state holding an equal or minority share in the new company alongside domestic or foreign capital. About 240 companies remain to be privatized, mostly small and medium companies in areas as diverse as chicken hatcheries and small hotels.[103]

Evidence of the resurgence of the private sector abounds. Newspapers and journals publish numerous articles that detail every feature of privatization and market generation, measuring gains and losses in market share, efficiency, salaries, and employees. Dozens of consultants hired by the government, the World Bank, private companies, and non-governmental organizations (NGOs) document the effects of tariff reform on costs or the obstacles to the operation of an efficient market. They examine worker satisfaction before and after privatization, or they detail the impact of higher producer prices on output. Private sector conferences chart the advances made by business and chronicle the delays and difficulties that continue to stifle new investment and growth. A proliferation of business magazines such as *Revista de Empresas, Economia*, and *Fórum Económico* profile new national and foreign entrepreneurs and evaluate the business climate. Government officials now sprinkle their discourse with references to "entrepreneurship," the "market," and "competition," drawing attention to the change in policy and ideology. Billboards and advertisements in the capital promote companies and their products and reinforce the dramatic shifts in practice and language. Thousands of conversations taking place every day in the street, in cafes, over the telephone and the Internet about business, prices, investment, and partnerships testify to the changed environment.

## Explaining privatization

With privatization now nearly complete, why and how did the government privatize? Two perspectives have tended to dominate the literature on why governments privatize. One view, labelled by Feigenbaum, Henig and Hamnett as the "economic perspective," presents the adoption of privatization as almost an economic necessity, "the inevitable consequence of neoclassical truths that

---

[102] Mozambique, Ministry of Planning and Finance, Technical Unit for Enterprise Restructuring (UTRE), 5, March 1998, p. 6.

[103] M. Mabunda, "Company Privatization, Restructuring Detailed," *Domingo* (15 August 1993), pp. 8–9, translated and reprinted in Foreign Broadcast Information Service (FBIS), *Africa* reports (13 October 1993), pp. 24–26; Mozambique, UTRE, 1998; Mozambique, Centre de Promoção de Investimento (CPI), "Situação de Projectos Autorizados (de 1985 a 31 de Dezembro de 1997)" (15 January 1998), mimeo.; Arahni Sont, former advisor to UTRE, personal communication, 8 June 1999.

dictate the retraction of a bulky, intrusive, and parasitic state." The other view, which they call the "administrative perspective," sees privatization as a largely technical exercise, a matter of deciding administratively whether share offerings or public bids are the appropriate mechanism for privatizing the economy.[104] Although many privatizations may display features associated with the administrative and economic perspectives, these two perspectives ignore the political intent of the privatization process. They leave out the conflicts and pressures, power struggles and motivations that may accompany even a seemingly innocuous asset sale. They seem particularly inadequate to explain the privatizations in Eastern Europe and Mozambique, where governments and social forces have restructured economies, changed political institutions, and refashioned ideologies.[105]

Examination of the variation present in the formulation and implementation of privatization leads Feigenbaum and Henig to conclude that, "privatisation is an intensely political phenomenon and ought to be analyzed as such."[106] To capture the political features of privatization, they propose a typology of strategies that recognizes the different political motivations and interests of the actors undertaking privatization, and their intended objectives. The typology ranges from "pragmatic privatizations," which are "short-term, often *ad hoc* solutions to immediate problems," to "systemic privatization," the most all-encompassing type of privatization. In systemic privatizations, the political motivations and the potential political ramifications of privatization strategies are the most obvious and most extensive.

Systemic privatization seeks (1) to lower people's expectations of what government can and should be held responsible for, (2) to reduce the public sector's oversight and enforcement infrastructure, and (3) to transform the interest group landscape to make it less supportive of governmental growth.[107]

The changes in Eastern Europe and Mozambique conform closely to the criteria contained in systemic privatization.

The commentary on Mozambique's privatization presents administrative, economic, and even political perspectives. World Bank reports on Mozambique portray the choice of privatization as the application of neo-classical "common sense" and explain its implementation as a technical exercise. One need only to get prices right, make markets more efficient, or solicit bids for the purchase of state companies to make it work. Some government officials reinforce the notion that the choice of privatization is an economic necessity achieved by employing the right "toolbox" of technical remedies when they state: "We think

---

[104] Feigenbaum, Henig, and Hamnett, *Shrinking the State*, pp. 38–39.
[105] Feigenbaum, Henig, and Hamnett, *Shrinking the State*, pp. 41–58, 167–72.
[106] Feigenbaum and Henig, "The Political Underpinnings," p. 186.
[107] Feigenbaum and Henig, "The Political Underpinnings," pp. 192–94.

that privatisation is part of the government's defined policy for conferring greater efficiency on our companies. The state's role is to regulate the system. The state should not be managing companies."[108] On the other hand, much commentary has avoided the pitfalls characteristic of the standard literature, and **has** recognized privatization as the "intensely political phenomenon" that Feigenbaum and Henig assert it is. As if they were ticking off the features of systemic privatization, critics of the process chronicle the shrinking public sector, note the application of neo-liberal solutions, delineate the interest groups who are in and out of favor, and chart the rise of private companies.[109]

However, many critics of the privatization process in Mozambique often depict it as a policy imposed from outside the country by the World Bank and the West. They thus continue the post-independence tradition of blaming policy choices and failures on exogenous factors. They portray the World Bank and the West as opportunists, taking advantage of the desperate situation that Mozambique was in during the mid-1980s to inflict their neo-liberal solutions on a weakened country.[110] It is true that the World Bank and Western influence has been pervasive, even ubiquitous in the last decade. With the fall of the Soviet Union, neo-liberalism now dominates the global agenda and neo-liberals work in nearly every major donor agency in Mozambique. They write position papers on, and give their responses to, most major policy decisions, whether these decisions concern financial overhaul, agricultural development, or land tenure.[111] The World Bank offers substantial, extensive technical advice on the various methods of privatization and it helps to finance the various government units in charge of the process. Donors frequently hire Western consultants, often with very little specific knowledge of Mozambique, to analyze everything from cashew production to informal trade. Donors then base their advice to the Mozambican government on the findings of consultants' reports. Some of these consultants bring their neo-liberal biases and perspectives to their analyses and only reinforce what the World Bank or Western donors want to hear. The World Bank and donors such as USAID or the Commonwealth Development Corporation (CDC) further entrench the turn towards privatization by financing existing or potential private sector projects.

Yet much of the critical literature on Mozambique theoretically misunderstands the relationship between the World Bank, Western donors, and the state. Moreover, it shares the empirical shortcomings of the administrative and economic perspectives by failing to examine **how** state elites have formulated and

---

[108] M. Mabunda, "Finance Minister Discusses Privatization," *Domingo* (15 August 1993), pp. 8–10, trans. and repr. in FBIS, *Africa* reports (20 October 1993), pp. 21–24.

[109] See especially Hanlon, *Mozambique: Who Calls the Shots?* and *Peace without Profit*.

[110] Saul, *Recolonization and Resistance*, pp. 74–81; Hanlon, *Peace without Profit*; Plank, "Aid, Debt, and the End of Sovereignty"; Mittelman, *The Globalization Syndrome*, pp. 99–107.

[111] Donors numbered about 250 organizations around the signing of the peace accord, 17 July 2000, <http://www.worldbank.org>.

implemented privatization in Mozambique, and **how** social forces have influenced the privatization process. Blaming the World Bank and Western donors for thrusting privatization on the Mozambican government ignores the ideological differences within the non-governmental organization (NGO) community in Mozambique and other African countries, how those differences can stall or shape policy recommendations emanating from the NGO community, and how they produce tensions between the World Bank and donors.[112] It does not acknowledge the internal divergences in understanding within the World Bank or the alterations that take place as policy recommendations travel from its head office in DC to resident missions in individual countries. Nor does it recognize the limits to the World Bank's capacity. According to Simon Bell, a World Bank senior financial economist who was formerly at their resident mission in Mozambique, "Of course, there is some element of force or bribery in the World Bank relationship with Mozambique, but Mozambicans never did anything they didn't really want to do. There was a bank privatization scheme in Tanzania that failed because the government didn't really want to do it. There has to be an intellectual buy-in, which there was in Mozambique."[113]

And if critics assume that the World Bank and Westerners speak with one voice, they also assume that the Mozambican state hears with one ear. They underestimate the ability of the Mozambican leadership to recognize and address its own economic difficulties. Even Sergio Vieira, a Frelimo member of the Assembly of the Republic and a vocal opponent of the turn to neo-liberalism, admitted, " 'We didn't need the World Bank to tell us it was wrong to heavily subsidise certain sectors of our economy'."[114] Furthermore, what critics do not take into consideration is that policy recommendations travel through sinuous routes into the office of the president and into the ministries and that when they are implemented, they travel out along the same tangled pathways. Along the way, in both directions, workers and smallholders, state and private company managers, provincial administrators and national ministers mold, thwart, and modify policies. What gets implemented may not resemble what major donors anticipated or wanted, but donors are unlikely to call attention to the gap between the recommendations and the reality for fear of exposing their own limitations.

I argue that the transition to capitalism in Mozambique reflects the features of systemic privatization outlined by Feigenbaum and Henig, and Feigenbaum, Henig and Hamnett, and mimics the pattern followed by the Eastern European countries that Róna-Tas describes. Political motivations and objectives have infused many aspects of the privatization process as they have done in other

---

[112] On divisions within NGOs and the complexity of their relationships with the World Bank, see P. Nelson, *The World Bank and Non-Governmental Organizations: The Limits of Apolitical Development* (New York: St Martin's Press, 1995).

[113] Interview, S. Bell, senior economist, World Bank-Mozambique, 18 February 1998.

[114] Sergio Vieira quoted in Askin, "Economic About-turn."

African countries.[115] The government's desire to respond to different social pressures and expectations, and its efforts to attract new elites, provide the justification for calling this privatization "systemic." The paralysis of many state firms in industry and agriculture hastened the shift to the private sector. The collapse of the Soviet Union and the loss of markets in the formerly socialist countries in Eastern Europe also drove the reforms and consolidated a faction within government that preferred neo-liberal solutions. The global dominance of neo-liberal doctrines combined with pressure by the World Bank set the parameters for change. In addition, with peace, foreigners became interested in the opportunities available in tourism, agriculture and fishing, energy, mining, and forests.[116] They were joined by existing and new national investors who were determined to purchase state firms located in potentially profitable sectors of the economy. Returning refugees also prompted the government to shape an agrarian strategy that addressed smallholders' concerns about land and local political authority. These factors explain **why** the government privatized.

However, the identification of those state companies to sell, oversight of the actual sale process, the selection of winners, and the rules of private sector operation were not simply the products of administrative or economic considerations. They reflected political struggles within Mozambique and the requirements of the government. They show **how** the government privatized and what the intentions were. If one examines just the implementation process, one finds that private domestic actors who benefitted from the reluctant reforms of the 1980s influenced the trajectory of privatization in the 1990s. Existing elites used their position to shape the privatization process. In addition, state officials decided what and when state enterprises were to be privatized. They governed who was eligible to purchase particular enterprises. They sought to balance competing interests in the country and, at the same time, they made the state a major player in proposed profitable ventures. The presence of continuities and discontinuities, intricately intertwined and not easily separated, leads me to describe the process of privatization as a case of "transformative preservation." The Mozambican state used the transition as a means to preserve some measure of state power and authority while it transformed the country. Below we analyze in more detail the characteristics of the implementation process as it occurred in Mozambique.

## The privatization process in Mozambique

The process for the sale of companies depended on the size of the company and the sector it was in, but, regardless of size, the government selected which firms were and were not privatized and what privatization method was employed.

---

[115] Tangri, *The Politics of Patronage*, pp. 38–61.

[116] J. Fiel, "Prós e Contras de Moçambique," *Exame* (Lisbona) (June 1993), pp. 84–90; "O deve e haver do país," *Exame* (July 1993), pp. 91–92.

It determined whether there was open or closed bidding on the sale of state assets, or a management/employee buyout, or a contracting out or leasing of management functions. For public and restricted tenders, which were the most common method of sale of the larger state companies, the government controlled the process of bidding and sale; it also directly negotiated with buyers in some cases. For example, the Ministry of Agriculture and Fisheries or the Ministry of Industry, Trade, and Tourism appointed organizations to identify those small and medium enterprises (less than 100 workers) to be privatized. The organizations conducted technical evaluations of the enterprises and defined the details of privatization for the ministry. In agriculture and industry, the Office for the Restructuring of Agricultural and Fishing Enterprises (GREAP) and the Office for the Restructuring of Industrial, Commercial and Tourist Enterprises (GREICT) respectively helped to study and coordinate the privatization process. The World Bank funded both offices but government members and consultants staffed them. Special national or provincial commissions connected to each ministry then handled the final evaluation and sale of the enterprise, depending on its cost and location.[117]

The largest sales also involved the highest levels of government. First, the Council of Ministers or the ministry of a particular sector identified which large state enterprises to privatize. The Technical Unit for Enterprise Restructuring (UTRE) then prepared a prospectus on the enterprise, working closely with the Inter-Ministerial Commission for Enterprise Restructuring (CIRE) chaired by the prime minister and a technical committee. UTRE also conducted studies on the financial and technical state of individual companies. Studies took up to a year on average and cost between $100,000 and $300,000 to complete.[118] When an enterprise was ready to be privatized, the prime minister nominated an Executive Privatization Commission (CEP) that pre-qualified bidders, evaluated proposals, and hammered out the final details with the winner of the bid. Alternatively, government ministers negotiated directly with buyers.[119] If the investment was more than $10 million, the Council of Ministers made the final decision.[120] The prime minister as the head of CIRE then confirmed the sale and gave final approval for the divestiture.[121]

Investors also had an organization to help them, but it was responsible to, and partially staffed by, the government. The Centre for Investment Promotion

---

[117] Mozambique, UTRE, 1995, p. 2; Mozambique, UTRE, 1998, p. 5. In 1994, the Ministry of Agriculture became the Ministry of Agriculture and Fisheries and the Ministry of Industry and Trade became the Ministry of Industry, Trade and Tourism (MICTUR). In 1999, the Ministry of Agriculture and Fisheries became the Ministry of Agriculture and Rural Development and MICTUR returned to being the Ministry of Industry and Trade. My usage changes accordingly.

[118] "Para uma privatização mais rápida," *Mediafax* (17 November 1994).

[119] Mozambique, UTRE, 1995, p. 2; UTRE, 1998, p. 5.

[120] Mozambique, Assembly of the Republic, Law 3/93 (8 June 1993), article 16.

[121] Mozambique, UTRE, 1998, p. 5.

(CPI), whose motto is "We are at the service of investors for the development of our country," aided investors by identifying opportunities, putting together investment proposals, and preparing bids. It prepared and distributed information on state companies to be privatized and on any changes in the legislation. It represented foreign and national investors in negotiations with government departments for the purchase of state companies. On behalf of an investor, it contacted the relevant agencies involved in the sale of a state asset. But the CPI performed that service for a fee of $\frac{1}{2}$ of 1 percent up to $50,000 once authorization occurred. Moreover, government closely guarded the actions of the CPI. The Ministry of Planning and Finance created the CPI and the CPI reported to the ministry. Before any proposals were submitted they went before the CPI's Investment Evaluation Board, which included representatives from the Ministry of Planning and Finance, the Central Bank, customs, and the sector relevant to the investment.[122]

Once a proposal was complete, the CPI worked with government officials to hammer out the terms of privatization.[123] Final decisions included the company's legal status, any tax incentives the government granted, the location of the company, and the time period that the contract occupied. Contracts specified the procedures for remitting profits abroad, the number and categories of workers to be employed (both foreign and national), what training schemes were to exist for Mozambican workers, and what goods could be imported and exported.[124]

Many investors have complained about the lengthy process of purchasing a former state company and making new investments as well as the degree of government involvement. They argue that the government sold many of the small and medium companies behind closed doors through direct negotiation between buyers and government officials.[125] Others state that the tendering process for state firms was not transparent. Some charge that bids were accepted after closing and selection was made on terms other than the price. Others complain that the sale price often seemed arbitrary and numerous times it was unclear how the price was determined. Many claim that this discouraged potential investors.[126] Furthermore, many investors argue that authorization for a project took much

---

[122] Mozambique, GPIE, *Investor's Guide to Mozambique* (Maputo: GPIE, 1992), pp. 75–76; Mozambique, CPI, "Summary of Main Investment Rules in Mozambique," brochure (May 1995).

[123] Investors have to submit three copies of their proposal to the CPI who has ten days to notify the investor whether the proposal is complete or not. Analysis and evaluation should take place within thirty days. If more than ninety days elapse, the investor can inform the CPI that it will begin implementing the project within thirty days (article 15).

[124] Mozambique, Law 3/93, article 14.

[125] F. Rafael, "Privatizações: Transparencia precisa-se," *Economia* (April/June 1993), p. 27.

[126] "Para uma privatização mais rápida"; Mozambique, Ministry of Industry, Commerce and Tourism (MICTUR), *Fourth Private Sector Conference in Mozambique* (Maputo: Montage Graphic, 1999), pp. 39–40.

longer than the thirty stated days and was expensive. Potential investors had too many requirements to fulfill and too much bureaucratic red tape to cut through in order to create a new company. Legislation was complicated and "restrictive." Costs of doing business were too high, and requirements to obtain visas, licenses and other pieces of paper frustrated investors. In some cases, the CPI acted more like a gatekeeper than a facilitator of private investment.[127]

The procedure and the complaints make clear that much government oversight accompanied privatization. The reasons for this were political and economic. Economic and political pressures brought about the reorientation of the economy towards market principles and privatization, but the government wanted to control the process in order to remain an active player in the economy. It also wished to gain the support of the constituency that encouraged and arose from restructuring. Whom the government targeted in the legislation and how the government treated different groups in the process of adopting a market economy expose the contradictory objectives in transformative preservation.

Policies and legislation currently attempt to address existing tensions within government and among diverse social forces. To redress the government's previous negligence of the family sector for example, the land law asserts that private investors must consult local communities when they apply for land and timber concessions.[128] The government's National Agricultural Development Plan (PROAGRI) also supports smallholders. It pledges to promote

the transformation of subsistence agriculture into one that is more integrated in the functions of production, distribution and processing, in order to achieve the development of a subsistence agrarian sector which contributes with surpluses for the market and the development of an efficient and participatory entrepreneur.[129]

These efforts to aid smallholders reveal that they have their advocates within government, but a faction that favors the expansion of private companies increasingly dominates the governmental agenda. The influence of a private sector faction is manifest in the institutions and the legislation we have already discussed, and this faction intends to benefit foreign and especially national

---

[127] World Bank, Southern Africa Department, Macro, Industry, and Finance Division, "Mozambique: Impediments to Industrial Sector Recovery" (15 February 1995), pp. xiii–xiv; Mozambique, MICTUR, *Third Private Sector Conference in Mozambique* (Maputo: MagicPrint Ltd., 1998), p. 52, pp. 78–79; Mozambique, MICTUR, *Fourth Private Sector Conference*, pp. 39–40; World Bank, "Mozambique Country Economic Memorandum: Growth Prospects and Reform Agenda," Report no. 20601-MZ (7 February 2001), pp. 49–50.

[128] Mozambique, Assembleia da República, Lei 19/97 (1 October 1997); S. Kloeck-Jenson, "Análise do Debate Parlamentar e da Nova Lei Nacional de Terras para Moçambique," Land Tenure Center-Mozambique (September 1997) and "A Brief Analysis of the Forestry Sector in Mozambique with a Focus on Zambezia Province," Land Tenure Center Project-Mozambique (December 22, 1998), draft mimeo.

[129] Mozambique, Ministry of Agriculture and Fisheries, "National Program for Agrarian Development PROAGRI, 1999–2003," Volume II-Master Document (February 1998), p. 48.

capital.[130] With regard to foreigners, legislation and policies recognize the skills and investment that foreigners are able to contribute to industry, agriculture, mining, tourism, and forestry in Mozambique. Government officials and institutions actively seek the participation of foreign capital, offering investment incentives, tax benefits, and attractive repatriation of profit options for those coming from abroad.

Yet a major objective of government legislative and institutional involvement is also to preference national investors. The prime minister of Mozambique, Pascoal Mocumbi, candidly stated in a 1997 speech to the First Pan-African Investment Summit that:

Privatisation must be perceived as a special moment for nurturing the national entrepreneurial class, which in many cases is still at birth. The development and consolidation of a strong national entrepreneurial class is one of the challenges my Government has undertaken, not withstanding the importance of the association of national entrepreneurs with foreign investors.[131]

Part of the reason for this preference is due to the historical weakness of national capital in Mozambique. During the colonial period, Portuguese settlers and foreign companies controlled most of the significant capital in the country – from the corner shop to the large sugar plantations. Capital investment by Mozambicans, especially Africans, was limited in the urban areas. In the rural areas, "progressive" African farmers who cultivated more than five hectares and received bonuses and credit from the colonial government emerged from the late 1950s. However, their share of total landholdings was small in comparison with that of colonial companies and settlers. Indians, who were involved mostly in commerce, accounted for a portion of the total capital. They were largely located in the capital and in northern rural areas.

Liberation did little to build up a national class whether black, white, or Indian. As the president of Mozambique has remarked: "After independence, the central planning system privileged the state and cooperative sectors. Although the Constitution at that time did not forbid the development of the private sector, in practical terms and for a variety of reasons private activity withdrew."[132] When the government then began to encourage investment and private sector initiatives, initially it favored foreign investors. It passed a law on direct foreign investment in 1984 giving the conditions under which investment could take place in the country. The terms and procedures that foreign investors should

---

[130] Even in PROAGRI, much emphasis is placed on the private sector as distinct from the family sector, see Mozambique, Ministry of Agriculture and Fisheries, "National Program," p. 51.

[131] Pascoal Mocumbi, Prime Minister of the Republic of Mozambique, "Address by his Excellency Dr. Pascoal Mocumbi," First Pan-African Investment Summit, "Privatisation in Practice: The Restructuring of State-Owned Enterprises in Africa into the next Millennium," Johannesburg, South Africa (17 March 1997), mimeo.

[132] "Mozambique Country Report," Corporate Location, 1992, p. 8.

follow were elaborated in subsequent decrees passed in the late 1980s and the 1990s. Moreover, originally the CPI was called the Office for the Promotion of Foreign Investment (GPIE) to aid foreign investors with identifying possible investment areas and preparing proposals to the government.[133]

Although Law 4/84 encouraged foreign investors to make investments in association with private or state Mozambican firms, the government did not address comprehensively the role of Mozambican nationals in the emerging privatization process until 1987. Serious attention to the position of Mozambican nationals likely stemmed from pressure by various domestic groups who claimed the process excluded them and who saw in privatization an opportunity to gain wealth. These were businesses that had remained in Mozambique in spite of the nationalizations after 1975. They consisted of former colonial agricultural companies such as João Ferreira dos Santos, the Entreposto Group, and the Madal Group that had the majority of their investment in Mozambique, and some external capital investments, mainly in Portugal. In addition, the group comprised many import-export businesses such as Gani Comercial, run mainly by "Indians." Furthermore, black Mozambicans who had, or wanted, agricultural land in the rural areas or small businesses in urban areas lobbied vociferously for more attention to be paid to national capital. Finally, Frelimo members in positions of political power or who sought investment opportunities also influenced the direction of government policy.

The government recognized the instability that might be caused by overlooking existing domestic groups and, conversely, it realized the potential political rewards it could gain by fostering national capital and granting land and firms to insiders. Thus, it reshaped the economic policy to reflect these political goals. Law 5/87 exempted or reduced the payment by national investors of customs duties and taxes on equipment and attempted to give national investors incentives and guarantees on their investments.[134] In order that "insiders" in the party could help to constitute national capital, the Fifth Frelimo Party Congress in 1989 withdrew restrictions on Frelimo party members with regard to their involvement in the private sector. It decreed that there was no limit to the number of workers that party members could have on their *machambas* (farms) or in companies, and it accepted that party members be allowed to accumulate capital.[135] This resolution released party members to participate in the private sector and gave the state the license to reward supporters with land and companies. The Constitution of 1990 also pledged government support to the growth of national capital, particularly small and medium companies.

---

[133] Mozambique, GPIE, *Investor's Guide*, p. 71; J. Mazive, "Legislação sobre Investimento em Moçambique," *Economia*, 6, 16, (Feb/Mar 1993), p. 31.
[134] Mazive, "Legislação sobre Investimento," p. 35.
[135] "Onde estão os empresários moçambicanos?" *Notícias* (21 December 1994).

Nationals continued to receive attention in subsequent legislation once privatization was fully underway. Law 3/93, of 8 June 1993, addressed nationals and foreigners together for the first time. The law ensured equality of treatment to both foreigners and nationals with regard to tax exemptions and fiscal benefits.[136] Decree 14/93 changed the GPIE to the Center for Investment Promotion and charged it with handling all investment proposals, be they foreign or national, thereby granting to national capital a resource that had previously only been available legally to foreigners.[137]

On closer inspection, Law 3/93 preferenced nationals. The law only required nationals to pay $15,000 in equity capital; while it required foreign investors to pay $50,000 when purchasing a company. Moreover the law stated that exceptions to equality of treatment " shall be those cases of projects or activities by nationals which by their nature or scale of investments and undertakings, may merit special treatment and support from the Government."[138] Many of the investment projects envisioned in the 1993 law attempted to contribute to the "training, expansion, and development of national entrepreneurs and Mozambican business partners" and to the creation of jobs for Mozambicans.[139]

Moreover, in spite of the equality of treatment clause in the 1993 law, the privatization process treated foreigners and nationals differently. After a small down payment, the process allowed nationals up to ten years to pay for a formerly state-owned company.[140] The legislation reserved approximately 20 percent of the equity in former state enterprises for the management and workers of the company. It stipulated that they had to have worked for the company for five years in order to be eligible for share purchase. Workers and management were eligible to acquire additional shares in those companies that were working well, competing effectively, and did not require substantial investments at the time of restructuring.[141] And although the law did not require private companies to contain a specific amount of national capital, in practice the CPI reserved about 26 percent of equity for national capital; in fishing, the percentage was 51 percent.[142] Nationals also qualified for tax exemptions and incentives if they exceeded the minimum investment of $15,000, while for foreigners the limit was $50,000.[143]

Credit schemes also targeted domestic capitalists, particularly those who invested in small and medium enterprises – the majority of firms in Mozambique.

[136] Mozambique, Assembly of the Republic, Law 3/93 (8 June 1993).
[137] Mozambique, Council of Ministers, Decree no. 14/93 (21 July 1993), article 4.
[138] Mozambique, Assembly of the Republic, Law 3/93, article 4.
[139] Law 3/93, article 7; "Quem privatiza quem em Moçambique?" *Notícias* (1 April 1995).
[140] Mozambique, Conselho de Ministros, Decreto 10/97 (6 May 1997), article 34.
[141] Mozambique, CPI, "Mozambique: Making Significant Headway," mimeo, 1994, p. 5; Law 15/91 (3 August 1991), article 16.
[142] "Mozambique Country Report," p. 16.
[143] World Bank, "Mozambique: Impediments," p. xiii.

Several of these schemes collapsed after only a short time, but with the assistance of the International Development Association (IDA), the government began a new project in 1999 to replace them. The Enterprise Development Project (PoDE) aims to support small businesses in industry and commerce with training schemes and credit. It addresses small (up to five workers) and medium (up to fifteen workers) businesses run by Mozambicans. One of its aims is to bring into the formal sector enterprises that are presently operating in the informal sector, such as woodworking, small machine repair, and dressmaking. This process of formalizing the informal sector is a phenomenon that is occurring elsewhere in Africa. Initially, the project is focusing on Sofala and Zambezia, but it will include other provinces later. It teaches business persons basic accounting, advertising and marketing techniques, and offers loans for improvements or expansion. This credit and training scheme joins other donor-funded projects that are meant to aid entrepreneurs in rural areas.[144] In aggregate these measures do not really equal the playing field with regard to the better capitalized, more experienced foreign investors. However, preferences to nationals reveal that they have enough influence to shape policy and that the state recognizes the potential rewards of enlarging domestic capital by favoring various national groups. Favoritism to national investors has helped build a new constituency of support for the state.

### Conclusion

The extensive role of the state in the implementation of privatization and market principles reveals the paradox in the neo-liberal perspective. Often proposed as a solution to excessive state intervention, privatization requires so many institutions and so much legislation to enact it that states with some degree of stability and legitimacy end up intervening greatly in order to carry out the process. Markets cannot be "unleashed"; they must be created and regulated. State firms cannot be sold like peanuts; they must be valued and restructured. Although a return to socialism is now improbable and the "demiurge" functions of the state have been drastically refined, nevertheless, state participation in Mozambique is pervasive. Government institutions and officials closely monitor and direct the privatization process, while constitutional pronouncements and legislation set the limits to private sector activity and regulate, promote, and encourage investors. Factions within government determine the particular characteristics of privatization and who the "winners" and "losers" in the process will be. The role of the state has altered but not disappeared: it seeks to shape the outcome of privatization as much as possible. These measures reinforce the claims made

---

[144] Jan Odegard, representative, UN Industrial Development Organization, Maputo, interview, 8 June 1999.

by Callaghy and Evans that states are instrumental to the formation of a free market, private sector economy. Rather than ignore them, scholars should look at what kinds of roles the state is adopting and to what end.[145]

The roles of different social actors also illustrate how blatantly political privatizations can be, in spite of attempts in much of the current literature to frame privatization as an economic or administrative exercise. In Mozambique, the government has tried to satisfy competing interests and to silence the voices of others through the process of restructuring and liberalization. Joined uneasily together in the new dispensation are the state, historically privileged social groups, new elites that arose following the transition to independence, and foreign capital. The existing private sector, as well as members of the Frelimo party and influential foreigners, have used their political connections and power to help structure the process of privatization. While workers, the urban and rural poor, and smallholders represent vociferous constituencies and have their spokespeople in government, the voice representing capital is clearly in the ascendancy.

Because the characteristics of privatization in Mozambican contain elements of change and continuity, I have referred to the process as one of "transformative preservation." It is path-dependent and reflects the influence of the colonial and socialist periods. It also allows for a continuing and prominent role for the state. Simultaneously, the adoption of market principles, the growth of private companies, and the adherence to capitalist ideology have altered the state's roles, generated new social actors, revealed new sources of support for the state, and introduced additional tensions. The next chapter examines the impact of restructuring and explores the meaning of state and capital relations for Mozambique.

[145] Callaghy, "Vision and Politics," pp. 164–65; Evans, *Embedded Autonomy*.

# 4    A privatizing state or a statist privatization?

> Privatisation – the remedy favored by the western doctors for all the econo-
> mic ills of the continent – does not represent as big a break with the previous dy-
> namic of the postcolonial State as people like to think.    Jean-François Bayart[1]

The impact of privatization raises important questions about state/capital relations in post-war, post-socialist Mozambique. Does privatization indicate the
withdrawal of state intervention in the economy and its replacement by a more
efficient private sector, or are these objectives both unrealized and unrealistic?
Will it result in a more productive economy which dispenses benefits not only
to large investors, but also to small producers; or is it designed to enrich the
few at the expense of the masses? Are we witnessing the creation of a stable,
independent, economically prosperous country or simply a recolonization of
Mozambique?

Three approaches attempt to conceptualize the state and capital relations
that are arising from privatization and all three pervade public and scholarly
discourse in Mozambique. The World Bank approach stresses the positive and
beneficial aspects of privatization, whereas skeptics of privatization emphasize
the loss of political and economic sovereignty that may come with the sale
of state assets and the influence of Western donors. Officials in the Mozambican government, as well as representatives of some non-governmental organizations, embrace a third position. They argue that privatization represents a
"smart partnership" or a marriage of interests between the private sector and
the government that can bring mutual benefits to both participants.

According to the neo-liberal arguments that characterize the first perspective, selling off state enterprises allows both the state and business to improve their overall performance. A key component of a broader structural
adjustment package promoted by the World Bank, privatization reduces the
weight of the state in the economy and leads to increased economic output
and greater development. Governments also benefit from the shedding of the

---

[1]  Bayart, *The State in Africa*, p. 86.

state sector. They are left free to engage in the business of politics and to provide services such as health and education while the private sector produces wealth.

This policy is a prescriptive application of two related theories: public choice analysis, and new institutionalism grounded in rational choice theory. They have been evident in economic policy approaches adopted by countries as different as Brazil and Bulgaria. Drawing upon key concepts from market theory in economics, public and rational choice theorists argue that political actors, just like economic agents in a market economy, tend to pursue their self-interest to achieve their maximum utility. One reason that state-run economies – and Mozambique offered a typical example – are poor guarantors of either economic prosperity or social welfare is that when the political and economic realms are so intertwined as they are in highly intervened economies, state actors tend to use intervention as a form of "rent-seeking," that is, as a means to enhance personal wealth or institutional power. Privatization serves the dual purpose of restructuring the state administration to operate more efficiently in the political realm and organizing the economy according to principles and priorities of the market. With the state and the economy now acting more autonomously, the chances of political and economic self-interest intermingling are reduced; each can be more efficient and hence more successful in its respective realm.[2]

As far as the World Bank, several NGOs, and many government officials are concerned, Mozambique has faithfully implemented the World Bank's privatization agenda for the country. In fact, it has followed the prescription so well that Mozambique's privatization program has been termed "the most successful in Africa" by World Bank officials and many Western donors.[3] The rapid pace and large number of state sector sales since 1992 comprise a large part of the criteria for "success", but the World Bank also includes company performance after privatization in its appraisal. In conversation and in the media, Simon Bell, a senior economist at the World Bank resident in Mozambique, pointed to the increased output and strong sales of Coca-Cola (a joint-venture between the Mozambican government and South African Breweries) as an example of privatization's "success."[4]

---

[2] See P. Self, *Government by the Market? The Politics of Public Choice* (London: Macmillan, 1993) for an explanation and critique of public choice theory. For a critical review of new institutionalism see C. Leys, *The Rise and Fall of Development Theory* (Bloomington: Indiana University Press, 1996), chapter 4 and for a critique of World Bank discourse, see Hibou, "The Political Economy." Theoretically, rational choice has begun to influence area studies in the US; practically, it enjoys much popularity with the World Bank and USAID. R. Bates, ed., *Toward a Political Economy of Development: A Rational Choice Perspective* (Berkeley, CA: University of California Press, 1988) applies the perspective to Africa.

[3] Baloi, "Privatizações são das mais"; "Programa de privatizações."

[4] Baloi, "Privatizações são das mais," and Bell, interview.

The increased consumption of Coca-Cola notwithstanding, critics of privatization in Mozambique take a rather different view. They argue that the privatization of state enterprises is reducing the provision of supplies and services to the poorest people in the poorest sectors of the economy because private investors do not find it profitable to market in those areas.[5] Resuscitating many of the arguments made by dependency theorists in the 1970s, critics furthermore insist that the state has relinquished its sovereignty and is now dependent on the dictates of foreign NGOs, investors and global markets. To the extent that Mozambican nationals are the beneficiaries of privatization, they are only the "comprador" agents for foreign capital, providing a facade of domestic involvement when, in reality, foreign investors control the actual wealth and power. Outsiders and their domestic allies then act together to weaken the state, or they use it to repress the very groups the state sought to champion at independence.[6] A weak state increasingly challenged by the inexorable logic of capital under the control of outsiders looks a lot like Mozambique's colonial past. Hence more than one critic has referred to recent events there as "recolonization": a return to the colonial days of foreign monopolies, super profits, and coerced labor.[7]

The third conceptualization does not adopt the perspective advanced by critics that Mozambique is the victim of global political and economic forces, nor does it accept the need for the state and economy to function as autonomous entities, a component that is so essential to the "hard" neo-liberal paradigm. Rather, proponents of the third approach argue that the state and the private sector, along with other sectors of the society, can form a partnership to pursue their interests. Although references vary on who constitutes the membership of the partnership, they always include both the private sector and the government as key players. Proponents also recognize that the partnership is a work in progress and not yet fully realized, but, nevertheless, they argue ideologically that a "marriage of interests" between forces inside and outside of Mozambique is both possible and desirable. President Chissano of Mozambique expressed his vision of the relationship between government and business to the Regional Investors' Forum in June of 1998: "We are keen to see this 'smart partnership' in practice. Economic prosperity requires a combination of forces including governments and the business sector to transform the region."[8] Several months later, the president used the word "partnership" five times in his opening address to the Fourth Private Sector conference, perhaps to underscore the extent to which he would like to see a partnership realized. He stated:

[5] J. Marshall, *War, Debt and Structural Adjustment in Mozambique: The Social Impact* (Ottawa: The North–South Institute, 1992); Mittelman, *The Globalization Syndrome*, pp. 102–7.

[6] Plank, "Aid, Debt, and the End of Sovereignty."

[7] Hermele, *Mozambican Crossroads*, p. 42; Hanlon, *Mozambique: Who Calls the Shots?*, pp. 243–47; *Peace without Profit*; Saul, *Recolonization and Resistance*, introduction and chapter 3.

[8] President Joaquim Chissano, speech, Regional Investors' Forum (16 June 1998).

I want to express my confidence in the development of a dynamic, responsible and broadly based local private sector. I believe in the constructive and complementary role that this sector can play in formulating and conceptualizing a vision of national development, in partnership with the government, trade unions and the community.[9]

The inclusion of "trade unions and the community" suggests a shift towards corporatist arrangements and the use of corporatist ideological messages. But subsequent references to partnerships only intermittently appeal to workers and other social actors while references to a relationship between the government and the private sector remain a constant. Later in the same speech, President Chissano argued that "we must promote actions aimed at creating and exploiting a tripartite partnership between the private sector, the public sector and the political leadership."[10] Here, the partnership membership seems to be confined to those who own, oversee, regulate, and manage business; "trade unions and the community" are dropped from the vision.

While the new emphasis on public-private partnership illustrates the degree to which the socialist message of yesterday has been greatly overridden, it is not as radical a departure from earlier Frelimo ideological appeals and economic policies as might first appear. It still allocates a prominent role to government in economic matters. The government is not only creating an environment that is "conducive to the achievement of a strong and sustained private sector in the country," as one World Bank analyst insisted;[11] it is to be a **partner** in the attempts to bring about development. The articulation and goal of a partnership between the government and the private sector draws on and pushes further an emerging emphasis on "good governance" within the donor community and international institutions. Stung by market failures in Asia and Eastern Europe, some international policy-makers have begun to concede the importance of regimes that can negotiate among and balance different interests and organizations. These regimes are streamlined, technical, and apolitical, not the interventionist governments of the past. "Good governance" approaches stress well-managed, incorrupt, legitimate regimes operating according to liberal-democratic principles, with properly functioning judicial systems and respect for human rights.[12] "Smart partnerships" aim to extend the boundaries of good

---

[9] President Joaquim Chissano, "Keynote Address," in Mozambique, Ministry of Industry, Commerce and Tourism (MICTUR), *Fourth Private Sector Conference in Mozambique* (Maputo: MICTUR, 1999), p. 1.

[10] President Chissano, "Keynote Address," p. 2.

[11] S. Bell, "Four Years of Private Sector Conferences: Where Have We Come From and Where Do We Still Have to Go?" in MICTUR, *Fourth Private Sector Conference*, p. 41.

[12] See World Bank, *World Development Report 1997* for a list of what "good governance" consists. At one point, the state is referred to as a "partner in its country's development" (p. 3), but here the use of partner is restricted (once again) to facilitating private sector growth and regulating social forces. Rhetorically, the Mozambican use of "partnership" may be building on the language of

governance to linkages with particular social groups. In theory, they consist of mutually beneficial alliances between government and economic agents to manage and negotiate the changes that have come with an increasingly global economy. Jessop refers to these types of partnerships as "heterarchic governance" where interdependence prevails and the expected benefits are as follows:

Individual economic partners give up part of their autonomy in economic decision-making in exchange for political influence and a better overall functioning of the system; and the state gives up part of its capacity for top-down authoritative decision-making in exchange for influence over economic agents and more effective overall economic performance.[13]

The belief that an alliance of government and economic forces can bring about development is a position whose origins can be found in the arguments of modernization theorists in the 1970s, and it is a message that Frelimo has used before. Frelimo incorporated many elements of modernization theory into its ideology following independence, particularly the notion that government had the ability to transform a developing society. Now uncoupled from their union with socialist ideology, several principles of modernization are being deployed to sanction the alliance of the state and the private sector to accomplish development goals. Although a workable partnership remains to be realized fully, Frelimo is fashioning both an ideological message and a policy agenda that incorporate previous discourses and that resonate with an emerging donor emphasis on "governance."

These three approaches reflect the major currents in the debate about the nature of capitalist development in Mozambique, but they address inadequately the process and outcome of privatization there. I argue that we should not be calling privatization a success, or a case of capitulation, or even a "smart partnership." The kind of unfettered capitalist development that strict neo-liberals might envision or recolonization analysts have feared is unlikely due to the particular historical context in which privatization has taken place. Just "unleashing markets" has not been sufficient to overcome the legacies of the colonial and the socialist periods; thus the pattern of capitalist penetration has been uneven and diverse. Equally, companies have pursued different investment and production strategies that have elicited distinct responses at the local level. Communities and their residents have shaped the nature and degree of capital penetration taking place. Both neo-liberals and recolonization theorists have failed to account for the path-dependency arising from Mozambique's past, the variations

the World Bank; in practice, the term applies to a much more expansive role of the state, as we shall see. For a critique, see F. Petiteville, "Three Mythical Representations of the State in Development Theory," *International Social Science Journal (ISSJ)*, 155 (March 1998), p. 122. The entire volume is a special issue on "Governance."

[13] B. Jessop, "The Rise of Governance and the Risks of Failure: The Case of Economic Development," *ISSJ*, 155 (March 1998), p. 36.

in entrepreneurial strategies, and the diverse responses on the ground that have helped to influence capital formation.

Moreover, while the implementation of privatization has constrained the ability of the ruling party to shape economic policy, there is no minimalist state here as neo-liberals might wish and no "puppet state" as recolonization analysts might decry. The state may have drastically reshaped the roles it plays in the economy but the streamlining process has produced a "leaner, meaner state," one that has been able to preserve itself through transformation. The Frelimo government has reconstructed its authority and re-invented itself. It has taken advantage of many opportunities to create a new constituency of private sector supporters for its economic agenda and to gain badly needed political legitimacy as a result. It has used its position to foster domestic capital formation, to forge links with foreign and national capital, to strengthen and consolidate so-called public companies, to participate in joint-ventures, and to invest in new mega-projects. So far, the occurrence of regular elections in which a sizeable portion of the electorate in selected parts of the country votes for the opposition may have curbed, but not halted, the ruling party's strong appetite for capturing a significant share of the investment entering the country.

The active role of the state, alongside the growing importance of private capital, seems to lend credence to the "good governance" or "smart partnership" approach. After all, links between the private and public sectors and government may be necessary components of the "new internationalization" that has arisen out of an increasingly global economy. As Evans argues, local and international economic agents in developing countries, with the encouragement and support of states, need to join forces to gain better access to information and to enhance their competitive chances. These alliances bring mutual benefits to both local and transnational capital but they depend on an active state to create the conditions for successful partnerships.[14] However, the concepts of "smart partnership" and "good governance" envisioned by "soft neo-liberals" are theoretically and empirically very problematic. Even if "governance" and "partnerships" were practiced in the idealized, technical, apolitical way in which they are theorized, they would still tend to exclude politics, to restrict participation and to ignore the demands of those affected by policy. As Kazancigil argues,

governance is at its best in horizontal co-ordination, partnership, negotiation, regulation, but not so good in responding to the need to aggregate demands and decide on issues that go beyond sectoral policies. In this mode, a plurality of stakeholders in a policy process, constituted as 'policy communities,' participate in horizontal co-ordination and negotiations. However, the game is rarely played among equals, and powerful groups

---

[14] Evans, *Embedded Autonomy*, pp. 182–85.

such as well organized firms, sectors or professions, which possess enough coherence and a strategic view of their own interests, generally carry the day.[15]

Through a link with private capital, the state intends to secure the authority that it did not achieve under socialism. To a certain extent, it has accomplished these objectives. It **has** enhanced its legitimacy, improved its capacity, and strengthened its authority. Yet the manner in which this process is taking place is producing antagonisms that are constraining the state. These antagonisms are not solely externally driven or provoked as many recolonization theorists claim. They are not simply between foreign and national capital, or foreign capital and the state; they are the products of sectoral, class, ethnic, and regional factions that are arising from and influencing the privatization process. Internal cross-cutting fragmentations and solidarities connected, but not limited, to the nature of capitalism contradict the state's intentions and undermine the twin objectives of development promotion and political stability. What we find in Mozambique is an unstable dynamic that its partners continually renegotiate, but which has a great possibility of collapsing at any time. In the end, references to a "smart partnership," reinforced by private sector advertisements that legitimate the new direction that the state has adopted, may serve a useful ideological function, but they cannot disguise the dangerous fluidity that constitutes the foundation of this project.

In this chapter, I evaluate the three conceptualizations of Mozambique's restructuring by exploring some of the distinguishing features of privatization. I trace which companies and sectors have been privatized. I discuss the sources and types of investment, the formation of new elites, and the alliances, conflicts, coalitions and factions that are taking place among different economic agents in the country. I then scrutinize the emerging roles of the state. I will show how the state shapes the character of capitalism and, in turn, how capital formation legitimizes but also constrains the state. Finally, I will evaluate the impact of the transition on the state, capital, and development in Mozambique.

## A privatizing state: investors and investment

### Foreign capital

Many proponents of dependency theory argue that foreign companies control capitalist development in less developed countries and that any development that occurs does so in accordance with the needs and demands of the world economy. African countries, they argue, lack the capacity for autonomous development because they lack an indigenous, independent capitalist class.[16] Furthermore,

---

[15] A. Kazancigil, "Governance and Science: Market-like Modes of Managing Society and Producing Knowledge," *ISSJ*, 155 (March 1998), p. 71.

[16] See discussions of the various positions on capitalism in Africa in D. Himbara, *Kenyan Capitalists, The State, and Development* (Boulder, CO: Lynne Rienner, 1993), chapter 1; Berman

the main role of states in these countries is to serve the interests of capital from developed, industrialized countries. In the present Mozambican context, elements of this perspective are evident in the application of the term "recolonization" to characterize the privatization process and investment by foreign companies. Saul refers to Mozambique's "resubordination to South African and global capitalist dictate" while Plank has forecast a scenario of "neo-colonial vassalage" for countries such as Mozambique, with the Western powers in full control of their administration and economies.[17] Such perspectives argue that, in the face of World Bank and IMF support for foreign investment, the Mozambican state and Mozambican nationals are simply serving the interests of external capital and foreign donors.

The interpretative framework has three components to it: foreign capital and its supporters, national capital, and the state. Examining first the claim that Mozambique has been resubordinated to "South African and global capitalist dictate," we analyze where and how foreigners are investing in Mozambique. The government has authorized the sale of nearly 1,000 state companies to foreign and national investors. The majority of the privatized companies are small and medium companies located in Maputo Province, and the majority (over 90 percent) of them have been sold to nationals. Agriculture and agro-industries (162 companies sold) and industry, commerce, and tourism sectors (434) account for the majority of companies privatized; construction (136) and transport (64) follow. In addition, the government has authorized both foreign and national investment in new projects. Total pledged investment from 1985 to 1998 (including new projects) reported to the Center for Investment Promotion is around $4 billion: approximately 70 percent of the investment is in agriculture and industry.[18]

Considering where and how foreigners have invested in Mozambique's economy reveals features that lend support to arguments that Mozambique is losing its sovereignty and is being "recolonized." Foreign investment is concentrated in the larger companies sold by the state and in the new mega-investment projects. As of 1997, foreign investment accounted for about 50 percent of the total equity of the medium to large companies sold by the state, even though

and Leys, *African Capitalists*, introduction and Leys, "African Capitalists and Development: Theoretical Questions," chapter 1.

[17] Saul, *Recolonization and Resistance*, p. 61 and Plank, "Aid, Debt and the End of Sovereignty," pp. 429–30.

[18] Mozambique, UTRE, *Information Bulletin*, 5 (March 1998), pp. 4–6 and Mozambique, CPI, "Situação de projectos," p. 5. 1998 was the last year in which the CPI identified investors in each sector by name; I therefore rely on data from this year rather than more recent years. The decision to reduce transparency by refusing to disclose investors is unfortunate. The 1998 figures include loans contracted from third parties also. Investment figures do not include investments made by individuals who do not rely on government institutions for financial help, or to seek partners, etc.

foreign investors only purchased 25 companies out of the 115 that were sold.[19] Foreign interests either have monopolies or significant investments in food and beverages, cement production, banking, cotton processing, and oil prospecting. In addition, foreigners have proposed new investments in huge, mega-projects in industry, tourism, and mineral resources as well as in proposed transport corridors linking Maputo in the south of the country with South Africa, Beira in the center with Zimbabwe, and Nacala in the north with Malawi. Total pledged foreign investment from 1985 to the end of 1998 was approximately $1.2 billion out of a total of approximately $4 billion. This figure did not include the investment planned for the corridor projects. If all of these projects are realized, foreigners will be heavily represented and very influential in key sectors of the Mozambican economy.

Furthermore, foreign investment in Mozambique is spatially imbalanced. The majority of actual and proposed foreign investment is earmarked for industrial and agricultural projects in the province of Maputo, while other provinces have received only around 20 percent of the total pledged foreign investment. Niassa Province, which is one of the northernmost provinces in Mozambique and the least developed, has received a paltry $600,000 in investment funds. Such skewed distribution reflects the historical legacy of development in Mozambique and the biases of foreign investors. During the colonial period, the capital and its environs received the bulk of investment for infrastructure, communications, and industry. Following independence, the Frelimo government continued the trend partly for pragmatic and partly for political reasons. Frelimo has drawn most of its support from a southern, urban base of constituents. Foreign investors find urban areas and industrial sectors easier to invest in and are drawn to the infrastructural advantages that Maputo offers. Because most foreign investors are interested in exports, Maputo's proximity to South African markets presents a great attraction. Furthermore, most of the planned projects will tie Mozambique even tighter into the global economy.

Foreign investment comes from approximately 45 countries; South Africa, Portugal, and Great Britain are the most prominent. South African and British investors have one of the largest investments ever in Mozambique, a $1.3 billion, aluminum smelting plant outside of Maputo.[20] In addition, South Africa has pledged around $100 million for 179 projects. These include the restructuring and rehabilitation of many formerly state-run tourist operations and hotels from Cabo Delgado to Inhambane Provinces, natural gas projects in Inhambane Province, and breweries, textiles, service stations, and flour mills in Maputo Province. There is also, of course, the famous Coca-Cola Sabco operation. This is a joint-venture between the Mozambican government and South African

---

[19] UTRE, "Privatisation in Mozambique" (1998), p. 6.
[20] CPI, "Situação de investimento" (1998), p. 5 and CPI, "Situação de projectos," p. 3, table 3.

Breweries. It consists of three factories dispersed throughout the country and the total investment is worth over $30 million. Finally, South African investors and the South African government, along with the Mozambican government, parastatals, and investors, are also actively involved in the creation of the Maputo Corridor. The project involves the improvement of road and rail links between the port of Maputo and Mpumalanga and Gauteng Provinces in South Africa. Road expansion has occurred but many aspects of the corridor project are not yet finalized. In future, while restrictions on capital export from South Africa and falling growth rates within South Africa may temper large investments, South Africans are clearly interested in Mozambique's industrial, agricultural, mineral, and tourist sectors, and this interest is expected to continue.[21]

Portugal is the second largest foreign investor in Mozambique. It has 225 projects pledged totalling $170 million.[22] As in the colonial period, the Portuguese monopolize cement production and dominate the financial sector. They also finance over half of the new or recently privatized banks in the country. With regard to other large projects, the Portuguese have invested in glass making, shipbuilding, flour mills, milk production, and beverages. Former Portuguese settlers returning from Portugal and South Africa also comprise many of the small and medium investors in Mozambique. They are reclaiming or repurchasing companies that they owned during the colonial period.[23]

In addition to British investment of $245 million in Mozal, Great Britain has 60 projects valued at $47 million. Lonrho dominates the British investment portfolio and, of course, has been in the country in some capacity since the colonial period. Other British investments are in small and medium companies in the hotel and tourist business. British Petroleum also began prospecting for oil in 1998.[24]

The presence of foreign capital in particular sectors, its concentration around Maputo, and the types of projects it has invested in perpetuate the colonial legacy, but it seems premature to proclaim the "recolonization" of Mozambique. First, the investment that is authorized is pledged not actual investment. Many of the schemes associated with the Maputo Corridor that are aimed at large foreign investors are in their infancy. Some investment may not materialize. The collapse of the huge tourist scheme proposed by the American investor, James

[21] See S. Nhantumbo, "Finance Minister Views Economy, Foreign Investment," *Notícias* (24 May 1994) reprinted in *FBIS, Africa* reports (15 June 1994), p. 12; C. Morna, "Mozambique," *Institutional Investor*, sponsored section, n.d., p. 16; and Mozambique, CPI, "Situação de investimento" (1999), table 5 and CPI, "Investidores" (15 March 1998), selected pages.

[22] CPI, "Situação de investimento" (1999), p. 7.

[23] CPI, "Investidores," n.p. See *BR*, III Série, 1986 to present, various years for notices regarding Portuguese companies and land requests/authorizations.

[24] CPI, "Investidores," various pages.

Blanchard III (deceased), and the withdrawal of the American oil company Enron following its declaration of bankruptcy in the United States, are rather vivid illustrations of empty promises made by foreigners.

Second, the degree and pace of foreign investment depends very much on domestic conditions in Mozambique and not just on the strength of the individual foreign investor. In the early 1990s, foreign investment in Mozambique was very sluggish. When Mozambique was arguably at its weakest and most dependent, many foreign investors avoided Mozambique. Institutional and economic constraints to investment, such as the low educational rate of Mozambican workers, bureaucratic red tape, poor infrastructure, corruption, a low resource base, and language difficulties, discouraged (and continue to discourage) potential investors. Investors were reluctant to invest in Mozambique despite the fact that the government was quite "soft" on the terms of payment for privatized companies owing to its "desperate" situation.[25] Before 1994, foreign investment in Kenya, Ghana, Nigeria, South Africa, and even Tanzania was greater than that in Mozambique.[26] World Bank officials lamented that privatization was slow, "sometimes excruciatingly slow."[27] Investment began to climb following the elections in both South Africa and Mozambique in 1994. Investors perceived that the political climate was more stable and the government more legitimate. With increased investor interest in the country, "ironically the government is in a stronger position *vis à vis* proposals and interestingly *vis à vis* the World Bank," argued one investor. The government can afford to be selective about the type of investor it wants: it cancels proposals if it does not find the terms attractive; it negotiates hard for the inclusion of nationals; and it is tough on the conditions of payment.[28] Thus, it hardly sounds as if foreign capital monopolizes the playing field in Mozambique.

Third, and most importantly, almost all foreign investment in Mozambique takes the form of joint-ventures with participation by the state or national investors. Except for some limited cases such as oil prospecting, very few large companies are owned outright by foreigners. Instead the state and/or national investors own shares and are represented on the boards of almost every company in which there is foreign investment. Some have dismissed the state and national presence in these joint-ventures as mere window dressing. For example, Hanlon observes that "many people . . . are anxious to be compradors-agents for the recolonisers."[29] There are several cases that support Hanlon's claim, where Mozambicans do nothing more than collect the director's fee and keep a seat warm at board meetings, but these should not be allowed to overshadow much

---

[25] Edward Farquharson, country manager, Commonwealth Development Corporation, Maputo, interview, 2 March 1998.
[26] Bennell, "Privatization in Sub-Saharan Africa," p. 1791.
[27] Bell, interview, 18 February 1998.    [28] Farquharson, interview.
[29] Hanlon, *Mozambique: Who Calls the Shots?*, p. 245.

more complex interactions and linkages between the state, the public sector, and foreign and domestic capitalists.

Images of the puppet state or comprador capital ignore two vital points. First, transnational corporations all over the world have changed in rather fundamental ways. According to Evans, the days of multinationals operating with "splendid independence" are gone. Foreign companies now need, and actively seek, domestic alliances, for vertically integrated partnerships that are more suited to their investment and production strategies.[30] In interviews, several foreign investors in Mozambique, particularly from the banking sector, reinforced Evans' claim. One banker said that her bank preferred a 50/50 national–foreign mix when investing in a company, because the combination proved more stable in developing countries. Another stated that in the negotiations over the financing of the Maputo Corridor, foreign investors "bent over backwards to include Mozambicans in the deal" because they were convinced that things would go more smoothly if Mozambicans were involved.[31] Nationals provide knowledge of the investment site, local tastes, fashions, or preferences, and they understand the nuances of investment, tax, and labor laws. In addition, they can navigate the intricacies of local and national bureaucracies and can open doors if they have government connections. Foreign companies thus have great political and economic reasons for forming alliances with national capital.

Second, national states and domestic actors have a variety of reasons for participating alongside foreigners and they play a variety of roles within these companies. They may serve as front men collecting stipends merely in exchange for associating themselves with the company, or they may see foreign connections as a way to get access to much needed capital, technology, markets, or know-how. Their roles may be integral to the company's survival or superfluous to its operation. In Mozambique, both the state and domestic capitalists seem to occupy many points on a spectrum ranging from "comprador" and "handmaiden" to serious investor and respected partner. This suggests that the motivations, capacities, and objectives of states and domestic capitalists in investment projects that may or may not involve foreigners are more complex, more significant, and more extensive than Hanlon and others have acknowledged. Abundant evidence from Mozambique joined with that from other countries in Africa amply illustrate the point and we turn to it below.

### The role of domestic capital

Like the claims made by dependency theorists, recolonization arguments tend to concentrate on the relations of exchange rather than on the relations of

---

[30] Evans, *Embedded Autonomy*, p. 184.
[31] Audet, interview; Scott Jazynka, independent financial and business consultant, Maputo, telephone conversation, 19 February 1998.

production that occur in most capitalist African countries. Focusing on exchange relations more often than not exposes the continuing asymmetrical nature of trade between developing and developed countries, with the balance clearly in favor of the industrialized West. Furthermore, exchange relations tend to attract attention because so many of the recent neo-liberal solutions proposed for Africa have rested on reducing budget deficits, opening markets, and expanding trade – that is, on issues directly related to exchange.[32] Several decades after independence, many African countries continue to export primary commodities while remaining heavily dependent on imports of machinery and other high-technology goods. They continue to rely on substantial loans to finance a number of social and economic projects, and international financial institutions influence the pace of their "reforms." An examination of the composition of trade and trade imbalances, and the sources of external pressure on government economic policy, therefore lends credibility to arguments that Africa remains dependent, or, in the Mozambican case, is being recolonized.

Yet, as standard critiques of dependency have long argued, the theory exaggerates the impact of external factors and neglects a country's internal dynamics.[33] Switching the focus from exchange to production moves the analysis from an examination of exogenous to endogenous influences on development and, most importantly, to those groups inside a country who are engaged in the production process. In Africa, the theoretical shift has directed researchers to the importance of the state, and the role of domestic as well as foreign capital in the process of capitalist development.[34] Limiting the discussion to the role of domestic capital for the moment, Berman and Leys strengthen the argument for paying attention to the role and nature of domestic capital and capitalist classes by noting that "there are functions that the internal capitalist class must perform for capitalist development to occur, and the conditions in which it operates, determine how well or badly these functions are performed."[35] Although they do not overlook the role played by foreign capital, they contend that foreign capital

---

[32] See Alice Amsden for a critique of the neo-liberal bias, "Editorial: Bringing Production Back In – Understanding Government's Economic Role in Late Industrialization," *World Development*, 25, 4 (1997), pp. 469–80.

[33] A. So, *Social Change and Development: Modernization, Dependency and World-System Theories* (Newbury Park, CA: Sage, 1990), pp. 132–33. P. Collier's examination of the general ineffectiveness of conditionality in Africa only reinforces the point, see his "Learning from Failure: The International Financial Institutions as Agencies of Restraint in Africa" in A. Schedler, L. Diamond, and M. Plattner, eds., *The Self-Restraining State: Power and Accountability in New Democracies* (Boulder, CO: Lynne Rienner, 1999), pp. 313–30.

[34] See for example J. MacGaffey, *Entrepreneurs and Parasites: The Struggle for Indigenous Capitalism in Zaire* (Cambridge: Cambridge University Press, 1987); J. Rapley, *Ivoirien Capitalism: African Entrepreneurs in Cote d'Ivoire* (Boulder, CO: Lynne Rienner, 1993); Himbara, *Kenyan Capitalists*; Berman and Leys, *African Capitalists*; Spring and McDade, eds., *African Entrepreneurship*. For criminal activities, see J-F. Bayart, S. Ellis, and B. Hibou, *The Criminalization of the State in Africa* (Bloomington, IN: Indiana University Press, 1999).

[35] Berman and Leys, *African Capitalists*, p. 3.

is quite selective about the sectors in which it chooses to invest. Therefore, "there must also be local, domestic, internal, 'national' (and, perhaps, 'indigenous') capitalists" who can contribute to capitalist development.[36] These capitalists can differ greatly from country to country with regard to their historical background, degree of political influence, social status, and level of skill, hence the importance of empirically grounded work on the nature of domestic capital in each country.[37]

Evidence from Mozambique provides additional support for the argument that domestic capitalists occupy an important role in the capital formation that is taking place. As in other African countries, their historical origins, skills and experience, proximity to political power, and their economic, political, and social alliances influence their capacities. Domestic capitalists have purchased 90 percent of the privatized state companies and participate in most of the proposed projects. They are present in almost every sector of the economy, most notably industry, commerce, tourism, and agriculture. Total pledged national investment in privatized companies and in new projects is around $328 million and, like foreign capital, the majority of it is concentrated around Maputo.[38] In the rest of the country, national investors occupy critical economic sectors such as agriculture, industry, and trade.

Four groups make up national capital; several have a history in Mozambique stretching back to the nineteenth century, while others only acquired the label of "capitalist" yesterday. Nearly all of them have some form of connection with the state; the importance of that connection varies inversely with how old they are. The older the enterprise, the more accumulation it has and the less dependent it is on the state, whereas recent domestic capitalists tend to be former government officials, Frelimo party supporters, or former managers of state companies who rely on the state to ease their entry into business. The different groups contain white, black, and so called "Indian" Mozambicans; some are huge, highly centralized companies with extremely diversified holdings throughout the country, while others are small, specialized, regional businesses. Their different characteristics suggest various systems of classification; I have opted to rank them in order of political and financial importance, from those with the most capital to those with the least capital. It is relevant to note, however, that there is overlap between the groups and that the situation in Mozambique is quite fluid, almost dangerously so. There are cross-cutting cleavages and alliances and therefore the status and composition of the groups can change.[39]

---

[36] Berman and Leys, *African Capitalists*, p. 11.
[37] See the contributions on Zaire, Senegal, Kenya, Nigeria, and Cote D'Ivoire in Berman and Leys, *African Capitalists*.
[38] CPI, "Situação de investimento" (1999), p. 4 and CPI, "Situação de projectos," p. 3.
[39] The situation in Mozambique mirrors what Bayart has found elsewhere in Africa, see *The State in Africa*, chapter 6.

The first group consists of powerful companies such as JFS, the Madal Group, and the Entreposto Group. Formerly they were colonial concessionary companies that remained after independence and they have managed to recover and expand most of their holdings in the past few years. They now have a formidable presence in the Mozambican economy, either through their wholly owned undertakings or through joint-ventures with the government. They have interests in industry and agriculture, commerce, and mining. Collectively and separately they dominate the import-export trade and have significant investments in cotton, copra, tobacco, and cashew production and processing. Their holdings stretch from fields of cotton and tobacco in Cabo Delgado and Niassa to flour mills in Maputo.

This group's claim to be "national capital" is paradoxical and controversial. Public discourse often labels the group as "foreign" and frequently criticizes its actions. In particular, JFS is often the target of negative media attention because at times it openly and dramatically flaunts state regulations. Ironically, JFS is probably the most "national" in the group, for the company got its start a hundred years ago in northern Mozambique. Many of its past and present owners were born in Mozambique, although most of its upper-level directors are recruited from Portugal. On the other hand, most of the share capital in Madal is Norwegian, while its directors are white Mozambicans or foreigners. Yet according to one of its managing directors, Madal is considered "part of the furniture", a national company, by the Mozambican government.[40] A key feature of these companies that is worth remembering is that they are successful enterprises existing within a former colony that is now part of a global economy. The categories of "national" and "foreign" become diluted in an increasingly global world. As a result of Mozambique's former status as a Portuguese colony and the longevity of these companies, often the directors and administrators of these companies come from Portugal, and the companies receive Portuguese or Norwegian or English investment, but they also make investments in other parts of the world and co-participate with foreigners as well as the state in investments within Mozambique.

The government's justification for calling this group Mozambican seems to be partly legal and partly nostalgic. At the time of independence, these companies had the bulk of their capital in Mozambique. They were legally registered in Mozambique and they were not subsidiaries of larger companies in Portugal or other countries. Any investments they had, or now have, in the rest of the world came as a result of their growth in Mozambique during the 1960s, not the other way around. Second, because the majority of their capital was in Mozambique at the time of independence, these companies decided to stay through the difficult period of state intervention. Their loyalty appears to have

[40] Nigel Pollard, managing director, Madal Group, Maputo, interview, 2 March 1998.

been rewarded. The government considers these companies Mozambican: on the lists of purchasers that each privatizing agency maintains, these companies are always listed as Mozambican companies. They have been amongst the major beneficiaries of the sales of assets by the state and co-participate with the state in many joint-ventures. They are also just as likely to have former government members as directors to facilitate relations with the state. For example, the managing director for Madal is a former minister of Industry and Energy and a longtime Frelimo supporter. Asked in an interview what those connections bring to Madal, another director noted that "having him does not mean that we can present lousy projects, but if the government sees that he supports a project, it increases our credibility."[41]

Another indication that companies like JFS and Entreposto are national is that they self-identify as Mozambican companies and they see others as "foreigners." For example, in a reference to attracting investment to Mozambique, the financial director of the Entreposto Group stated, "The Entreposto Group wants foreign investment in Mozambique but it should play according to the rules and not be granted special conditions to come to Mozambique."[42] However, these capitalists, like other capitalists, foreign or domestic, care about profit: the actions they engage in to realize it invite the public ire, although the complaints are often couched in anti-Portuguese sentiment.

Today JFS, Entreposto, and Madal are the largest national companies in Mozambique. They have extensive investments and are considerably diversified. The Madal group, whose base is in Zambezia Province, has been in Mozambique since the nineteenth century. It was one of the largest copra-producing concessions during the 1940s, making huge profits on the sale of copra to neutral countries during World War II.[43] It also expanded into cattle and other agricultural enterprises by independence. Presently, it continues to have copra and cattle but has also invested in timber, fishing, mining, and phosphate prospecting in joint-ventures with the government or alongside other investors.[44]

In the case of JFS, the state intervened in some of its companies following independence, but after 1986 began to reward JFS for its "loyalty" by giving it the options on state land that was going to be privatized. The current interests of JFS include sisal, rice, cotton, and tobacco production, industrial processing, marketing, and import-export trade. It wholly owns six companies, is a shareholder in several others, and is engaged in joint-ventures with the state to produce tobacco, cotton, and other products throughout Mozambique.[45]

The Entreposto Group formed in the 1940s, and its major shareholders were the Mozambique Company, an old concessionary company dating from the

[41] Pollard, interview.
[42] Odete Nunes, financial director, Entreposto Group, Maputo, interview, 8 April 1998.
[43] Vail and White, *Capitalism and Colonialism in Mozambique*, p. 256.    [44] Pollard, interview.
[45] João Ferreira dos Santos, "Brief Presentation of João Ferreira dos Santos Group," mimeo.

nineteenth century, and the National Cotton Company, a large cotton concession in Manica and Sofala. It had industrial, commercial, and agricultural concerns throughout Mozambique by the 1960s. In 1968, it began to invest in Portugal and presently controls shares in twenty-five companies in Portugal in the auto industry and food distribution sectors. It also has investments in Spain and Brazil. Like JFS, it survived the nationalization period, and like JFS it has diversified its investments in Mozambique. The company is now involved in timber, cotton, and cashew processing, edible oils and soap factories, security services, and the import-export trade. Alone and in association with the state, the Entreposto Group participates in around eighteen companies in Mozambique.[46]

The second tier of domestic interests shares with the first group a long historical association with Mozambique. Many of the companies in this tier have been in Mozambique since the nineteenth or early twentieth centuries, and many investors in this group can trace their origins to Portugal, India, Pakistan, China, and even Greece. While they maintain links to relatives or firms from their country of origin, or continue some of the customs and religious practices of these countries, most hold Mozambican passports and consider themselves Mozambicans. They remained in Mozambique after the revolution, survived the period of intervention and nationalization, and have now expanded or strengthened their holdings with and without forming links with foreigners or the state.

Like the large companies, this business stratum influences the state in many ways and seek benefits from it – in fact several of its members are Parliamentarians – but its capital and existence are independent of the state. These investors figure prominently in national industry and commerce; some also dominate the economies of particular provinces, engaging either in import-export or retail trading networks in the rural areas. In the capital of Maputo, for example, Alkis Macrópulos, a businessman of Greek origin, has been a loyal supporter of Frelimo, but he also has investments in Mozambique that pre-date independence. He owns PROTAL, a factory that produces condensed milk, and his family owns 80 percent of a plastics factory that was one of three factories created out of the privatization of the former state plastics company, Emplama. In addition, the Macrópulos family holds shares in the Polana Hotel, the Crown Cork Company, and a tobacco company.[47]

A firm of Indian origin, Has Nur has also emerged as a substantial player. Has Nur has operated for 100 years in Mozambique, and it is owned by the Unus family. The father and son who comprise its major shareholders were both born in Nampula but carry Portuguese passports, indicating that they have also

[46] Nunes, interview, 8 April 1998; "Group Entreposto – Expanding in Mozambique," n.p.; "Companhia de Moçambique tem novo Presidente," *Agora: Economia Política Sociedade*, 11 (June 2001), p. 16.

[47] CPI, "Investidores," various pages; *BR* (3 May 2000), pp. 454–55.

maintained links with Portugal. The business began in the commerce of agricultural crops and consumer goods in Nampula Province, but it has expanded into industry and agricultural processing. The government granted the company a cotton concession in the north and it purchased a former state cashew factory outside of Maputo. It also has invested in a foreign-national-state joint-venture in a large flour mill in the center of the country. It trades agricultural products such as cashews, and distributes consumer goods such as beverages, textiles, clothing, and shoe products from Beira and Maputo to rural areas.[48]

Following the example of Has Nur, there are several regional players who are investing beyond their provincial strongholds. One is the AGT Group, the parent company for a number of different operations, with a base in Nampula but an agenda that will give it a national identity. One of its subsidiaries is Gani Comercial, a large wholesale commercial operation that forms the foundation of the group. It was founded by Abdul Gani Tayob, who came to Mozambique from British India in 1918.[49] The rest of the subsidiaries engage in every kind of wholesale and retail trade from automobiles and construction materials to supermarkets. The AGT Group operates in six of the country's ten provinces and has an extensive rural trade network in Nampula and Zambezia. The group is also involved in salt extraction, cotton and cereals production, stock raising, textiles, and beverages. Moreover, it trades a number of agricultural products within the country and abroad, and owns two cashew processing factories in Angoche and Nacala (now closed). All together, the business employs about 3,000 people all over the country.[50] Several years ago, one of its former directors, who has since died and who was a Frelimo alternate representative to parliament, was accused of using the cashew factories as a cover for drug smuggling. These charges were never proven and were eventually dropped.[51] However, the great media attention that the case received and the rumors that circulated around it revealed the anti-Indian sentiment that resides just beneath the surface in Mozambique.

These first two groups have fashioned links with the state, they rely on government officials for advice and special treatment, and they may be members of parliament. Particularly if they are large companies, they may be involved in joint-ventures with the state. But their existence pre-dates the independent government and they are businesses first, using political tools to protect or improve their business interests. This is not the case for most members in the third group, who were in government and politics first and who partially owe their economic existence or expansion to patronage and clientelistic networks, as is

---

[48] *BR*, III Série (22 September 1993), pp. 554–55; UTRE, *Information Bulletin*, 5 (1998), appendix 3.

[49] I. Verdier, *Mozambique – 100 Men in Power* (Paris: Indigo Publications, 1996), pp. 70–71.

[50] "Ikbal Gafar nasceu."

[51] D. Foi, "Comerciantes indianos, traficantes ou não?!", *Savana* (9 June 1995).

so common in the rest of Africa.[52] They are new and recent capitalists who moved from politics into business. Many, but not all, are black Mozambicans. They are former or current government officials, Frelimo party members, members of the armed forces, and former managers and directors of state companies. Frelimo members used to be subject to a law that prohibited them from owning companies or employing workers. Since it was overturned in 1989, Frelimo members have applied for land concessions in agriculture or made investments in industry, particularly in the south. In addition, many new capitalists, using their connections to the state and the party, are now on the boards of banks, breweries, and bottling plants; they are presidents, directors, and managers of companies. They control large agricultural enterprises or process cashews or run tourist outfits. They are also busily forming links with the first and second groups so that considerable overlap amongst the groups is emerging.

For a small segment of this group, political connections have merely provided an entry into business circles: now this segment is much more interested in being entrepreneurs than political power-brokers. Given that opportunities were denied to Africans during the colonial and command periods, it is not surprising that black Mozambicans especially need to rely on the state in order to acquire business interests. In this sense, Mozambique's version of "black empowerment" – the attempt to encourage black business interests that has become so popular in South Africa – has many similarities with its neighbor. Black Mozambicans benefit from state policies and legislation that enable them to purchase shares in companies or form partnerships with foreigners or the more established capitalists in Mozambique. They are forming banks, appearing on company boards, managing firms, and owning factories. They are shopkeepers, retail traders, industrialists, consultants, agricultural producers, and concessionaires. Some such as Egas Mussanhane, the president of the cooperative bank, CREDICOOP, or Américo Magaia, the director of FACIM (Mozambique's international trade fair) and a shareholder in a textile mill and other businesses, do have links to the government and the Frelimo party, but they also have economics degrees, business experience, and a genuine interest in management and finance.[53]

Yet the overlap and linkages between business and politics enjoyed by many of the new domestic capitalists moves beyond empowerment to favoritism and privilege. The new domestic capitalists in Mozambique are former prime

---

[52] Bayart, *The State in Africa*; Tangri, *The Politics of Patronage*.

[53] Egas Mussanhane, director, CREDICOOP, Maputo, interview, 8 April 1998; Américo Magaia, director-general, FACIM, Maputo, interview, 18 March 1998; CREDICOOP has an interesting list of investors. It includes more established capital, such as that of Alkis Macropulos and Gani Comercial, as well as the "newer" capital of Mussanhane and Jacinto Veloso, see *BR*, III Série (24 May 1995), p. 433.

ministers as well as the current prime minister, and former ministers of Defence, Justice, State Security, Economic and Social Affairs, Trade and Industry, and Agriculture. Frelimo parliamentarians and the wives and children of current and previous presidents have also invested in industry, commerce, and agriculture.[54] The higher the political profile, it seems, the greater the business interests. At least three of the former ministers are now presidents of commercial and investment banks, which have grown rapidly in recent years as a result of the privatization of the banking system. Portuguese capital dominates most of the newly private banks, but the banks also contain investments and participation by prominent Mozambicans. Graça Machel, the former first lady and Education minister and current wife of the former president of South Africa, Nelson Mandela, has invested in the Banco Internacional de Moçambique (BIM) and is the president of the bank's General Assembly, while the president of the Board of Directors is the former prime minister, Mario Machungo.[55] A former minister of Justice also directs another bank, the Banco Comercial e de Investimentos (BCI), and it includes investments by black and Indian Mozambicans, old and new money as well as Portuguese capital.[56] These banks often serve as the basis for holding companies that have purchased former state companies or are investing in new projects in transport, minerals, and industry.

Beyond finance, this third group is also involved as investors, directors, and concessionaires in industry and agriculture. The current prime minister, Pascoal Mocumbi, is on the Board of Directors of Lafinanciére Moçambique, one of four Mozambican companies to acquire a total share of 11 percent in the Companhia Industrial de Matola. This large flour mill is a joint-venture between the Mozambican state (45 percent), a consortium of three foreign companies (44 percent) and four Mozambican companies (11 percent).[57] Lafinanciére is a holding company consisting of many Mozambicans with ties to the Frelimo party, and its stated purpose is to develop "national entrepreneurs" and to invest along with others in "all branches of the national economy."[58] At least seven of its shareholders are also members of Promove and Pira, two projects whose aims are to provide material, technological, educational, and social support to former Frelimo combatants. The president of Mozambique, members of the armed forces, businessmen, and women who fought in the Liberation struggle are also members of these veterans associations.[59]

---

[54] See selected issues of *BR*, III Série: for example, *BR* (16 August 2000), pp. 967–68; *BR* (6 September 2000), p. 1087; *BR* (29 November 2000), pp. 1470–71 and references to *BR* below.
[55] *BR*, III Série, 11 September 1996, p. 877; "Banco Internacional de Moçambique-Em franca expansão," *Fórum Económico* (Março 1998), pp. 18–20.
[56] "Paixão de investidores lusos reluz em Moçambique," *Domingo* (13 July 1997). BCI also has links with Machel's Community Development Foundation.
[57] "CIM Privatizada," *Mediafax* (29 December 1994).     [58] *BR*, III Série (30 June 1993), p. 345.
[59] *BR*, III Série (7 December 1994), p. 848; *BR*, III Série (8 March 1995).

Furthermore, Eneas Comiche, the former minister in the Presidency for Economic and Social Affairs and one of the leading architects of privatization, is himself the chairman of the board of several companies engaged in the manufacture of bicycles, textiles, and metal products, and serves under Machungo in BIM. He is also on the board of the Foundation for Community Development (FDC), a non-governmental organization that funds development projects. Graça Machel founded and chairs FDC and many Mozambicans with ties to the Frelimo party are participants.[60] Another member of the government, Armando Guebuza, who is a former minister and now the head of the Frelimo party in parliament, runs a powerful holding company called Moçambique Gestores (MG, Mozambique Managers) that has invested in several projects, many of them in the transport sector.[61]

Not to be left out, members of the armed forces have also become businessmen. Former chiefs of staffs and generals have formed their own companies, invested in existing businesses, and proposed new development projects. Of particular note are the interests of the white Mozambican, Jacinto Veloso, and those of João Mpfumo. A major-general, Veloso served in the revolution from its inception in 1963, participated in the joint military commission set up during the period of transition to independence, and brokered the Nkomati Accord in 1984. His posts in government following independence were numerous. He now owns and runs a consulting firm and holding company, JV Consultores, and was a founding member of CREDICOOP, the only wholly Mozambican-owned bank. He has invested in former state companies such as an air transport company and a dairy, and made new investments in pharmacies, a casino, a trading company, and a paper and printing company in the capital.[62] Equally, the retired general, João Americo Mpfumo, has formed a holding company to finance investments in fishing, and he is a minority shareholder in one of the first private health clinics in Mozambique, Clínica Cruz Azul in Maputo.[63] As a long-serving member of Frelimo, he, too, participates in the projects that aid former combatants. In addition, the military have apparently submitted a plan to develop commercially a large and valuable tract of land they control along Kenneth Kaunda Avenue. It is in one of the most expensive parts of Maputo, just down the street from the US Embassy.[64]

[60] Verdier, *Mozambique – 100 Men in Power*, pp. 94–95; J. Hanlon, "Mozambique's Banking Crisis," *Moçambique On-line*, English version of an article published in *Metical*, 1073 (17 September 2001), <http://www.mol.co.mz/noticias/metical/2001/en010917.html>.
[61] Mozambique, UREA, "Mapa das empresas alienadas no Ministério da Agricultura em 23.05.95" (1995), mimeo., n.p.; "Reconciliações," *Metical*, 599 (4 November 1999); "Negociação inacabada," *Metical*, 608 (18 November 1999).
[62] UTRE, *Information Bulletin*, 5 (1998), appendix 3; CPI, "Investidores," various pages; *BR* (21 July 1993), p. 405; *BR* (29 September 1993), p. 562; *BR* (24 July 1996), p. 670; *BR* (12 March 1997), pp. 168–70; *BR* (29 March 2000), pp. 307–8.
[63] *BR* (14 April 1993), p. 208; *BR* (6 October 1993), p. 583.
[64] Source wishes to remain confidential.

In agriculture, the participation of individuals with past or present political connections is equally evident. From the provincial to the local level, governors as well as village administrators have received land grants as gifts. In Gaza Province government officials at the district and provincial levels and former state farm managers benefitted from the division of the CAIL state farm. Similarly, the distribution of land in Sofala Province went not only to small producers, but also to large commercial and agricultural interests and government officials. A former governor of Sofala has 200 hectares in a cotton scheme around Búzi.[65] As far north as Cabo Delgado Province, officials have allocated plots to themselves in the N'guri irrigation scheme on the Mueda Plateau while members of the military have received titles to "military warehouses, garages, and machine shops."[66]

At the national and local level, then, Frelimo officials and supporters in the party and the government clearly use political connections and status to gain economic power. Yet how widespread the connections are between politics and business is unclear. Mozambique law requires that all companies publicly register their shareholders, capital, and statutes in the weekly government bulletin on which much of the information we have just recorded is based, but the bulletin contains incomplete information on shareholders and capital, and lacks data on companies. Moreover, a 1990 law requires ministers to declare their assets to the minister of State Administration, but he is not required to make the information public. An effort in parliament to require the public declaration of assets failed; rarely do members volunteer information about their investments (Sergio Vieira, a Frelimo parliamentarian, is a notable exception). In reply to one source who asked "how members of the public could denounce corruption on the part of top officials, if they had no access to the lists of assets," the former minister of State Administration, Alfredo Gamito stated, " 'I have no idea. I don't know'."[67] Existing evidence and anecdotal reports suggest that links with business extend to lower-level bureaucrats. As one newspaper editorial claimed, civil servants are "using the taxes paid by the productive sector as the financial basis of their own businesses which, by and large, imply growing levels of extortion from the productive sector."[68] Evidence is also mounting that corruption is an integral part of the relationship between business and politics.[69]

---

[65] G. Myers, J. Eliseu, and E. Nhachungue, "Segurança e conflito em Moçambique: estudos de caso sobre acesso á terra no período do pós-guerra," Land Tenure Center, University of Wisconsin and Ministry of Agriculture (December 1993), pp. 29, 64, 89.

[66] H. West, "Creative Destruction and Sorcery of Construction," *Cahiers d'Etudes africaines*, 147, XXXVII-3 (1997), p. 687.

[67] "Ministers' Assets," *Mozambiquefile*, 224 (March 1995), p. 20.

[68] "E caríssimo investir em Moçambique," *Mediafax* (6 July 1995), p. 2.

[69] G. Harrison, "Corruption as 'Boundary Politics': The State, Democratisation, and Mozambique's Unstable Liberalisation," *Third World Quarterly*, 20, 3 (1999), pp. 537–50. The violent deaths of Carlos Cardoso, the editor of *Metical*, and António Siba-Siba Macuácua, the acting head of

Given the means that many members of this third group have used to gain entrance into the private sector and what some of them do with their money, this group is the most susceptible to the label of "comprador capital." Some of them lack business skills and their capital is limited. While the CPI claims to reserve a part of enterprises to be privatized for national investors, some argue that the national investors are just front men.[70] Foreigners also pay nationals to participate in the proposal and equally pay them off when the bid is won, or Mozambicans occupy minor positions in newly created companies. Moreover, like the elites of West Africa depicted by Bayart and Amselle, members of this group are attracted to cars, commodities, vacations, and large estates, hardly productive uses of their money.[71] Some can be seen driving Mercedes and BMWs around Maputo, and they are building grand houses in fashionable parts of town. In spite of the fact that many have been stalwart Frelimo supporters, their conspicuous consumption and, in several cases, their corrupt behavior, have caused alarm.[72] Men and women on the street recognize the incongruity between the earlier Frelimo emphasis on equality and the increasing stratification that now characterizes life in the country, and the differences among excessive consumerism, blatant corruption, and productive investment.

Applying the label of "comprador" to this type of national interest is too simple, however. It ignores how deeply entrenched in Mozambique's economic life these individuals have become, how they are beginning to act collectively, how they organize private sector conferences to promote dialogue between the state and the private sector, and how they use their access to the state as much as their access to foreign capital. These same bank presidents and parliamentarians, company directors and prime ministers, entrepreneurs and party members are also the heads and directors of business associations in Mozambique such as the Industrial Association of Mozambique, the Private Sector Association of Mozambique, and the Chamber of Commerce. Like their counterparts in Russia and Hungary, they have stitched together intricate, interlocking directorships with other domestic and foreign capitalists. They have formed holding companies such as the Sociedade de Participações de Investimentos (SPI, Investment Participation Company), the Sociedade de Controlo e Gestão de Participações

---

Banco Austral, may indicate that corruption is firmly entrenched in the highest echelons of the political system. Both men were investigating a series of non-performing loans to key Frelimo and Renamo figures made by Banco Austral (formerly Banco Popular de Desenvolvimento) and alleged incidents of fraud within the Banco Comercial de Moçambique (BCM). See Hanlon, "Mozambique's Banking Crisis."

[70] Hermele, *Mozambican Crossroads*, p. 42; Hanlon, *Mozambique: Who Calls the Shots?*, p. 220–27 and *Peace without Profit*, pp. 129–31; M. Simpson, "Foreign and Domestic Factors in the Transformation of Frelimo," *Journal of Modern African Studies*, 31, 2 (1993), p. 335.

[71] Bayart, *The State in Africa*, p. 98; J.-L. Amselle, "Socialisme, capitalisme et précapitalisme au Mali (1960–1982)" in H. Bernstein and B. Campbell, *Contradictions of Accumulation in Africa* (Beverly Hills, CA: Sage, 1985), p. 258.

[72] Hanlon, "Mozambique's Banking Crisis."

Financeiras (SCI, Control and Management of Financial Participation Company), and MG to pool their resources in order to invest in new undertakings such as the Maputo Corridor, civil construction, or the brokerage business.[73]

The economic and social lives of elites also intertwine. As elites elsewhere in Africa have done, Mozambique's upper crust has relied on "mechanisms of reciprocal assimilation" to tie themselves together personally and professionally.[74] They are members of social and athletic associations. For example, Armando Guebuza and several other prominent Mozambican businessmen and politicians formed Ngiyana, an association to defend the interests of the Ronga culture and language. Although Ngiyana was practically moribund in 1999, its ethnic identity draws attention to the kinds of networks among the elite that are likely to form in the future.[75] In addition, several of those with military connections belong to a sports club frequented by security and military officers. Members of the sports club also control a company whose objective is to recover property formerly belonging to the intelligence services.[76]

Mozambique is so small that the high-profile entrepreneurs and politicians can be seen dining in the restaurants of their friends. They might choose Umgumi, in which the wife of a top official is alleged to have a share, or Restaurante Sheik, whose owner, Yok Chan, epitomizes the characteristics of the third group. Of Chinese descent, Yok Chan formerly managed several state companies and was the national director of Tourism from 1986 to 1990. He is now on the boards of several companies, is the Chair of the Mozambican Association of Hotels and Tourism, and is a member of the Mozambique–South Africa Chamber of Commerce. As a Ronga speaker, he is also a member of Ngiyana, even though clearly he is not fully Ronga by birth.[77] Thus, this third group of domestic capital is no mere agent to foreign capital, it is one of the cornerstones of the transformation process, "straddling" the boundaries between the local and the global economy, and moving among the economic, political, and social arenas of Mozambique.

Completing the category of domestic capital are thousands of African and Indian shop owners, producer and marketing cooperatives, industrial shareholders, provincial, regional, and local traders, and large farmers. They may own consumer goods stores selling clothes, electrical goods, packaged foods, canned and bottled drinks, school supplies, books, magazines, and newspapers. They may run hotels, restaurants, clubs, and cinemas in the cities and towns or they

---

[73] *BR* (9 April 1997), pp. 268–69; *BR* (5 January 2000), pp. 8–10; *BR* (18 October 2000), p. 1269.

[74] Bayart, *The State in Africa*, p. 150.

[75] P. Machava, "'Ngiyana morreu? Não, apenas está moribunda," *Savana* (8 January 1999), pp. 2–3.

[76] Verdier, *Mozambique – 100 Men in Power*, p. 152.

[77] Oh, how fluid ethnicity is! See Verdier, *Mozambique – 100 Men in Power*, pp. 40–41; *BR* (10 November 1993), p. 648 and *BR* (2 August 2000), pp. 914–16.

may operate hatcheries and flour mills, engage in retail and wholesale trade, or produce copra, tobacco, rice, and wheat on landholdings in the countryside. They may be in the formal or the informal economy or both. They may also form part of a small group of managers, technicians, and workers who have been allocated shares in former state enterprises. Because this group lacks the national political connections or the economic strength of the previous three groups, it justifies a separate category. But members of the group have few social and cultural characteristics in common. They are highly educated or they are barely able to read or write. They are recent immigrants or old money. They have just acquired their property, or they are long-term, loyal managers who now own former state enterprises such as fruit or fishing, or they are established traders whose families have lived in Mozambique for generations. They are urban and they are rural. They depend on the market and are subject to its vicissitudes, but often they are overlooked in the literature on privatization.[78]

The commercial sector contributes most of the members of this category as there are approximately 10,000 licensed traders and thousands of shopkeepers in the country.[79] They are mostly of Indian and African origin. They range from traders who operate on a national level to provincial traders in Maputo or Nampula to the small rural traders who only operate in a few villages. For this last group, the border between what is formal or informal is quite porous, calling attention to the inadequacy of these categories when applied to Africa. For example, it is possible to find goods in Maputo shops that have been brought into the country illegally. It is also not uncommon for shopkeepers to move goods more quickly by dumping them into the informal economy. The mobility and low prices of the informal sector provide an attractive venue for the sale of surplus ironing boards, sheets, extension chords, and clotheslines, from which the formal economy takes a hefty cut. Some traders also find the informal economy handy for the transmission of second-hand clothes, bricks, and even food aid, or whatever item they happen to buy in bulk that week. Yet, whether formal or informal, many members of this group accumulate capital without being connected to prominent politicians.

Given the varying characteristics of domestic capitalists in Mozambique, is it helpful or illuminating to call them a class? Can their interests be readily distinguished from those of foreign investors and are those interests important enough to bring cohesion to a disparate group? The historic circumstances of most domestic capitalists, the policy environment, and the political expressions and objectives of some groups of domestic capitalists suggest the emergence of a national class identity, but cross-cutting alliances and cleavages weaken the chances for a coalescence around something called "national capital."

---

[78] The material presented here is based on selected newspaper and journal articles from *Savana, Demos, Notícias,* and *Tempo* covering the years 1994 to 1998.

[79] World Bank, "Mozambique Country Economic Memorandum," p. 7.

We shall examine the evidence for class formation first. Whether investors are foreign or national, the environment in Mozambique can be discouraging. Unreliable weather, a lack of capital markets, a cumbersome bureaucracy, the lack of incentives to invest, poor infrastructure, and unclear laws on land are among the issues with which all investors have to contend.[80] But national investors also face additional obstacles. The historic circumstances of national capital distinguish it quite starkly from foreign capital. Although domestic capitalists control a majority of the privatized firms, they only account for around 9 percent of the total pledged investment. With the exception of a few large agro-export businesses and large import-export firms, most national investors are concentrated in small and medium enterprises. Nationals' lack of capital, know-how, and technology make it difficult to compete with foreign companies for credit.[81] Their task is not made easier by the fact that banks are reluctant to give credit to small and medium firms where nationals are concentrated because they feel that these enterprises are not financially sound. A survey also confirmed that lack of credit was a big complaint amongst small and medium entrepreneurs.[82]

By contrast, foreign investors mostly have a stake in large enterprises. They invest in businesses with a high return or in areas where they know they will have a monopoly, for example, in cement or in oil refining. Foreigners have capital, technology, know-how, and access to foreign markets which makes investment easier. Banks prefer to do business with them, and governments of their respective countries and international institutions also give them grants and loans. They benefit greatly from these infusions of capital, yet neo-liberals rarely acknowledge the more privileged position of foreign *vis à vis* national investors.[83]

Since the banking system is alleged to discriminate against nationals, government policy has created institutions and funds that aid nationals managerially and financially as chapter 3 discussed. The policy instruments exist because domestic capital has united around issues that distinguish them from foreign capital and they pressure the government to help them. An identity as a Mozambican capitalist class is surfacing in the several national banks and holding companies that have sprung up. Comprised mostly of Frelimo members, they have minority shares in many sectors of the economy. The identity also is manifest in the pronouncements of some nationals, mainly those black Mozambicans who have moved recently from politics to business. For example, Egas Mussanhane, a black Mozambican who is the head of the Private Sector Association of

---

[80] "Mozambique Country Report," Corporate Location (1992) p. 8; MICTUR, *Fourth Private Sector Conference*, pp. 19–24.

[81] "Quem privatiza quem em Moçambique?", *Notícias* (4 January 1995); Egas Mussanhane, director, CREDICOOP, interview, 8 April 1998.

[82] "Onde estão os empresários moçambicanos?", *Notícias* (21 December 1994).

[83] "Estado 'facilita' créditos a empresas estrangeiras," *Demos* (15 April 1998), p. 6.

Mozambique and a founding member of CREDICOOP, the only 100 percent Mozambican-owned bank, readily distinguishes between foreign and national capital in his analysis of the Mozambique economy. He sees two private sectors in Mozambique, one characterized by large firms dominated by foreign capital and the other consisting of small and medium firms run by nationals. He understands that there are some issues that the two sectors have in common and on which they can work together, but he surmises that once these are resolved, foreign capital will readily abandon national capital. He is not against foreign capital *per se*, but he sees a concentration of investors from particular countries rather than a diversification of foreign investors. According to him, "it is important to have an equilibrium of capital in the country." Worst of all, he argues, "No one is thinking of national capital. The main obstacle is that government is not creative in its thinking about how to help national capitalists. To provide support requires an innovative attitude and a desire for national capital to become part of development. Then the solutions are unlimited."[84]

Furthermore, public discourse contributes to the formation of a national class identity through the use of nationalistic rhetoric, arguments about recolonization, the expression of anti-foreign sentiments, and pleas to aid national capital. Newspaper articles ask, "Where are the national entrepreneurs?" and allege that nationals have been left out of the privatization process, or they criticize the sale of a state company to a foreigner for a "trifle." They run interviews with former combatants of the liberation struggle who voice their concerns that the country is being sold to foreigners. The media also publishes complaints by nationals about the apathy of government credit institutions designed to help small domestic industrialists.[85] Clearly, there are differences between foreign and national capital regarding the areas of investment, their financial strengths, access to credit, and treatment by the state that merit attention by the media, by scholars, and by policy-makers.

But if this foreign versus domestic antagonism bubbles to the surface of conversations in the cafes and corridors of Maputo, there are also examples of cooperation between nationals and foreigners, such as that found by Evans in the informatics industry in Brazil. National companies are supplying foreign companies with local materials, or acting as local franchises for multinationals. Domestic capitalists are co-investing with foreign companies in former state companies that have been privatized, such as textile factories, flour mills, breweries, and agricultural toolmaking. They hold minority shares alongside foreigners in new projects such as the Maputo Corridor, tourist complexes, casinos, air transport, fishing, and finance. In the end, it is not easy to identify

---

[84] Mussanhane, interview.
[85] "Privatizar por privatizar será política de desenvolvimento?", *Notícias* (1 November 1996); A. Chiúre, "Artur Vilanculos: As frustrações de um veterano," *Savana* (16 August 1996); "Associações económicas zangadas com o IDIL," *Domingo* (27 October 1996).

readily a domestic capitalist class in Mozambique. References to a "domestic class" may serve as a useful heuristic device in calling attention to the neglect of the range and the strength of domestic capitalists, but they attribute cohesion and unity to a group that is in fact quite disparate and cannot be categorically counterpoised against the "foreign capitalist class."[86] This observation seems to apply to other countries in Africa also. In spite of the eagerness of Berman and Leys to find domestic capitalist classes in Africa, what is most revealing in their study is how fractured the indigenous capitalist "classes" are. In Zimbabwe, for example, this "class" clearly is divided not only by nationality (foreign and indigenous) but also by race (white settlers versus black capitalists), while in Côte d'Ivoire, the foreign capitalists are themselves divided.[87] The point to be drawn from these divisions is that capital configurations in selected countries derive from the particular historical circumstances prevailing in each place.

Capitalism in Mozambique cannot be framed solely as a rivalry between national and foreign capital. Instead there are fragmentations within the two groups and alliances that cut across the national–foreign divide. These fragmentations and alliances are amongst sectors, regions, and ethnic groups. They are between those reaping the rewards of privatization and those groups, such as smallholders and labor, who are suffering its effects. They are between manufacturing and agro-export firms and commerce. They are between north and south, between Indians and black Mozambicans, between manufacturers and consumers, and between owners and workers. They split and fragment but also fashion and unify capital into peculiar configurations. These hinder the formation of a local class that can act consistently or collectively as an engine of capitalist development. At the same time, they call our attention to what may be one of the most interesting characteristics to emerge from transitions, that is, the "recombinatory strategies" that different agents employ to navigate the privatization process. Grabher, Stark, and others, and Stark and Bruszt have detailed how informal networks and associative ties are shaping transformations in distinctive ways in the former socialist countries of Eastern Europe.[88] Below we examine the cleavages and commonalities among social actors that are emerging in Mozambique.

### Sectoral unity and division

Several foreign and national companies in Mozambique have formed alliances between sectors for their mutual benefit. Despite the historic antagonism

---

[86] Migdal, *et al.*, eds., *State Power and Social Forces*, p. 19, make a similar point.

[87] T. Ostergaard, "The Role of the 'National' Bourgeoisie in National Development: The Case of the Textile and Clothing Industries in Zimbabwe" in Berman and Leys, *African Capitalists*, pp. 115–37 and J. Rapley, "The Ivoirien Bourgeoisie" in Berman and Leys, eds., *African Capitalists*, pp. 39–68.

[88] Grabher and Stark, eds., *Restructuring Networks*; Stark and Bruszt, *Postsocialist Pathways*.

between trade and industry, many links between these two sectors exist. For example, Dimac, a national company that trades in construction material, is supplying CIMPOR, the new foreign construction firm. Two domestic import-export distributors, ENACOMO and Gani Comercial, have moved into industry by buying a cashew processing factory, while the domestic trading company, Has Nur, has co-invested with an American company in MOBEIRA, a flour mill in Beira. Other traders have invested in textile factories. Foreigners and nationals are also working together to link vertically Mozambique's vast raw cotton production to the manufacture of textiles. They have renovated a textile factory in northern Mozambique and also undertaken the production of cotton in contract-farming arrangements with smallholders. Such links challenge the notion of a national–foreign rivalry and also illustrate the possibilities for tying together commerce and industry, and agriculture and industry in a country historically dominated by import-export activity.

However, there is also serious sectoral fragmentation. These examples expose the divisions that cut through the Mozambican economy regardless of nationality. First, although the government launched a comprehensive industrial policy in the last few years, commercial interests seem to have the most influence with the Ministry of Industry and Trade (formerly MICTUR).[89] Second, government policies and company practices harm manufacturing and agro-processing industries. The textile and cashew processing industries, which will be discussed in more detail in the following chapters, offer two examples of industries that have been undermined. Customs duties and tax incentives favor the export of raw cashews and raw cotton for processing and use abroad rather than encouraging them to remain inside the country for use by domestic industry. Informal trade in second-hand clothes and unregulated cross-border trade further undercut the ability of industry to compete effectively in domestic and international markets.

### Class and gender struggles in the countryside and the city

If commerce appears to be privileged over industry, both of these sectors are favored over that of agriculture. To be sure, agriculture has received the second most national and foreign investment since privatization began. But this amount represents a fraction of what agriculture is worth, considering that it contributes 33 percent to Mozambique's gross domestic product (GDP), and employs 80 percent of its workforce.[90] The Ministry of Agriculture and Rural Development also does not receive budgetary allocations proportional to agriculture's position in the economy.

---

[89] Odegard, interview.
[90] Mozambique, CPI, 1995, "Investment in Mozambique's Agricultural Sector," CPI Report for Investors (July 1995), mimeo., p. 7.

The reasons for the neglect are not hard to discover. As in the past, the government is experiencing difficulties controlling parts of the countryside. Intra-sectoral clashes that pit domestic agricultural producers against national and foreign wholesalers, retailers, processors, and exporters reveal an emerging class struggle. Smallholders challenge traders and agro-export industries in clashes over prices and land. Land-titling programs and schemes to increase production have neglected smallholders, but as smallholders have always done, they are using their voices and their access to production to challenge unfair practices.[91]

Gender struggles and issues also permeate the countryside. Women participate extensively in agricultural production, undertake most household duties and child care, and comprise a growing percentage of informal traders. Yet rural surveys, credit schemes, extension programs, and private company practices tend to privilege men and neglect the work that women do. Many rural assessments of agricultural output, smallholder income, or even food security assume that the male is the head of household, use male interviewers to gather data, and rely on male informants for information about crops, trees, harvests, and income.[92] Moreover, women participate greatly in cotton production and, in some parts of the country, both receive and keep the income from cotton sales, alone or jointly with their husbands. However, cotton concessionary companies frequently issue to men the cotton cards on which to record the yearly amount of cotton sold and the income received. Donor-assisted extension programs often teach new techniques to men or offer new varieties of crops or trees to men, even though women are largely responsible for planting and taking care of crops. In the cashew trade, licensing practices tend to discriminate against female cashew traders.[93]

Women challenge these attempts to marginalize them from productive activities, control over income, and debates about land. Within households, they have cooperated, negotiated, or fought with their husbands for rights to share or control resources, or resorted to subterfuge against domineering males by hiding money or other assets. In the southern parts of Mozambique where male migration to cities or the mines in South Africa is particularly pronounced, women are extensively involved in the sale of cashews, maize, and other agricultural products and often decide alone what to purchase with their income. Associations such as the Organization of Mozambican Women, which has the status

[91] Chapter 6 investigates the conflicts in cotton and cashew production and processing in more detail.
[92] See M. Pitcher with S. Kloeck-Jenson, "Homens, Mulheres, Memória e Direitos aos Recursos Naturais na Província da Zambézia" in R. Waterhouse, and C. Vijfhuizen, eds., *Estratégias das Mulheres, Proveito dos Homens: Género, terra e recursos naturais em diferentes contextos rurais em Moçambique* (Maputo: Universidade Eduardo Mondlane, 2001), pp. 147–79.
[93] Abt Associates, "Structure, Conduct and Performance of the Cashew Subsector in Nampula Province," draft mimeo. (January 1998), p. 35.

of a non-governmental organization but has renewed links with the Frelimo party recently, aid women to find jobs in agriculture or industry, to start new businesses, or to seek redress against abusive spouses. Donors such as CARE, the Danish and Dutch governments, the Swiss aid agency, Helvetas, and others try to target women in projects such as the construction and repair of local water wells, the processing of sunflowers and sesame seeds, maternity care, girls' education, and the provision of credit for micro-enterprises.[94] Women also use their voices and their feet to protest against unfair treatment by spouses, kin, and companies.

Class and gender struggles extend to the city, where privatization and liberalization have seriously affected workers. As might be expected in a formerly socialist country, many laws exist that acknowledge and protect the rights of labor; trade unions are numerous and well organized in most branches of industry; and the media covers labor issues in great detail. During the privatization process, government officials repeatedly encouraged foreign and national investors to retain Mozambican labor and nearly every investment law refers to the importance of training Mozambican workers. Despite these efforts, unemployment has risen sharply since the adoption of structural adjustment in 1987 and has brought stinging criticisms of the government's handling of privatization from ordinary Mozambicans. Union officials and journalists repeatedly claim that 100,000 workers have been dismissed from their jobs with salaries up to 2 years in arrears, and little or no severance pay, regardless of whether the firm is owned by nationals or foreigners. In civil construction, logging, and mining, 12,000 workers have lost jobs; in transport and communications, the figure is around 30,000. In the cashew processing industry, where women constitute a large percentage of the workforce, approximately 90 percent of the industry's 8,000 to 10,000 workers have either been dismissed or are facing dismissal, or they have not received salaries since 1997.[95]

Notwithstanding assurances from the head of the government body responsible for privatizing the large state companies that "the reduction of the labor force is temporary,"[96] union officials and journalists point to the rise of prostitution, the increase in child labor, and the growth of the informal economy as indicators of the reduction in formal sector jobs. They also emphasize the poor working

[94] "Participação da mulher na ordem dos 30 por cento," *Notícias* (14 April 1998). For a full-length study of issues affecting rural women, see Waterhouse and Vijfhuizen, eds., *Estratégias das Mulheres*.

[95] B. Bango and C. Lopes, "1o de Maio negro para os trabalhadores," *Savana* (1 May 1998); C. Nhancale, "Milhares de operários desempregados-Jeremias Timane de SINTICIM," *Savana* (1 May 1998), and A. Sefane, "Privatizações 'produziram' 30 mil desempregados," *Notícias* (4 November 1997); J. Manjate, "Governo deve clarificar a sua posição sobre o sector do caju," *Notícias* (4 May 1998).

[96] M. Juma, general director of UTRE, quoted in A. Matavela, "O impacto das privatizações," *Savana* (1 May 1998).

conditions and low salaries for those who remain employed, whether workers are in national or foreign companies, and they stress the disparity between the rich and the poor in the country.[97] One World Bank official, when asked about the growing inequality as a result of the privatization policies adopted by the Mozambican government, responded rather complacently: "clearly there is differentiation going on: there are rich elites now whereas everyone was poor together in the 1980s."[98] In the emerging class and gender struggles in the city and countryside, national and foreign capital occupy common ground in their determination to keep costs down at the expense of male and female smallholders and workers.

### Ethnic discord and regional imbalance

Racial, ethnic, and regional conflicts also permeate Mozambique and they dilute attempts at class or national unity. Most of the traders are Indian while export-dependent, agro-processing, and domestic industry owners are white or black Mozambicans or foreigners. As intermediaries, Indians are often in a contradictory position. In the cashew trade, they are resented by smallholders for offering low prices, even though many times the retail traders are being squeezed by the wholesalers on whom they depend for credit during the buying season. In the cotton sector, on the other hand, smallholders appreciate the higher prices offered by Indians. Consumers also prefer to buy cheaper second-hand clothes from Indians than purchase more expensive, domestically produced cloths, or imports of new clothing. Yet many African consumers as well as industrialists view Indians as parasites who undermine productive activities and charge high prices. Some argue that the government protects Indians because of their electoral support for Frelimo. They also charge that Indians discriminate against Africans. These sentiments can be seen in comments made by the president of a small opposition party in a respected weekly paper – "The President of the Republic is totally compromised by the Indians"[99] – and in articles accusing the Indians of racism or of having received their fortunes through drug trafficking.[100]

The increasing number of returning Portuguese and the arrival of many white South Africans are also reintroducing racial tensions within Mozambique after a period in which they seemed nearly moribund. Black Mozambicans accuse

---

[97] Bango and Lopes, "1o de Maio"; J. Manjate, "Despedimentos e salário mínimo na festa do trabalhador," *Notícias* (1 May 1998); Mozambique, GREAP, "Documento final do Seminário sobre o balanço do processo de reestruturação do sector empresarial do Estado," mimeo. (November 1997), pp. 10–11.

[98] Bell, interview.

[99] W. Ripua, President of PADEMO, "Deputado Mogne é racista," *Savana* (2 June 1995).

[100] Foi, "Comerciantes indianos"; A. Elias, "'Indianização' ameaça unidade do islão," *Savana* (30 June 1995).

returning Portuguese of racism and resent their reappropriation of valuable urban and rural properties.[101] Several Portuguese and white South Africans contribute to growing fears by making racist comments about Mozambicans, verbally abusing black Mozambicans in public places, and frequenting shops, cafes, and restaurants that seem implicitly to be for "whites only." Ethnic differences are also emerging, although they are more muted than elsewhere in Africa. While Renamo has been strongly associated with promoting the ethnic interests of several central and northern groups, the issue is not confined to the opposition. Some government officials and prominent Mozambicans are also playing the ethnic card, as indicated by the formation of Ngiyana: apparently, the association arose in response to the dominance of Shangaan speakers in Frelimo.[102]

Added to the ethnic and racial divisions created by privatization are the regional imbalances that privatization has exacerbated. Most of the privatization is located in the south, especially around Maputo. Of the approximately 1,100 investment projects that have been authorized (including new investment and privatized former state companies), 60 percent are in Maputo Province. Maputo Province has also received a majority of national and foreign investment.[103] The development bias in favor of the south is rooted in the colonial period, but it has been reinforced by post-colonial policies and political loyalties. The south is a Frelimo stronghold. The purchase or receipt of property and companies by Frelimo party members in Gaza, Inhambane, and Maputo reinforce their presence in the south. By contrast, the center and north of the country are largely agricultural and Indians dominate the commercial networks. Many provinces lack infrastructure and credit. Their roads are poor, or impassable during the rainy season.[104] The north is also a Renamo stronghold: Renamo won the most agriculturally productive provinces in the country, Zambezia and Nampula, in the 1994 and 1999 elections. These disparities are unlikely to change in the near future.

Taken together, several of the issues may aid class formation or they may be indicators that the making of a united "class" of domestic capitalists in Mozambique is problematic, if not impossible. Unifying and fragmenting tendencies presently interact with each other in a creative dynamic as capitalism consolidates in Mozambique. It is evident that alliances will continue to form across sectors or that foreign and domestic capitalists with state support will dominate increasingly aggressive workers and smallholders. Moreover, alliances between domestic and foreign investors within industries such as textiles and cement, or between sectors such as trade and agriculture, illustrate that

---

[101] J. Massinga, "Não a neocolonização!", *Notícias* (12 July 1995), letter to the editor.
[102] Verdier, *Mozambique – 100 Men in Power*, p. 77.
[103] CPI, "Situação de Projectos Autorizados," pp. 2–3; CPI, "Situação de Investimento," p. 5.
[104] MICTUR, *Third Private Sector Conference in Mozambique* (Maputo: Mictur, 1997), pp. 62, 69.

they have ignored national, regional, and ethnic differences to secure a profit from their investments, much as foreign and domestic entrepreneurs have done elsewhere. But it is equally evident that differentiation and fragmentation will impede elite unity and that struggles in the city and countryside will constrain the state. Though the issues and configurations are different, the Mozambique restructuring experience exhibits similar features to those in Eastern Europe.

## A statist privatization

A key determinant in the eventual outcome of privatization and liberalization policies is the state. It is the matrix through which the sectoral, ethnic, class, and regional alliances and struggles occur in Mozambique. The state facilitates and disrupts linkages among distinct groups of capital, not only foreign and national capital, but also old and new national capital, and white, Indian, and black capital. It contributes to and prevents fragmentation between owners and workers, companies and smallholders, men and women. It generates constituencies and can be sustained or constrained by them. But the Mozambican state goes beyond being a facilitator or generator of capital relations; it is also a key player in the development of the private sector. Besides implementing policies to favor its supporters, the government has made very strategic decisions about which enterprises to sell and which not to sell, and it has formed solid partnerships with the private investors in important sectors of the economy.

The government has privatized much, but what it has **not** privatized demonstrates rather vividly the extent of continued state intervention. The government retains a percentage of total investment. In some capacity, the government is present in almost every major economic undertaking from agriculture to mining to Mozal to the Maputo Corridor. The state still owns and in some cases operates key strategic sectors in the economy such as communications, transportation, and electricity. In turn, many of these strategic sectors also make investments of their own in a dazzling array of companies from cable television to casinos to toll roads.[105] Moreover, the government has formed partnerships with **all** of the major investors: foreign and domestic investors; black, white and Indian investors in industry, agriculture and commerce; investors in the north and the south. It has used joint-ventures as a mechanism to attract much needed foreign capital and as a means for the state to retain a share in large or important industrial or agricultural undertakings. It has purchased minority shares in medium to small companies to aid national capital and to benefit from any profits. Together with the participation of individuals and groups that are or were part of the state and party apparatus, these links make the state a powerful actor in the process of privatization and likely to be implicated in its outcome.

---

[105] CPI, "Investidores," various pages.

There are three tiers of state proprietary intervention in the economy: first, the continued existence of state-operated enterprises most of which are now called "public companies"; second, the investment of these public companies in other companies either in conjunction with other public companies or with private investors; third, direct state participation in joint-ventures where it holds an equal or minority share along with the private sector. In the first tier, there exist state enterprises in which the state has retained majority proprietorship. These companies include telecommunications, electricity, insurance, the railroads, ports, the post office, and the national airline. Their volume of business puts most of them amongst the 100 largest companies in Mozambique. All of these companies are now called *empresas publicas* (public enterprises) and increasingly they have secured strategic private partners or have concessioned services to the private sector, but ownership remains in the hands of the state. Government officials are active on company boards, and major company decisions involve lengthy consultation with the appropriate government ministry. For example, the Minister of Planning and Finance sits on the Board of Telecomunicaçoes de Moçambique (TDM, Mozambique Telecommunications), the telecommunications company, and he chose TDM's managing director. The state has retained most of these companies because they are "cash cows," producing substantial profits for the government, or because they are located in strategic sectors that the government considers vital to the country's sovereignty. In contrast to many of the state companies that were selected for privatization, these companies are in good shape. At least seven of them are among the top twenty companies in the country according to the volume of business transacted.[106] In the cases of TDM and Electricidade de Moçambique (EDM, Mozambique Electricity), for example, the companies are reasonably well run, make their accounts public, turn profits, do not carry too much debt, and are fairly responsive to the demands of those consumers who can pay for their services.

In addition, the government may be reluctant to privatize companies that employ high numbers of workers because it fears the potential political costs of such a move. Consider the Portos e Caminhos de Ferro de Moçambique (CFM, Ports and Railways of Mozambique) the public ports and railways company, which is the largest employer in the country. CFM itself has stated that to be more "efficient," its workforce of around 18,000 has to be pruned to around 6,000 to 7,000 workers.[107] Without a redundancy plan that includes secure employment, however, the addition of such numbers into the already sizeable pool of unemployed labor might court protests that could destabilize the country.

[106] "As 100 maiores empresas," *Metical*, 624 (13 December 1999).
[107] N. Saúte, "There is No Privatisation Without Solving the Problem of the Workers," interview with Rui Fonseca, *Xitimela*, 3, nos. 5/6 (January–December 1998), pp. 18–19; N. Saúte and B. António, "Rationalisation of the Work Force," *Xitimela*, 6 (June 2001), pp. 43–51. Actual numbers of workers vary from 20,000 to 18,000. Here I use the latest figures.

Thus, in spite of rather incessant pressure by the World Bank and international donors, especially the US, to privatize CFM, the state has so far resisted.[108]

State ownership does not mean, however, that public companies are not being run like capitalist enterprises or that management services have not been concessioned out to private companies. The management of CFM repeatedly refers to the necessity of "restructuring" and "rationalizing" CFM so that it makes a profit. The company no longer depends on state subsidies and manages its own accounts. While it has remained under state control, presently it is engaging in "smart partnerships" with the private sector to increase its capital, upgrade its port and rail technology, break into regional markets, and participate in international trade.[109] Like the private sector, it follows macroeconomic trends closely and keeps up with international developments. Similarly, the national telephone company, TDM, has aggressively sought private business partners to upgrade its telephone lines, acquire appropriate technology, expand and modernize its services, and install digital equipment.[110] These activities suggest that state companies have also responded to the "new internationalization" of the twenty-first century. They are increasing market share and becoming more competitive through strategic links with the private sector.

Second, these public enterprises themselves are also prominent investors in the country. They are shareholders in recently privatized state companies and they are extensively involved in new investment, particularly in sectors and businesses that have connections with their own enterprises. For example, TDM has many investments in services and communications. Its subsidiaries are engaged in television and radio services, Internet service provision, and repair of company vehicles. They also have investments along with the private sector in satellites and insurance.[111] Linhas Aéreas de Moçambique (LAM, Mozambique Airlines), the national airline, was slated for privatization but the government hastily withdrew it, claiming that it was unhappy with the bids. However, another explanation for the withdrawal is also plausible: LAM has reported profits in the last few years. LAM is also an investor in the Polana Hotel, one of the finest hotels in Southern Africa, as well as the beautifully renovated Rovuma Hotel. Both are in Maputo.[112] Finally, CFM is also busy expanding.

---

[108] See the CFM magazine *Xitimela* for CFM's position. The donors' position was discussed by Tim Born, Infrastructure division chief, USAID, interview, 2 March 1998 and David Arkwright, deputy chairman, Maputo Corridor Company, interview, 24 March 1998. CFM has not avoided strikes by staying public, see "CFM: Grevistas e administração não dialogam," *Metical*, 1046 (8 August 2001).

[109] N. Saúte, "There is no Privatisation," p. 16 and p. 19; "Smart Partnerships for the New Millennium," *Xitimela*, 5, nos. 8/9 (June 2000), pp. 62–64.

[110] TDM, *Annual Report*, 1998, 1999.   [111] TDM, *Annual Report*, 1996.

[112] "Privatizadas 15 empresas que renderam 16.3 milhões de dólares," *Notícias* (7 April 1998); CPI, "Investidores," various pages. As this book was going to press, *Savana* reported that the Aga Khan Fund for Economic Development had bought LAM's shares in the Polana Hotel, see " 'Polana' nas mãos de Aga Khan," *Savana*, 425 (1 March 2002), p. 24.

Through its new holding company, it has invested in the Sociedade Terminais de Moçambique (STM, Mozambique Terminals Company), the terminal that handles goods coming in or going out of the southern part of the country by road or railway. The investment consists of a joint-venture (50/50) between a Portuguese company, Tertir, and CFM.[113] CFM, along with many Mozambican investors, is also a shareholder in Sociedade de Desenvolvimento do Corredor de Maputo (SDCM, Maputo Corridor Development Company), a company that forms part of the TransAfrica Concession, a consortium of investors that is developing the Maputo-Witbank toll road.[114] Finally, CFM controls 49 percent of the recently privatized Malawi Railways which links northern Mozambique to Malawi. If it seems strange that a public enterprise in Mozambique has purchased part of another country's former state railway company, it is worthwhile to recognize that state companies from other countries are equally investing in Mozambique. Transnet, the national railroad of South Africa, gained the right to manage part of CFM's rail line in southern Mozambique. Investments by public enterprises in one country in projects in other countries cast doubt on many of the objectives behind privatization claimed by the World Bank, but more importantly, they direct our attention to the complexity of investment in a globalizing world. The old polarities of national versus foreign, state versus private sector, public versus private enterprises do not seem to make sense anymore or to reflect accurately the tensions that globalization produces. Domestic, foreign, public, and private investors are seeking strategic alliances that can operate in a competitive, international, and highly technological environment.

Finally, the Mozambican state has remained as a partner in joint-ventures with the private sector in some of the largest and potentially lucrative companies and in medium and small companies too. It has retained a share where there is substantial foreign investment or where the enterprise was in working order at the time of sale, or was considered strategic. To manage these investments, the government is creating an Office for the Management of State Participation (GGPE, Gabinete de Gestão de Participação de Estado) which will oversee state participation in the companies in which it retains a share.[115] Examples of direct participation abound; here I shall just cite a few. In industry, the state has retained a share in many large companies, and frequently in those that have attracted foreign investment. In the cement company, now called Cimentos de Moçambique, the state retains a 49 percent stake alongside the 51 percent share of CIMPOR, the Portuguese investor. In cashew and fruit processing, beer and milk production, and glass and metalworking factories, the government has retained as little as a 15 percent share in some cashew factories to as much as

[113] D. Cumbane, "Novo Terminal rodo-ferroviário," *Fórum Económico*, 4 (June 1998), p. 46.
[114] "CFM Diversifies its Intervention", *Xitimela*, 3, nos. 5/6 (January/December 1998), p. 36.
[115] Mario Guimaraes, consultant, UTRE, interview, 4 March 1998.

45 percent in the Companhia Industrial de Matola, a flour mill.[116] In agriculture, the government has granted concessions to foreigners and nationals and in most cases has retained an equal or minority share in the private company. In other sectors, whether they are recently privatized or contain new investments, the findings are similar. The total pledged investment may be as great as $1 billion or as small as $700,000; it may be in industry or transportation, in hotels or agriculture; it may be with Mozambicans or foreigners, in Manica or Maputo; but the state controls an equal or minority share in select companies.

## Conclusion

In a previous chapter, we traced the means through which the state managed and regulated the privatization process. From the creation of government bodies that handled the valuing and sale of companies to the passage of legislation that aided national investment, the state has used a variety of measures to shape the outcome of privatization. In this chapter, we have seen that state influence and intervention can also be found on the proprietary level. State and Frelimo party officials have received a share of many of the companies that have been sold and they also participate actively in management. They are bank presidents and company directors; they sit on boards of directors and they form consortia. More directly, the state co-participates in many joint-ventures with foreign and domestic capital. Furthermore, it retains large public companies such as telecommunications and electricity. In turn, these public companies invest in other companies. Thus, the state and state companies are visible in almost every sector from agriculture to tourism. State officials are behind the selection of managers and directors, the state appears frequently in shareholder agreements and will soon have its own department from which to manage its investments.

Continued state intervention in the economy simultaneously weakens World Bank claims that privatization has been a "success" and challenges arguments that Mozambique is losing its sovereignty. What these connections reflect instead is the ability of the state to adapt to changing national and international circumstances and to find a number of counterparts (foreign and domestic capital) who share its new agenda. These linkages are what government officials are referring to when they speak of "smart partnerships," and they reflect the state's continuing ability to engage in transformative preservation through legislation, ownership, and institutions. Partnerships allow the state to maintain some control in companies. They offer new and/or domestic capital the chance to gain experience or security, and they allow foreign capital to secure political influence and local knowledge.

---

[116] See UTRE, *Information Bulletin*, 5, 1998.

Yet such a characterization glosses over the demands generated by heterar-chic governance in a less developed country in the twenty-first century. What is occurring in Mozambique is not a "smart partnership" but a troubled al-liance between state and capital that is reconfiguring the economic and political landscape of Mozambique. Partnerships compromise the state's capacity to act autonomously; they reduce the ability of the state to respond flexibly and innovatively to political challenges and threats. As Evans argues, "The new internationalization clearly complicates the politics of state involvement."[117] Local elites shift loyalties to the transnational firms with which they are in al-liance and are not as easily controlled by the state. The state, too, finds that while it may help capital to consolidate, it may also be required to conform to some of capital's dictates. In extreme cases, these dictates can corrupt, even "crimi-nalize" the state, undermining its legitimacy.[118] Creative tensions and unstable coalitions proliferate in this type of environment, endangering both political stability and economic development. In the two chapters on manufacturing and agriculture that follow, I explore these issues in more detail.

[117] Evans, *Embedded Autonomy*, p. 205.
[118] Bayart, Ellis and Hibou, *The Criminalization of the State*.

# 5    Continuities and discontinuities in manufacturing

Industry is the dynamising factor for economic development.

Third Frelimo Party Conference, 1977[1]

Industry must develop a dynamic, modernising role in the economy, stimulating its qualitative transformation and growth.

Ministry of Industry, Trade, and Tourism, 1997[2]

The sale of state enterprises in the manufacturing sector accounts for about half of all privatizations that have taken place in Mozambique. The government has sold breweries, bottling plants, textiles, plastics, and chemical factories. These companies produce mainly for the domestic market but have the potential to export abroad. While Mozambican nationals have purchased the majority of enterprises, foreign investment accounts for much of the value of total investment. It is concentrated in large factories such as brewing or bottling that dominate their respective sectors. In addition, many major new projects that are underway or that have been proposed contain significant foreign investment. As of 1999, approximately $6 billion have been pledged for these projects, and if the investment is fully realized, it will exceed the investment by those companies that have bought existing firms. The new projects include the creation of road and rail transport corridors linking ports in Mozambique with South Africa, Zimbabwe, and Malawi. The purpose of these corridors is to foster free trade zones and to encourage the growth of industry along the route. The government also is promoting iron and steel projects in Maputo and Beira, eco-friendly resorts, and the construction of petro-chemical plants. Of the proposed "mega-projects," only the construction of the $1.3 billion Mozal Aluminum Smelter finished ahead of schedule in June 2000. The rest of the projects await completion.[3]

---

[1] Frelimo, "Central Committee Report," p. 53.
[2] Mozambique, Ministério da Indústria, Comércio e Turismo, "Industrial Strategy Policy," approved by Council of Ministers, Resolution no. 23/97 of 19 August 1997, Government Gazette Series No. 33, 2nd supplement, p. 2.
[3] CPI, "Mozambique Means Business-Mega Projects," 17 July 2001, <http://www.mozbusiness. gov.m2/megapro.htm>.

This chapter explores the structure and conditions of industry following privatization and the adoption of market principles. Relying on general surveys and case method analysis, it investigates former state enterprises that have been sold to the private sector. It analyzes both those that have been rehabilitated and those factories that have collapsed. It discusses the environment in which the formal private sector now works, the obstacles it encounters, and the expectations it has of the state. Equally, I examine proposed new investment and the environmental, social, and economic issues it raises for the Mozambican government and its citizens.[4] I conclude with an analysis of the continuities and discontinuities that characterize the relationship between manufacturing and the state since privatization.

Statistical errors, gaps, and lapses frustrate the study of manufacturing. Reliable data on the value and volume of production, salaries, and employment by individual firms and sectors within manufacturing are poor and difficult to obtain. According to one source, the Ministry of Industry and Trade, which oversees the sector, depends on the voluntary submission of production and employment data by individual companies. Many of them fail to supply the ministry with the information.[5] With most sales completed and many new investment projects in the final stages of negotiation, however, a considerable number of surveys, studies, and newspaper articles have begun to evaluate the impact of privatization on productivity, prices, and working conditions, while other sources have examined the challenges and opportunities faced by the emerging private sector in Mozambique. The World Bank has sponsored several surveys examining the effect of restructuring as well as workers' perceptions of privatization. In addition, several annual private sector conferences have taken place since 1994, and they provide useful information on the outcome of privatization over time. At these events, government officials, representatives from non-governmental organizations and delegates from a wide array of private companies meet to discuss the constraints that the private sector faces and how they can be alleviated. From a more critical perspective, an immense number of newspaper articles have reported on conditions in particular factories with the return to private ownership. Several recent academic works also have called attention to the more deleterious aspects of privatization in Mozambique. Where appropriate, I have relied on this material to analyze the current state of manufacturing. In addition, I use case method analysis to analyze specific firms and sectors. Material for this analysis derives from factory visits, discussions with

---

[4] The chapter does not discuss the informal sector in Mozambique. Although much of it is concentrated in trade, anecdotal evidence from Maputo and surveys in Nampula Province indicate that there is a sizeable informal economy in handicrafts, beer brewing, alcohol distilling, food production, and textile manufacture and finishing. The forthcoming work of Natalina Monteiro and Nina Bowen should give researchers greater insight into how the informal sector works.
[5] Odegard, interview.

management, and interviews with representatives from industry, government, and non-governmental organizations.

Assessments of Mozambique's policy changes usually are careful to note that the changes are too recent to determine conclusively their effects. Nevertheless, two flaws characterize several studies of Mozambique's transition in the industrial sector. First, the studies rest on an assumption that privatization itself is responsible either for the success or failure of a company. They assume that the very act of selling a state company to a private owner can explain its growth or paralysis. Second, several of the studies assume that the state's role with regard to the newly privatized companies already is, or ought to be, minimalist. They ignore the diverse roles that the state plays or might play to alleviate the challenges or expand the opportunities of the industrial sector.[6] Even those studies and articles that are critical of the prevailing neoliberal discourse in Mozambique assume that private agents or the World Bank now control most economic activity and that the national state has little role to play.[7]

I argue that multiple factors account for the current conditions in recently privatized enterprises in Mozambique. In some cases, privatization may correlate with improvements or with bankruptcy, but it cannot be cited as the sole cause of either success or failure. Nor can it be assumed that privatization *per se* automatically creates a market economy. Instead, other factors such as the condition of the state enterprise at the time of sale, the characteristics of a company's buyer, the availability of credit, the market for a company's product, and political and economic constraints and opportunities are also responsible for the situation of a particular company after privatization. Although this argument does not yet receive much attention within Mozambique, research on the emerging capitalist economies of Eastern Europe now commonly asserts that the ingredients for a market economy go beyond mere removal of planning and state control. I draw on the insights of that research in this chapter.[8] I illustrate the factors influencing success or failure in Mozambique by comparing the

---

[6] World Bank and the Government of Mozambique (WB/GOM), "Mozambique: Evaluating the Impact and Effectiveness of the Enterprise Restructuring Program," Preliminary Discussion Draft, July 22, 1996, mimeo.; F. de Vletter, "Privatization and Labour in Mozambique: Worker and Management Perceptions," report prepared for the World Bank and UTRE (October 1996), mimeo.; F. de Vletter, no title, report prepared for the World Bank and Utre (1998), mimeo.

[7] J. Hanlon, " 'O Dono de Moçambique é o FMI' " in D. Sogge, ed., *Moçambique: Perspectivas sobre a Ajuda e o Sector Civil* (Amsterdam: Gemeenschappelijk Overleg Medefinanciering, 1997), pp. 17–41.

[8] See D. Bartlett, *The Political Economy of Dual Transformations: Market Reform and Democratization in Hungary* (Ann Arbor, MI: University of Michigan Press, 1997), chapter 6; B. Eichengreen and R. Kohl, "The External Sector, the State and Development in Eastern Europe," Working Paper 125, Berkeley Roundtable on the International Economy (March 1998); K. Meyer, "International Production Networks and Enterprise Transformation in Central Europe," *Comparative Economic Studies*, 42, 1 (Spring 2000), pp. 135–50.

different outcomes of a selected sample of former state companies that have been sold to the private sector.

Second, I claim that while the state's role has undoubtedly changed with the adoption of neo-liberal policies, it has not become the minimalist state that neo-liberals favor and critics malign. In fact, the directors of both existing and proposed firms have sought out and relied on the state to reduce constraints and expand opportunities for private investors. Unaware of, or unconcerned with, the prevailing orthodoxy regarding the dangers of state involvement, many investors both expect and actively lobby the government to intervene to further their interests. For example, although total manufacturing output has grown following privatization, individual Mozambican firms, like their Eastern European counterparts, confront a legacy of structural constraints that affect business relationships and choices in the present. To overcome constraints such as a lack of capital, a low skilled workforce, the absence of business networks, and poorly developed or volatile markets, capital, particularly national capital, frequently calls on the state for help. Such reliance on the state may be temporary (e.g. related to conditions prevailing at that particular moment) or confined to specific areas (e.g. the education of the workforce), but it calls attention to several concerns. It suggests that neo-liberals have not acknowledged sufficiently the ways in which new economic actors in a transitional economy may actually need the state. Moreover, regardless of the reason, such reliance by private economic actors on the state indicates that the impetus for involvement rests not solely with the state but also with social forces. Again, much of the anti-statist literature tends to neglect the ways in which private actors look to the state for support and for favors: the actions of these private actors thereby reinforce the state's political propensity to intervene. Finally, the range of roles that the state plays, together with some of the enduring structural characteristics of industry in Mozambique, imply that alongside the ruptures introduced by privatization and the market, there runs a certain continuity. Evidence of this continuity surfaces institutionally and ideologically, linking the colonial and early post-independence periods with the present. Scholars have noted similar patterns with regard to the transitions in Eastern Europe which indicates that Mozambique's experience is not unique.[9]

## An aggregate assessment of industry

Following a downturn from 1990 to 1994, industrial production has nearly tripled since 1995. Sectors that have experienced recent growth are mostly low-wage manufactures producing for domestic consumption: food and beverages, tobacco products, textiles, footwear, graphic arts, and chemical products such

---

[9] Hausner, Jessop, and Nielsen, eds., *Strategic Choice*; Stark and Bruszt, *Postsocialist Pathways*.

as soap, detergents, matches, and toothpaste. These sectors account for the greatest share of production in manufacturing and they are the same sectors that contributed so greatly to manufacturing at independence. Together food, beverages, tobacco, clothing, textiles, and footwear account for 79 percent of total manufacturing output and they have seen production increases of nearly 200 percent between 1995 and 1999.[10] At present, manufacturing does not contribute greatly to exports, but that likely will change. With the completion of a new aluminum smelter, aluminum should figure greatly in exports in the near future, alongside the more traditional exports of semi-processed agricultural goods (sugar, cotton, tea, copra), fishing products, especially shrimp, and raw cashews. Mozambique also exports electricity and gains revenue from migrant labor remittances and the transit trade.

Surveys of selected samples of industrial companies support the positive results of the aggregate statistics. They find that the number of paralyzed firms decreased and sales increased after privatization. Sales increases were particularly dramatic in the case of larger enterprises.[11] One survey of 111 companies shows that whereas before privatization approximately 58 percent of the companies were paralyzed or semi-paralyzed, after privatization only 13 percent remained inoperable. Approximately three-quarters of the privatized firms in the sample were active and around 10 percent were being rehabilitated. Productivity increased by 250 percent while real salaries were up by 40 percent within two years following privatization. Employment levels even slightly increased rather than decreased as expected following privatization. However, the number of workers in the sample had decreased by 20 percent in the two years prior to privatization, possibly because individual firms were attempting to be more attractive to potential buyers by "rationalizing the workforce."[12]

Since the results show a positive correlation between privatization and increases in productivity and salaries, the surveys conclude that change in ownership is responsible for the positive increases in productivity and output. As one World Bank/Government of Mozambique survey states, "The present analysis assumes that the observed changes in the performance of the sampled firms were due solely to changes in their ownership structure. It does not take into account possible changes caused by the changing macro-economic environment of the country." The survey's justification for this assumption rests on the claim that "anecdotal evidence suggests that changes in the macro-economic environment

[10] Mozambique, MICTUR, "Balanço da Actividade Industrial Referente ao 1 Trimestre de 1999" (12 April 1999), mimeo., appendices 2–3.
[11] WB/GOM, "Mozambique: Evaluating the Impact," p. 3. A later, slightly larger study of 150 firms found similar results, see World Bank, Regional Program on Enterprise Development, Africa Region, *Survey of Mozambican Manufacturing Firms* (Washington, DC: World Bank, 1998) and WB, *Mozambique Country Economic*, pp. 11–12.
[12] Study cited in de Vletter, no title (1998), p. 4.

have not had a positive impact on the enterprises remaining in state ownership, most of which have continued to decline and many have in fact ceased
production."[13]

For supporters of privatization, these findings offer vindication for their
belief in the virtues of private ownership. Unfortunately a number of serious methodological flaws weaken the claims of the surveys. First, the World
Bank/Government of Mozambique survey finds a positive correlation between
private ownership and increases in productivity. The survey then uses that correlation to assert causation – to claim that privatization alone causes improvements in sales and productivity. The confusion of correlation with causation is
an error of interpretation of the most basic sort and it undermines the survey's
credibility. Second, the survey relies on anecdotal evidence regarding the poor
results by state firms to inflate the importance of privatization to increases in
sales and productivity. It also relies on anecdotal evidence to dismiss competing
explanations for increases or declines. It may be the case that private ownership
is the reason for increases in output, yet without a quantitative and qualitative comparison with a variety of state firms – not just the ones that are doing
poorly but also those such as TDM and LAM which are doing well – that claim
convincingly cannot be made.

Third, privatization has not taken place in a vacuum. It is part of a series of
changes that have occurred over the last ten years. These include the promotion
of structural adjustment policies, the end of the war in 1992, two democratic
elections in 1994 and 1999, and increased regional integration, particularly with
South Africa following its own adoption of democracy. Given the range and intensity of these changes, it is quite plausible that the end of the war, for example,
would have prompted the recovery of many enterprises, regardless of whether
they were state or privately owned. At the aggregate level, asserting a direct
causal relationship between recent improvements or declines in manufacturing
and privatization *per se* would appear to be quite problematic. Most importantly, the changed policy environment that has resulted from the government's
adoption of market principles and its promotion of the private sector has seen
an upsurge in the availability of credit and grants to the private sector from the
World Bank, the African Development Bank, the Commonwealth Development
Corporation, USAID and other granting and lending agencies. Simultaneously,
the government drastically reduced subsidies to state enterprises in the years
preceding privatization. The grants, aid, and advice to private firms, which
were not available to state firms, have enabled many private firms to begin or
resume operations, to purchase new machinery, to increase production, and to
train workers. Yet supporters of privatization often conveniently overlook these
"subsidies" to the private sector when they credit private ownership with the

---

[13] WB/GOM, "Mozambique: Evaluating the Impact," p. 2.

improvements in production and profits. They also fail to recognize that many state companies, however poorly they may have performed during the period of official state sponsorship, were badly neglected during the war and after the government adopted structural adjustment. It seems prudent then to consider the recent improvements and declines in Mozambique's manufacturing sector as the outcome of multiple causes. The methodological resolution to the dilemma is not to assert a direct causal relationship between the sale of a state company to private investors and its improvement or decline, but to treat privatization as part of a set of broader changes within Mozambique's political economy. It cannot be stressed enough that a vital component of these changes consists of subsidies (grants and loans) to the private sector.

Two surveys conducted in 1996 and 1998 by an independent consultant for the World Bank and UTRE employ a broader set of criteria in order to judge the impact of privatization. Rather than examining productivity and sales, they explore workers' **perceptions** of the changes brought or not brought by privatization. They are explicitly comparative and examine working conditions in state versus private companies as well as in nationally-owned versus foreign-owned private companies. These comparisons allow us to isolate more clearly what the perceived effects of private ownership have been. More importantly, the comparisons between foreign and national capital allow us to draw distinctions between different types of private investors and the skills and capital they bring to their companies. Although by no means comprehensive, the findings do begin to expose some of the multiple factors influencing the current practices of companies in Mozambique.

One study was undertaken in 1996 and then a follow-up study of virtually the same population was done in 1998. The sample in 1998 interviewed 1,099 workers – 415 were from state-owned companies and 684 were from privately-owned companies. In turn, the workers interviewed in private companies were split almost equally between foreign-owned and nationally-owned companies. The study examined 65 companies: 23 were state enterprises and 42 were private. For most of the companies, managers, workers, and trade union representatives responded to questionnaires. The majority of the firms in the sample were in manufacturing, but it also included companies in agriculture and fishing, trade, transport, construction, and other sectors. Most of the companies were located near the southern capital of Maputo, but the survey also selected a very small number of companies in Chimoio, Beira, and Quelimane, cities in the center and north of Mozambique.

The studies explicitly recorded workers' perceptions of privatization, rather than the actual effects of the change to private ownership. The questions not only asked workers what they thought about privatization, but also asked them to comment on their levels of satisfaction with regard to a broad range of issues including management, salaries, benefits, productivity, and equipment.

Asking about particular areas of firm activity allowed for comparison and cross-checking with the more general answers about privatization. The study also cross-checked workers' answers to questions about working conditions against the responses of management to the same questions. Moreover, the surveys followed virtually the same sample population over a two-year period so it was possible to measure changes in company performance and in workers' perceptions over time. Unfortunately, the reader is not told whether this working population was male or female, but indirect remarks suggest that most of those interviewed were male.

An examination of the failure rates for companies between the initial survey and the follow-up study offers the first indication that privatization alone does not explain performance. In the two-year period between the first and second study, approximately 15 percent of the initial sample population of 101 companies were either paralyzed or nearly paralyzed by 1998. The percentages of the state-owned versus privately-owned companies that had collapsed or nearly collapsed during the two-year period were 17 percent and 14 percent, respectively. The figures for state firms refute the anecdotal evidence used by the World Bank/Government of Mozambique study regarding the collapse of state firms. In fact, the rates of failure in the sample nearly were similar for state versus private firms.[14]

At the aggregate level, the 1998 survey revealed that workers' perceptions of the conditions in state versus private firms did not diverge that greatly. Workers in both state and private firms complained about low salaries and inadequate safety measures. Contrary to what one might expect, most of the state workers thought that privatization would be "good" and most of the private workers thought it had been "good," but both groups feared for their future and thought retrenchments would surely take place. Differentiating the data into state versus private firms, and the private firms into foreign versus national companies, yields a more complex picture of company performance in Mozambique. In the state enterprises, workers held contradictory and rather surprising positions about working conditions and management. On the whole, the majority of workers responded that state companies were undercapitalized, had poor equipment, bad management, and did not work to capacity. They complained that salaries were too low and that safety measures, such as protective clothing, were not adequate. The answers support evidence from other sources such as newspaper accounts and interviews cited in previous chapters regarding the inadequate financial, physical, and administrative conditions of state firms. However, contrary to what might be expected, most workers expressed satisfaction with the degree of

---

[14] de Vletter, "Privatization and Labour" and no title (1998). Below I discuss in detail the findings from the 1998 survey. I want to thank Fion de Vletter for allowing me access to the data, and I want to stress that the interpretation of this data is my own.

regularity of salary payments, their hours of work, their holidays, and the overall working environment. Most workers felt that management treated them well, tolerated trade unions, and were sensitive to workers' needs. These responses challenge the common portrayal by neo-liberals of state companies as either mechanisms for rent-seeking by state elites or in a state of paralysis.

Regarding privatization, a majority of those who worked in state enterprises expected that privatization would bring new injections of private capital – just as neo-liberal supporters argue. But slightly less than half also expected retrenchment in the event of privatization of their company, and about one-third simply did not know whether management, or working conditions, or salaries, or worker-management relations would improve. They also did not know that they were eligible to participate in Employee Share Option Schemes in the event their companies were privatized. These schemes allow workers to buy shares in a newly privatized company, and the government has touted them as evidence that it is not selling off Mozambique's assets completely. Yet few of these schemes seem to be fully operational.[15] Most workers in the survey were unaware of how the schemes work, who is eligible to participate, or how they are administered. To summarize the responses of workers in state firms: they criticized conditions in state firms, but they were not wholly dissatisfied with their working environment. They were unsure or unclear about what privatization offered and they did not know that they could participate in their companies through share purchase.

The responses of workers in privatized firms justifies the doubts expressed by state workers about the impact of privatization. About 48 percent of workers in private firms reported that they thought privatization was "good" but just over a third of them thought it was "bad." Although many reported that their companies increased production and made profits, slightly under half feared for their company's future. A majority reported that the working environment was the same or worse than before, and that plant equipment, access to protective clothing, the quality of management, and relations with management were also the same or worse than previously. These responses do not suggest that privatization has provided substantial and positive changes, at least from the workers' points of view.

When asked about their particular situation, just over half of those interviewed thought that they were worse off personally than they had been before. Over half reported that their salaries were the same or worse than before, as was the regularity of the payments of their salaries, holidays, and general benefits. For about 20 percent of workers, some benefits that state enterprises used to

---

[15] Exceptions are Vinte/Lam, the scheme for LAM workers, "Airline Sale to Go Ahead," *Mozambique INVIEW*, 109 (16 May 1999), p. 1 and GETCOOP, the scheme for workers in EMOSE, *BR* (12 April 2000), pp. 370–72.

provide such as transport to and from work, food, training opportunities, and sanitary assistance have ceased in the private firms. Thus, from the workers' perspectives, privatization has not produced significant improvements in their salaries or working conditions. Such a situation may be part of the economic reality introduced with privatization, but it may bring political costs for the government.

Assessing the impact of privatization becomes more complicated once the private sector is broken down into foreign versus national investors. The privatization process has generated a lot of controversy in Mozambique over the relative merits and weaknesses of foreign-owned versus nationally-owned firms. The findings of the 1998 study for the World Bank and Utre reinforce a generally held perception that foreign-owned companies in Mozambique are better capitalized and better equipped than domestic companies, but they give a dismal picture of worker-management relations in both foreign and domestic firms. As I do, the 1998 Utre Study uses a broad definition of domestic capital and labels a company "domestic" if it is a former colonial company with a majority of its capital in Mozambique, or if Indians or black Mozambicans own it, wholly or in the majority. According to the survey, an absolute majority of workers in foreign companies answered that both the volume and quality of production increased following privatization. By contrast, less than half of the workers in national companies thought that productivity rose in national companies, and only one-third thought that the quality of production improved. Furthermore, about 40 percent of workers answered that the machinery in foreign-owned companies was better or much better than it was before privatization. Only 21 percent of workers in nationally-owned companies argued that the machinery was better than before.

With regard to working conditions and relations with management, however, the differences between foreign-owned and nationally-owned companies narrowed. Although management in both national and foreign firms asserted that improvements had been made in many areas, workers disagreed. They responded that salaries, bonuses, and holidays were the same or worse than before privatization. A majority of workers in national and foreign firms also stated that the extent to which companies paid salaries on time was the same or worse than before. Moreover, just because companies were called Mozambican, that did not inspire their managers to provide educational support, training on the job, better food, more transport, or higher salaries for workers any more than foreigners did. In addition, being a national company did not mean that management was better or more available to listen to workers' complaints, or more just when it dismissed workers. In all of these categories, workers in both national and foreign companies felt that conditions were worse than before or stated that some provisions had been dropped all together. Finally, one-third of workers in both nationally-owned and foreign-owned companies responded that relations with management were worse or even much worse than before. One-third of workers in nationally-owned companies, as opposed to one-fifth in foreign-owned companies, said that relations with managers improved with privatization.[16]

By and large, whether companies were nationally-owned or foreign-owned, whether they were highly capitalized or operating on a shoe string, their owners appeared to act like what they were, capitalists. To make a profit, both nationals and foreigners trimmed the "fat" such as transport, training, and meals at work. Both tried to get away with what existed before by paying the same salaries, keeping the same working hours, and allowing the same holiday time for workers. Management may have improved in one-third of the private companies, but in most cases it was the same or worse than during the state-run period according to workers. Given these negative responses, it is surprising that privatization has not been more politically explosive. The reasons may have to do with the timing of retrenchments, the weakening of trade unions, and the way the government marketed privatization.

In some cases, the government reduced employment *before* companies were privatized, thus new owners have avoided potentially explosive confrontations with remaining workers. Once enterprises were privatized, the entity with legal responsibility to those workers dismissed from state firms became unclear. Workers found it difficult to make demands for employment or back wages against an enterprise that no longer legally existed. Several sources have put the total number of workers dismissed due to various reasons at 100,000 by 1996 or about a 40 percent reduction in the workforce from peak levels of employment. Further retrenchments have continued since 1996 as privatized firms have rationalized their work forces, changed the structure of their businesses, or collapsed.[17] Moreover, the severance of their long alliance with Frelimo has weakened trade unions, and other political parties have not offered viable political avenues for worker grievances. Furthermore, in the beginning, the government carefully crafted a message that stressed the economic benefits of privatization, alluded to sacrifices that had to be made, and promised to defend the rights of workers. Into the early 1990s, it delivered this message in an uncertain economic climate. Perhaps these factors dissipated more

[16] The discussion above was based on de Vletter, no title (1998), pp. 14–27 and appendix, "Empresas privatizadas."

[17] That retrenchments preceded privatization is supported by the surveys discussed above and by trade unions. See Forum de Concertação Social, "Desempenho da economia durante o ano de 1995: Posição do movimento sindical," mimeo. (22 April 1996), and J. Manjate, "Despedimentos e salário mínimo na festa do trabalhador," *Notícias* (1 May 1998). On continuing retrenchments see A. Matavela, "O impacto das privatizações," and C. Nhancale, " 'Milhares de operários desempregados'," *Savana* (1 May 1998). For examples of worker complaints against old state firms, see "200 trabalhadores reclamam o seu dinheiro," *Domingo* (1 March 1998) and "Nampula," *Tempo*, 1435 (2 May 1999).

sustained and organized responses by workers to what was a clear pattern of restructuring.

The aggregate information from these sources calls attention to how the private sector operates and what privatization brings to Mozambique's industrial sector. The sale of existing manufacturing firms to private investors and the proposed new major projects certainly indicate that the policy environment for the industrial sector has altered profoundly in the last few years. New owners with new management styles, increased investment in particular zones of the country, reductions in employment levels at existing units, and individual efforts to respond to the demands of global and regional markets indicate that the structure of manufacturing has changed. Several of the companies purchased by foreigners have increased the quantity and quality of production, in some cases way beyond the output of the former state enterprise. As in Eastern Europe, some foreign-owned factories in Mozambique are better financed and equipped with more modern machinery than those run by nationals, but that should not be surprising. Many foreign investors possess more capital than national investors, particularly Africans. Furthermore, foreigners have been able to purchase (wholly or jointly) larger factories that were in better shape at the time of sale. They have purchased companies that the state prioritized so their initial starting point is stronger than that of the small and medium companies that the state neglected and that most nationals have purchased. Once foreign investors make improvements to some of these large factories, they are more able than nationals to capture greater market share, as they have done in many countries in Eastern Europe.

### From the general to the specific: a look at sectors and firms

The aggregate data suggest that output has increased but it gives little insight into the constraints and opportunities that companies confront. Sectoral and firm-level data such as interviews, factory visits, and newspaper articles reveal in more detail the diverse outcomes of privatization. Moreover, they expose the multiple factors that may be contributing to these outcomes. In the first category are the "success" stories, where companies function efficiently and production is rising. This is the outcome that supporters of privatization so often project. In a second category exist companies that appear to have been purchased for speculative purposes. Speculators rob them of their remaining equipment, selling it off piece by piece or using it for scrap. They then convert the remaining shell to a warehouse for imports of clothing or food. Last, there are the unfortunate firms. Some firms in clothing, wood furniture, rubber tires, the production of industrial chemicals, and other manufacturing sectors face stiff competition from cheap imports or the informal sector. In other sectors, companies remain paralyzed or they produce way below capacity. Many of these companies have old or broken equipment and new owners lack the liquidity or the interest to make substantial, but necessary investments. Of the firms that Mozambicans have purchased, for example, "less than 20 percent of the money pledged by nationals has actually been paid," indicating that like state firms, some private firms are strapped for cash.[18] As a result, although the industrial sector as a whole is growing, particular sectors such as metal working or individual firms such as those in plastics or glassware are experiencing slow growth, stagnation, or decline.[19]

I examine first the performance of former state companies that were sold to private investors and are doing well. Many of these contain a majority of foreign capital and most of them face very little competition. Because the Mozambican economy is so small, one or two companies tend to dominate each sector. Positive results for one company in a sector can often explain why the entire sector is doing well. I illustrate some of the features of the privatizations by examining the Coca-Cola franchise and several breweries that dominate the beverage sector; Topack, a company that has great market share in the plastics sector; and Sabrina, a finishing company in clothing.

Foreign capital comprises the majority of the shares in Coca-Cola, Cervejas de Moçambique (Mozambique Beer, which has a factory in Beira and one in Maputo), and Topack, yet in each case the government has retained a percentage. As proponents of privatization might expect, these companies have added new machinery or made additional investments. All three have bought new equipment and interestingly they produce for the domestic market. Thus they depend on general improvements in the rest of the economy in order to do well. Coca-Cola has been celebrated as a shining example of the benefits of privatization and it epitomizes the well functioning, privately-owned firm.[20] Formed in 1994, the company is a joint-venture between the Mozambican state and the South African Bottling Company (SABCO), which has the franchise to make all Coca-Cola products. One of its plants is located just outside Maputo on the site of one of the production units that belonged to the former state bottling company. Following the purchase, SABCO made substantial investments in new machinery in order to increase production capacity and to expand the product line. Between 1994 and 1997, sales increased by about 400 percent. Moreover, its workforce has increased from 76 employees at the time of the sale to around 280 persons now working three shifts.[21]

Cervejas de Moçambique also has been hailed as the great success story of privatization in Mozambique. It consists of two breweries, one in Maputo and one in Beira that were sold by the state in 1995 for a total of $14 million to a Dutch subsidiary of South African Breweries.[22] Production tripled only one

---

[18] de Vletter, no title (1998), p. 4.    [19] MICTUR, "Balanço," appendix 3.
[20] Baloi, "Privatizações são das mais."
[21] "Mozambican Demand is 100 million Litres Per Year," *Investir*, 0, 3 (November, 1997), pp. 1–2.
[22] UTRE, "1998 – Consolidating the Gains," p. 7.

year after privatization and may have increased more had retailers passed onto consumers the benefits of a sharp tax cut in the price of beer which took place at the beer company's insistence. Throughout the 1990s, production continued to increase: sales in the first trimester of 1999 were 14 percent above the same period in 1998.[23] The company was one of the first enterprises in Mozambique to issue shares for sale on the Mozambique Stock Exchange.[24]

Other companies such as Topack, a plastics company, share some of the features of Coca-Cola and the breweries. Topack is one of five privatized companies created out of the former state plastics company. It is the largest of the five and the last to be privatized, but presently it is the only one in full operation (another factory got implicated in a drug scandal in early 2000).[25] Just prior to privatization Topack was nearly in ruins. Workers had sold or appropriated any easily transportable materials to compensate for the state's failure to pay their salaries. Most of the machinery was obsolete and had to be sold for scrap metal when the factory was privatized. The company had 11 drivers but no cars. Since privatization the new owners have reduced the workforce from 180 workers to 130 and would like to further reduce it to 80 workers. Purchased for around $700,000, the new owners have made major investments in the company including a $1.5 million investment for a machine that makes plastic crates. They have reorganized the production process and productivity has shot up.[26]

The company makes every kind of plastic imaginable for Mozambique's domestic market, from the distinctive green and white sacs emblazoned with the symbol of the Polana Hotel to the yellow and red sacs of Shoprite, Southern Africa's version of Sainsbury's or Safeway. They make plastic buckets for carrying water and collecting cashews; crates for holding beer and soft drinks; and containers for oil and vinegar, or milk, or gasoline. And just recently, they purchased a new machine that will make plastic medicine bottles for Mozambique's pharmaceutical industry. This purchase apparently dovetails with a government decision to raise tariffs on imports of plastic containers which has sparked some criticism. According to Petropharm, a pharmaceutical company, Topack lobbied the government to raise tariffs on imports of plastic containers in June of 1997 to protect the domestic plastics industry. Newspaper accounts claim the increase in tariffs from 7.5 percent to 35 percent jeopardized

[23] "Beer Tax Cut," *Mozambiquefile*, 241 (August 1996), p. 23 and MICTUR, "Balanço," p. 6.

[24] *BR* (2 February 2000), p. 113.

[25] In February 2000, several national newspapers and international journals reported that police had seized 300 kg of methaqualone powder (used to make Mandrax) from Plasmex, another one of the privatized plastics factories. Plasmex is owned by the Mozambican government (20 percent), Andre Timana (30 percent) and Jacinto Nhamoneque (30 percent), though only an international journal identified the owners. It is not known whether they have been charged or not. See M. Vesely, "Africa – Highway to Drug Hell?", *African Business* (April 2000).

[26] Joaquim Campos d'Olivieira, Administrator, Topack, interview, 7 June 1999, Maputo; and *BR* (6 September 2000), pp. 1038–104. The state retains 20 percent.

Petropharm because it made prohibitive the cost of importing plastic containers for pharmaceuticals.[27] But the protection appears to have encouraged Topack to invest in the manufacture of medicine bottles inside the country. The case is illustrative because it reveals some of the emerging conflicts within the private sector and the need to build better linkages among private companies within Mozambique. It shows that protectionism can lead to investment and it demonstrates that the government can effectively respond to the demands of private capital. All of these observations run counter to the logic of neoliberalism.

The final example is a clothing company, Sabrina, that is performing well, but where difficulties persist and the future looks uncertain. Unlike the other companies we have featured, its ownership is mostly national capital and it produces for export. Sabrina used to be part of the state-owned clothing company called Soveste. Soveste consisted of four garment finishing units located in Maputo, all of which were sold between 1994 and 1996. A group of Mozambicans bought Sabrina and foreign participants account for a small percentage of ownership also. It produces good quality shirts and school uniforms mainly for the South African market, supplying retail outlets such as Tie Stop, Woolworth's, Dunns, and Edgars. Since privatization, sales have climbed steeply and it has the capacity to expand even more. It employs approximately 400 workers, many of whom worked for the company when it was state-run. The majority of these workers are females who make around $50 a month which is considered a very good wage for Mozambique (as of 1999). Although there is no on-site creche for children, the company does provide basic medical care and a subsidy for transportation. Company management maintains good relations with the union and at present there is a spirit of collaboration among workers and directors in the factory.[28]

Yet, Sabrina also illustrates vividly the challenges of doing business in Mozambique. Second-hand clothes inundate the Mozambican market and their low cost undercuts the price of locally produced goods. In some instances, the avoidance of customs charges by traders decreases the price even further. As in the rest of Africa, the practice has become so widespread that even in the most remote rural areas of Mozambique, consumers may purchase a pair of used Dockers or a dress by Erika at the local market. Without a viable market for its finished goods in Mozambique, Sabrina must therefore produce for the intensely competitive export market. Presently it has only managed to break into South Africa, although other markets may open up. For example, it is rumored

---

[27] "Industriais queixam-se de elevados custos de produção," *Notícias* (6 March 1998).
[28] B. Langa, "Sul-africanos sustentam indústria de confecções," *Domingo* (29 March 1998); Factory visit and interviews with Abdul Azziz, administrator; Américo Magaia, administrator; Frank Roomer, manager, Sabrina, 10 June 1999.

that American textile manufacturers want to take advantage of Mozambique's low cost of labor to produce for the US market.[29]

Although the low cost of Mozambican labor makes Sabrina an attractive competitor in the South African clothing market, nevertheless, it struggles against huge obstacles. The lack of industrial development in Mozambique makes the company extremely import dependent for all of its inputs. To make the shirts and uniforms that are its specialty, the company must import every component that goes into the final product, everything from the bolts of cloth that the buyer favors, to the scissors that cut the cloth, to the sewing machines that female Mozambicans run all day to fashion the shirts and uniforms, to the irons that press them. The shirts' buttons and the thread used to sew them on are imported, as are the plastic collar inserts that keep the collar stiff, and the pins that hold the shirts together neatly in their imported plastic bags that go into the imported boxes in which the shirts will be shipped to their destination in Johannesburg. Even the floor supervisor is imported from Hong Kong, because he has the skills and training to understand the whole operation from start to finish. In the end, what makes Sabrina competitive is the low cost of Mozambican labor. It is a reminder of the limits of globalization. Borders are not now so porous nor workers so mobile as to make meaningless the cost of labor in one country versus another. But the business is very cutthroat even with low labor costs. Bureaucratic red tape at customs and overcrowded roads to the market in Johannesburg threaten Sabrina's comparative advantage. According to one of the administrators, even a delay of twenty-four hours loses business.[30]

While factories such as Coca-Cola, Topack and Sabrina are doing relatively well, success in a particular factory's traditional area of specialization is not guaranteed by any means nor even sought after in some cases. In the second category of companies are those that have been privatized but whose new owners are quite consciously and deliberately reneging on agreements or not even using factories for their intended purpose. The new owners of this category of companies operate them on a shoestring, or use them for the purpose of speculation. They strip the company of its remaining assets; they "de-industrialize" in order to make money. Later they may turn any remaining buildings into warehouses. According to Madalena Zandamela, a trade union secretary, some prospective owners win the bid to purchase a new company knowing full well that they do not have the money to buy it.[31] Moreover, some new owners are "individuals without capital, parasites lacking management capacity and competence," and they are ruining companies throughout the country.[32]

---

[29] W. Shoulberg, "Levi Stress," *Home Textiles Today* (8 March 1999).
[30] Langa, "Sul-africanos sustentam" and factory visit, Sabrina.
[31] Bango e Lopes, "1o de Maio."
[32] J. Timane, general secretary of the National Sindicate for Civil Construction, Timber and Mining (SINTICIM) quoted in Nhancale, " 'Milhares de operários'."

Some owners may run the factory as before but renege on agreements they made at the time of purchase. In one example of a factory in Maputo that makes plastic shoes, workers accused the new owner of violating agreements he made to pay back wages and to provide technical training when he bought the factory. They said that the new owner avoided these commitments, using the income from sales to purchase things for himself. When asked about these irregularities, the new owner replied that "I take the money that I want from the business, because the business is mine."[33] Although this practice is not illegal, it does indicate that despite agreements at the time of sale, owners can sidestep their responsibilities, even when they have the money to honor them.

In other cases, unscrupulous owners use the factory's assets to enrich themselves and regressively restructure their factories by asset stripping. According to the secretary general of SINTICIM, the trade union for workers in construction, timber, and mining,

These individuals use the last resources the enterprises have to buy BMWs, Mercedes, and to construct and furnish their houses. And, after using up the money that the companies have, they transform them into warehouses for selling "roupa de calamidades" [disaster relief clothing donated to Mozambique but then sold to Mozambicans], avoiding the responsibilities they agreed to during the bid.[34]

The story of failed commitments or de-industrialization is repeated all over the country in Manica, in Zambezia, and in Nampula. In Nampula some former factories now store and sell second-hand clothes. Ironically, one of these establishments is on the same road as a dormant, but well-equipped, textile factory. In Manica, workers at one beverage plant suddenly found they were without work because the new private owners had failed to honor the commitments they made during the process of privatization. In Manica as well as Maputo, the government has repossessed companies in order to keep them running and to send a message to other companies that speculation and noncompliance will not be tolerated.[35]

Finally, there are quite a large number of companies that have been bought that operate poorly or have collapsed. They run the gamut of the manufacturing spectrum from flour mills to furniture factories and, like the previous category, they can be found in every province. They differ from the second category in that their decline is largely owed not to intentional sabotage but to pre-existing or emerging economic conditions that thwart their efforts (though the line is blurred). In 1998, the General Secretary of Mozambique's national union put the

---

[33] C. Nhancale, "Novo patrão acusado de desvio de fundos da sua própria empresa," *Savana* (6 June 1997), p. 2.

[34] Timane quoted in Nhancale, " 'Milhares de operários'," p. 3.

[35] "Privatisation Nears Completion," *Mozambiquefile*, 247 (February 1997), p. 7; Arnold Sowa, privatization specialist, World Bank, Washington, DC, interview, 26 June 1997.

number of companies that were not doing well at around 243. Of these, around 40 were completely paralyzed.[36] These companies may have been former state companies that, at the time of privatization, had obsolete or broken equipment, huge debts, and salaries in arrears which the sale contract then stipulated had to be paid. At the time of purchase, the private owner was then faced with enormous responsibilities, not only to pay the purchase price but also to make investments and to pay workers. According to a spokesman for GREICT, the government body responsible for privatization of firms in industry, trade, and tourism, "These privates can't manage to pay everything. Many times they don't pay salaries. The state tries to arrange payment but after the sale, it can't control the situation."[37]

The textile industry illustrates the challenges. Although the industry was among the first to be privatized, only one firm in the south is fully functioning. Many other firms are paralyzed throughout the country and their workers have received no pay for years.[38] For example, after receiving some private investment from Portugal in the early 1990s, the Texmoque factory in northern Nampula Province is still not working.[39] When operational, the factory will employ 1,000 workers and have the capacity to produce 1.2 million square meters of textiles. Yet, from the point of production to the point of sale, the factory must overcome hurdles that so far it has not managed to resolve. The cotton it needs for its 20,000 spindles must be available and of the right quality, but Nampula Province exports most of its considerable cotton crop to foreign markets where it receives a better price and brings in foreign exchange. Assuming cotton were available, it must be constantly tested and classified to make sure it is of the right quality for Texmoque's spindles. Even if the factory were to restart production, not only would it face competition from second-hand clothing but also it would pay high transport costs to ship cloth to the south of the country. Consumers are more numerous in the south and have greater buying power, but poor and inconvenient roads in Mozambique hinder north–south trade and drive up costs. The company could export, but cheaper Chinese and Indian cloth undercut that option.[40]

The collapse of a factory is all the more noticeable as one moves away from the relatively prosperous southern capital of Maputo to regions where opportunities to work are extremely limited. In these areas, collapse can provoke political conflict with workers who have lost their jobs and send provincial governors and industrialists hurrying to Maputo to ask for assistance. In Manica Province alone, nine of thirteen state-owned companies that were sold in the

[36] "243 empresas privatizadas estão numa situação de crise," *Notícias* (4 May 1998), p. 6.
[37] Raimundo Matule, economist, GREICT, Maputo, interview, 17 April 1998.
[38] Langa, "Sul-africanos sustentam," p. 13.
[39] G. Gauth, "Governo empenhado na recuperação da indústria textil," *Notícias* (3 June 1998).
[40] Factory visit, Texmoque, Nampula Province, 4 May 1994.

province collapsed, throwing hundreds of people out of work. One of them, a furniture company, had actually been refurbished following privatization and was functioning. It then shut down when the owner was unable to secure new credit and could not repay loans.[41]

## Demands on the state and the state's capacity to respond

Regardless of whether individual companies are successes or failures, all of the private sector encounters tough conditions in Mozambique, just as the private sector has faced challenges in the former Soviet Union and in other parts of Africa. Over the past few years, successive private sector conferences have referred to the myriad difficulties of doing business in Mozambique, from the red tape and expense of obtaining visas for foreign investors to the high cost of securing credit for national investors. The country's weak infrastructure, poorly trained workforce, complex legislation, and "archaic" bureaucratic practices at customs increase the costs of production. For example, the representative of Cervejas de Moçambique (Mozambique Beers) noted in 1996 that "each import involves, on average, fifty pieces of paper, processed through ten offices, and handled by fifteen people."[42] Although many customs operations have now been subcontracted to a private company that has streamlined procedures, investors continue to criticize corruption, processing delays at the borders, and excessive bureaucracy.[43]

Moreover, no matter how "efficient" the private sector is, it cannot overcome the disparities between doing business in the relatively well-developed capital of Maputo and trying to conduct it in the more isolated regions to the north. Post-colonial practices have only reinforced the favoritism that was shown towards the south by successive colonial administrations. Maputo houses all the national governmental offices and has tarred roads that connect it to nearby South Africa, good communications, and a fairly reliable supply of electricity and water. Most businesses in the Maputo area have telephones, faxes, and email. Their workers are better educated and more skilled. It shares a border with South Africa and has access to the market there. These features stand in stark contrast to those that characterize some of the northern cities. Up north, Nampula city's roads are notorious for the number of potholes they contain. Outside Quelimane, capital of Zambezia Province, the roads quickly turn to dirt, sand, or gravel which makes them quite impassable during the rainy season. Training centers for workers are few and far between, and sometimes the

---

[41] "Privatisation Nears Completion," p. 7.
[42] C. McDougall, "Prospects for the Foreign Investor: A *Cervejas de Moçambique* Perspective," Paper 11 in Mozambique, MICTUR, *Second Private Sector Conference in Mozambique* (Maputo: Cowling Davies and Associates, 1996), p. 55.
[43] Mozambique, MICTUR, *Fourth Private Sector Conference*, pp. 19–24.

only communication between the larger cities and towns and the countryside is by radio. Plans might be underway to exploit Nacala's claim as the best natural deep-water harbor on the east coast of Africa, but that has not prevented resentful remarks that "the team that designed the project lives in Maputo."[44] Indeed, in the last few years, those private investors who have ventured north of Maputo, even those who have settled in Mozambique's second-largest city of Beira, have discovered what Mozambicans from the Limpopo to the Rovuma rivers have known since colonialism: that the north has great agricultural and industrial potential, but successive governments and investors have proved unable or unwilling to take advantage of it. For those projects and companies that have sought to tap the potential, the risk is high. Failures, which are common, have dramatic consequences on local populations because there are so few alternatives. Thus the collapse of a large timber project or a cattle farm or cashew factory can leave hundreds of people destitute.

When investors and representatives of international institutions discuss solutions to these impediments to doing business in Mozambique, they invariably allude to the role of the state. For some the cause of the problem is simple: too much government. And a simple solution follows: get the government out of the economy. Speaking at a private sector conference in 1998, Simon Bell, the resident senior financial economist for the World Bank resorted to pop psychology to analyze the challenges facing Mozambique and how they could be solved. He argued that what was needed was a change in "mentality": "we need to stop being constrained by Mozambican reality and start **'thinking outside of the box'**" – a "box" being psychology's current metaphor for destructive patterns of behavior. For government, his example of **"thinking outside of the box"** was that:

The hand of Government on the private sector must be light – and we must continually challenge and review the role and function of the Government in private sector activity. What this means in practice, for example, is that the Government should move well beyond FIAS's Red Tape Study of Bureaucracy in Mozambique, to stop tinkering around the edges and start setting totally new rules of the game.

To set the new rules of the game, he exhorted government to "start **thinking outside of the box** to create an environment which is conducive to the achievement of a strong and sustained private sector in this country."[45]

Therein lies the recurrent paradox of World Bank prescriptions. They advocate a minimalist state **and** a conducive business environment. Government is condemned for being too involved and encouraged to withdraw. Anything short

---

[44] Mozambique, MICTUR, *Fourth Private Sector Conference*, p. 51.
[45] S. Bell, "Four Years of Private Sector Conferences: Where Have We Come From and Where Do We Still Have to Go?" in Mozambique, MICTUR, *Fourth Private Sector Conference*, p. 41. The boldface and use of capitalization are his.

of setting totally new rules of the game is criticized as dysfunctional behavior. Then government is called on to create a favorable environment for business. Yet creating such an environment requires the capable state institutions that minimalist prescriptions proscribe.

Interestingly, many investors in Mozambique instinctively seem to know that a minimalist state is not the answer. Although most investors join the World Bank in criticizing the heavy hand of the state, they call for a much greater role to be played by government than do World Bank representatives. At a conference on the private sector in 1998, investors sought greater dialogue between the public and private sectors, more government promotion of business opportunities, and concerted efforts to reduce the barriers to doing business in more isolated parts of the country.[46] These requests require more than a minimalist or passive state; they require state institutions that actively oversee and regulate private sector behavior. They require a state with regulatory capacity – a custodian, to use Evans' term – so that it can prevent customs irregularities and other corrupt practices that businesses and not just government officials engage in. Moreover, those northern regions that present real challenges to the unfamiliar investor require a state in order to bring industry into being and to give it every encouragement to consolidate and thrive.

Minimalists will observe that Mozambique does not begin to approximate the Weberian bureaucratic ideal and to sanction any kind of state involvement is to reinforce the clientelistic and personalistic behavior that is so commonly associated with states in Africa. Indeed, we have already seen how government officials and Frelimo supporters have used their access to the state to secure factories and farms. But the politics that characterize African states will not be eliminated by hobbling the state with only a minimal amount of involvement in the economic arena. Stripping the state of its capacity will simply drive personalism and clientelism underground. It will create a more sinister type of "embeddedness" than the one that might be achieved by recognizing that the state needs to be involved in development. Continued state involvement will certainly satisfy political objectives of the Frelimo party and that may actually be what government officials intend when they speak of a "partnership" with the private sector. A partnership allows Frelimo to reward its own and to build a new constituency of supporters. But institutionalizing different types of state involvement, such as partnerships or regulatory committees, also forces the state to be more accountable. A *bona fide* "partnership" makes state actions visible, while regulatory commissions show the state in the role of overseer and expose political machinations and favors. These types of involvement reveal in different ways and in various venues the capacity and authority of the state. If the state performs these roles well, it may build political legitimacy. If it does

---

[46] Mozambique, MICTUR, *Fourth Private Sector Conference*, pp. 47–49, p. 55.

not, at least there is an identifiable institution against which social forces can mobilize for change.

Some might object that, so far, I have really focused on the privatization of former state companies. These were already quite run down when the government sold them and they may have deteriorated too greatly to be rehabilitated, private owner or not. Moreover, their "pre-existing" conditions hobble them from the start and, in fact, they may require a more active state simply because they are still coping with unresolved issues from the previous period of state intervention. It is thus incumbent upon the state to at least resolve some of these difficulties before withdrawing to a more minimalist stance.

With new investment, however, it could be argued that one is able to see how a good investment climate and a minimal state can pay handsome dividends. New investment and new proposals might offer examples of "thinking outside of the box." New investors start with a clean slate: they do not inherit poorly trained workers or a deteriorating plant or bad debts. They can determine their own plant capacity, borrow the money they require, and train their own workforce. In Mozambique, several new major projects are underway, other ambitious proposals are in the pipeline, and the potential the country offers generates much excitement among local and foreign investors. Among those projects under construction or consideration are Coca-Cola bottling plants in the center and north of the country, an aluminum smelting plant near Maputo, and a series of transport corridors. Investors have planned two iron and steel projects in the south and center of the country, while others have positioned eco-tourist developments and game parks along the coast and in the interior of the country.

If the upward trajectory of Coca-Cola's fortunes are any indication, these new projects may bring considerable benefits both to Mozambique and to their owners. The positive results from its bottling plant outside Maputo prompted Coca-Cola, with the **state as partner**, to build two other bottling plants: one in the country's center and the other in the far north near Nampula which has just been completed. The company has already invested $45 million and expects to invest up to $85 million in the coming years. The plant in the center of the country has a capacity to produce around 4 million crates of soft drinks per year and employs around 165 workers. Expected to open shortly, the plant in Nampula will be the largest one in the country. It is expected to produce about 6 million crates of soft drinks per year and employ 200 workers.[47]

Another new investment that is generating employment and promises to have great multiplier effects on the rest of the economy is the newly completed aluminum smelter outside of Maputo. Referred to as the "talk of the town" by the CPI in Maputo, it tops the list of the "mega-projects" already constructed

[47] "Investimentos da Coca-Cola atingirão 85 milhões de dólares," *Notícias* (11 June 1999), p. 13; "Mozambican Demand," pp. 1–2.

or under consideration in Mozambique. Its shareholders are Billiton of the UK with 47 percent, the Industrial Development Company of South Africa, a South African governmental corporation that aids private sector investment, with 24 percent, Mitsubishi of Japan with 25 percent and the Mozambican government with 4 percent.[48] Total investment was projected to be around $1.3 billion (the largest in the country) but at its completion (six months ahead of schedule in June 2000) it came in at $100 million under budget.[49] When fully operational in 2001, the company expects to produce earnings of about $400 million per year on sales of aluminum to markets abroad and to employ about 900 people.[50]

Mozal is not an isolated investment. Instead, its creation is linked to the development of the Maputo corridor, a grandiose series of networked projects revolving around road and rail links between South Africa and Mozambique. The scheme includes public and private investment from the two neighboring countries, from the region, and from the rest of the world. It includes a commitment to improve infrastructure and proposals for new investments in tourism, mining and energy, industry, and agriculture on both sides of the border. For Mozambique, these projects include a $1.1 billion proposed iron and steel plant, the rehabilitation or construction of several tourist complexes near Maputo, petro-chemical plants, and electricity.[51] Although the Maputo Development Corridor gets the most attention and has progressed the farthest, corridors are also proposed for Beira and Nacala. Like the Maputo Corridor, they are integrated schemes linking together infrastructural improvements in the region with developments in tourism, mining, manufacturing, and agriculture.

These new projects reinforce the need for a state that can calculate the social costs and benefits of a proposed undertaking. They require also a state that can enforce judiciously rules and regulations regarding employment practices, tax payments, land use, and the environment. Several of the new proposed developments have already raised serious questions for the government with regard to their opportunities and drawbacks. For example, a viability study of the Maputo Iron and Steel Project forecast that it will bring about 1,200 jobs to Mozambique and contribute around 8 percent to the GDP, but only *after* five years are spent recovering the initial expenditure. The company will have to import most of the materials for its construction, it will have to relocate and disrupt approximately 2,000 households, and it is unlikely that the investment will create many upward and downward linkages with the rest of the Mozambican economy. Moreover, it is projected that the Maputo Iron and Steel Project "could consume more than

[48] *Mozal News*, 1 (December 1998), p. 3.
[49] "Final Results – Part 1," *AFX News Ltd.* (29 August 2000).
[50] J. Walker, "Maputo's Aluminum Plant Set to be a Winner," *Sunday Times Business Times* (17 May 1998); *Mozal News*, 1, p. 1.
[51] David Arkwright, deputy chairman, Maputo Corridor Company, Johannesburg, South Africa, interview, 24 March 1998; "Maputo Development Corridor," 1998, mimeo.

four times the current industrial water consumption in Maputo" and place heavy demands on the water supply. Wastewater from the plant may also seriously disrupt fishing in the Maputo Bay. These findings have caused alarm among local populations that may be affected, and they have looked to government to address their fears.[52]

Furthermore, the aluminum smelter project illustrates that government involvement was necessary even after approval was granted. With construction underway, demands on government accelerated, not declined. The capacity of the Ministry of Industry and Trade was so tied up with the day-to-day details regarding Mozal that the ministry had little time for anything else. First, both the ministry and provincial government mediated a number of labor disputes and land conflicts at the construction site and continue to do so now that the company is beginning production.[53] Second, Mozal's demand for engineers prompted an "internal brain drain" in the country so that many other companies lost engineers. Perhaps the "market" could have responded to the shortage, but at present there are no private engineering schools in the country, only an underfunded, understaffed public institution. Third, Mozal's use of heavy trucks tears up the roads near the site. Since the roads are not expected to be privatized, the Ministry of Transport and Communications must fix them.[54] Fourth, mounting concerns about environmental effects, the use of the Maputo port, and other issues prompted the formation of an Inter-Ministerial Committee led by the Ministry of Industry and Trade and five other state institutions. The committee discusses and monitors company matters on a regular basis.[55] Once other mega-projects materialize, no doubt these demands on government capacity will intensify.

New projects in developing countries also need aid and encouragement from state institutions to bring them into being and on-going support as they get established. Almost all of the proposed mega-projects include participation from the Mozambican government and the South African government, not only because these states hope to gain something but also because companies feel reassured by state participation. With regard to the Maputo Corridor, at least three Mozambican government ministries are involved in the coordination of road and rail links with industrial and mining projects. On the South African side of the border, government institutions engage in planning, but they are also providing financial assistance to investors. With regard to most of the mega-projects, the Mozambican government has granted tax breaks and established

[52] GIBB Africa (Pty) Ltd., "Draft Findings of the Environmental Impact Assessment for the Maputo Iron and Steel Project (MISP)," May 1998, pp. 37, 126–37.

[53] S. Nhaca, "Governo atento a eventuais conflitos com as populações," *Notícias* (24 February 1998); "Strike Fears at Mozal Factory," *Indian Ocean Newsletter* (11 November 2000).

[54] Odegard, interview.

[55] J. Rungo, "Governo e empresários cada vez mais próximos," *Domingo* (5 April 1998).

industrial and commercial free zones where investors benefit from reduced customs duties on imports.[56] One news report noted with regard to Mozal that its "profitability is dependent upon the numerous fiscal advantages given by the Mozambican government and the low cost of electricity used by the factory."[57] For new small and medium businesses, the government has additionally instituted funding programs.

Company directors acknowledge the aid that government provides even if they are also aware of its drawbacks. Just prior to construction, representatives from those companies that control the majority of shares in Mozal praised the "invaluable help and encouragement which they had received from the beginning" from the Mozambican government, and they profusely thanked the governments of Mozambique and South Africa when the project was completed.[58] The managing director of Coca-Cola equally realized the importance of government, even though he was irritated with some aspects of government involvement. With the state as a partner, Coca-Cola built a new bottling plant in Nampula. The company manager pointed out that having the state as a partner was frustrating because there were often bureaucratic delays and "the state has often more pressing priorities than investment in industrial and distribution activities."[59] But Coca-Cola's managing director also held his partner accountable, and he had certain expectations from the state. He stated that Coca-Cola and other businesses in the north were appealing to the government "to recognise that the future of the country and its people is irrevocably linked to the economic potential and development of the north of the country."[60] Recognition included a governmental commitment to reduce the historical imbalances between the north and south of Mozambique.

At the end of the day, whether one is talking about the privatization of former state companies or new investment projects for road and rail, or steel and iron, or hydroelectric power, lurking beneath the surface is the role of the state. The discussion is not **if** the state should be involved, but as Evans has stated, **"what kind"** of involvement it will be. Sales of former companies to private capital or new investment in mega-projects illustrate different types of state involvement – from a mediator and regulator to a promoter and facilitator of investment. Some of the intervention has caused delays, spawned corruption, served personal and political goals, and hindered production, but these will not disappear by dismantling the state. Further, minimizing state involvement means minimizing the kinds of state intervention that can be helpful to society and to development generally. These interventions include policing the environmental impact of a

---

[56] G. Mavie, "Construção da Mozal começa em Julho próximo," *Notícias* (16 May 1998), p. 7.
[57] "Strike Fears at Mozal Factory."
[58] Mavie, "Construção da Mozal"; "1st Aluminium Produced," 18 June 2000 <http://www.mozal.com>.
[59] Mozambique, MICTUR, *Fourth Private Sector*, p. 47.     [60] *Ibid.*, p. 47.

company's operation, monitoring negotiations between management and labor, protecting the land-tenure rights of local populations, and taking a comprehensive approach to the **national** as opposed to the regional or local impacts of particular projects. Such actions invariably restrict the maneuverability and even profitability of individual companies. But private investors seem to expect some of the other sorts of state involvement, such as working together with industry to realize an investment or providing an advantageous business environment. To perform these roles the Mozambican state needs resources, better training, higher salaries, and the streamlining of bureaucratic procedures. Although it seems to be making a huge effort to court and satisfy the private sector, state capacity is stretched.

### Conclusion

The success or failure of a company following privatization cannot be attributed simply to the sale of a former state company to a private owner. The outcome of a firm's privatization is intimately linked to national and global economic trends. It depends on multiple factors such as the condition of the plant and its assets prior to the sale, the motivations of the new owner, access to credit and inputs, national and global market conditions, and the type of state involvement. If Coca-Cola illustrates the best case scenario, then the sale and subsequent paralysis of a furniture factory in Manica Province represents the worst case. In the case of Coca-Cola, a foreign company with ample resources and much experience, bought a plant in relatively good condition to produce soft drinks for a growing market. State institutions were transparent and supportive of the undertaking. Profits and production rose.

The failure of the furniture company in Manica Province represents the other extreme of privatization. Despite the sale of the state company to a private owner and the owner's commitment to restructuring, the factory still collapsed. A lack of credit and the inability to repay loans forced the owner into bankruptcy. The company's location in the central part of Mozambique probably explains why banks were reluctant to grant loans and why the government was less helpful than it has been to grand projects, such as Coca-Cola and Mozal, located near the capital. Thus, the impact of privatization in manufacturing has been marked by contrasts. Some sectors flounder while others flourish. While some companies see their profits rise, others are paralyzed. These examples suggest that privatization in manufacturing has not been the "success" story that the World Bank has claimed.

Moving away from individual companies to consider the aggregate effects of privatization on manufacturing, the findings are revealing. Both change and continuity characterize manufacturing today. There is now a greater desire for regional integration and an interest in investments that will link countries in the region. Export-led development that was previously based on agricultural processing has now shifted to include the products of heavy industry such as aluminum, iron, and steel. Environmental considerations weigh heavily in decisions to allow or prohibit the construction of an industry. The promotion of corridors brings us a little closer to the realization of the borderless world advocated by proponents of globalization.

There is also a noticeable break from the period of state-run companies, when the private sector was suppressed. From a state that once hobbled opportunities for private accumulation we now have a state that hastens it. Before, the state intervened to produce shovels and bricks, shirts and soft drinks, to run funeral parlors, and to operate shoe stores. Now in telecommunications, electricity, and transport, it may still plan, invest, and produce, but it does this in association with private sector actors, and it must now take into account the demands of the market. In other arenas such as textiles and beverages, it polices and promotes, encourages and occasionally begs, but it is not a producer or competitor. Instead, Mozambicans of all ethnic backgrounds are the investors, sometimes alone but often in partnerships with foreigners. These foreigners are not the Russians and Romanians of the 1980s, but South African, British, Portuguese, and other investors responding to the "marketing" of Mozambique conducted by the Center for Investment Promotion.

More dramatic institutional ruptures may still occur, but there are also great structural and ideological continuities in Mozambique that are worth remembering. The structure of manufacturing has not changed greatly since the 1970s. The food and beverage sector still accounts for 30 percent of industrial output in the country, followed by textiles, clothing, and footwear. There is some heavy manufacturing of metal and chemical products that are also remnants of late colonial development. As in the past, most industries in Mozambique depend greatly on imports. Similarly, certain ideological predilections endure. Like governments of the late colonial period and the immediate post-independence period, this government espouses high modern principles. As many of its predecessors did, it has a penchant for grand schemes that promise to transform Mozambique and Mozambicans. In fact, certain ideas have been around so long that they provoke cynicism and disgust. One disgruntled Beira businessman at the Fourth Private Sector Conference in 1998 remarked that he wished people would stop talking about the Beira corridor being "new" as it had been discussed for at least 100 years. The same observation could be made about the iron and steel projects.

Unfortunately, except for the talk about corridors in Nacala and Beira, most of the projects are centered around Maputo, as in the past. Maputo has received the bulk of investment and probably will continue to do so. There is also continuity in the kinds of political considerations that businesses must make when doing work in a developing country. In Mozambique, as in many other countries in Africa, political interests tend to be intertwined closely with economic objectives when the pie is small. The government uses economic rewards to dispense patronage, and punishes its enemies by withholding economic opportunities. Investors must adjust to these exigencies if they expect to do business, but when they do so, they sometimes perpetuate them. Some efforts to focus on the accountability of business and not just on the accountability of government must be undertaken if this climate is to change. Finally, there is a continuity of forgetting those on the ground and a continuity of resistance from those forgotten. Attention to these "mega-projects" ignores or forgets the contribution that local knowledge or local craft industries can make. The neglect of local concerns parallels the contempt of officials for local input during the colonial period and during the period of communal villages and state-run companies. But just as before, domestic social forces are helping to shape the outcome by demanding inclusion in decisions that affect their future. This time, they challenge a government that some of them have elected to represent their interests and that, in the next election, they could quite conceivably vote out of office. These continuities and discontinuities reflect the historical character of the developmental process and draw our attention to the constraints and opportunities that attend its every step.

# 6    Capital and countryside after structural adjustment

Privatization and liberalization in agriculture and agro-processing have been protracted and highly contentious. Investors express frustration at the numerous barriers that confront them once they are outside of the capital, larger cities, and towns. As state planners discovered just after independence, poor infrastructure and communications can lead to critical delays in the supply of necessary inputs such as fertilizers and pesticides, and equally can thwart the timely export of cotton or maize. Poor or inadequate governmental presence in the provinces can stall the completion of the necessary paperwork for exports and imports and force company managers to travel to Maputo, thus increasing the cost of doing business. Conflicts with other companies or with rural inhabitants over land, prices, or output may languish for years in overstretched local tribunals, or may be resolved by the local application of the "might is right" doctrine.

Yet it is in many of the more remote provinces that one finds Mozambique's prime agricultural areas. Nampula and Zambezia in the north are responsible for producing some of Mozambique's major exports, including cotton, cashews, sugar, tea, and copra, and for supplying the domestic food market with maize, rice, peanuts, beans, and fruit. To those investors willing to bear the risks, the possible returns on their investments can be substantial. Agricultural output has been growing steadily since the peace accords in 1992 and demand for cashews, maize, and sugar is high.[1] Even with devastating floods in the south of the country during early 2000, newspaper accounts predicted a good agricultural year for the rest of the country. The potential offered by agriculture thus attracts interested investors, in spite of the risks.

This chapter argues that the impact of the return of capital to rural Mozambique is broader and more complex than neo-liberal partisans and their detractors suggest. As neo-liberals might expect and recolonization critics fear, reforms in agriculture and agro-processing are redefining the role of the state. Privatization and liberalization have constrained the ability of the ruling party to shape economic policy and have allowed powerful private actors to dominate particular sectors and to determine patterns of production. Yet, state interests

---

[1] Mozambique, Ministry of Agriculture and Fisheries, "National Program," p. 27.

have not completely receded. In the case of joint-ventures in cotton, the government has tried to use privatization to gain badly needed political legitimacy on the local level and to create a new constituency of supporters for its economic agenda. As it has done with other strategic sectors, it has retained a percentage of the ownership in order to gain economic benefits and to exercise control over the actions of the emerging private sector. For example, although the interaction between the government and cotton interests has been too problematic to be called a "smart partnership," it has drawn attention to the different configurations that can characterize a market economy. By contrast, the cashew industry has illustrated the potential hazards involved in privatization and liberalization. There, conflicts of interest between and within the state, the private sector, smallholders, and workers have produced policy incoherence, institutional paralysis, and devastating economic results.

The process of capitalist penetration in agriculture has been more uneven and diverse than either neo-liberals or recolonization critics anticipated. All of the emerging capitalist enterprises seek profits, but they have pursued different investment and production strategies to meet their objectives, and they have interacted with the state administration in discrete ways. In addition, local communities have developed distinct responses to the government's privatization policies and to the actions of particular companies. Assorted strategies and responses suggest that the restructuring of agriculture and agro-processing has had a varied impact across regions and that multiple state institutions have had to juggle constantly the diverse interests of the countryside.

## From nationalization to privatization

The sale of state enterprises in agriculture (including fishing) has accounted for approximately 20 percent of the total number of enterprises privatized in the country as of 1998. The value of investment in agriculture and agro-industry (which equalled around $550 million as of 1997) occupies a distant second behind the value of investment in industry which stands at about two billion dollars (excluding Mozal). Investment in agriculture and agro-processing is approximately evenly split between foreign and national investors if the state's share of investment is included in the total figure. Top foreign investors have been Lonrho of Great Britain followed by Portuguese and South African investors. They have invested in the agricultural production and processing of cotton, sugar, tobacco, maize, and cashews for the domestic and export markets. The on-going rehabilitation of sugar also brings Mauritius into the pool of foreign investors. Mauritian investors have spent approximately $70 million to renovate the former Sena Sugar Estates' factories in Sofala and Zambezia Provinces. Regarding national investors, João Ferreira dos Santos, the Madal Group, and the Entreposto Group emerge as the major players with investments in cotton, timber, tea, and copra. Smaller national investors have interests in timber, tobacco, cotton, livestock, and chicken hatcheries.[2]

Since the state continues to "own" the land in Mozambique, "privatization" in this context means the right to use land over a period of time and the right to own any fixtures or capital equipment that are included in a sale or placed on land once a contract is signed. Where agricultural activities such as cotton or tobacco production involve relationships with hundreds or thousands of smallholders and require large investments, the state has preferred to establish joint-ventures with companies, although outright sales to investors do occur. In joint-ventures, investors usually have a controlling interest alongside the state. The state's contribution to the partnership consists of the equipment, infrastructure, and land (sometimes as much as 200,000 hectares) of an old state farm. If the joint-venture is a cash cropping enterprise such as cotton or tobacco, the state often grants monopolistic-monopsonistic buying rights over family sector households that produce these crops. In cotton, the government has joint-ventures with both prominent domestic companies such as João Ferreira dos Santos and the Entreposto Group and foreign companies such as Lonrho. Similar arrangements also characterize sugar, tea, or copra in provinces such as Zambezia or Maputo, although many of the privatizations in these areas have occurred more recently. The dominance of Madal in Zambezia Province virtually insures that the government will both cater to it and supervise it. In tea, the government has sold off parts of the state tea company, EMOCHÁ, to several foreign investors and to a company with which it is intimately acquainted, João Ferreira dos Santos.

The production arrangements for cashews are somewhat different and lately they have caused much controversy. Possibly because cashews are also food crops, contract farming arrangements have not characterized its production. Moreover, alone among the agricultural export crops, cashews can be exported raw without processing. Until recently, Mozambique has added value by processing raw cashews in factories that are located near the most productive cashew areas, mainly Gaza and Nampula Provinces. During both the colonial and socialist periods, successive governments protected the processing factories with restrictions and high tariffs on raw cashew exports, thus vertically linking the production, processing, and export of cashews. Policy reforms during the 1990s severed that link. The government relaxed restrictions on the export of raw cashews, breaking the integration between production and processing. The reforms both exposed and created opposing interests that clashed over whether to trade raw cashews or to process them. Some of these interests include the same powerful agricultural companies that are in cotton or sugar. They are not

[2] Mozambique, CPI, "Investidores"; "Local Sugar on the Shelves Again," *Mozambique INVIEW* (16 March 1999), pp. 9–10.

only involved in trying to increase the production of cashew trees, but also they trade and process cashews. They are thus implicated in the controversy over the future of the cashew industry.

Those state enterprises that exhibited the greatest potential for lucrative returns thus have gone to politically important domestic investors and to foreign and domestic investors with access to capital. The state also has concessioned smaller areas of prime agricultural land to former or current national and provincial government officials, Frelimo party members, returning Portuguese settlers or their descendants, and ordinary Mozambicans. All together, private individuals and companies have requested approximately 4 million hectares throughout the country.[3] While state agencies have favored entrenched and powerful interests, they have been slow to give individual title to smallholders, have rarely divided state farms into smaller parcels, and have not financed worker buy-outs. Where a particular sector such as sugar or copra requires substantial investments, moreover, state institutions have kept competition in that sector to a minimum.[4]

Although as a whole Mozambique is not a densely populated country, authorizations of land in the more arable parts of the country have prompted a number of land conflicts with local residents. In the peri-urban zones around Maputo, Beira, Quelimane, Nampula, and other towns, *deslocados* (dislocated people) from the war who may have arrived as many as 15 years ago, and residents who are native to the area, have found that the government has conceded land they have been farming for over a decade to a former Portuguese settler, or a government official, or a white farmer from South Africa. Within irrigated areas or within regions suitable for cotton, tobacco, and maize growing, new titleholders have moved in, shunting aside rich as well as poor smallholders. In the south of Maputo Province, smallholders complained that a large eco-tourism project encroached on their lands and interfered with their ability to use water, to obtain medicinal plants, and to occupy sacred forests for their ceremonies.[5] Meanwhile, in Zambezia Province in the north of Mozambique, approximately 300 to 400 smallholder families were embroiled in a conflict with the beneficiaries of the parcelization of the Zambezia Company. In a peri-urban community outside of Quelimane, residents complained in 1998 that, without even consulting them, the Zambezia Company sold land on which they have been growing rice for over a decade. Some residents saw their crops plowed under to make

---

[3] For the reason behind this figure, see M. Pitcher, "What's Missing From 'What's Missing'? A Reply to C. Cramer and N. Pontara, 'Rural Poverty and Poverty Alleviation in Mozambique: What's Missing from the Debate?'," *Journal of Modern African Studies*, 37, 4 (December 1999), p. 703.

[4] Myers and West, "Land Tenure Security" and Myers, *et al.*, "Appendices."

[5] "Blanchard acusado de usurpação de terras," *O Popular* (12 May 1999). The government has revoked the concession owing to the death of the investor.

room for other uses of the land, or they were told to leave, while others waited anxiously to find out what would happen next.[6]

The debate about land control is often framed as a conflict between foreigners and nationals. Foreigners have certainly benefitted from government land allocation but, as pointed out above, one of the ways that Frelimo has taken advantage of privatization has been by rewarding its own supporters with land concessions. Renamo also apparently privatized land under its jurisdiction in the early 1990s in order to reward its backers.[7] In reality, the land conflicts are rooted in complaints about the fairness and the transparency of current allocation procedures. And desire for land is historically grounded in a perennial insecurity about economic survival as well as dynamic cultural interpretations about the symbolic meaning of land. Local and national government officials have granted land concessions (with use rights for a period of fifty years given to large companies) without consulting or acknowledging the rights of local communities and individual producers to have access to land. As a result, smallholders feel insecure about their tenure and are reluctant to make investments in land about which they feel uncertain.

Furthermore, land policies and practices often disregard the cultural and economic connections that women have with land. Current land titling practices disproportionately favor men, because title-granting agencies discriminate against women and/or women lack the means or the information to request titles. Moreover, participants in debates on land reform either have assumed that customary practices are rooted in patriarchy and therefore that "tradition" discriminates against women, or they have overlooked women's active participation in agricultural production and household decision-making. They have misinterpreted or ignored customary practices that enable women to have access to land, and they have not acknowledged the ways in which women have negotiated and continue to negotiate land rights.[8]

Through a number of non-governmental organizations such as the Rural Mutual Aid Association and the National Union of Peasants, smallholders have actively resisted state and private sector maneuvers to take their land.[9] They

---

[6] "Camponesas protestam e prometem lutar pela sobrevivencia," *Savana* (14 November 1997); *muene*, Dona Ana, Quelimane, Zambezia, interview, 25 May 1998 (with Scott Kloeck-Jenson); smallholder Dona Ana, Quelimane, Zambezia, interview, 25 May 1998 (with Scott Kloeck-Jenson).

[7] Myers, "Segurança e conflito," p. 19.

[8] H. Gengenbach, " 'I'll Bury You in the Border!': Women's Land Struggles in Post-War Facazisse (Magude District), Mozambique," *Journal of Southern African Studies* 24, 1 (March 1998), pp. 7–36; M. Pitcher, "Conflict and Cooperation: Gendered Roles and Responsibilities within Cotton Households in Northern Mozambique," *African Studies Review*, 39, 3 (December 1996), pp. 81–112; Waterhouse and Vijfhuizen, eds., *Estratégias das Mulheres*.

[9] Fieldwork (with Scott Kloeck-Jenson), Mutange, Zambezia Province, 20–27 May 1999; Janet Assulai, legal advisor, Associação Rural de Ajuda Mútua (Rural Mutual Aid Association), interview, Maputo, 19 May 1998.

even won some concessions in the 1997 Land Law, such as the requirement that "local communities" be consulted before commercial companies or individuals acquire land.[10] However, defining who belongs to a community, where the community geographically begins and ends, and who will take decisions on behalf of the community pose enormous difficulties. In addition, the 1997 Land Law has several weaknesses that may undermine women's access to land. First, although the law claims that women have the right to land titles and the right to inherit land, there is as yet no mechanism to insure those rights are respected. Second, in its deference to local communities, the law may have undercut local informal and gendered approaches to resolving land conflicts.[11] Nevertheless, the existing law represents a significant improvement over earlier drafts that gave little consideration to local needs and practices.

Once again, in Mozambique, as in the rest of Africa, the countryside is the locus for struggles over policy, resources, and power. In the rest of this chapter, we examine the restructuring of the cotton sector and the controversy within cashews in order to illustrate concretely the constraints and the potential generated by the privatization and liberalization of agriculture and agro-processing. The debates taking place within these two sectors also reflect the fragmentation within government as well as the tensions among government departments, donors, and an array of social forces within Mozambique.

## The creation of joint-ventures (JVCs) in cotton[12]

### Impact on revenue and efficiency

The majority of Mozambique's population engages in small-scale agricultural production as its main economic activity. Smallholders provide 75 percent of the agricultural output in the country and it is among smallholders that recovery must occur if Mozambique is to achieve economic and political stability. Of those who are involved in agriculture, around 250,000 smallholders depend for their major source of income on the sale of raw cotton to ten large cotton processing companies.[13] The way in which the government has privatized and liberalized the cotton sector therefore has far-reaching implications for hundreds of thousands of family sector producers. Furthermore, the outcome of changes in the cotton sector reveals some of the constraints and opportunities that other agricultural sectors likely confront.

---

[10] Lei 19/97 (1 October 1997).    [11] Gengenbach, "'I'll Bury You in the Border!'", p. 36.

[12] Parts of this section on cotton are drawn from a longer article of mine, see Pitcher, "Recreating Colonialism or Reconstructing the State? Privatisation and Politics in Mozambique," *Journal of Southern African Studies*, 22, 1 (March 1996), pp. 49–74.

[13] Mozambique, Conselho de Ministros, "Estrategia para o desenvolvimento de algodão," 30th Session (22 September 1998), p. 2.

As legal entities, many of the private cotton companies have been in operation for about ten years, though JFS has been managing part of the former cotton state farm of Nampula in the Namapa area since 1986. The situation is still quite fluid and, because world prices of cotton keep dropping, it will probably remain so in the next few years. Yet it is possible to determine whether restructuring has brought the economic and political benefits anticipated by policy-makers and theorists. Has privatization enhanced revenue generation and economic efficiency? Have public-private partnerships improved or complicated the state's regulatory functions? Has transformation made political leaders more accountable, or more legitimate, in rural areas? In cotton, the trajectory of reform is now long enough that we have some answers to these questions.

First, the state did not receive any revenue from the "sale" of these enterprises. It merely concessioned the land and the equipment on it in return for the promise of private investment in infrastructure and equipment. However, the state has benefitted from the restructuring of cotton through increased taxes, increases in exports of ginned cotton, and increases in foreign exchange. Total cotton production in the country increased by 60 percent between 1990 and 1998; exports of ginned cotton have increased correspondingly and brought in almost $15 million in 1998. Cotton's contribution to the value of exports has been approximately 10 percent, and Mozambique also has saved on foreign exchange by supplying some of its textile factories with nationally produced cotton. Moreover, cotton companies all over the country pay a tax to the Cotton Institute that is equal to 3.5 percent of their revenue from exports of family sector produced cotton.[14]

Second, each cotton company has the exclusive right to purchase cotton from smallholders in a designated "zone of influence" under its jurisdiction. These zones of influence can sometimes encompass as many as 200,000 hectares. This right has encouraged some companies to make necessary capital improvements and to provide inputs, but along with the right, companies also have shouldered a duty to purchase all cotton grown in their area of influence. Thus, the 250,000 smallholders who produce cotton have been guaranteed a market for their cotton and have obtained a cash income from their sales.[15] The context in which these exchanges have taken place is important. It underscores the point that privatization cannot be separated from other economic developments such as the emergence of markets and the reliable supply of goods. Producers want to

---

[14] Mozambique, Ministério da Agricultura e Pescas (MAP), Instituto de Algodão de Moçambique (IAM), "Assunto: Ponto de Situação das Companhas do Algodão (4 Trimestre de 1998)", N/Ref. 08/GAB/IAM/99 (29 January 1999) and MAP, IAM, "Assunto: Ponto de Situação das Companhas do Algodão (1 Trimestre de 1999)", N/Ref. 24/GAB/IAM/99 (23 April 1999).

[15] Mozambique, Conselho de Ministros, "Autorizaçao do Projecto 'Sodan' ", Resolução Interna, no. 3/91, 24 May 1991 and "Autorização do Projecto 'Lomaco-Montepuez' ", Resolução Interna, no. 4/90, 28 May 1990.

sell cash crops because there are consumer goods available, a situation which is far different from the harsh years of the 1980s. While incomes from cotton sales have been low (the average return in 1998 was $125 per hectare), they have allowed producers to purchase items such as soap, cloth, and oil for their everyday needs.

Third, special high-input schemes have enabled some producers to save money and to make substantial investments in labor-saving machinery such as grain milling equipment. On these schemes in Cabo Delgado Province, LOMACO, a joint-venture between Lonrho and the government, has supplied inputs for cotton production and other crops such as maize and beans on specially-designated blocks of land or on dispersed parcels of land. Depending on how much aid each farmer needed, LOMACO helped to prepare the land, supplied pesticides and insecticides, and helped farmers get credit. Output on these schemes in the late 1990s was approximately one ton per hectare in comparison with 530 kilograms per hectare achieved by ordinary smallholder production. The scheme has proved so attractive to farmers that each year, other smallholders try to join. The scheme has expanded from 300 producers in 1993 to about 1700 in 1998. In all, total land area devoted to high-input cotton in 1999 was approximately 2,000 hectares, up from 1,100 hectares in 1993.[16]

Fourth, several of the contracts that the government made with cotton companies require the companies to improve the techniques for cotton production, obtain and distribute selected seeds and pesticides, develop varieties, and train professionals who can provide advice to cotton producers. For example, LOMACO initiated an extension program and received financing from the World Bank to maintain it. The program has provided seeds, pesticides, and technical support to family, cooperative, and private producers. It also has established separate experimental fields where variety trials are conducted. Further, it has trained extension workers who then convey new techniques and approaches on cotton and food production to producers.[17] Finally, the arrival of the companies has increased salaried employment. Cotton companies have employed around 20,000 seasonal and permanent workers to supervise cotton production, purchase cotton at the markets, gin and bale it.[18]

These JVCs have been more able than the former state enterprises to increase output and deliver financial returns to producers, but it is important to

---

[16] LOMACO visit, May 1994 and Mozambique, MAP, IAM, "Assunto: 4 trimestre de 1998," appendix 2A. At its inception, the scheme was called the PUPI (Pequenas Unidades de Produção Intensiva, small units of intensive production) scheme. They have now been transformed into Peasant Associations, E. Muhate, director, IAM, personal communication, 17 June 2000.

[17] Mozambique, Conselho dos Ministros, "Contrato de Fomento entre o Governo da RPM e a LOMACO." In the cotton sector, private producers or *privados* are commercial farmers that have at least a minimum of 20 hectares devoted to cotton production.

[18] A. Mataveia, "Governo sob forte pressão dos empresários," *Savana* (29 May 1998).

ask under what conditions the increases have occurred. What most critics find objectionable about private sector production is not that it is more efficient than state enterprises, or that it is profit-making, but that profits are often made under exploitative conditions. Looking at many of the cotton joint-ventures, those who argue for recolonization would find much to be concerned about. These companies have operated virtual monopolies with little or no competition. State enterprises operated in a similar fashion, but at least in the early years of the Frelimo government, management was ideologically committed to changing the relations of production. This is not the case with the JVCs. Managers in these companies pursue profits. At the ginning factories, markets, and their own direct production fields, the companies use seasonal labor. They do not have the same moral obligations as the state to keep employees on the payroll throughout the year. Companies lobby the government hard to keep down their highest variable cost, which is the cost per kilo of seed cotton purchased from smallholders.

Supported by their contracts, the large companies also try to prevent rivals in their zone of influence from informing producers about other crops or from negotiating contracts to buy their cotton. This strategy bears similarities to the practices of companies in the colonial period, particularly to the period prior to the liberalization of the cotton concessionary scheme in the 1960s. As in that period, most producers living today within the zones of influence of cotton JVCs must produce cotton if they expect to receive cash. Since consumer goods have been increasingly available, most producers have opted to grow cotton even if they would have preferred to grow maize, as some of them indicated in interviews.[19]

Revenue from cotton production would be greater if productivity were higher, but it has not been. First, beyond the hoe and the machete, the family sector or smallholders have lacked access to tractors or more sophisticated tools for the preparation of land and planting. Second, pesticide application by family sector producers has been erratic due to delays in arrival, their high cost, and corruption by those individuals in charge of supplying them to the family sector. During the 1998 season, for example, producers in the zone of influence of SODAN, a joint-venture in Nampula Province between João Ferreira dos Santos and the government, complained that a company agent had demanded wine and chickens in return for applying pesticides. Moreover, the agent had diluted the pesticides with water, clearly undermining their effectiveness.[20] Third, individual and company behavior has lowered productivity. Based on past experience, family sector producers and some companies are still uncertain about

---

[19] Interview with producer, SODAN area, May 1994 and see Myers and West, "Land Tenure Security" for similar findings in the LOMACO zones, p. 61.

[20] "E preciso subornar capatazes para assistirem ás machambas," *Notícias* (27 February 1998).

the future, even the immediate future. Producers are therefore hesitant to accept pesticides on credit or invest in tools. They are afraid that by the time the crop is harvested there will be no market for their crop, yet they will still be expected to pay back the advance on pesticide application or agricultural tools. Company managers in Africa frequently criticize this behavior, attributing it to backwardness or irrationality. In reality, it reflects producers' uncertainty about the future, which in turn contributes to their risk aversion – a logical approach given Mozambique's past.

Risk aversion equally plays a role in the strategies of the companies. For example, when it first undertook cotton production in Cabo Delgado, LOMACO had ambitious plans to mechanize part of the production process, increase pesticide and fertilizer applications, and create a "middle class" of smallholders with its high-input schemes. Although its direct and high-input production schemes showed high returns per hectare, LOMACO has modified both schemes. Regarding direct production where the company uses mechanization, fertilizers, and pesticides, LOMACO has reduced total hectarage by two-thirds since 1994. The low world price of cotton did not make this approach compensatory anymore. Furthermore, company representatives claimed the high-input schemes were too much responsibility and too costly, and they wanted to change them. They argued that the company took all the risk in the supply of inputs. Producers were "free riding" off the company, defaulting if they experienced financial losses. Farmers did not have to shoulder any of the risks themselves because they lacked collateral. They gave priority to their own family plots first and then worked on the high-input scheme. In addition, because admittance to the scheme favored men and not women, women did not see the land on the scheme as "theirs" and were reluctant to work on it, so there were labor shortages.[21] To address these issues, LOMACO has in recent years encouraged high-input producers to form associations where they pool resources and labor.[22] The objective here may be for the associations to assume collective responsibility for loans with which to purchase inputs such as pesticides and machinery. In that way, the associations rather than the company shoulder the risk of cotton production.

While output has increased greatly in the past decade, it is still unclear whether cotton is compensatory for smallholders given the monopsonistic practices of companies, the risks, and the prevalence of corruption. But producing cotton may no longer be their only option. There are active labor markets in

---

[21] C. Coetzee, director, N'Ropa, LOMACO, interview, 9 May 1994.

[22] The elimination of high-input schemes has not off set LOMACO's financial difficulties. Although the Montepuez operation was considered to be profitable, LOMACO's undertakings in the rest of Mozambique were in debt and Lonrho's shares in the company were in the process of being transferred to the state for re-sale as of 2000. Erasmo Muhate, director, IAM, personal communication, 17 June 2000.

many of the cotton zones. These appear to be siphoning producers away from cotton as family members search for off-farm income. Ultimately the situation may force companies to seek more cooperative relations with smallholders. In addition, markets for other cash crops, such as tobacco, sunflower, maize, and cashews, are growing, and these may attract people away from cotton. The presence of traders in the zones of the cotton companies also has inspired producers to demand a higher price and has complicated the position for the concessionary companies. Each year, associations of larger producers (who may sell to whomever they wish), will contract separately with individual traders to buy their harvests. But what frequently occurs is that these traders will also try to buy from smaller farmers who are under obligation to sell to the concessionary company in their area. Since 1995 at least, two Indian trading firms, Ibramugi and Issufo Nurmamade, have offered higher producer prices for cotton than concessionary companies. These trading companies have claimed they supply seeds and fertilizers to smallholders during the year, while the concessionary companies have argued that the traders are simply encroaching on areas that are under their jurisdiction.[23] The truth may lie somewhere in-between, but the impact is such that small producers have heard about the higher prices paid to larger producers and have demanded the same compensation at the cotton markets run by the concessionary companies. So far, companies have reached compromises with producers or producers have capitulated to local government and agro-export company pressure, but the incidents are revealing. The actions of the traders introduce competition where no real market exists and, in doing so, they challenge the dominance of the concessionary companies. While companies do not face regular competition at present from other buyers or employers, they may have to increase productivity, lower risks, or raise prices in order to attract people away from other job opportunities or other competitors in the future. These measures might raise output and increase revenues for producers.

### Regulatory powers, "smart partnerships," and a renegotiation of legitimacy

When we move away from issues of efficiency and increased revenue, the ability of these joint-ventures to bring about systemic change in Mozambique becomes more problematic. As rational choice theorists advocate, privatization has institutionalized new, slimmed down roles for state administration. Restructuring means for the most part that the state no longer plays the role of "demiurge." Although the Cotton Institute is a buyer of last resort and the state is a part

---

[23] Conflicts between traders and companies occur every year, for 1998–99 see Mozambique, MAP, IAM, "Assunto: Ponto de Situação das Campanhas do Algodão (1 Trimestre de 1999)," p. 3.

owner in these joint-ventures, it is not directly responsible for developing cotton production. It has left company management to the private sector and it now plays the custodian for the most part: mediating and regulating conflicts and company behavior. It tries to employ quality standards that apply to the sector as a whole and to curb financial abuses by companies or their employees. It also plays midwife to, and practices husbandry for, the private sector. It gives tax exemptions or other financial incentives to companies to get started and, if pressured, it seeks compromises on prices and tax payments during individual years. With the adoption of the "Strategy to Develop Cotton," it intends to expand its midwifery and husbandry roles by standardizing the time and place of markets for purchasing cotton from smallholders, encouraging more dialogue between producers and traders, and adopting measures that will improve the quality of cotton so that it is more in line with international standards. It sees its role as "regulating, promoting, and supervising" the development of cotton through technical and administrative measures.[24]

The state still forms part of the ownership structure of some of the major cotton concessionary companies. Also, it has pledged to aid the sector with the adoption of a comprehensive strategy. It would seem that conditions are ideal for labelling the arrangement a "smart partnership" of the kind that government leaders have called for with such insistence lately. But the relationships that have developed among the cotton companies, the state, and smallholders support Jessop's claim that partnerships introduce constraints and dilemmas for all participants. Second, they are characterized by power imbalances that may shift and change over time. Jessop notes that partnerships have to operate within the "broader political system" and to the extent that the state has to be sensitive to political demands and pressures, "it reserves to itself the right to open, close, juggle, and re-articulate governance not only in terms of particular functions but also from the viewpoint of partisan and global political advantage."[25] State responses to public pressure can therefore work to the disadvantage of its private sector partners. On the other hand, the nature of capitalism produces contradictions and conflicts that get reproduced in or can destabilize the partnership. The need to shed labor or the bankruptcy of a firm that is a partner of the state can obviously have an impact upon the state's legitimacy and strain the public-private partnership. State departments and officials also develop private interests that may supersede concerns about the public good.

The dilemmas produced by public-private partnerships also place enormous demands on a state's capacities and throw open to question the technical, apolitical model of "governance." The state must encourage cooperation in order to achieve certain goals, but it must also allow competition in order to resolve

---

[24] Mozambique, Conselho de Ministros, "Estratégia."
[25] Jessop, "The Rise of Governance," p. 39.

conflicts and/or inspire innovation. It must weigh openness to new members or responsiveness to social demands against the security and potential stability of a more closed, restricted group of partners. Third, the state must retain the ability to govern and respond creatively to different challenges. It must balance "governability" and "flexibility." Finally, and most importantly, partnerships pose a dilemma for governments between accountability and efficiency. Efforts to find efficient solutions to economic problems may compromise the government's accountability to the larger public. The development of individual, specialized interests arising out of partnerships may clash with the government's claim to represent the national good. At the same time, social demands that force the government to be accountable may interfere with objectives that would promote the partnership.[26]

In cotton production, incidents where the state has had to discipline behavior illustrate these complaints and dilemmas. The incidents suggest more a "troubled alliance" than a "smart partnership." Most theorists agree that regulatory or disciplinary duties by states are critical to the success of any privatization effort.[27] The government-run Cotton Institute has tried to engage in these duties by forging an important role as mediator between the state and companies, companies and producers, or between two companies. From the perspective of the companies, however, this role has made the state an unreliable partner. For example, until 1996, it seemed that the largest cotton joint-ventures were very influential in the setting of the producer price for cotton. The prevailing world price of cotton served as a baseline for the negotiations and the different interests negotiated within that framework. Family sector and private producers were not involved in price-setting, and so it was up to government representatives to see that they got a fair price.[28]

Apparently, the government did not perform that function adequately; in 1996, producer protests over the low prices and fears by government officials of the return of political instability in the countryside prompted an increase in the producer price. The Cotton Institute and the National Commission of Salaries and Prices (which includes representatives from Agriculture, Finances and Labor) raised the producer price substantially, such that it was 60 percent of the export price. Since then, companies have protested vociferously that they cannot make profits given the producer price. Company directors even formed their own association to articulate more strongly their collective interests. The government has made concessions by decreasing the producer price in line with

[26] Jessop, "The Rise of Governance," pp. 39–42.
[27] For a discussion of the need for regulation see Adam, *et al. Adjusting Privatization*, pp. 19–22.
[28] Erasmo Muhate, director, IAM, Maputo, interview, 8 April 1994. In theory, the producer price is a minimum not a maximum price and companies are expected to negotiate higher prices directly with producers; in practice, the producer price set by the government is the price offered, except in those instances where there is competition.

decreases in the world price, reducing the tax on cotton exports and guaranteeing the supply of credit at a particular exchange rate. But at the request of producers, the Cotton Institute has continued to intervene to set the price rather than have the companies or "the market" determine it.[29] Conflicting objectives of the government and the companies thus strain the partnership.

State officials also frequently must police the activities of companies. Each year, the Cotton Institute has to arbitrate squabbles between companies or between companies and producers. For example, SAMO and SODAN have contiguous zones of influence. One company will sometimes try to poach producers from the other company by offering slightly better prices to those producers living near the border between the two companies. More often, disputes will occur among private producers, independent traders, and the big cotton concessions over who has the right to purchase cotton produced by private farmers. Independent traders will offer a better price to private producers even though the privates have already contracted with the large companies, or vice versa. The Cotton Institute must intervene to keep the companies from fighting over the producers. It must also insure that companies and private producers honor their contracts, particularly with regard to running cotton markets following the harvest and paying the producers in a timely manner. In 1999, for example, the Cotton Institute had to reprimand sharply LOMACO for giving producers "credit" instead of cash for their cotton. Finally, the government has canceled the contracts of those cotton companies that could not fulfill their duties.[30] Here again, feuds among the companies and differences between the government and the companies challenge the stability of the partnership.

Of greater seriousness are those circumstances where the Cotton Institute suspects a company of illicit activity, as occurred with SODAN. In March of 1998, the Cotton Institute sent a letter to JFS expressing its concern that SODAN had been under-invoicing its cotton exports. Later that year after having been contacted by a former general director of SODAN, a reputable newspaper, *Metical*, reported that SODAN had been under-invoicing sales of cotton abroad and under-reporting the weight per bale of cotton, thus robbing Mozambique of approximately 1.5 million dollars in foreign exchange. The paper also alleged that employees of the Cotton Institute had aided SODAN in the scam. Over a period of years, they had consistently under-weighed bales of cotton for

---

[29] Associação Algodoeira de Moçambique, "Preço de algodão anunciado pelo CNSP no dia 21.05.98," letter to Minister of Agriculture and Fisheries (26 May 1998), mimeo.; "Alternativas de compensação do diferencial entre os preços aprovados pelo governo e os propostos pelas empresas para o algodão, na campanha agricola 1997/98" (29 May 1998); "Mozambican Government Announces Minimum Cotton Prices," Panafrican News Agency Daily Newswire (10 July 2001), Lexis/Nexis, <http://www.lexis-nexis.com>.

[30] Muhate, interview, 8 April 1994; Carlos Pinto, agent, SODAN, interview, 12 June 1995; director, IAM-Nampula, interview, 23 June 1995; director, Armazens Ibramugi, interview, Nampula, Nampula Province, 3 July 1995; Mozambique, IAM, "Assunto," p. 3.

SODAN.[31] Once the story broke, the Cotton Institute disciplined the suspected workers and reorganized work patterns in the classification section. It then skillfully used the media and its own moral and political pressure to embarrass SODAN, to force them to pay some of the value of the under-invoiced cotton, and to account for missing cotton.[32] These areas where the state has to engage in regulatory or disciplinary action mitigate against the possibility of a stable partnership. As a part owner, the state knows it is partially accountable for the activities of these companies and therefore it is interested in curbing abuses that they may commit. Many company representatives are also acutely aware that they are working with a state that once favored workers over bosses, peasants over company officials. They also depend on the state and they try not to cross the line of what is acceptable, but violations do occur.[33]

However, the large companies do take advantage of the state's participation. Any disciplinary action that the Cotton Institute has engaged in has been no more than wrist slapping, as the SODAN case illustrated. SODAN was never subject to any judicial inquiry or civil proceeding. The reason is that the state is caught in a contradiction. The state is partially accountable, but its interests are intertwined with those of the companies. It is reluctant to impose stiff penalties if companies exceed the terms of their contracts or go beyond the bounds of what is acceptable conduct. In this respect, companies can take advantage of the "partnership." Second, the Cotton Institute does not have the authority, the personnel, or the resources to prosecute companies that engage in wrongdoing. Third, state officials do not exert much leverage in the day-to-day operations of the joint-ventures. Representatives from both the Ministry of Agriculture and Rural Development and the Ministry of Finances sit on the companies' Board of Directors, but the board only meets twice a year. The joint-ventures have also hired a few state officials, who now see their interests as more aligned with those of private capital than with those of the state.[34] These officials have emerged from, and are supported in government by, a "neo-liberal faction," consisting of prominent Frelimo members who "have converted, with a vengeance, to the new orthodoxy" of privatization and market principles.[35]

---

[31] "Correspondencia," *Metical*, 259 (6 July 1998).

[32] IAM, letter to Sr. Marcelino Mosse, journalist for *Metical*, "Assunto: Respostas ao seu fax desta manhã," N/Ref 42/GAM/IAM/98, 7 July 1998, mimeo.; parts of the letter were then published in *Metical*, "IAM crê que sim," 262 (9 July 1998).

[33] At the Second National Land Conference, Maputo, 25–27 May 1994, Carlos Henriques, director of Lomaco-Montepuez, felt compelled to defend LOMACO publicly against charges that the company had abused its water rights in Chokwe.

[34] Manuel Martins, former director, Sodan-Namialo, Namialo, Nampula Province, interview, 17 May 1994; Carlos Henriques, director, Lomaco-Montepuez and Celia Jordão, World Bank extension work coordinator, Montepuez, Cabo Delgado Province, conversation, 5 May 1994; Muhate, interview, 8 April and 7 June 1994.

[35] Simpson, "Foreign and Domestic Factors," p. 335.

These incidents suggest that the state is unwilling to be a silent partner along-side concessionary companies, but also that it is unable to discipline company behavior as much as it would wish. Partnership stifles its flexibility and com-promises its social welfare functions. Reforms to the sector submitted by the Cotton Institute in 2000 recognize these constraints and dilemmas. Several of the proposed reforms actually try to reduce the power of companies and break up the partnerships. They encourage the formation of associations of family and private farmers to balance the power of the companies. They advocate a reduction in the role of state in the JVCs so that it can act with more autonomy but, at the same time, the reforms argue for an increase in the powers of the Cotton Institute. Moreover, the reforms suggest that the state ought to play a greater role in financing individual private producers.[36]

Even if state administrators have performed their regulatory functions poorly and the virtues of partnerships are in doubt, what are the prospects that these reforms may help to rebuild the legitimacy of the Mozambican state in the countryside or contribute to the political survival of the Frelimo regime? These are important additional considerations, given that rural areas have played such a significant role in undermining both the colonial regime and the post-colonial, socialist one. Four developments affected or created by restructuring may pro-vide the answer: the revival of traditional authorities; the position of Frelimo appointees; the blurring of public and private duties; and the growth of a new or born-again elite. First, the new cotton enterprises have relied on traditional authorities and Frelimo-appointed administrators to carry out their activities. To staunch the deterioration in relations between the government and its popu-lace, Frelimo officially resurrected traditional authorities, particularly *regulos* or chiefs, as well as their subordinates, after the peace accord. Government officials needed to reinsert them into the political framework because some of the traditional authorities had considerable legitimacy in their communities. For example, fifty-eight out of seventy-three producers in three districts of Nampula who answered a question regarding *regulos* or their subordinates stated that tra-ditional authorities had the most authority in their communities, and producers approached them to settle land conflicts and social problems. Four informants stated that *regulos* and government-appointed officials had equal authority.[37] A study sponsored by the Dutch embassy in the western part of Nampula also found that *regulos* retained legitimacy and prestige among the peasantry in spite of attempted humiliation by Frelimo supporters.[38]

---

[36] Mozambique, Conselho de Ministros, "Estrategia"; R. Miguel, "Nampula: guerra de algodão continua" and "Vai ser um fiasco," *Domingo* (27 August 2000), p. 12.

[37] HS, Monapo, Meconta, Mecuburi Districts.

[38] L. Metselaar, R. Gonçalves, O. Baloi and F. Maiopue, "Relatório da missão de levantamento de dados nos distritos de Malema, Lalaua, Ribaué e Murrupula na Província de Nampula," Maputo (March 1994), pp. 13–15.

Moreover, it is not a coincidence that the government recognized traditional authorities around the time that privatization occurred. To produce cotton properly, companies need the participation of local authorities at various stages of the cotton cycle. Many of these authorities have experience from the colonial period, and they can remind or encourage producers to clear their fields properly before planting. Their participation helps to ensure that cotton seeds are planted on time and that pesticides are administered in the proper amounts. They supply labor for direct production activities and transmit advice on new techniques. They can also convey important information about prices or the location of markets. Thus companies require individuals who are respected in their communities and/or have power to act as liaisons between producers and the companies.[39] Companies have bought the support of traditional authorities by paying them salaries for participating in the cotton scheme and granting them bonuses for increased output. After years operating unofficially on the sidelines, *regulos* in particular have welcomed the opportunity to receive an income, to heighten their prestige, increase their power, and to help their communities.[40] That these outcomes are contradictory and by no means guaranteed is a risk that all parties have decided to take.

Fashioning a link between traditional authorities and joint-ventures ties these local authorities into the government's agenda, making them participants in the new strategy and therefore accountable. Over time, their legitimacy may be tied to the fortune of the joint-venture, just as in the colonial period the legitimacy and illegitimacy of traditional authorities depended on how they navigated colonial economic pressures. Traditional authorities have become acutely aware of this link. In an interview, one *regulo* lamented that the people in his community were threatening to reject him because he had not been able to secure hoes and shovels for them to use on their fields. He said that his people did not want him if he could not help them. Another argued that he did not have much influence but that could change if the fortunes of his community improved.[41] These statements suggest that the legitimacy of these traditional authorities is acquired not assumed, negotiable not axiomatic.

Second, the arrival of companies has helped to build a relationship between Frelimo-appointed officials and traditional authorities though these new relationships have not been without complications and conflict. Officials must carefully mediate relations among chiefs, companies, smallholders, and themselves. They must perform a tricky balancing act where they aid companies,

---

[39] A. Machado, director, Family Sector Production, SODAN, conversations, 17–26 May, 1994 and see also A. Dinerman, "From 'Abaixo to 'Chiefs of Production': Agrarian Change in Nampula Province, Mozambique, 1975–87," *Journal of Peasant Studies*, 28, 2 (January 2001), pp. 60–63.

[40] *Regulos* 1–6, interviews, Monapo; *regulos* Mukapera and Varua, Corrane, Meconta District, Nampula Province, interviews, 14 June 1995.

[41] *Regulos* 1–6, interviews, Monapo.

strengthen relations with those chiefs who are respected, and respond to the needs of smallholders.[42] Authority and legitimacy remain contested for appointees as well as traditional authorities and may depend to a significant degree on the actions of the companies.

The third development concerns the blurring of public and private functions. The expectation of the Frelimo-led government has been not only that companies would help to re-negotiate political legitimacy at the local level, but also that they would support certain financial burdens. The government cannot afford to perform many of the duties that are normally expected of a financially stable state administration so the companies have done them. These duties have fallen outside of the companies' contractual agreement with the state, and they have benefitted people who are not directly employed by the companies. They thus fall beyond the boundaries of what would be considered a private duty. For example, some companies have rebuilt roads and provided electricity, while others have given bicycles and even cars to state and local authorities.[43] In return, the companies expect loyalty. The impact on the state may be grave: these activities blur the boundaries between public duty and private obligations, jeopardizing the state's autonomy and legitimacy.

Finally, guaranteed markets, the availability of consumer goods, the recognition of traditional authorities, and schemes to give producers a larger income do appear to be forging a new or born-again elite in some of the cotton areas of Mozambique, which may increase Frelimo's legitimacy in the long run. Frelimo's improved performance in Nampula during the 1999 national elections indicates that perhaps it has won some support from groups who either championed or simply tolerated Renamo. In the campaign to remake itself, Frelimo has created a new group that owes its fortunes to joint-ventures and the government. Together with state officials who have benefitted from privatization, *regulos* and their subordinates who have been revived, and those companies that have made investments, this group may become a powerful rural constituency that the Frelimo-led government can rely on for support. But the schemes for producers bring risks. The better-off producers created by these schemes are dependent on the companies. If the companies decide to end the schemes or to pull out of cotton all together, as they periodically threaten to do, these producers may not survive and may blame both the company and the government for their misfortune. Moreover, the differentiation that is occurring may introduce new tensions into the countryside for which both the national state, local authorities, and companies are unprepared. Clashes in Montepuez and the deaths

---

[42] *Chefe de posto*, Netia Administrative Post, Monapo District, Nampula Province, interview, May 1994; president, N'Ropa, Montepuez District, Cabo Delgado Province, interview, 4 May 1994; *regulo* of N'ropa, Montepuez District, Cabo Delgado Province, 12 May 1994.

[43] Company visits: Agribuzi, Buzi, Sofala Province; SODAN, Namialo, Nampula Province; and LOMACO, Montepuez, Cabo Delgado Province, 1994 and 1995.

in a prison there of over eighty members of the opposition party in late 2000 should serve as a warning that political and economic stability cannot be taken for granted in rural Mozambique.[44]

## The cashew controversy

If the restructuring of cotton has produced rather equivocal results, the same cannot be said for the cashew sector. There, liberalization and privatization have provoked the greatest condemnation and had the most negative effects of any restructuring in the country. The case crosses and blurs the line between intentional sabotage and unanticipated misfortune. It is a tragedy and a travesty: those involved have suffered greatly while others manipulated the changes in cashews to their advantage. It illustrates many of the rivalries we have discussed, such as the conflicts among agriculture, trade, and industry; nationals and foreigners; blacks, whites, and Indians; workers, smallholders, men, and women; and how these rivalries influence the government. It also demonstrates clearly the pivotal role that a state plays in the making (or unmaking) of a market.

The controversy began with the privatization of the factories that process raw cashews collected from thousands of smallholders. Many people in the country see cashews as something authentically Mozambican, a national symbol. Their cultivation and harvest do not carry the negative connotations that have been associated with the production of cotton. Mozambicans see the processing of raw cashews as something that they do well and exports of processed cashews have brought in much revenue in the past. Thus it was quite important to the government that the sale of cashew factories go to nationals and that the public view it as a successful privatization. According to well-informed sources within the business community, however, during the competition for the sale of the processing factories, neither foreign nor domestic investors showed interest in purchasing them. With interest sluggish, government officials lobbied behind the scenes, using nationalistic arguments and promising support to attract important domestic investors.

The appeal was successful. Those who finally purchased the factories included some old established Indian companies such as Has Nur and the AGT group that have been in Mozambique a long time, and a former state company called ENACOMO that the government sold to Mozambican nationals. Black and Indian entrepreneurs, including the wife of a former Minister of Agriculture, also purchased some of the factories. These newly privatized companies joined an existing group of around six private cashew processing factories that the state either had returned to their former owners, such as Anglo-American in Gaza, or had never nationalized. These latter included Companhia de Caju do

---

[44] "83 morreram numa 'cadeia de transito'," *Metical*, 878 (12 December 2000).

Monapo belonging to the Entreposto Group and Indústrias de Caju Gordhandas Valabhdas in Nampula. At the end of the privatization process, nationals had the majority of shares in the former state factories.[45]

With regard to the purchase of cashew processing factories by domestic investors, the deal was sweet. Domestic investors "bought" most of the factories way below their listed sale prices. Domestic investors of four of the seven factories that were privatized only made down payments that averaged around 17 percent of the purchase price, and they received a grace period of one year before starting payments. In addition, the government agreed to assume $12 million in debt that all seven companies had accumulated.[46] Although the government did manage finally to sell the state factories, this privatization can hardly be termed a "success." The government went to considerable lengths and made enormous financial sacrifices to achieve it.

Just as the factories were sold, another vexing problem arose. A study of the cashew industry commissioned by the World Bank found that cashew production had dropped and producer prices were low. Instead of suggesting that the Ministry of Agriculture undertake reforms to improve production, the study attributed cashew's poor performance to protectionism and pricing. It highlighted policies that prohibited the export of raw cashews in order to protect domestic industry and oligopolistic practices among a handful of specially licensed wholesale traders that kept producer prices down.[47] To give incentives to producers to increase output, the World Bank recommended a phased-in liberalization of raw cashew exports and the elimination of the requirement that wholesale traders have licenses. The license requirement had restricted the number of traders, who were then able, in classic oligopolistic fashion, to set a low price paid to producers but then highly mark-up the wholesale price offered to factories. According to the World Bank rationale: "The elimination of licenses will introduce more transparency in the trading system and promote competition among traders. Increased competition *should* then boost producer prices, and thereby output growth" (my emphasis).[48] Further, the World Bank noted that under existing conditions, the value added in the industry "has, in recent years, been either marginal or negative" and that by processing raw cashews, Mozambique was actually losing foreign exchange. Since the industry had just been privatized and was in the process of rehabilitation, the recommendation suggested that a period of "temporary

[45] Leite, "A guerra do caju," p. 5, footnote 8 and table 8; UTRE, "Privatisation in Mozambique," 1998, appendix entitled "Lista dos Investidores," p. 1; CPI, "Investidores," 1998.

[46] H. Hilmarsson, "Cashew Pricing and Marketing in Mozambique," World Bank Working Paper, second draft, n.d., p. 21.

[47] Hilmarsson, "Cashew Pricing and Marketing," pp. 3–6. By restricting its focus only to the potential effects of market liberalization of cashews rather than examining the obstacles to increased production of raw cashews, the study biased its conclusions from the start.

[48] World Bank, "Mozambique: Impediments," p. xvii.

(reasonable) protection" would allow the industry to adjust to raised producer prices and to adopt more efficient techniques. The study stated that what constituted "reasonable" would be a 15 percent tax that decreased over a three-year period.[49]

The Ministry of Industry and Trade regulates trade and processing in the cashew sector. Pressured by the World Bank and the IMF, the Ministry of Industry and Trade substantially lowered tariffs on exports of raw cashews following the report. Previously, tariffs consisted of a 30 percent tax on the difference between the producer price and the border price.[50] The ministry decided to lower tariffs to 20 percent of the difference between the farmgate price and the border price in 1995/96 and then to 14 percent in 1996/1997. Simultaneously, it abolished a provision that local industry be supplied first with raw cashews before exports took place. As a result of these measures, the price of raw cashews became more competitive and foreign buyers, mostly from India, became interested in their purchase to supply a growing processing industry in India. Freed from the restriction to sell locally, wholesale traders within Mozambique responded by selling abroad. The sale abroad of raw cashews broke the vertical integration of production, processing, and trade.

National uproar followed the news that the government had lowered tariffs and allowed the sale of raw cashews. Every newspaper in the capital attacked the World Bank's arrogance for dictating a policy change for cashew, and they invoked arguments about "national sovereignty" to demand that the World Bank stop interfering in Mozambique's affairs. Industrialists, coalescing around the Association of Cashew Industrialists (AICaju) which had formed in 1992, deplored the apparent favoritism towards traders within the Ministry of Industry and Trade. They argued that without the tariff, they could not compete with the more favorable prices offered by India. They lacked cash and had not had time to renovate the factories, so they could not make a profit on processed cashews at that purchase price. Most did not buy raw cashews for their factories and, within two years, the majority of the factories had stopped working. Industrialists then lobbied for the re-imposition of tariffs and a grace period to revitalize factories.[51]

---

[49] World Bank, "Mozambique: Impediments," pp. xvii.

[50] Hilmarsson, "Cashew Pricing and Marketing," p. 15.

[51] *Metical*, under the direction of its editor, Carlos Cardoso, spearheaded newspaper criticism of the government's cashew policy. See the *Metical* page in *Demos*, "Confusão total no caju" (8 October 1997), p. 12; "Alternativas de sobrevivencia" (29 October 1997), p. 6; "Governo dá golpe final à indústria de Caju" (5 November 1997), p. 6 and also the *Metical* issue on cashews, no. 569 (23 September 1999). See also R. Miguel, "A Frelimo é totalmente contrária à desindustrialização do caju," *Domingo* (9 November 1997), pp. 16–17; S. Moyana, "A guerra do caju," *Savana* (13 June 1997), pp. 2–4; and Manjate, "Governo deve clarificar"; J. Hanlon, "Power without Responsibility: the World Bank and Mozambican Cashew Nuts," *Review of African Political Economy*, 83 (2000) summarizes the position of the industry and that of the World Bank, pp. 36–39.

Joining the chorus of protests were the labor unions. Arguing that the state still retained 90 percent of the ownership of the cashew factories since the down payments had been so small, the unions pleaded with the government to resolve the crisis. Repeatedly, they noted that thousands of jobs had been lost because there were no cashews; they had all been sold to India. At a demonstration, one sign carried by a protesting worker read "To export cashews enriches India and impoverishes Mozambique."[52] Acting on orders from the president, the ministry kept the tariff at 14 percent. The decision pleased neither the World Bank, who thought the tariff was still too high, nor the industrialists and the labor unions, who argued it was too low. The result was that the government nearly courted a break with its party in parliament. Frelimo parliamentarians vehemently denounced the decision not to raise tariffs as harmful to the country's national industry and passed a measure in late 1999 asking the government to raise the tariffs once again.[53] The government responded by raising the surtax to 18 percent, but it was too late to revive the collapsed factories. To add insult to injury, the world price then slumped from $700 per ton to $415 per ton in 2001.[54]

If the story ended there it would be a tragedy; additional revelations make it a travesty. Government officials, the World Bank, and critics have neglected or obfuscated several facets of the cashew debacle including prices, production, the timing of the liberalization, and the perceived conflict between traders and industry. First, despite optimistic calculations made by the World Bank that prices and production would increase with liberalization, prices to producers have only increased to about 50 percent of the border price and production of raw cashews is still under 50,000 tons per year. Moroever, world prices have dropped since 1999 and producer prices for raw cashews in 2001 were half what they were in 1999. These are hardly the glowing results the World Bank predicted.[55] The sluggish price and output response is due to production constraints and oligopolistic behavior. Cashew trees in Mozambique are old and suffer from diseases; war and neglect have diminished even further their productivity. Without support to farmers for new varieties, new plantings, and the cleaning of old trees, there will not be a response to price increases. Relative

---

[52] Manjate, "Governo deve clarificar." The sign resurfaced in March 2000 in a strike at Mocajú, where workers had not been paid in a year and were demanding their salaries, see "Prossegue manifestação na Mocajú," *Metical* (23 March 2000).

[53] Miguel, "A Frelimo é totalmente contrária," pp. 16–17; *Metical*, "A Frelimo contra o Governo," *Demos* (3 December 1997), p. 4; "Missão do FMI em Maputo," *Metical*, 604 (12 November 1999).

[54] P. Fauvet, "World Bank Crushes Mozambique's Cashew Industry," *Business Report* (23 May 2001), p. 2.

[55] "Moves to Rescue Cashew Industry," *Mozambiquefile*, 272 (March 1999), pp. 6–8; Fauvet, "World Bank Crushes."

to other crops and opportunities, cashew production may be unattractive, and Mozambique's poor roads also impede attempts at expanding the crop. Some smallholders lack sufficient labor or knowledge to care for trees properly and thus give priority to food crops.[56] The lack of attention to these constraints not only reveals the World Bank's undue emphasis on market mechanisms to solve every problem, but also exposes the relative weakness of the Ministry of Agriculture and Rural Development in relation to the Ministry of Industry and Trade within government. The position of the Ministry of Agriculture regarding the difficulties in cashew has barely been heard.

Moreover, oligopolistic practices continue to keep the price lower than ex-pected because the government has liberalized the trade without liberaliz-ing the wholesale traders. Again, this issue seems to reveal the weakness of agriculture in relation to trade in Mozambique. In the north of Mozambique, wholesalers and exporters of cashews overlap. There are about a dozen cashew trader/exporters and they are well-organized in the Commercial, Industrial and Agricultural Association of Nampula (ACIANA). Barriers to entry in the whole-sale and export trade still remain. As long as a dozen traders can control prices paid to retailers who, in turn, control prices paid to thousands of producers, the price of cashews will not be high enough to act as an incentive.[57] Even though the government has increased minimum producer prices for cashews, small-holders have claimed that agro-processing companies and retail traders have cheated them and that the set producer price for cashews also has discouraged competition.[58] Some smallholders have pointed out that official price sheets for cashews have been replaced by counterfeit sheets to fool them. Furthermore, a report that examined cashews in Nampula argued: "Relations among par-ticipants within the cashew marketing system are extremely antagonistic and characterized by opportunism and lack of confidence."[59] Farmers have stated that the prices offered by traders do not encourage them to grow more cashews or they view traders as unreliable. Traders cannot be trusted to have cash on hand or to show up regularly to buy cashews.[60] Moreover, Frelimo parliamentarian, Abdul Carimo, has insisted that smallholders buy goods from, and sell cashews to, the same traders. Producers have complained that traders offer inflated prices

---

[56] C. Cramer, "Can Africa Industrialize by Processing Primary Commodities? The Case of Mozambican Cashew Nuts," *World Development*, 27, 7 (1999), pp. 1256–58; P. Mole, "An Economic Analysis of Smallholder Cashew Development Opportunities and Linkages to Food Security in Mozambique's Northern Province of Nampula," Ph.D. dissertation, Michigan State University (2000).

[57] Moyana, "A guerra do caju," pp. 2–4; Leite, p. 11; Cramer, "Can Africa Industrialize?", p. 1258.

[58] "Camponesas são lesados na venda de culturas de rendimento," *Notícias* (24 April 1998).

[59] Abt Associates, "Structure, Conduct and Performance of the Cashew Subsector in Nampula Province," appendix H, draft mimeo. (January 1998), p. 11.

[60] Abt Associates, "Structure, Conduct and Performance," pp. 11 and 20.

for consumer items, robbing them of the little money they earn from cashew sales.[61]

A second, neglected aspect of the cashew crisis concerns the timing of liberalization. Critics have denounced liberalization as another example of World Bank arrogance and bullying of the government. Yet as early as 1991–92, the government had already granted to a select group of traders (including the former state company for cashew) the right to export a proportion of the raw cashews. The loosening of restrictions on exports of raw cashews occurred **before** the World Bank recommended liberalization and **before** the privatization of the state enterprises for cashews. Thus liberalization did **not** suddenly affect the ability of processors to gain raw cashews in 1995–96; exports of raw cashews had already increased to approximately 21,600 tons by 1993–94.[62] More than half of the production for 1994 was sold abroad, again **before** the so-called liberalization of 1995, yet few articles mentioned this occurrence.

The third issue concerns the apparent distinction between industrialists and traders. While the differences in the interests of industrialists versus traders are substantial, critics of the cashew policy have often overlooked the fact that traders and industrialists in Mozambique are sometimes the same people. Those wholesale traders who were granted the right in 1993–94 to export raw cashews did so at a time when the producer price was about one-third of the world price. At that time, they made huge profits on their sales and continued to do so following official liberalization.[63] When the government then began to privatize in 1994, several of these same traders bought some of the cashew processing factories. By purchasing former state companies, several of those who had been wholesale traders also subsequently became "industrialists." When official liberalization occurred in 1995, some company directors in the private processing factories wore their industrialist hats to complain about the effects of liberalization, but they put on their trading hats to continue to export raw cashews – as they had done before official liberalization. For example, the AGT (also known as Gani) Group owns two cashew processing factories but has exported raw cashews throughout the 1990s. As the administrator unashamedly admitted, "'Gani is a commercial enterprise. Even before we embraced industry, we were exporting cashews."[64] The AGT group exported $10 million of cashews in 1995.[65] JFS and Has Nur, two other owners of cashew factories, also have

---

[61] A. Carimo, quoted in AIMNews, 10899E, "Cashew Bill under Debate" (22 September 1999), <http://www.sortmoz.com/aimnews>. In some areas of Nampula, producers have access to at most one or two retail traders. Unless producers are willing to travel long distances to encounter more competition, the "free market" simply does not exist. Fieldwork, Nampula Province, 1994, 1995.

[62] Hilmarsson, "Cashew Pricing and Marketing," p. 14; Leite, "A guerra do caju," pp. 10–11, p. 28–29, p. 43, table 2.3.

[63] Hilmarsson, "Cashew Pricing and Marketing," p. 13.    [64] Moyana, "A guerra do caju," p. 2.

[65] Foi, "Comerciantes indianos."

participated in the sale of raw cashews. As of late 1997, the processing factories of Has Nur and AGT were not operational, while JFS was processing as well as trading cashews.[66]

Thus one of the reasons why the government perhaps did not liberalize the wholesalers (though there are some new players from India) is that they include companies that have historically supported the government and they agreed to "buy" or at least to appear to "buy" the cashew processing factories. It is thus unlikely that the government would move against them. What many have portrayed as a battle between industrialists and traders includes a group of people wearing two hats and hedging their bets on the world price of cashews. When the world price is high, the group sells raw cashews. If the world price drops, perhaps the value added by processing will look more attractive. If production increases, perhaps these investors will process **and** trade, as I expect they intended to do when they purchased the factories in the first place. Regardless of the choices they have made, their oligopolistic control of the market has allowed them to continue to take advantage of producers.

The fourth aspect of the travesty concerns the role of the government. It may be that the World Bank forced the government to liberalize the trade of cashews, as critics and even the president of Mozambique have argued.[67] But some journalists have stated that members of the government and the Frelimo party used their positions to help one company to break into the market for raw cashews and that, in turn, they benefitted from this company's activities. Several journalists have alleged that at least one of the trading companies, Saba, is linked to powerful members of the Frelimo party. They claim that the company used this link to gain credit from the state bank (before it was privatized) and to avoid paying export taxes. On the pages of the weekly journal, *Savana*, the company convincingly refuted the allegations regarding preferential access to credit and non-payment of the export taxes. It showed canceled checks that indicated payment of the export tax to customs officers in the port of Nacala. It stated that while it did receive financing from the Banco Popular do Desenvolvimento, BPD had received the pre-export loan from Equator Bank.[68] Equator Bank confirmed in an interview that it had indeed financed the bank that financed Saba, but also that it had extended pre-export financing to other large exporters of cashews as it has done for many years. Equator extended pre-export financing to the state bank from the time of its arrival in 1979 and it continues to extend credit to large private companies now that privatization has taken place.[69]

[66] "Governo dá golpe final"; Leite, "A guerra do caju" implicitly speaks to this point also, see p. 18, p. 27–28, p. 45, table 7.

[67] Hanlon, "Power Without Responsibility"; "Poverty Forced Acceptance of Cashew Diktat-Chissano," *AIMNews*, 2526 (25 June 2001), <http://www.sortmoz.com/aimnews>.

[68] Moyana, "A guerra do caju," pp. 2–4.     [69] Audet, interview.

Regarding Saba's links to Frelimo, whether the leadership of Frelimo supported this company or gained revenue through its links with this company remains unclear. What is known is that this company was one of the few new companies to have benefitted from the so-called liberalization of trade and that it is a company comprised of black Mozambicans. Saba was a lucky entrant in a market mostly dominated by established trading firms, many of them former large colonial companies or smaller companies owned by Indians. Historically, black Mozambicans have not been involved in the export of cashews. Saba thus posed a threat not only to those investors who bought factories and then lacked raw cashews to process, but also to established trading companies. Applied by others to denigrate the company, the word *paraquedista* (parachutist) captures the resentment at Saba's sudden good fortune. According to Saba's directors, the antipathy was not just because the company was new, but because it was black: "It is a question of racism, because we are the first blacks to enter into the business of cashew exports, in an area that was always monopolized by Asians and whites."[70] However, it also seems to be a question of favoritism, because few other firms have entered the market. In addition, if members of the Frelimo party or the state have benefitted from the high profits to be made from exports of raw cashews, the policy of liberalizing exports without liberalizing the exporters makes perfect sense.

Finally, it is fair to say that the real losers have been the producers and the workers in the cashew factories. With regard to the plight of producers, the World Bank is to blame for assuming that its best case scenario would be realized. It wrongly assumed that producers would receive higher prices and that the government would follow its recommendations to the letter by eliminating licenses for traders along with the export tax. But the government should also shoulder the blame for not liberalizing the traders when it liberalized trade, for pressuring national investors to buy the cashew factories, and for not making loans available for rehabilitation. Collectively, the World Bank, the government, and the industrialists/traders also should bear responsibility for what has occurred to workers at the processing factories. Reports have suggested that from 3,000 to 10,000 workers have lost or are in danger of losing their jobs.[71] For most of these workers, salaries in arrears, periodic layoffs, and the threat of dismissal have plagued them throughout the 1990s. Even before privatization, several of the cashew factories were not operational because of damage from the war, high debt, a lack of raw materials, or broken

---

[70] Moyana, "A guerra do caju."

[71] "SINTIC culpa Governo e BIRD pela situação dos trabalhadores," *Notícias* (6 June 1998); "Moves to Rescue Cashew Industry." Some of the workers in the rural factories are also producers, so they have been hurt twice.

machinery.[72] In addition to a shortage of raw cashews, private owners now encounter bureaucratic impediments to securing necessary imports and they lack credit. These factors can also result in layoffs or closure.[73] Under these constraints, it thus seems incredible that either the World Bank study or a later study by the accounting firm of Deloitte Touche could make any claims about what the value added would be if the factories did any processing. If these factories were capable of positive added value then some of their owners would not have sold the raw cashews abroad. In addition, some of the very same industrialists who complained about how many jobs were lost were the ones who exported raw cashews.

In the end, there has been rather bad faith all around and enormous obstacles to the processing of cashews in Mozambique. The solutions appear to be to improve production, to rehabilitate the factories, and to break the wholesale trading oligopoly. These will require cooperative efforts by the Ministry of Agriculture and the Ministry of Industry and Trade, by the agro-processing industry, by the World Bank, and by smallholders. Ironically, national and international criticism of the World Bank probably has increased the government's leverage with the bank on this issue. Moreover, within government, the influence previously exercised by traders has now shifted somewhat to agriculture and industry. The development of a master plan to improve production, an increase in donor support for new plantings and rehabilitation of existing trees, and the reimposition of the 18 percent surtax on raw cashew exports are the most visible manifestations of the various power shifts.[74] Whether the renewed focus on production and processing will yield tangible results remains uncertain.

## Conclusion

Critics have remarked that the re-creation of concessionary companies in cotton and the undue influence of the World Bank in the cashew sector are indicative of the recolonization that is occurring in Mozambique and indeed throughout Africa. Granting monopsonies to cotton companies and selling raw cashews, rather than adding value through processing, do seem like horrifying regressions. But exclaiming the return of colonialism underestimates the range and

---

[72] "Será relançada actividade do sector do caju," *Notícias* (28 October 1992); "Trinta mil toneladas ficaram retidas no campo em Nampula," *Notícias* (15 February, 1993); "Reestruturação do sector afecta negativamente os trabalhadores," *Notícias* (27 November 1994); "Ex-Caju de Moçambique em Reabilitação," *Diário de Moçambique* (29 December 1994); J. Morais, "Não há dinheiro para comprar castanha," *Notícias* (24 November 1995).

[73] Cramer, "Can Africa Industrialize?", p. 1259.

[74] Visits to selected cashew-growing areas, Nampula Province (May–June 1994), Zambezia Province (May 1998); Rich Newberg, team leader, Rural Incomes Office, USAID, Maputo, interview, 2 June 1998.

complexity of the relationships that state, capital, and countryside have established during the transition. References to recolonization ignore the contradictory roles that the state has adopted and devalues the diverse responses of social forces from industrialists to smallholders.

The formation of joint-ventures in cotton has changed the relations between the state and the economy in anticipated and unintended ways. As expected, the state has withdrawn from its role as economic manager. It is no longer a demiurge. Private cotton companies have returned and rehabilitated processing facilities all over the country. Cotton smallholders have responded also to the restructuring of the cotton sector. Both food and cotton production have increased in the last decade. Producers have access to an income and consumer goods. Both foreign and domestic trade have risen. Furthermore, the contract-farming arrangement for cotton has allowed the government to reintegrate traditional authorities into positions of authority without formally incorporating them into local government institutions.

At the same time, restructuring has brought new tensions and challenges. Cotton companies have enjoyed great privileges in their zones of influence and have taken on some of the functions that state agencies normally engage in, though not without resentment at the capital outlay required. A new or resurrected elite has arisen out of those that have been handed land or encouraged to expand. There is a new national bourgeoisie in the making with roots in the Frelimo party. There are old capital interests who remained in Mozambique after the revolution as well as new foreign arrivals. These developments exacerbate income inequalities in rural areas and provoke conflicts among traders, agricultural companies, and cotton producers over land, prices, and commodities.

In cashew, the situation is much worse. Chicanery and poor judgment characterized the privatization of cashew factories and the liberalization of the raw cashew trade. Reluctant buyers purchased factories in poor condition. Sales of the factories were contingent on a policy that protected the factories and prevented the export of raw cashews, but the government had unofficially abandoned this policy at the time of sale and then officially overturned it. With production stagnant, factories collapsed.

The outcome of the transition in cotton and cashew calls attention to the changing and contradictory roles of the state. In cotton, partnerships with the private sector have brought constraints and opportunities. They give the state a chance to exert leverage on companies, but state officials have sometimes lacked the means and the will to use that leverage. Equally, partnerships can force unpleasant choices on the government. Government officials have to choose between their loyalty to the partnership or their desire to serve the general interest. But, at least in the cotton sector, government officials appear to be making a conscious effort to redefine their roles to become mediators, liaisons, overseers, and protectors of companies and producers, even if these roles and the interests they serve often clash. In cashews, perhaps because institutional responsibility and accountability are not well defined, officials work behind the scenes to favor certain groups over others. State involvement is hidden, secretive, and duplicitous. The interests of traders seem paramount, while the interests of workers and smallholders are marginalized.

The activities of the state in cotton versus cashews suggest that the question, "what kind of state involvement?", cannot be answered definitively in Mozambique. The label "intermediary state" may still capture best the contrasting roles the state plays and the contradictory outcomes these roles produce. As the transition continues in Mozambique, then, social forces may greatly influence the kind of capitalism that will take root and the kind of state that will govern it. We have already seen how these social forces are consolidating in the private sector, how entrenched capital is recombining with new foreign investors and political elites to pressure government for favors or protectionism. But there is a role here too for workers and smallholders, for those less privileged by the move to a market economy. Throughout Mozambique's history, smallholders and workers have demonstrated their ability to shape the projects of the state and capital through negotiation as well as resistance, and they are just as active now. There is a vocal opposition in Mozambique, expressed not only through local leaders but also through the ballot box and the print media. Nowhere has this been more evident than in the cashew crisis, where critics repeatedly condemned the influence of the World Bank and demanded that the state alleviate the crisis. This time, they may help to shape a market economy that will distribute benefits more evenly than in the past. They may help to create a state that will be more accountable to the public than previous regimes.

# 7    The end of Marx and the beginning of the market? Rhetorical efforts to legitimate transformative preservation

Over the past quarter century, Mozambique has twice experienced decisive institutional and ideological ruptures. Independence brought profound changes, such as the juridical abolition of many oppressive colonial laws and the replacement of the Portuguese colonial government by an independent, socialist, and nationalist Mozambican one. In the workplace and on the streets, institutionalized forms of racial and ethnic segregation declined. State economic intervention nearly eliminated settler farms in agriculture and vastly reduced the role of the private sector in industry and agriculture. Discursively, the new government intertwined the languages of socialism, nationalism, and modernism to express its multiple and momentous goals. The iconography of the early post-independence period generated by the National Directorate of Propaganda and Publicity represented the revolution's objectives by glorifying those who had been oppressed before and depicting them in new, liberated roles as a result of the Frelimo victory. Inspired by the political art of the Russian Revolution, revolutionary posters in Mozambique reproduced the Soviet image of the heroic male blacksmith with his hammer to symbolize the struggle of workers. Many early posters incorporated the five-pointed red star to symbolize Mozambique's solidarity with other socialist countries. Replacing the Soviet sickle with the Mozambican hoe, the iconography also addressed the critical role that small-holders were to play in the new Mozambique.[1]

The transition from socialism to capitalism, from the one-party state to a notionally democratic one, also represents a sharp departure from the institutions and policies introduced since independence. Gone is the demiurge state whose multiple plans set every price and tried to track every import. Gone are the production targets for every factory and every state farm from Maputo to Cabo Delgado. The state is no longer a foe of private capital, it is a "partner." The party secretary no longer paces the floor of northern textile factories nor

---

[1] A sophisticated analysis of the iconography of the Soviet Union can be found in V. Bonnell, *Iconography of Power: Soviet Political Posters under Lenin and Stalin* (Berkeley, CA: University of California, 1997). For a thorough survey of Mozambican political poster art, see B. Salstrom and A. Sopa, *Catálogo dos Cartazes de Moçambique-Catalogue of Mozambican Posters* (Maputo: Arquivo Histórico de Moçambique, Universidade Eduardo Mondlane, 1988).

supervises cotton production in the countryside. Dynamizing groups do not meet to discuss the quotas at the state farm, and a vanguard party is not using the state to carry out its revolution. Now, the Frelimo government, or more accurately, the Chissano government, accounts for its actions at the ballot box every five years and must confront a persistent, if incoherent, opposition party at the polls and in parliament. Now, government ministers are more likely to address private sector conferences and investor forums than attend peasant rallies and worker demonstrations. Global markets, available infrastructure, and the cost of labor influence whether investments will be made in Mozambique. When investment does take place, the private sector largely decides where capital will go and what projects will get funded. As neo-liberals anticipated, the state largely has withdrawn from economic decision-making, the markets now function, albeit inadequately, and private actors now control much economic activity. Advertisements for rental cars and cell phones, insurance and bank loans, are the new icons. They have replaced the state-commissioned posters and murals of yesterday.

However, the transformative process equally incorporates institutional, political, and procedural continuities. Some practices and institutions usefully could be characterized as "interrupted continuities"; that is, they disappeared or declined after the colonial period, but they have resurfaced in the current transition. These continuities are at least partially what critics have in mind when they refer to current developments in Mozambique as "recolonization." The decision to embrace an economic system that shares structural features with that which prevailed in the colonial period invariably helps to revive that legacy. The presence of the past is also reinforced by the manner in which the government has chosen to pursue capitalism and democratization and the ways in which various social forces in Mozambique have sought to influence recent developments. "Recolonization" appears evident in the rise of traditional authorities when so much of Frelimo policy sought to condemn them; in the return of Portuguese settlers or their relatives to reclaim businesses or parcels of land; in the *de facto* recreation of racial and ethnic hierarchies at work and in the social spaces of cities such as Maputo and Beira.

But when we re-examine the features of the supposed "recolonization" that is taking place, what is so striking about some of them is that they are not being "reintroduced" following a period of disappearance, but rather they were there all along. They survived the earlier transition: they are long-term continuities. The use of stamped, lined paper to apply for visas or business licenses is a superficial example; a more substantive one is the compromises with traditional authorities that Frelimo party secretaries made at the local level. Furthermore, the largest companies in Mozambique today have their roots in the colonial period and they used the socialist period to strengthen their position. The government preference for large-scale, capital-intensive projects was not just a socialist pre-occupation but a colonial obsession. The obsession continues to-day, shorn of some of the grandiose language of yesterday. The past – the real and the imagined, the recent as well as the distant – is the setting in which social actors construct the present.

In addition, the charge by critics that outsiders have imposed the ideas of neo-liberalism on Mozambique rings rather hollow when one considers that the Frelimo party-state also borrowed the ideas of Marx and Lenin from abroad. Mia Couto draws our attention to the continuity and unsuitability of foreign ideas when Deolinda, the main character in "The Secret Love of Deolinda," embraces a foreign investor on the streets of Maputo because he looks like Marx. The reader might recall from our earlier reference to Deolinda that, during the socialist period, she had been given a button with a picture of Marx to wear on her lapel at her factory job. Outraged at the presence of a white foreigner on her breast, her father made her take it off. Yet she continued to kiss her picture of Marx every night before she went to bed. As the story moves forward in time, the government exchanges the rhetoric of socialism for the discourse of the market. Western non-governmental organizations and private investors replace the vanguard party. In turn, Deolinda transfers her attachments too – an act which culminates in her embrace of a bearded foreign investor who looks like Marx.[2] In depicting the ease with which Deolinda transfers her attachment from Marx to the foreign investor, Couto both criticizes the zeal with which some Mozambicans embrace anything that appears to come from outside and exposes the tendency to treat foreign ideas as if they are interchangeable. Couto seems to be saying that Mozambicans have readily exchanged Marxism for market principles, yet without really understanding the distinction between the two. Nor do they recognize what actually links the two ideas together; both are foreign; both are in a sense imported from abroad; and both may not suit Mozambique. Foreign ideas and actors, then, were at least as influential in the choice of socialism as they were in the choice of neo-liberalism. Their uninterrupted presence in one form or another also calls attention to the continuities that characterize Mozambique.

Importantly, the command economy has left its legacy, too, as it has in the former Soviet Union and in Eastern Europe. Mozambique's socialism may not have been institutionalized to the extent that it was in Hungary or Romania, but neither was the rupture as great. After all, the ruling Frelimo party has been in power continuously since 1975. As researchers have found in other post-socialist countries, there is a degree of path-dependence to the current trajectory of capitalism. It is evident in the way privatization has been implemented, in who benefits from sales of state assets, in who participates in grand projects, and in the roles of the state. Both the advocates of neo-liberalism and their

---

[2] Couto, *Every Man is a Race*, pp. 112–13.

critics have underestimated the extent to which post-command states – those who occupy its institutions as well as existing social forces who may have cooperated with and challenged them – have captured and reshaped the neo-liberal agenda. Technical and administrative approaches treat former command economies as if they are blank slates. They ignore the politics of privatization. The irony actually may be that some privatizations are "successful" precisely because they have been captured by old networks, inclusive of state institutions and state elites.

To argue that transitions are path-dependent, however, is not to assume that their outcomes are predetermined at the start. What we have in Mozambique can really best be described as "transformative preservation," a dynamic but contradictory process of blending rupture with replication, of joining discontinuity to continuity. It can be found in the structure and institutions of post-transition Mozambique and in the recombinatory strategies that many actors have adopted to navigate the transition. Moreover, it is unmistakably evident in the discourse used to legitimate change. This chapter concludes study of the transition from a command state to a market economy by examining this discourse, just as the initial chapters analyzed the ideologies of the independent, revolutionary state. Rhetoric and visual imagery are the most obvious manifestations of transformation. They symbolically commence and complete a process of change. Presidential addresses and policy directives are often the first indications that a shift is underway. Official statements reinterpret the past, mold the present, and project the future. Images convey new ideas and aspirations, express desires, and inculcate values. The language that social groups employ in their everyday conversation or during moments of conflict both reflect and challenge these new forms of expression and the objectives they seek. These discursive approaches and responses are just as integral to the process of transformation as institutional restructuring. They are as consciously constructed as procedures for selling state enterprises. The themes, ideas, and images they employ are just as complex and intricate as the social configurations that have emerged from privatization and liberalization.

### The official rhetoric of transformative preservation

After independence, the revolutionary state tried to project its utopian vision through a complex ideology refracted through party conferences, state-commissioned posters, slogans, and murals. The message emanated from a centralized core and its dissemination took place through official channels from government ministers to Frelimo party secretaries. Ultimately, the state had little control over the responses to its message, but at least party ideologues were reasonably confident that the message was formulated and transmitted to the public as they intended. The ideological themes of nationalism, socialism, and modernism complemented and contradicted each other, but they were nevertheless readily identifiable as organizing principles of the new government. They faced little rhetorical competition, at least at the level of formulation and articulation.

Now that opposition parties challenge the ruling party at the polls and the ownership and management of farms and factories are more dispersed, the discursive power of the state is more diffuse. Messages dispatched by radio and the print media express a plurality of contradictory and competing viewpoints. These multiple voices impede the formulation of a totalizing ideology that can give meaning and authority to the significant changes that Mozambique has undergone. Similarly, even were a coherent ideology to be formulated, its transmission to the public would compete with alternative interpretations of what is occurring. For example, are we witnessing "the dawn of an African renaissance" as several African leaders have pronounced in recent years? Or is Africa in "crisis" as others have claimed? Is globalization undermining Mozambique's national sovereignty, or is it offering the country new opportunities to achieve growth? These highly divergent interpretations of contemporary events are recurrent themes in news articles, and there are many more. To organize a legitimating discourse amidst such a multitude of rival narratives must be particularly challenging.

Yet the need for such a discourse is great. The state today cannot rely on revolutionary victory and the tropes of liberation and struggle to carry it along. Instead, the government must explain what looks like the defeat of a project that it once wholeheartedly embraced at an ideological level. It must legitimate the transition that Mozambique has undergone, justify its own role in it, and gain supporters for its project. Evidence of this legitimating discourse is emerging. State officials are crafting a message about the transition through public and private speeches or interviews.

Five authoritative themes recur throughout these messages and together they support an over-arching government strategy aimed at transformative preservation. The first is a decidedly neo-liberal theme, where government speeches refer frequently to the benefits of competition and the efficiencies to be gained from relying on the market rather than the state. They discuss the expected benefits to economic development brought by a dynamic private sector, and, less often, they promote liberal freedoms and democratic values. President Chissano expresses well the central objective of neo-liberalism when he argues "our government is deeply committed to establishing a favorable business climate."[3] Notably, there are few attempts to explain why socialism failed or even to apologize for government mistakes during the socialist period. Rather, today's emphasis is on the benefits that the private sector allegedly will bring.

---

[3] President Chissano, "Keynote Address," *Fourth Private Sector*, p. 4.

Although the use of neo-liberal buzzwords regarding the market, competition, investment, and efficiency are the most noticeable indications of a rupture with the past, several of the themes actually re-mix elements from the colonial and socialist periods. In particular, the state continues to be accorded a large role in economic undertakings. Chissano's 1997 speech to the Assembly of the Republic pays much attention to the government's role in resolving problems brought by privatization, in stimulating investment, and in protecting and re-training workers.[4] Even in speeches to the private sector, government officials present the state as a guarantor, protector, and facilitator of capital investment and corporate growth. These might be seen as roles typically associated with more activist governments in developmental states, those who practice mid-wifery and husbandry, to use Peter Evans' terms. But it is noteworthy that the roles seem to extend much beyond what neo-liberal prescriptions envisage for "transitional" countries. Mozambican government officials stipulate more and more often that the government can be a partner. We have already referred to the two senses in which the president uses the word "partnership." In one usage, the president envisages a partnership as one that includes government, capital, and labor. Here, government appears to be a neutral third party in what is practically a corporatist project. The government is interested in stabilizing the relationship between workers and employers. In other cases, the use of "partner" comes closer to the reality we have observed. It describes a state that directly or indirectly forms joint-ventures with capital to retain assets, maintain power, obtain profits, and gain prestige for state directors. Yet the term also obfuscates. It hides the inequalities and power imbalances that may characterize public-private relationships. To speak repeatedly of partnerships is to seek to legitimate what is already a reality in Mozambique – that the state is an active player in the restructuring process.

The themes of nationalism and modernism are also quite strong. Government officials make references to developing Mozambique, promoting policies that benefit Mozambicans, and embracing the nation's rich and diverse cultural heritage. This latter sentiment is reflective of a kind of "new nationalism" that has been popularized by the transition in South Africa, where cultural and linguistic diversity within a nation-state paradoxically is seen as an integral part of the national character of that state. In Mozambique, features of the "new nationalism" are evident in the Constitution of 1990 which praises and protects Mozambique's linguistic and cultural diversity, and in the 1997 Land Law which acknowledges the role of "communities" in deciding how local land will be used. Nevertheless, more common understandings of the term "nationalism," such as loyalty to the nation-state, or the pursuit of national as opposed

---

[4] President Chissano, "O Estado da Nação," Comunicação do Presidente Joaquim Chissano a Assembleia da República," (17 March 1997) (Maputo: Bureau de Informação Pública, 1997).

to individual or class interests, are also evident. In speeches directed at the private sector, government officials pay special attention to the importance of Mozambican entrepreneurs and express support for Mozambican projects. The dialogue includes references to "smart partnerships" between Mozambicans and foreigners because the government wishes to see Mozambicans included in potentially lucrative arrangements. What's attractive about the use of the term "partnership" is that it implies that the participants in the arrangement are on equal footing. One is not beholden to the other, or subordinated to the other. For a government that critics frequently accuse of having sold-out to neoliberalism, it is attractive to depict Mozambique as a partner, not as an apprentice or slave to foreign investors or the World Bank.[5] Furthermore, government officials use public occasions and business conferences to encourage private sector actors to be patriotic and to benefit Mozambique. They also frequently launch projects and schemes designed to alleviate poverty. These measures continue the discourse of nationalism that began with the Frelimo victory in 1975.[6]

A "low" rather than "high" modernism also permeates public discourse. Government officials now direct their modernist inclinations towards particular grand projects rather than incorporating them into an over-arching plan to create a scientific, rational social order. Supported by investors and international institutions, government officials express preferences for large-scale electrification schemes and corridors that criss-cross the country. Discussions about high-speed train lines, giant eco-tourism projects, dams, and iron and steel plants reflect a continued obsession with big, high-technology undertakings that will tame nature and tie Mozambique firmly to the twenty-first century. Phrases such as "spatial development initiatives," "industrial free zones," "the rationalization of the workforce," and "operational management" reveal the continuing adaptability and appeal of modernist notions. The recent completion of a billion dollar aluminum smelting plant accompanied by official pronouncements about the enormous benefits that the project will bring provides the most concrete manifestation of the fascination with modernism on the part of officials. Promises of a better future provide a convenient distraction from the hardships that characterize so many Mozambican lives.

Finally, successive governments in Mozambique since the colonial period have frequently portrayed the country as part of a larger community, and they have relied on and incorporated ideas and aid from abroad. Up to 1974, the primary influence on the colonial government came from Lisbon. After independence, other socialist countries as well as the Nordic countries donated

---

[5] Even the World Bank has adopted the term when referring to its relationship with Mozambique, see L. Landau, *Rebuilding the Mozambique Economy: Assessment of a Development Partnership* (Washington, DC: World Bank, 1998).

[6] "Em Foco: Presidente de Moçambique conta com Portugal para a eliminação da dívida," *Moçambique*, 21 (April 1999), pp. 6–8.

ideas, personnel, and funds. The government also considered vital the support of the constellation of other independent countries of southern Africa. Today, the government continues to acknowledge the importance of the region, including South Africa, to the Mozambican economy. The Mozambican government equally praises the efforts by foreign non-governmental organizations, investors from abroad, and international financial institutions in Mozambique. It emphasizes the virtues and benefits of internationalization and regionalization, though government speeches carefully balance their references to globalization with promises to shield local actors from any harmful effects.

It may be difficult to call this combination of themes an "ideology" if by that we mean a totalizing discourse. It is even more diffuse and fractured than that constructed just after independence. It contains several elements such as internationalization and nationalism, and neo-liberal capitalism and a continuing statism that conflict with and contradict each other. And it is hard to find among Frelimo party documents a coherent articulation of all the themes in any way comparable to the ideological pronouncements found in the documents of the Third Frelimo Party Congress of 1977 or in the "socialist realism" of revolutionary poster art. Moreover, the message is much harder to control than during the colonial or socialist periods. It competes with contrasting messages coming from opposition parties, independent newspapers, business journals, billboard advertising, radio programs, fax machines, satellite televisions, and the Internet.

## Messages of legitimation in images and text

Multiple sources inside and outside Mozambique, however, do complement the government's message; it is not a lone voice. International institutions and foreign investors also speak the language of competition, efficiency, markets, and investment. These same actors articulate the themes of regionalization, internationalization, and modernism as do Mozambican entrepreneurs. Many Mozambican investors employ the discourse of nationalism in order to lobby the government to protect and support their businesses. As might be expected, the government is drawing its base of support largely from those with whom the message resonates. Urban, educated, middle-class people who are the main beneficiaries of the reforms serve as one of Frelimo's core constituencies. In addition, Frelimo still relies on its traditional bases of support in the rural areas of the south, and in the northern province of Cabo Delgado where the revolutionary movement started. Thus, once again the government appears to have combined the old with the new.

Since the government directs much of its message towards strengthening the loyalty of the private sector, I have explored the extent to which articles and advertisements in business and economic magazines complement or challenge this message. I examined articles in four magazines: *Xitimela*, the journal of the Mozambican port and railways parastatal, whose publication is partly financed by the Spanish government; *Revista de Empresas* (Business Review), a bi-monthly magazine aimed primarily at domestic investors, directors, and managers as well as those nationals interested in business; *Fórum Económico* (Economic Forum), a quarterly business journal geared towards foreigners and nationals in the Mozambican market, which is owned by a Portuguese company but staffed by Portuguese and Mozambican writers. The fourth magazine, entitled *Moçambique*, is a slick, polished publication produced quarterly by the Portugal–Mozambique Chamber of Commerce. It is aimed at those Portuguese and Mozambican investors who run the largest enterprises and are involved in substantial economic undertakings. These four magazines broadly represent the range of groups that support the growth of the private sector and have benefitted from it: domestic and foreign investors, government institutions and officials, neo-liberal economists, managers, and middle-class consumers. In addition, the parastatal magazine, *Xitimela*, also addresses its workers in the port and railways sector.

To different degrees, the content of the magazines reinforces many of the messages emanating from government. Like the government, the magazines are up-beat and positive about Mozambique's future. They embrace the characteristics of modernism. They welcome the turn towards capitalism, and they emphasize the virtues of more open markets and greater integration in the global economy. At the same time, they reveal the fault lines that are arising from the transition: the debates about the role of the state; the viability of partnerships; the use of land; local versus foreign investors; and owners versus workers. What the journals do not discuss is equally revealing. Like the government, they refrain from lengthy discussions of the immediate past, except to note that it achieved poor results. They ignore the war, except in passing, and most of them rarely concern themselves with ethnic identities, traditional authorities, or the plight of smallholders. They paper over the inequalities and injustices that are accompanying privatization. Indeed, one is hard pressed to find within the slick pages of the journal, *Moçambique*, the country that is still listed by the World Bank as one of the poorest countries in the world.

Advertisements constitute another contribution to the emerging discourse that government speeches, interviews, and company profiles articulate. Advertisements in Mozambique are found on billboards or on the sides of buildings in the urban areas. They are also printed in newspapers and in the national and international business journals that have proliferated since Mozambique began to privatize. It was in advertising that I expected to find the embodiment of transition, for nothing is more indicative of a rupture with socialism than a commercial advertisement that markets a commodity, or a corporate advertisement that highlights a private company's worthy qualities. Advertising is, after all, the "language of capitalism," visually wrought.[7] Though the decentralized nature of their creation mitigates against the production of a coherent set of ideological constructs, the mere existence of advertisements reinforces a core element of contemporary capitalism, commodity fetishism.[8] The principal purpose of an advertisement is to get a consumer to buy the brand-name product that is its subject. To accomplish this goal, the advertisement must convince the consumer of the importance of insurance, or the value of staying in one hotel versus another. It must link the drinking of a Coca-Cola to qualities or ideas that the viewer finds meaningful.[9] Similarly, a corporate advertisement tries to convey a company's business philosophy, to build confidence or trust in its services, and to construct a favorable image of the company in the minds of the public. Because they highlight the qualities of companies rather than market specific products, corporate advertisements act to legitimate capitalism in its entirety.[10]

Surveying those advertisements placed in business journals, I found many examples of advertisements that market commodities or seek to establish an "'environment of confidence'" for particular companies and their services.[11] As might be expected, businesses designed advertisements for the clientele that were likely to read these types of journals, principally domestic and foreign business people, but also government representatives, officials from international institutions, and the moneyed tourist. There were advertisements for hotels, rental cars, and airlines directed at foreigners. There were advertisements for farm equipment and animal rations geared towards the owners and directors of agricultural enterprises; advertisements for electrical cables, batteries, ship repair and metal containers aimed at those associated with industry or transport. There were advertisements for all kinds of services likely to be needed by small and large investors: banking, insurance, cable television, equipment rental, import-export, and consulting. Scattered throughout every journal also were corporate advertisements that aimed to create credibility for an existing firm, to establish name recognition, and to develop trust in particular companies. The presence of numerous advertisements of this type are indicative of the changes that have occurred recently. Because the private sector has only recently emerged in Mozambique, companies must raise public awareness about their activities and instill confidence.

[7] M. Cross, "Reading Television Texts: The Postmodern Language of Advertising" in M. Cross, ed., *Advertising and Culture: Theoretical Perspectives* (Westport, CT: Praeger, 1996), p. 1.
[8] R. Goldman, *Reading Ads Socially* (NY: Routledge, 1992), pp. 35–36.
[9] Goldman, *Reading Ads Socially*, see chapter 1.
[10] H. Keyishan, "'We Bring Good Things to Life'/ 'We're Always There': The AdWorld of GE," in Cross, ed., *Advertising and Culture*, pp. 49–60.
[11] E. Barnouw quoted by Goldman, *Reading Ads Socially*, p. 86.

Collectively, the advertisements illustrate the particular timing and manner of Mozambique's participation in the "new internationalization." Mozambique's entrance into the global economy at the end of the twentieth century means joining a world where the service sector now dominates and the advertisements reflect this. Mozambique continues to rely on traditional exports of raw materials such as cotton, cashew, tea, tobacco, and sugar, and on the provision of transport services for goods going to and from South Africa, Zimbabwe, and Malawi. Yet it is also seeks to appeal to, and provide services for, the more global tourist, the foreign investor, and representatives of international institutions and non-governmental organizations. At the same time, advertising markets a variety of services to Mozambique's small, but cosmopolitan, domestic elite.

Merely by attempting to sell products, services, or a company name to a select public, advertisements reinforce the transition to a market economy. Trust in the private sector and a thriving consumer culture may not yet be realities in Mozambique, but many advertisements are not intended to reflect reality. They are trying to inculcate new tastes by enticing the viewer to adopt the values they market or share in the fantasy they construct. To convey their messages, advertisements rely on the written word as well as visual imagery. As a medium and as a conveyer of reified ideals, advertising thus shares characteristics with the iconographic tradition of the socialist period. Both the socialist period, with its political posters and murals, and the capitalist period, with its ubiquitous advertisements, try to shape what is not yet there, to envision a utopian world or, at least, a different world.[12] When the socialist political posters called attention to the role of women in defense and in production during the 1980s, they were not just acknowledging the contributions that women had already made to an independent Mozambique. They were trying to secure the loyalty and support of women at a time when resistance to collectivization and the modernist aims of the party was increasing and when Renamo was escalating the number of attacks. The posters also anticipated a future in which women would be more appreciated than they were at the time. Yet they presented that future as if it already existed. Similarly, an advertisement for crystal or a cable television that states "We are producing for you" or "We are bringing communication to you" is not speaking to the current ability of Mozambicans to purchase crystal or cable television, since most cannot afford them. It is imagining a future in which Mozambicans will be able to purchase these commodities.

As in the previous period, the ability to convince depends on the advertiser's familiarity with cultural and historical images that resonate with viewers. In the same way that party ideologues employed images of peasants, or cashew trees, to strike a chord with Mozambican smallholders after the revolution, the current dilemma for the advertiser in Mozambique is to find ways to use cultural

---

[12] J. Fowles, *Advertising and Popular Culture* (Thousand Oaks, CA: Sage, 1996), p. 101.

symbols and history to entice the audience to buy products or use services. Advertisements have to go beyond selling a product to speak to social relations. Their function, like the iconography of socialism, is thus paradoxical. They must shape tastes and beliefs, but they must do so by relying on established meanings and frames of reference that have significance for viewers.[13] Not surprisingly, the motifs and images that some of the advertisements in Mozambique employ replicate more complex and contradictory themes that the government emphasizes. Many of them are optimistic and strident, presenting change as for the better, but without explicit references to past failures. Some juxtapose images of an imagined past with those of the present, or blend claims to tradition with claims to modernity to get their message across. They make references to continuity and to change. They stress the importance of regionalization and internationalization, or they may privilege Mozambique as a place where opportunity abounds. Some appear to be consciously constructing a link with a mythical glorious past (but not a socialist one) at the same time that they speak to the new political and economic orientation of the Frelimo government.

To illustrate these points, I examine several advertisements in depth. I do not undertake here an exhaustive, quantitative survey of advertisements in business magazines to illustrate the extent to which numerically they support the themes that the government emphasizes. Nor do I mean to suggest that viewers interpret these advertisements or identify with the values expressed in advertisements as advertisers may have intended. Indeed, as Fowles argues, one reason that advertisements are so numerous and so symbolically charged is that the capitalist beliefs they are trying to convey meet with some resistance on the part of intended recipients. He states: "Proselytizers are not always welcomed. Most consumers believe in moderation, some enjoy periods of nonconsumerist relapse, and a stalwart few refuse to convert at all."[14] In Mozambique, where domestic viewers have not been "trained" to respond to advertising, this may be even more the case. I interpret selected advertisements in order to show how they might be speaking to the themes that the government addresses and thus might be reinforcing efforts to engage in transformative preservation.[15]

---

[13] See Goldman, *Reading Ads Socially* for a more detailed discussion of the different strategies and objectives of advertising.

[14] Fowles, *Advertising and Popular Culture* pp. 101–2.

[15] The responses of two groups to a questionnaire of mine informs my interpretation. One audience consisted of ten Mozambican professors, government officials, and college students who had attended a lecture I gave on privatization in Mozambique. Following the lecture, I gave them a questionnaire in which I asked them to comment on the content of the messages in the advertisements, whether they had a favorable or unfavorable reaction to the advertisement, etc. Following the five advertisements, I then asked them to comment on the process and impact of privatization in Mozambique. A second audience consisted of twenty-two American college students who had spent a semester with me learning about the history and cultures of Mozambique. A comparison of the similarities and differences in their responses requires further study and is not addressed here.

Several advertisements by foreign investors concentrate on themes such as globalization and the future in order to emphasize changes and Mozambique's links to the rest of the world. Internationalization is often represented by globes with the African continent in a prominent position. The advertisement placed by Ferpinta explores the theme of transformation and globalization in a very dramatic way (see figure 7.1). The advertisement depicts a bright orange fetus swirling around in amniotic fluid that is a turquoise color with flecks of white. The amniotic fluid resembles the earth as seen from the outside the earth's atmosphere, and is an obvious allusion to globalization. Coupled with the words, "My Africa," the unborn child is meant to represent the dawning of a new generation on the continent of Africa, the birth of a new era in which Africa benefits from globalization and all of its associated properties, such as privatization and free trade. The text of the advertisement hails the peace, development, and prosperity that will be realized as this new generation in Africa matures. But just as the purpose of pre-natal care is to ensure a healthy baby, so also the text of the advertisement notes that in order to realize a prosperous future work must begin in Africa today. Ferpinta, the company that has placed the advertisement, wants to work together with others to generate wealth and realize opportunities for the "Men of tomorrow."

An advertisement by another Portuguese investor, Grupo José de Mello, also stresses the future of Africa and notes the importance of working together to realize success (see figure 7.2). The group uses the caption of its advertisement, "The future is this way," in two senses: the first refers to the potential of the African continent, and the second refers to the strength and breadth of the company. The continent's potential is represented by a map of Africa with the desert areas highlighted in khaki and the forested areas in green. Superimposed on the map is text referring to the activities that Grupo José de Mello engages in "with local partners" in each country, for example, banking, insurance, naval repair, etc., in Mozambique and insurance in Guinea-Bissau. Below the text are several photographs showing some of the Group's undertakings. There is a picture of one of its ships and a photograph of one of its insurance offices. Not only is the advertisement marketing the company's services, but also it is a corporate advertisement seeking to legitimate the company's name in the minds of viewers. The implication is that if viewers want to participate in Africa's bright future, they need to be a "partner" with Grupo José de Mello.[16]

---

[16] José de Mello is the parent company of CUF, a large Portuguese industrial-financial conglomerate that had investments in colonial Mozambique. After 1974–75, most of its investments were nationalized in both Portugal and Mozambique; it began recovering its companies in Portugal from the mid-1980s and investing in Mozambique in the 1990s. In 2000, José de Mello merged its financial activities with those of Banco Comercial Portugues, see José de Mello, Home page, 30 November 2001 <http://www.josedemello.pt>.

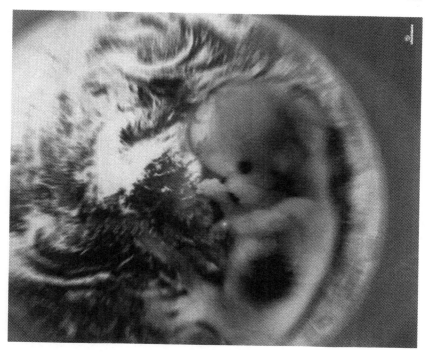

# ÁFRICA MINHA

Esta será sem dúvida a África da Nova Geração. Terra de Paz, desenvolvimento e prosperidade.
O Continente do Futuro. Futuro esse, que queremos partilhar, gerando riqueza e oportunidades
para os Homens do amanhã. E, para isso, é preciso começar já hoje. Vai daí, o **GRUPO
FERPINTA** está presente em ANGOLA e MOÇAMBIQUE, convicto de que juntos
faremos mais e melhor. Em nome de uma África de todos.

Figure 7.1 Ferpinta Group, advertisement, courtesy of Leonel Pires, General
Marketing Manager, Ferpinta Group.

Figure 7.2  José de Mello Group, advertisement, courtesy of Fernando Pereira Marques, Director of Communication, José de Mello Group.

The attention to the importance of partnerships is intensified in an advertisement by IMPAR, an insurance company in Mozambique that has recently merged with another insurance company[17] (see figure 7.3). Consistent with the make-up of the company (which used to be a joint-venture between foreign and national investors), and the service it is marketing, the advertisement stresses the importance of working together. It depicts a relay race in which one runner hands off a baton to another, followed by a caption in bold that says "Success is the result of teamwork." The text then reads, "In the world of business, entrepreneurial success depends greatly on the partners with whom we work. IMPAR is without a doubt your best partner for the protection of your personal or business assets, proposing professional solutions for your insurance needs." The advertisement builds on the themes of "smart partnerships" stressed by the government, asserting that partnerships such as that between the insurer and the insured will guarantee a positive outcome. Unlike the other advertisements just cited, it does not make explicit reference to a future that is brimming with potential, but like the other ads it implies that there is an upward trajectory in market economies that will be realized if certain measures and specific actors are involved. In this ad, the company suggests the upward trajectory by depicting a race in which the obvious purpose is to reach the finish line first. In this race, it appears that a black arm and hand is receiving the baton in the race from a white hand and arm. The inclusion of black and white hands and arms may have been intended to promote racial harmony by suggesting that blacks and whites can work together, just as blacks and whites worked together in the joint-venture IMPAR. But the picture can be interpreted in other ways. The handing of the baton to the black runner rather patronizingly suggests that Africans need the help of whites in order to achieve victory. Alternatively, one could also see the exchange as one where it is now Africa's turn to participate in the race, to take the baton and go, but that the opportunity has been made possible by the hand that is giving up the baton. Consistent in all three interpretations is the belief that the race will produce great opportunities for its participants. This message displays the optimism of neo-liberal prescriptions regarding the market and private investment.

The advertisements by new investors and newly formed joint-ventures emphasise a bright future, the benefits of globalization, and the virtues of partnerships. The advertisements of old or established businesses in Mozambique treat these themes somewhat differently. They do not restrict time to the present and the future; they also play on the past, although it is a reconstructed past. The advertisements of established companies juxtapose tradition with modernity

---

[17] The merger resulted in a new company, SIM (Seguradora Internacional de Moçambique), SARL. BIM, whose parent company is Banco Comercial Portugues in Portugal, has 20.82 percent of the capital in the new company, see BCP, Home page, "Fusões por Incorporação," 30 November 2001, <http://www.bcp.pt>.

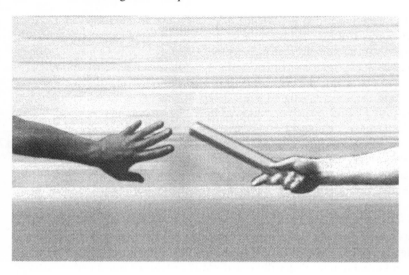

# O sucesso é o resultado do trabalho em equipa.

No mundo dos negócios o sucesso empresarial depende muito dos parceiros com quem trabalhamos.

A ÍMPAR é, sem dúvida, o seu melhor parceiro para a protecção do património empresarial ou pessoal, ao propôr-lhe soluções profissionais para as suas necessidades de segurança.

IMPAR

COMPANHIA DE SEGUROS
DE MOÇAMBIQUE

Figure 7.3   IMPAR, advertisement. IMPAR has merged with another company.

and endow both with positive features. Take the commodity advertisement for the Polana Hotel (see figure 7.4). The Polana is one of the oldest and most luxurious hotels in Mozambique. Built during the colonial period, it was completely restored and modernized in the early 1990s as the civil war in Mozambique began to wind down and privatization began to increase. Visually and textually, both the Portuguese and the English versions of the advertisement try to convey the Polana's history while appealing to global guests with modern demands. The advertisement presented here shows an image photographed from beyond the clear, blue swimming pool in the back of the Polana. The photo is shot from below so that the white, four-story hotel framed by palm trees commands a grand, imposing presence filling up the entire frame in the wide-angle shot. In the Portuguese version of the ad, the photo is followed by the claim that "the doors of the Polana Hotel are open to guests from all over the World." Following this assertion, the words "Polana Hotel" are repeated and then followed by the adjectives, "Tradition and Reputation." A short description of the hotel follows, remarking on its colonial past and its location on the Indian Ocean. It is exclaimed that its five-star rating makes it the pride of the national hotel industry **and** of Sub-Saharan Africa. To the side and below the text, four smaller pictures with accompanying descriptions suggest a very modern hotel with few roots in tradition and one that is too new to have earned a reputation. One picture shows a computer with printer (although one might note that both are out of date) set in a large conference room with a podium and a viewing screen. There is also a photo of a fitness center with modern nautilus equipment and a hotel room where we are told there is a refrigerator and a television with twelve international channels. Below the elegant logo of the Polana Hotel, telex, telephone, fax numbers, and an email address are given, reinforcing the Polana's claim to modernity.

There are two types of contrasts that are worth mentioning. First, the advertiser consciously attempts to emphasize tradition as well as modernity. The product is of course aimed at visitors, and these are visitors who clearly are quite accustomed to having all the modern services available to them, from fitness equipment to fax machines. At the same time, the advertisement uses the past to legitimate the present. It contrasts visual and verbal claims to modernity with a visual and verbal emphasis on "tradition" and "reputation". These are attributes that are earned **in** time and **over** time. The Portuguese version of the advertisement anchors that time frame in the colonial period, describing the Polana as a "magnificent building of colonial splendor"[18] It uses the hotel's grandeur to synecdochically represent an era and in doing so, it reduces colonialism to a period of splendor and magnificence, obscuring its associations

---

[18] The English version of the ad changes the reference from "a magnificent building of **colonial** splendor" to "a white majestic edifice."

As portas do Hotel Polana estão abertas
aos hóspedes de todo o Mundo

# HOTEL POLANA
## Tradição e Requinte

O Hotel Polana encontra-se
instalado num magnífico edifício
de esplendor colonial,
debruçado sobre o Oceano
Índico. Alicerçado num
esmerado serviço cinco estrelas
constitui o orgulho da hotelaria
nacional e da áfrica austral.

O Centro de Conferências oferece a tranquilidade
eficiente de um serviço esmerado para reuniões
com o seu moderno sistema de comunicações, e
serviço de Secretariado, assim como para
banquetes e recepções do mais alto nível.

A Piscina de um azul prístino sob o sol de
África e o Ginásio com os melhores
equipamentos, proporcionam belos momentos
de lazer e de recondicionamento físico, assim
como o repouso necessário ao equilíbrio físico
e mental.

Tanto o Salão de Chá como o Restaurante
Terraço apresentam um cardápio
cosmopolita digno da qualidade e conforto do
seu ambiente.

As Suites e os Quartos confortáveis, equipados
com instalações técnicas avançadas e
decorados com requinte, oferecem uma ou
duas casas de banho, frigobar, TV com 12
canais internacionais e serviço de Chá & Café.

**MAPUTO • MOÇAMBIQUE**

Av. Julius Nyerere, 1380.
Caixa Postal 1151 • Telex 6 - 278 POLANA MO
Telef. +258 1, 491001/7 • Fax + 258.1.491480
E-MAIL: MAR. @ HPOLANA.UEM.MZ

Figure 7.4 Polana Hotel, advertisement, courtesy of Deolinda Stilwell,
Marketing and Public Relations, Polana Hotel.

with forced labor and systematic repression. Of course, many advertisements for luxury hotels market their elite exclusivity. What is distinctive about this advertisement is that it consciously trades on an invented notion of the colonial past to attract those visitors who wish to "experience" Africa ("I stayed in a colonial hotel"), without having to endure any of its inconveniences.

The other contrast exists beyond the photo, beyond the advertisement for the Polana Hotel. It has to do with the organization of space in the capital city. It is the contrast between what Gordimer recalled as the "sybaritic luxury" of the hotel and the hardship prevalent elsewhere.[19] Barely two miles away from the comforts of the hotel is the real Maputo, the city where most urban residents live, the overcrowded suburbs of Xipamanine or Zimpeto. Unlike the jacaranda-lined boulevard that sweeps in front of the Polana, the pot-holed main streets of the suburbs convey a huge assortment of busses, carts, automobiles, animals, and people to their final destinations. These streets connect with a tangled array of twisted pathways that run between the cane or cinder-block houses where thousands of urban residents live. Often drenched by water during the rainy season and engulfed with the smoke from charcoal fires during the winter, these severe conditions are "home" to all but the wealthiest Mozambicans. Nothing better illustrates the stark inequalities that characterize the city of Maputo than the image of a Mozambican woman with a baby on her back and a bucket of water balanced on her head making her way through the muddy streets of Zimpeto. Contrast this with the image of a hotel guest stepping off the marble platform in front of the Polana into one of those ubiquitous Range Rovers that are the vehicle of choice for the foreign non-governmental organizations that operate in Mozambique. The luxury that the Polana markets to tourists may in fact be exactly what they are getting, but it does not reflect in the slightest what many Mozambicans themselves experience. The images conveyed by the advertisement mask the contradictions that are so apparent in this transformation: the inequalities between elites and the poor, between those who are accumulating wealth and those who have lost formal economy jobs.

Whereas the Polana Hotel draws on a "tradition" that has never existed for most Mozambicans in order to market a fantasy overnight stay to "guests from all over the world," other businesses rely on historical references to suggest continuity. Some of the oldest companies in Mozambique allude to the past to convey a sense of stability, to suggest that they are trustworthy because they have survived so much. A past that goes back at least a hundred years is the magic number. What a century communicates to the knowledgeable reader is that the company has been in Mozambique almost from the beginning of the creation of formal colonialism, weathered independence, endured the socialist period, stuck it out during the civil war, and successfully navigated the transition.

---

[19] N. Gordimer quoted in Sidaway and Power, "Sociospatial Transformations," p. 1468.

To the reader lacking any familiarity with Mozambican history, the claim to continuity challenges the stereotype of Africa as a place of turbulence. The conclusion the reader draws then is that the company is a sound operation, not a speculative one, and that it must surely know Mozambique, even if the reader does not. The claims to continuity distinguish these companies not only from new undertakings by foreigners, who may or may not know Mozambique, but also from the recent investments by Mozambican businessmen-in-the-making.

Corporate advertisements by Banco Standard Totta de Moçambique, João Ferreira dos Santos, and CFM aptly illustrate the reliance on historical continuity to convey stability and trustworthiness. BSTM is the only private bank that survived the transition to socialism. It is now one of the major banks in Mozambique. In the advertisement considered here (see figure 7.5), it wants to get across this sense of continuity by suggesting that it is "a bank with roots." The picture is a shot from below of the bank's main offices in Maputo. The bank's logo and a semi-circle of green leaves – an allusion to ancient Greece, no doubt – are superimposed on the photo. The image projects a timeless, classical structure that has ably withstood adversity, emerging almost unchanged from the turbulent past. Lest the reader feel that such links to the past imply old-fashioned ways of doing things, she is reassured that this is a "young bank with more than 100 years of experience." The written text that accompanies the advertisement tells the reader that the bank uses modern electronic equipment and offers a variety of services. However, the bank's age guarantees that clients and the business community will receive a "solid service, secure and of extreme confidence." The juxtaposition of the youthful with the old, of the experience gained from continuous operation with the willingness to incorporate new technologies, helps to legitimate the notion of transformative preservation. Here is a transition that, for all its differences with the socialist period, has roots in the past. Such links bring stability.

The corporate advertisements of JFS and CFM echo the theme of one hundred years. Both companies, the former a private company and the latter a parastatal, are trying to generate confidence by implying that they have been through a great deal. JFS (figure 7.6) adds a nationalistic twist to its story of continuity by stating that the sole focus of its efforts has been to construct a better Mozambique. JFS began its operations in 1897 and remained in the country after the declaration of independence and Frelimo's official adherence to Marxism-Leninism in 1977. Its owners were born in Mozambique and most of its assets were in Mozambique. These features appealed to the nationalistic strand in Frelimo's post-independence orientation and the government spared the company from nationalization. Although times were rough, the company emerged from the socialist period and the war as one of the largest companies in Mozambique. The company details the extent of its business activities in the text of the advertisement. The advertisement is a celebratory one, commemorating

# UM BANCO DE RAIZ

## BANCO STANDARD TOTTA DE MOÇAMBIQUE

Operando em Moçambique, há mais de 130 anos, tendo como principais accionistas o Banco Totta & Açores (Grupo Champalimaud) e o The Standard Bank of South Africa Limited oferece aos seus Clientes e ao Empresariado um serviço sólido, seguro e de extrema confiança, suportado por um sistema electrónico moderno.

Em operações cambiais e comerciais, a nível nacional e internacional, o **BANCO STANDARD TOTTA DE MOÇAMBIQUE** responde de uma forma rápida e eficiente às mais exigentes solicitações, desde a abertura e movimentação de contas em moeda nacional e em divisas, ao financiamento de projectos e crédito, em qualquer tipo de moeda, garantias bancárias, operações correntes de invisíveis e abertura de créditos de importação e exportação.

COM RAÍZES PROFUNDAS NA BANCA MOÇAMBICANA

### UM BANCO JOVEM COM MAIS DE 100 ANOS DE EXPERIÊNCIA

Phone: (258 1) 42 30 41 /5 • Fax: 42 69 67 - 43 08 86 - 42 30 29 • Telex: 6223 DERBY MO - Swift BSTM MZ MA • P.O. Box. 2086 - 1119 - Maputo - Moçambique

Figure 7.5  Banco Standard Totta de Moçambique, advertisement, courtesy of Frederico Lehrfeld, BSTM.

Figure 7.6 João Ferreira dos Santos Group, advertisement, courtesy of José Borges, Director General, JFS Group.

the company's 100 years in Mozambique from 1897 to 1997. It draws on nationalistic and developmentalist themes to gain the trust of the reader. The sharp blue-and-orange logo of the company is contrasted with the photo below. It shows a manicured field of tea bushes interspersed with tall trees, through which two people are walking. The photo reminds the reader that the bulk of JFS's operations relate to the production and purchasing of crops such as tea, cotton, and tobacco. The scene appears to be in the north of the country, where the founder of the company got his start and where JFS now concentrates most of its agricultural undertakings. The irony of the advertisement is that many Mozambicans have serious doubts whether JFS has constructed a "better Mozambique." Newspapers frequently call attention to various scandals that involve JFS employees, such as allegedly underinvoicing cotton sales abroad or improperly classifying cotton to justify paying producers a lower price. To the reader who does not know this history, however, the advertisement honors a solid company with experience and loyalty to Mozambique.

Lastly, I turn to an advertisement by CFM (figure 7.7). Here, too, the company is capitalizing on the perceived legitimacy associated with a hundred years of operation and implying that it will last into the next century. It thus addresses both ends of the timeline, the past and the future, and, in so doing, tries to evoke a sense of security in the viewer. The advertisement presents the past

Figure 7.7  CFM-Portos e Caminhos de Ferro de Moçambique, advertisement, courtesy of António Libombos, Director of Communication and Image, CFM.

as seamless, as flowing without complication into the present. Although CFM was a parastatal in the colonial period and is a parastatal now, instability has characterized much of its recent history. The colonial war disrupted CFM operations and Renamo sabotaged rail lines repeatedly after independence. Transport traffic at the port of Beira and on the central line from Beira to Harare fell drastically after Mozambique adhered to United Nations' sanctions against Rhodesia (Zimbabwe) in the late 1970s. Moreover, the South African government deliberately diverted traffic from CFM's southern line into and out of Maputo and at its ports at approximately the same time. Sharp reductions in the use of migrant labor by the gold mines of South Africa further cut into rail traffic on the southern line. These events greatly diminished the previously sizeable income that Mozambique had derived from the transit trade. To those who are familiar with this history, the advertisement suggests that any company with such a turbulent past is definitely prepared to face the millennium. Those who do not know it might imagine that here is a company that has been rock solid for over a century and has the experience to navigate the approaching one. Moreover, the photo used in the advertisement is reminiscent of several shots of Mozambique's ports taken by José dos Santos Rufino, a well-known chronicler of the colonial landscape in the 1920s.[20] There are thus visual links with the past.

The use of English and the image represented in the advertisement also call attention to the role of transport in facilitating and fostering globalization. The use of English in its bi-lingual (Portuguese-English) company magazine reveals a clear intent on the part of CFM to appeal to a foreign audience. The company would especially like to regain the lucrative transit trade with South Africa, but other English-speaking countries in Southern Africa represent potential clients also. The photograph looks out over the water from a dock in Nacala, Nampula Province, inviting the reader to imagine all the ships that come in and go out of Mozambique from other parts of the world. The advertisement is expansively spread across two pages with the text on one page and the CFM logo and small drawings of a ship, a dock, and a train on the facing page. CFM is spelled out in English and Portuguese, one under the other. The only indications that CFM continues to be a state company are the letters E.P. (Empresa Publica, or Public Enterprise) after the Portuguese rendition of the logo. Otherwise, this is an advertisement for just another company seeking to drum up business, not a state company seeking to preserve its assets, enhance its power, and protect its workforce in a transition to capitalism.

Collectively, these advertisements reinforce as well as influence the messages delivered by state authorities. They illustrate how the activities of elite social agents in the transformative process can buttress official positions and even

---

[20] See Rufino, *Albuns Fotográficos*, Vol. 2, p. 98. I'd like to thank Eric Allina-Pisano for directing me to this source.

share their contradictions. Yet the interests of these elites do not merely serve the state's agenda, they also determine and define it. In the present climate, this iterative process serves to empower both parties, but it could also weaken them should their interests diverge. Legitimating transformative preservation, then, is not only a structural endeavor, but also a discursive one involving both the state and select social groups.

## Concluding transformation

"When future historians write their assessment, will they write that Mozambique successfully made the transition from colonialism to independence, from war to peace, from one political party to many, from an economy directed by Marx to one directed by the market?.... Or will they simply say there was insufficient vision to sustain these changes and no willingness to put national interest ahead of personal gain?"[21]

Unfortunately, polemical evaluations such as this permeate debates about Mozambique's transition. Some observers insist on portraying economic and political change as something that can be realized merely by having sufficient vision and a greater commitment to the national interest. Particular ideological choices and institutional commitments certainly do influence outcomes, but these are insufficient to bring about a transition either to a command **or** a market economy. Whether the "vision" is a socialist one or a free market one, elites actively frame legitimating discourses to justify their choices and to project representations of imagined futures. A Department of Propaganda may control these discourses or multiple channels may disseminate them, but they are conscious and consistent efforts to structure the ideas that govern the economic agenda.

Moreover, in Mozambique as in other countries, the design of state institutions and the officials who occupy them have energetically contributed to the transformative process. Too often, observers have seen the state as a hindrance or a handmaiden, a weak bystander as capital engorges itself on a country's riches, or a debilitating nuisance interfering with the efficiency of the market and the pursuit of profit. The Mozambican experience illustrates that the state has played a pervasive, complex, and contradictory role. It has reinvented itself to suit global requirements. It has divested but at the same time it has reconfigured its power. Its current discourse tries to legitimate the present course of action and obscure the previous one. Its policies try to create support while state representatives participate actively in the sale of state companies and the allocation of land. Most importantly, social forces continue to express their grievances and aspirations, to and through, state institutions. Businesses rely on the state for assistance and urban workers appeal to it for protection.

---

[21] Dennis Jett, former American ambassador to Mozambique, quoted in "Jett, Polemical to the Last," *Mozambiquefile*, 241 (August 1996), p. 22.

State institutions coopt and control, manage and facilitate these social groups, but also they reflect the divisions that permeate the social order. Socialists have underestimated and neo-liberals have overlooked the ways in which existing social forces have shaped policy choices and influenced institutional arrangements. In the Mozambican case, international actors inhibited the realization of a transformative project rooted in "high modernism" of the "left-wing variant."[22] But the state's "inconclusive encounters" with smallholders and the existence of a residual private sector from the colonial period also nibbled away at the project over time. Similarly, the interaction of existing social agents with state institutions hastens and thwarts economic restructuring now. It subjects reforms to political struggles, to the unstable cleavages and alliances that characterize the competition for power in transitional countries.

What are these social forces that influence the trajectory of transition in Mozambique and what are their characteristics? The globalization of capitalist ideas and institutions in the twenty-first century means that states as well as investors must respond to the demands of global finance and take into account global markets. But they appear to be responding in a manner derived from their specific historical-institutional context. In Mozambique, elites who emerged during the period of the command economy are joining elites who pre-date independence to form or manage companies. Foreigners seek domestic partners with know-how and connections in order to navigate the culture of business in Mozambique. Domestic investors pursue the capital of foreigners to help insinuate themselves into Mozambique's new economic configurations. Foreign investors are forming "partnerships" with the state or public companies to invest in railroads or aluminum plants or bottling plants. Former government officials are running banks, and black Mozambicans with economics degrees are managing factories and starting consulting companies. Though the actors and configurations are slightly different, the previous command economies in Eastern Europe also reveal the capture of markets and firms by former elites and institutions. The multiplicity of patterns that are emerging from these alliances mean that specific local configurations still condition the effects of globalization.

Established and emerging rivalries parallel these new alliances and they undercut the ability of capital to converge around shared goals. There are competing factions of black nationalists, Indians, white Mozambicans, and foreigners. The interests of traders conflict with those of agriculture and industry, and smallholders are arrayed against concessionary company owners. Racial and regional antagonisms also fester. The characteristics of these conflicts and the ways in which they are expressed also draw on the distant and not so distant past. Some conflicts, such as those between cotton companies and rural smallholders, are nearly flashbacks to the colonial period. They are rooted in recurrent

---

[22] Scott, *Seeing Like a State*, p. 88.

struggles over the price of cotton or the treatment by cotton authorities. Yet these conflicts creatively employ language and forms of expression from the socialist period to address contemporary challenges. In one cotton conflict that I witnessed in 1995, smallholders were talking excitedly about making a banner to string up across the road in front of the cotton market. On it they wanted to inscribe the words "Peasant Strike." Listening to them protest against low cotton prices, I was struck by how the language of the socialist period had not been lost on these smallholders, even though these same people had spoken disparagingly of the "abaixo" government, when Frelimo used to say "Down with colonialism" and "Down with chiefs." In the peasant strike, however, the smallholders were using some of the lessons of socialism regarding the rights of peasants and the strength of collective organization to challenge government administrators in a democratic state and company officials in a capitalist country. They also blended these lessons with words used during the colonial period by referring occasionally to the company that worked in their area as a *patrão* (boss). When I spoke with several of the striking smallholders, I discovered that they interpreted their situation as one where they were suffering at the hands of a company. The *patrão* was exploitative, but if they worked together they might win concessions. They united behind the village chief or *regulo* and his assistant, the *cabo*, their recently rehabilitated "traditional authorities." Both men were angrily denouncing the way that the current structure of the cotton system left smallholders few options for gaining an income besides producing cotton. These claims harkened back to the period of the liberation struggle when Frelimo spoke of the colonial cotton regime in similar terms. This time (1995), when a district government official arrived to plead with the producers to sell at the established price, they stood firm and the government and company representatives left empty-handed. The producers said they were seeking "justice" and they did achieve a short-lived success. The following year, the price of cotton nearly doubled. Subsequently, falling world prices have undermined the gains that smallholders secured that day.

Interestingly, the cotton conflict illustrates that not only winners but also losers of reform measures are weaving together colonial and post-colonial, socialist discourses to interpret and understand change. The strategies that more diffuse and less powerful social forces such as smallholders employ to mitigate uncertainty draw on lessons learned during the colonial period as well as the independent one. As capitalism consolidates in Mozambique, social forces will continue to amalgamate or break apart, and how they do so will engender new challenges for the state. Over time, the state may face increased pressure to favor capital or to protect workers; to support landowners or to defend smallholders; to attract foreigners or to sustain Mozambicans. How well the state is able to manage and manipulate these configurations will determine eventually the wisdom of its commitment to transformative preservation and the kind of capitalism that Mozambique will have.

Mozambique's transition from a command economy and an authoritarian state to its capitalist and nominally democratic circumstances today carries all the signs of a clean break with the past. Since the late 1980s, the Frelimo government has slashed expenditures and cut state intervention, signed a peace accord and held elections. It has sold over 1,000 companies to the private sector, in one of the largest sales of state assets in Africa. The government has altered its planning methods, management practices, investment strategies, and ownership. Now the state no longer is responsible for formulating production targets; instead, private actors make that decision. In place of elaborate plans formulated at the national level, thousands of decisions take place at the local level with regard to inputs, outputs, and labor. The state does not use murals and incentives to exhort workers to achieve higher production targets. Rather, private companies use advertising to lure consumers to purchase their products, and they combine threats with bonuses to increase productivity. These efforts have made Mozambique a model for the success of neo-liberal programs and won praise from the World Bank and Western donors.

The effects of reforms have been equally dramatic, but much more unequal than neo-liberal supporters acknowledge. Growth rates for the country have soared over the last five years and a construction boom has hit the capital of Maputo. Beneficiaries of the transition are building homes, frequenting new restaurants, buying cars, and taking cruises. By contrast, urban slums ripple out in all directions from the capital, as the unemployed – privatization's losers – turn to informal trade, to begging, or to prostitution, to make ends meet. Already swelled by those who fled the war in the 1980s, the slums struggle to accommodate the steady influx of rural people who exchange the countryside for the city in their search for work. These developments alone suggest that the changes have been profound and non-transient.

Yet I have argued throughout that there remain discursive and institutional continuities that link the period of Marx to the current period of the market. The threads of the past are stitched into the fabric of the present in Mozambique, as they are in Romania or Hungary. They are manifest in the persistent influence of foreign ideas and in attachments to those values believed to be associated with modernity. Current discourse also draws on historical symbols and images that resonate with listeners. At a structural level, former state officials have taken advantage of the tumultuous changes to become bank directors and chief executive officers. Social networks comprised of old and new elites have captured resources, and former state institutions have redefined their roles in order to retain their power. These historical continuities, whether they date from the colonial or command experience, do not suggest stasis or a lack of dynamism. Rather, they attest to the resilience of state institutions, and the imaginative responses to change by social actors. Transformation in Mozambique begins and ends with the vibrant, complex interaction of the state and social forces, but it is an interaction bound by history.

# Bibliography

## PRIMARY SOURCES

### INTERVIEWS

Arkwright, David. Deputy chairman, Maputo Corridor Company. Johannesburg, South Africa. 24 March 1998.

Assulai, Janet. Legal advisor, Associação Rural de Ajuda Mútua. Maputo. 19 May 1998.

Audet, Lisa. Vice-president and representative, Equator Bank. Maputo. 3 March 1998.

Badenhorst, Caspar. Director, Agribuzi. Buzi, Sofala Province. 14 April 1994.

Bell, Simon. Senior economist, World Bank. Maputo. 13 July 1995; 18 February 1998.

Biriba, Sr. Director, Serviços Provinciais do Caju da Zambezia. Quelimane, Zambezia Province. 20 May 1998 (with Scott Kloeck-Jenson).

Bliss, Sid. Team leader, Expanded Rural Enterprises, USAID. Maputo. 17 March 1998.

Born, Tim. Infrastructure division chief, USAID. Maputo. 2 March 1998.

Chefe de posto. Netia Administrative Post, Monapo District, Nampula Province. May 1994.

Coetzee, C. Director, N'Ropa-Production Unit, LOMACO. Montepuez District, Cabo Delgado Province. 9 May 1994.

Direcção Provincial de Agricultura. Quelimane, Zambezia Province. Email communication. 8 June 1998.

Director. Instituto de Algodão de Moçambique-Nampula. Nampula, Nampula Province. 23 June 1995.

Director. Armazens Ibramugi. Nampula, Nampula Province. 3 July 1995.

d'Olivieira, Joaquim Campos. Administrator, Topack. Maputo. 7 June 1999.

Factory visit. Sabrina. Maputo. 10 June 1999.

Factory visit. Texmoque. Nampula, Nampula Province. 4 May 1994.

Farquharson, Edward. Country manager, Commonwealth Development Corporation. Maputo. 2 March 1998.

Francisco, Virgilio. Assistant director-general, SODAN. Namialo, Nampula Province. 25 April 1994.

Galamba, António. Former director of Banco Standard Totta de Moçambique. Maputo. 9 April 1998.

Goncalves, Victor. Director, João Ferreira dos Santos. Maputo. 16 February 1994.

Group Interview (GI). Abdul Azziz, administrator; Américo Magaia, administrator; Frank Roomer, manager. Sabrina textile factory. Maputo. 10 June 1999.

GI. *Regulos*. Netia, Monapo District, Nampula Province. 21 May 1994.

GI. Rural producers. Netia, Monapo District, Nampula Province. May 1994.

GI. Rural producers. Mecuburi District, Nampula Province. June 1995.

Guimaraes, Mario. Consultant, UTRE. Maputo. 4 March 1998.

Haque, Zacarias. Director, Favezal. Quelimane, Zambezia Province. 21 May 1998 (with Scott Kloeck-Jenson).

Harding, Alan. Consultant, CPI. Maputo. Conversation. 7 June 1994; 13 July 1995.

Helling, Louis. Independent consultant. Maputo. Conversation. 14 February 1998.

Henriques, Carlos. Director, Lomaco-Montepuez. Montepuez District, Cabo Delgado Province. Conversation. 8 May 1994.

Henriques, Carlos, director, Lomaco-Montepuez and Celia Jordão, World Bank extension work coordinator. Montepuez District, Cabo Delgado Province. Conversation. 5 May 1994.

Henriques, Rogério. Regional director, Madal Group. Quelimane, Zambezia Province. 21 May 1998 (with Scott Kloeck-Jenson).

Household Surveys (HS) (15 informants). Montepuez District, Cabo Delgado Province, May 1994.

HS (30). Netia Administrative Post, Monapo District, Nampula Province. May 1994.

HS (30). Corrane, Meconta District, Nampula Province. June 1995.

HS (30). Mecuburi District, Nampula Province. June 1995.

HS (21). Mutange, Namacurra District, Zambezia Province. May 1998 (with Scott Kloeck-Jenson).

Jazynka, Scott. Independent financial and business consultant. Maputo. 11 April 1998.

Machado, Antonio. Former director, Family Sector Production, SODAN. Nampula Province. Conversations. 17–26 May, 1994.

Magaia, Américo. Director-General, FACIM. Maputo. 18 March 1998.

Mahomede, Abdul Hamide and Abdul Rasside Mahomede. Owners, ARPEL. Quelimane, Zambezia Province. 21 May 1998 (with Scott Kloeck-Jenson).

Martins, Manuel. Former director, Sodan-Namialo. Namialo, Nampula Province. 17 May 1994.

Matule, Raimundo. Economist, GREICT. Maputo. 17 April 1998.

Muhate, Erasmo. Director, Instituto de Algodão de Moçambique. Maputo. Interviews, 8 April 1994, 7 June 1994; personal communciation 17 June 2000.

Mussanhane, Egas. Director, CREDICOOP. Maputo. 8 April 1998.

*Muene*. Dona Ana, Quelimane, Zambezia Province. 25 May 1998 (with Scott Kloeck-Jenson).

Neves, Carvalho. Representative, Fund for Community Development. Maputo. 30 May 1994.

Newberg, Rich. Team leader, Rural Incomes Office, USAID. Maputo. 2 June 1998.

Nunes, Odette. Financial director, Entreposto Group. Maputo. 8 April 1998.

Odegard, Jan. Representative, UN Industrial Development Organization-Mozambique. Maputo. 8 June 1999.

Pinto, Carlos. Agent, SODAN. 12 June 1995; 1 July 1995.

Pollard, Nigel. Managing director, Madal Group. Maputo. 2 March 1998.

President. N'Ropa, Montepuez District, Cabo Delgado Province. 4 May 1994.

*Regulo*. N'ropa, Montepuez District, Cabo Delgado Province. 12 May 1994.

*Regulo* Mukapera. Corrane, Meconta District, Nampula Province. 14 June 1995.

*Regulo* Varua. Corrane, Meconta District, Nampula Province. 14 June 1995.

*Regulos* nos. 1–6. Netia, Monapo District, Nampula Province. Names of informants are confidential. 21 May 1994.

*Regulos* nos. 1–2. Mecuburi District, Nampula Province. Names of informants are confidential. June 1995.

Ribeiro, João Manuel Sousa. Director-general, Companhia da Zambezia. Quelimane, Zambezia Province. 21 May 1998 (with Scott Kloeck-Jenson).

Salimo, Sr. and Sr. Tayoob. Traders. Nampula Province. Conversation. 7 May 1994.

Smallholder. Dona Ana, Quelimane, Zambezia Province. Informant wished to remain confidential. 25 May 1998 (with Scott Kloeck-Jenson).

Sont, Arahni. Former advisor to UTRE. 3 April 1998; personal communication, 8 June 1999.

Sowa, Arnold. Privatization specialist, World Bank. Washington, DC. 26 June 1997.

Sueia, Hermes. Director, UREA. Maputo. 17 July 1995.

Tschirley, Dave. Agricultural economist, Michigan State University/Ministry of Agriculture and Rural Development Food Security Project. Personal communication. 7 July 2000.

Viana, Violenda. Representative, Organização das Mulheres Moçambicanas. Nampula, Nampula Province. 25 April 1994.

Wilson, Ken. Personal communication with regard to Tete, 8 May 1998.

Zucula, Paulo. Ministério de Agricultura e Pescas. Maputo. 20 July 1995.

ARCHIVES

Arquivo Histórico de Moçambique (AHM), Maputo, Mozambique.

AHM, Fundo do Governo Geral (GG), Portugal, Província de Moçambique, Comissão de Estudos de Planos de Fomento, Grupo de Trabalho da Promoção Social. "Promoção da população rural integrada nas regedorias." 1962.

AHM, Secção Especial (SE), Portugal, Província de Moçambique, Serviços de Centralização e Coordenação de Informações (SCCI), "Prospecção das Forças Tradicionais-Distrito de Moçambique," by J. Branquinho, 1969.

AHM, SE, Governo do Distrito de Cabo Delgado, SCCI, "Análise da Situação do Distrito desde 14 Setembro 1962 a' 31 Dezembro 1971."

Hoover Institution (HM). Stanford University (SU). Palo Alto, California. Keith Middlemas Collection (KMC), Department of Special Collections, Reels A21-A23, Box 8 77036-8M.07. Forty-nine interviews conducted with business people, government officials, foreign diplomats in Maputo, Mozambique between January 1976 and November–December 1976.

## PRINTED PRIMARY SOURCES

GOVERNMENT AND PARTY DOCUMENTS

*Anuário da Província de Moçambique*, 1972–1973.

Assembleia da República. Lei 19/97. 1 October 1997.

Assembly of the Republic. Law 3/93. 8 June 1993. (English translation).

Banco de Moçambique. Centro de documentação e informação do Banco de Moçambique. "Indicadores financeiros das principais empresas de Moçambique (segundo os balanços de 31 de Dezembro de 1974)." Documento Informativo no. 6. 9 February 1976.

Direcção de documentação e estudos económicos. "Capitais dominantes nas principais empresas de Moçambique." Estudos macroeconómicos e de conjuntura no. 1. 5 September 1977.

Banco Popular do Desenvolvimento, "Trabalho realizado nas empresas estatais agrárias do distrito do Chokwe." Mimeo. 1984.

*Boletim da República (BR)*. I, III Série. 1975–2001 (formerly *Boletim Oficial de Moçambique*).

Centro de Promoção de Investimento (CPI). "Mozambique: Making Significant Headway." Mimeo. 1994.

"Summary of Main Investment Rules in Mozambique." Brochure. May 1995.

"Situação de projectos autorizados (de 1985 a 31 de Dezembro de 1997)." 15 January 1998.

"Investidores." 15 March 1998.

"Situação de investimento." 1998.

"Investment in Mozambique's Agricultural Sector." CPI Report for Investors. July 1995.

"Mozambique Means Business-Mega Projects." <http://www.mozbusiness.gov.mz/megapro.htm>

Chissano, Joaquim. "O Estado da Nação," Comunicação do Presidente Joaquim Chissano a Assembleia da Republica. 17 March 1997. Mozambique: Bureau de Informação Publica, 1997.

Chissano, Joaquim. Speech. Regional Investors' Forum. 16 June 1998.

Conselho de Ministros. "Autorização do projecto 'Lomaco-Montepuez'." Resolução Interna. no. 4/90. 28 May 1990.

"Autorizaçao do projecto 'Sodan'." Resolução Interna. no. 3/91. 24 May 1991.

"Contrato de Fomento entre o Governo da RPM e a LOMACO."

"Estratégia para o desenvolvimento do algodão." Aprovada na 30 sessão do Conselho de Ministros. 22 September 1998.

Decree no. 14/93. 21 July 1993. (English translation).

*Constituição*. Maputo. 1990.

Frelimo. Comité Central. Departamento de Política Económica. "Envio de materiais elaborados para uma palestra proferida no seminário sobre 'Problemas e tarefas para a organização e gestão das empresas da indústria e da construção'." 51/cc/DPE/89. 25 May 1989.

Frelimo-Mozambique Liberation Front. "Documents of the Second Congress of FRELIMO-Mozambique Liberation Front." Niassa, Mozambique. July 1968.

Frelimo Party. "Economic and Social Directives." Third Congress of Frelimo (3–7 February 1977). Trans. and repr. by Centro Nacional de Documentação e Informação de Moçambique (CEDIMO). Documento Informativo no. 6, Série E. 1 June 1978.

"Central Committee Report." Third Congress of Frelimo (3–7 February 1977). Trans. and repr. by CEDIMO. Documento Informativo no. 7, Série E. 6 June 1978.

"Statutes." Third Congress of Frelimo (3–7 February 1977). Reprint by CEDIMO. Trans. and repr. by CEDIMO. Documento Informativo no. 9, Série E. 14 June 1978.

*Out of Underdevelopment to Socialism*. Report of the Central Committee, Fourth Congress. Maputo: Frelimo Party, 1983.

Gabinete de Promoção do Investimento Estrangeiro (GPIE). *Investor's Guide to Mozambique*. Maputo: GPIE, 1992.

Gabinete de Reestruturação de Empresas Agrárias e Pescas (GREAP). "Documento final do Seminário sobre o balanço do processo de reestruturação do sector empresarial do Estado." November 1997.

Machel, S. "Independência implica benefícios para as massas exploradas." Speech. 3 February 1976.

*Mozambique: Revolution or Reaction?* Oakland, CA: LSM Information Center, 1975.

Ministério da Administração Estatal. II Seminário sobre a reforma dos orgãos locais e o papel da autoridade tradicional. Maputo. 19–23 April 1993.

Ministério da Agricultura. "Reunião do sector estatal agrário." Maputo. 13 February 1979.

"Reunião do Conselho Consultivo Alargado." April 1981.

"Regulamento para a cultura do algodão." Diploma Ministerial 91/94. 29 June 1994.

Departamento de Estatística Agrária. "An [sic] Preliminary Analysis fo [sic] the Size of Land Holdings in the Family Sector in Mozambique using Information from the 1993 Ministry of Agriculture Survey of the Family Sector." May 1994.

Departamento de Projectos. "Contribuição para o estudo da vulnerabilidade social das familias camponesas (aspectos metodologicos)," by V. Pankhova. 1990.

Direcção Nacional de Organização da Produção Colectiva, Gabinete de Apoio a produção da província de Nampula (GAPRONA), n.t. Reunião do sector estatal agrário. 13 February 1979.

Direcção de Economia Agrária. Sector de Análise de Unidades Economicas (SAUE). "Dossier das Empresas Estatais Agrárias da Província de Nampula." Maputo. January 1988.

Direcção Provincial de Agricultura da Zambézia. "Relatório a 2a Reunião do Conselho Agrário Nacional." 25–30 April 1977.

Ministério da Agricultura e Pescas, Instituto do Algodão de Moçambique (IAM). "Assunto: Respostas ao seu fax desta manhã." N/Ref 42/GAM/IAM/98. Letter to Sr. Marcelino Mosse, journalist, *Metical*. 7 July 1998.

"Assunto: Ponto de Situação das Campanhas do Algodão (4 Trimestre de 1998)." N/Ref. 08/GAB/IAM/99. 29 January 1999.

"Assunto: Ponto de Situação das Campanhas do Algodão (1 Trimestre de 1999)." N/Ref. 24/GAB/IAM/99. 23 April 1999.

Ministério da Indústria e Comercio. Gabinete de Controlo de Produção Industrial e Comercial. "Recomendações Gerais as Comissões Administrativas." 1976.

Ministério da Indústria, Comércio e Turismo. *Second Private Sector Conference in Mozambique*. Maputo: Cowling Davies and Associates, 1996.

*Third Private Sector Conference in Mozambique*. Maputo: MagicPrint Ltd., 1998.

*Fourth Private Sector Conference in Mozambique*. Maputo: Montage Graphic, 1999.

"Balanço da Actividade Industrial Referente ao 1 Trimestre de 1999." 12 April 1999.

"Industrial Strategy Policy." Approved by Council of Ministers, Resolution no. 23/97 of 19 August 1997. Government Gazette Series No. 33, 2nd Supplement.

Ministério das Finanças. "Relatório sobre a situação actual do desenvolvimento agricola e propostas de alteração à política de crédito." Maputo. September 1978.

"Servir os Interesses das Largas Massas é o Objectivo da Reestruturação da Banca." Repr. by CEDIMO. "A Reestruturação da Banca da Moçambique." Documento Informativo, 3, Ser. A. 1 March 1978.

Ministry of Agriculture and Fisheries. "National Program for Agrarian Development-PROAGRI, 1999–2003." Vol. II-Master Document. February 1998.

Ministry of Planning and Finance. Poverty Alleviation Unit. "Rural Livelihoods and Poverty in Mozambique." By A. Addison and I. MacDonald. Background document for the "Poverty Reduction Strategy for Mozambique." February 1995.

Technical Unit for Enterprise Restructuring (UTRE). "Privatisation in Mozambique," nos. 1–5. March 1995–March 1998.

Mocumbi, Pascoal. "Address by his Excellency Dr. Pascoal Mocumbi, Prime Minister of the Republic of Mozambique." First Pan-African Investment Summit. "Privatisation in Practice: The Restructuring of State-Owned Enterprises in Africa into the next Millennium." Johannesburg, South Africa. 17 March 1997.

Mozambique-Portugal. "Conversações no Ambito da Reestruturação da Banca em Moçambique." CEDIMO. n.d.

National Planning Commission. "Economic Report." Maputo. January 1984.

"Programa de emergencia." September 1976.

Província de Nampula. "Programa geral de reabilitação agrária dos Distritos Prioritários." By A. Ismael and D. Chereua. May 1989.

Provincia de Gaza. Unidade de Produção do Baixo Limpopo. "Relatório da U.P.B.L. por ocasião da I reunião nacional do sector estatal agrário." Macuse, Zambezia. 12 February 1979.

Recenseamento da População. 1980.

"Relatório da Província da Zambezia ao III Conselho Agrário Nacional." June 1978.

"Strategy and Program for Economic Rehabilitation, 1987–1990." Report prepared by the Government of Mozambique for the meeting of the consultative group for Mozambique. Paris, July 1987; Maputo, June 1987.

The Constitution of the People's Republic of Mozambique. Maputo: Minerva Central, 1980.

Unidade para a Reestruturação das Empresas de Agricultura (UREA). "Mapa das empresas alienadas no Ministério da Agricultura em 23.05.95." 1995.

"Sector Estatal Agrário Relacão das Empresas." Mimeo. n.d.

NEWSPAPERS AND PERIODICALS

A Tarde 1985
A Voz da Revolução 1979–1981
Africa Journal (Lisbon) 1984
Africa News 1984
African Business 1982
AFX News Ltd. 2000
AIMNews 1999–2001 <http://www.sortmoz.com/aimnews>
Business Report 2001
Christian Science Monitor 1983
Comércio do Porto 1986
Demos 1997–1998
Diário de Moçambique 1982

*Diário de Notícias* 1983
*Domingo* 1993–1998
*Economia* 1991–1994
*Exame* 1993
*Expresso* 1981, 1998
*Foreign Broadcast Information Service (FBIS) Reports on Africa* 1993–1994
*Financial Gazette* (Harare) 1987
*Financial Times* 1984–1987
*Forum Económico* 1997–1999
*Investir* 1997
*Jornal de Notícias* (Oporto) 1985
*Mediafax* 1994–1998
*Metical* 1998–2001
*Moçambique* 1997–1999
*Mozal News* 1998–2001 <http://www.mozal.com>
*Indian Ocean Newsletter* 2000
*Mozambiquefile* 1996–1999
*Mozambique INVIEW* 1997–2000
*Mozambique Revolution* 1964–1973
*New African* 1980
*New Internationalist* 1989
*Notícias* 1976–1998
*O Popular* 1999
*O Tempo* (Lisbon)1988
*Pan African News Agency* 2001 <http://www.nexis-lexis.com>
*Primeiro do Janeiro* (Oporto) 1982
*Revista de Empresas* 1996–1997
*Savana* 1994–1999
*Semanário Económico* (Lisbon) 1987
*South* 1987
*Sunday Times Business Times* 1998
*Tempo* 1976–1998
*The Daily News* 1989
*The Guardian* 1984
*Wall Street Journal* 1980
*Washington Post* 1980
*Weekly Mail* 1988
*Xitimela* 1997–2001

## SECONDARY SOURCES

### BOOKS AND ARTICLES

Abrahamsson, H. and A. Nilsson. *Mozambique: The Troubled Transition, From Socialist Construction to Free Market Capitalism.* Trans. by M. Dally. Atlantic Highlands, NJ: Zed Press, 1995.

Adam, C., W. Cavendish, and P. Mistry. *Adjusting Privatization: Case Studies from Developing Countries.* Portsmouth, NH: Heinemann, 1992.

Adam, Y. "Mueda, 1917–1990: resistência, colonialismo, libertação e desenvolvimento." *Arquivo*, 14 (October 1993), 9–101.

Aharoni, Y. *The Evolution and Management of State-Owned Enterprises*. Cambridge, MA: Ballinger, 1986.

Alden, C. *Mozambique and the Construction of the New African State: From Negotiation to Nation-Building*. Basingstoke: Palgrave, 2001.

Alexander, J. "Things Fall Apart, The Centre Can Hold: Processes of Post-War Political Change in Zimbabwe's Rural Areas." In N. Bhebe and T. Ranger, eds., *Society in Zimbabwe's Liberation War*. Portsmouth, NH: Heinemann, 1996, 175–191.

——— "The Local State in Post-War Mozambique: Political Practice and Ideas about Authority," *Africa*, 67, 1 (1997), 1–26.

Alpers, N. *Ivory and Slaves in East Central Africa*. Berkeley, CA: University of California Press, 1975.

——— "Gujarat and the Trade of East Africa, c. 1500–1800," *International Journal of African Historical Studies*, IX, 1 (1976), 22–44.

Alves, J. 2000. "Privatizing the State Enterprise Sector." In B. Ferraz and B. Munslow, eds., *Sustainable Development in Mozambique*. Trenton, NJ: Africa World Press, 2000, 58–63.

Amsden, A. "Editorial: Bringing Production Back in – Understanding Government's Economic Role in Late Industrialization," *World Development*, 25,4 (1997), 469–80.

Amselle, J.-L. "Socialisme, Capitalisme et Précapitalisme au Mali (1960–1982)." In H. Bernstein and B. Campbell, *Contradictions of Accumulation in Africa*. Beverly Hills, CA: Sage, 1985, 249–66.

Anderson, P. "Portugal and the End of Ultra-Colonialism," *New Left Review* 15 (May-June, 1962), 83–102.

——— "Portugal and the End of Ultra-Colonialism 2," *New Left Review*, 16 (July-August, 1962), 88–123.

——— "Portugal and the End of Ultra-Colonialism," *New Left Review*, 17 (Winter 1962), 85–114.

Andersson, H. 1992. *Mozambique: A War Against the People*. New York: St. Martin's Press, 1992.

Ariyo, A. and A. Jerome,"Privatization in Africa: An Appraisal," *World Development*, 27, 1 (1999), 201–13.

Azarya, V. "Reordering State-Society Relations: Incorporation and Disengagement." In D. Rothchild and N. Chazan, eds., *The Precarious Balance: State and Society in Africa*. Boulder, CO: Westview Press, 1988, 3–21.

Barker, J. "Gaps in the Debates about Agriculture in Senegal, Tanzania and Mozambique," *World Development*, 13, 1 (1985), 59–76.

Bartlett, D. *The Political Economy of Dual Transformations: Market Reform and Democratization in Hungary*. Ann Arbor, MI: Michigan University Press, 1997.

Bates, R. *Beyond the Miracle of the Market: The Political Economy of Agrarian Development in Kenya*. New York: Cambridge University Press, 1989.

Bates, R., ed. *Towards a Political Economy of Development: A Rational Choice Perspective*. Berkeley: University of California Press, 1988.

Bayart, J.-F. *The State in Africa: The Politics of the Belly*. New York: Longman, 1993.

Bayart, J-F., S. Ellis, and B. Hibou. *The Criminalization of the State in Africa.* Bloomington: Indiana University Press, 1999.

Bennell, P. "Privatization in Sub-Saharan Africa: Progress and Prospects during the 1990s," *World Development*, 25, 11 (1997), 1785–1803.

Berg, E. "Privatisation in Sub-Saharan Africa: Results, Prospects and New Approaches." In J. Paulson, ed. *African Economies in Transition*, Vol 1: *The Changing Role of the State.* New York: St. Martin's Press, 1999, 229–89.

Berman, B. and C. Leys, eds. *African Capitalists in African Development.* Boulder, CO: Lynne Rienner, 1994.

Berry, S. *No Condition is Permanent: The Social Dynamics of Agrarian Change in Sub-Saharan Africa.* Madison, WI: University of Wisconsin Press, 1993.

Bienen, H., and J. Herbst. "The Relationship Between Political and Economic Reform in Africa," *Comparative Politics* (October 1996), 23–42.

Bonnell, V. *Iconography of Power: Soviet Political Posters under Lenin and Stalin.* Berkeley, CA: University of California, 1997.

Boone, C. "States and Ruling Classes in Postcolonial Africa: The Enduring Contradictions of Power." In J. Migdal, A. Kohli, and V. Shue, eds., *State Power and Social Forces: Domination and Transformation in the Third World.* Cambridge: Cambridge University Press, 1994, repr. 1996, 108–40.

" 'Empirical Statehood' and Reconfigurations of Political Order." In L. Villalón and P. Huxtable, eds., *The African State at a Critical Juncture.* Boulder, CO: Lynne Rienner, 1998, 129–41.

Bowen, M. "Socialist Transitions: Policy Reforms and Peasant Producers in Mozambique." In T. Bassett and D. Crumney, eds., *Land in African Agrarian Systems.* Madison, WI: University of Wisconsin Press, 1993, 326–53.

*The State Against the Peasantry: Rural Struggles in Colonial and Postcolonial Mozambique.* Charlottesville, VA: University of Virginia Press, 2000.

Bratton, M. and N. van de Walle. *Democratic Experiments in Africa: Regime Transitions in Comparative Perspective.* New York: Cambridge University Press, 1997.

Brus, W. and K. Laski. *From Marx to the Market: Socialism in Search of an Economic System.* Oxford: Clarendon Press, 1989.

Bunce, V. *Subversive Institutions: The Design and the Destruction of Socialism and the State.* New York: Cambridge University Press, 1999.

Caballero, L. *The Mozambican Agricultural Sector- A (sic) Background Information,* Swedish University of Agricultural Sciences, International Rural Development Centre, Working Paper no. 138. Uppsala: Swedish University of Agricultural Sciences, 1990.

Caballero, L., T. Thomsen and A. Andreasson. *Mozambique – Food and Agriculture Sector*, Rural Development Studies no. 16. Uppsala: Swedish University of Agriculture, 1985.

Cahen, M. *Mozambique: La Révolution Implosée, Etudes sur 12 ans d'indépéndance (1975–1987).* Paris: Editions L'Harmattan, 1987.

"La Crise du Nationalisme," *Politique Africaine* 29 (Mars 1988), 2–23.

"Check on Socialism in Mozambique – What Check? What Socialism?", *Review of African Political Economy*, 57 (1993), 46–59.

Callaghy, T. "Vision and Politics in the Transformation of the Global Political Economy: Lessons from the Second and Third Worlds." In R. Slater, B. Schutz, and S. Dorr, eds., *Global Transformation and the Third World*. Boulder, CO: Lynne Rienner, 1993, 161–257.

Callaghy, T. and J. Ravenhill, eds. *Hemmed In: Responses to Africa's Economic Decline*. New York: Columbia University Press, 1993.

Casal, A. "A crise da produção familiar e as aldeias comunais em Moçambique," *Revista Internacional de Estudos Africanos*, 8–9 (January–December 1988), 157–91.

Casal, A. "Discurso socialista e camponeses africanos: legitimação política-ideológica da socialização rural em Moçambique (FRELIMO, 1965–1984)," *Revista Internacional de Estudos Africanos*, 14–15 January–December 1991), 35–75.

Castel-Branco, C., ed. *Moçambique: Perspectivas Económicas*. Maputo: Imprensa Universitária, 1994.

Castel-Branco, C. "Problemas estruturais de industrialização." In C. Castel-Branco, ed., *Moçambique: Perspectivas Económicas*. Maputo: Imprensa Universitária, 1994, 31–86.

Castro, Armando. *O sistema colonial Português em Africa*. Lisbon: Editorial Caminho, 2nd edn., 1980.

Chabal, P., ed. *Political Domination in Africa: Reflections on the Limits of Power*. Cambridge: Cambridge University Press, 1986.

Chazan, N. "Patterns of State-Society Incorporation and Disengagement in Africa." In D. Rothchild and N. Chazan, eds., *The Precarious Balance: State and Society in Africa*. Boulder, CO: Westview Press, 1988, 121–48.

Chingono, M. *The State, Violence and Development*. Aldershot: Avebury, 1996.

Clarence-Smith, G. *The Third Portuguese Empire, 1825–1975: A Study in Economic Imperialism*. Manchester: Manchester University Press, 1985.

"The Roots of the Mozambican Counter-Revolution." *Southern African Review of Books*, 2, 4 (April/May 1989), 7–10.

Collier, P. "Learning from Failure: The International Financial Institutions as Agencies of Restraint in Africa." In A. Schedler, L. Diamond, and M. Plattner, eds., *The Self-Restraining State: Power and Accountability in New Democracies*. Boulder, CO: Lynne Rienner, 1999, 313–30.

Collier, R. "Combining Alternative Perspectives: Internal Trajectories versus External Influences as Explanations of Latin American Politics in the 1940s," *Comparative Politics*, 26, 1 (October 1993), 1–29.

Comaroff, J. and J. Comaroff, eds. *Civil Society and the Political Imagination in Africa: Critical Perspectives*. Chicago, IL: University of Chicago Press, 1999.

Couto, M. *Every Man is a Race*. Trans. by D. Brookshaw. Portsmouth, NH: Heinemann, 1994.

Covane, L. *O Trabalho Migratório e A Agricultura no Sul de Moçambique (1920–1992)*. Maputo: Promedia, 2001.

Cramer, C. "Can Africa Industrialize by Processing Primary Commodities? The Case of Mozambican Cashew Nuts," *World Development*, 27, 7 (1999), 1247–66.

"Privatisation and Adjustment in Mozambique: A 'Hospital Pass'?", *Journal of Southern African Studies*, 27, 1 (March 2001), 79–103.

Craveirinha, J. "The Tasty 'Tanjarines' of Inhambane." In S. Gray, ed., *The Penguin Book of Southern African Verse*. New York: Viking Penguin, 1989, 355–60.

Cravinho, J. "Frelimo and the Politics of Agricultural Marketing in Mozambique," *Journal of Southern African Studies*, 24, 1 (March 1998), 93–113.

Cross, M. "Reading Television Texts: The Postmodern Language of Advertising." In M. Cross, ed., *Advertising and Culture: Theoretical Perspectives*. Westport, CT: Praeger, 1996, 1–10.

Davies, R. *South African Strategy Towards Mozambique in the Post-Nkomati Period: A Critical Analysis of Effects and Implications*, Research Report no. 73. Uppsala: Scandinavian Institute of African Studies, 1985.

de Alcántara, C. "Uses and Abuses of the Concept of Governance." *International Social Science Journal*, 155 (March 1998), 105–13.

de Brito, L. "Une relecture nécessaire: la genese du parti-Etat FRELIMO," *Politique Africaine*, 29 (March 1988), 15–27.

Dinerman, A. "In Search of Mozambique: The Imaginings of Christian Geffray in *La Cause des Armes au Mozambique. Anthropologie d'une Guerre Civile.*" *Journal of Southern African Studies*, 20, 4 (December 1994), 569–86.

Dinerman, A. "From 'Abaixo' to 'Chiefs of Production': Agrarian Change in Nampula, Province, Mozambique, 1975–1987," *Journal of Peasant Studies*, 28, 2 (January 2001), 1–82.

Economist Intelligence Unit. *Quarterly Economic Review of Tanzania and Mozambique*. 2nd Quarter, 1979. EIU: London, 1979.

Egero, B. *Mozambique: A Dream Undone*. Uppsala: Scandinavian Institute of African Studies, 1990.

Evans, P. "The State as Problem and Solution: Predation, Embedded Autonomy, and Structural Change." In S. Haggard and R. Kaufman, eds., *The Politics of Economic Adjustment: International Constraints, Distributive Conflicts, and the State*. Princeton, NJ: Princeton University Press, 1992, 139–81.

*Embedded Autonomy: States and Industrial Transformation*. Princeton, NJ: Princeton University Press, 1995.

"The Eclipse of the State? Reflections on Stateness in an Era of Globalization," *World Politics*, 50 (October 1997), 62–87.

Evans, P., D. Rueschemeyer, and T. Skocpol, eds. *Bringing the State Back In*. Cambridge: Cambridge University Press, 1985.

Feigenbaum, H. and J. Henig. "The Political Underpinnings of Privatization," *World Politics*, 46, 2 (January 1994), 185–207.

Feigenbaum, H., J. Henig, and C. Hamnett. *Shrinking the State: The Political Underpinnings of Privatization*. Cambridge: Cambridge University Press, 1998.

Ferraz, B. and B. Munslow, eds. *Sustainable Development in Mozambique*. Trenton, NJ: Africa World Press, 2000.

Finnegan, W. *A Complicated War: The Harrowing of Mozambique*. Berkeley: University of California Press, 1992.

First, R. *Black Gold: The Mozambican Miner, Proletarian and Peasant*. New York: St. Martin's Press, 1983.

*Focus on Mozambique*, pamphlet reprinted from *The International Review for Chief Executive Officers*. n.p.: Sterling Publications, 1994.

Fowles, J. *Advertising and Popular Culture*. Thousand Oaks, CA: Sage, 1996.

Fry, P. "Between Two Terrors," *Times Literary Supplement* (9–15 November 1990), 1202.

Geddes, B. "The Politics of Economic Liberalization." *Latin American Research Review*, 30, 2 (1995), 195–214.

Geffray, C. *A Causa das Armas: Antropologia da guerra contemporânea em Moçambique*. Trans. by A. Ferreira. Oporto: Edições Afrontamento, 1991.

Geffray, C. and M. Pedersen. "Nampula en guerre." *Politique Africaine*, 29 (1988), 28–39.

Gengenbach, H. "'I'll Bury You in the Border!': Women's Land Struggles in Post-War Facazisse (Magude District), Mozambique." *Journal of Southern African Studies*, 24, 1 (March 1998), 7–36.

Goldman, R. *Reading Ads Socially*. New York: Routledge, 1992.

Grabher, G. and D. Stark, eds. *Restructuring Networks in Postsocialism: Legacies, Linkages, and Localities*. New York: Oxford University Press, 1997.

Grosh, B. and R. Mukandala. *State-Owned Enterprises in Africa*. Boulder, CO: Lynne Rienner, 1994.

Habermeier, K. "Cotton: From Concentrations to Collective Production," *Mozambican Studies*, 2 (1981), 36–57.

Hall, M. and T. Young. *Confronting Leviathan: Mozambique Since Independence*. Athens, OH: Ohio University Press, 1997.

Hanlon, J. *Mozambique: The Revolution Under Fire*. London: Zed Books, 1984.

*Mozambique: Who Calls the Shots?* Bloomington, IN: Indiana University Press, 1991.

*Peace Without Profit: How the IMF Blocks Rebuilding in Mozambique*. Portsmouth, NH: Heinemann, 1996.

"'O Dono de Moçambique é o FMI'." In D. Sogge, ed., *Moçambique: Perspectivas sobre a Ajuda e o Sector Civil*. Amsterdam: Gemeenschappelijk Overleg Medefinanciering, 1997, 17–41.

"Power Without Responsibility: The World Bank and Mozambican Cashew Nuts," *Review of African Political Economy*, 83 (2000), 29–45.

Hanlon, J. "Mozambique's banking crisis," *Moçambique on-line*, English version of an article published in *Metical*, 1073 (17 September 2001), found on website <http://www.mol.co.mz/noticias/metical/2001/en010917.html.>

Harbeson, J., D. Rothchild, and N. Chazan, eds. *Civil Society and the State in Africa*. Boulder, CO: Lynne Rienner, 1994.

Harris, L. "Agricultural Co-operatives and Development Policy in Mozambique," *Journal of Peasant Studies*, 7 (April 1980), 338–52.

Harrison, G. "Democracy in Mozambique: The Significance of Multi-party Elections," *Review of African Political Economy*, 23, 67 (1996), 19–34.

Harrison, G. "Corruption as 'Boundary Politics': The State, Democratisation, and Mozambique's Unstable Liberalisation," *Third World Quarterly*, 20, 3 (1999), 537–50.

Harsch, E. "Privatization Shifts Gears in Africa: More Concern for Public Acceptance and Development Impact but Problems Remain," *Africa Recovery*, 14, 1 (April 2000), 8–11, 14–17.

Harvey, D. *The Condition of Postmodernity: An Enquiry into the Origins of Cultural Change*. Cambridge, MA: Blackwell, 1990, repr. 1994.

Hausner, J., B. Jessop, and K. Nielsen, eds. 1994. *Strategic Choice and Path Dependency in Post-Socialism: Institutional Dynamics in the Transformation Process*. London: Edward Elgar, 1994.

Hedges, D., ed. *História de Moçambique: Moçambique no Auge do Colonialismo, 1930–1961*. Vol. 3. Maputo: Departamento de História, Universidade Eduardo Mondlane (UEM), 1993.

Hedges, D. and A. Chilundo. "A contestação da situação colonial, 1945–1961." In D. Hedges, ed., *História de Moçambique*, Vol. 3. Maputo: Departamento de História, UEM, 1993, 197–257.

Hedges, D. and A. Rocha, "Moçambique durante o apogeu do colonialismo portugues, 1945–1961: a economia e a estrutura social." In D. Hedges, ed., *História de Moçambique*, Vol. 3. Maputo: Departamento de História, UEM, 1993.

Herbst, J. "The Politics of Privatization in Africa." In E. Suleiman and J. Waterbury, eds., *The Political Economy of Public Sector Reform and Privatization*. Boulder, CO: Westview, 1990, pp. 234–54.

"The Structural Adjustment of Politics in Africa," *World Development*, 18 (1990), 949–58.

Hermele, K. *Mozambican Crossroads: Economics and Politics in the Era of Structural Adjustment*. Bergen: Christian Michelsen Institute, 1990.

Himbara, D. *Kenyan Capitalists, The State and Development*. Boulder, CO: Lynne Rienner, 1994.

Hobsbawm, E. "The Future of the State." *Development and Change*, 27 (1996), 267–78.

Hobsbawm, E. and T. Ranger, eds. *The Invention of Tradition*. New York: Cambridge University Press, 1983.

Huntington, S. *Political Order in Changing Societies*. New Haven, CT: Yale University Press, 1968.

Hyden, G. "Civil Society, Social Capital, and Development: Dissection of a Complex Discourse," *Studies in Comparative International Development*, 32, 1 (Spring 1997), 3–30.

Inkeles, A. and D. Smith. *Becoming Modern: Individual Change in Six Developing Countries*. Cambridge, MA: Harvard University Press, 1974.

Isaacman, A. "Peasants and Rural Social Protest in Africa." In F. Cooper, A. Isaacman, F. Mallon, W. Roseberry, and S. Stern, *Confronting Historical Paradigms: Peasants, Labor and the Capitalist World System in Africa and Latin America*. Madison, WI: University of Wisconsin Press, 1993, 205–317.

*Cotton is the Mother of Poverty: Peasants, Work and Rural Struggle in Colonial Mozambique, 1938–1961*. Portsmouth, NH: Heinemann, 1996.

Isaacman, A. and B. Isaacman. *Mozambique: From Colonialism to Revolution, 1900–1982*. Boulder, CO: Westview Press, 1983.

Jackson, R. and C. Rosberg. "Personal Rule: Theory and Practice in Africa." In P. Lewis, ed., *Africa: Dilemmas of Development and Change*. Boulder, CO: Westview, 1998, 17–43.

Jessop, B. "The Rise of Governance and the Risks of Failure: The Case of Economic Development," *International Social Science Journal*, 155 (March 1998), 29–45.

Jones, S. "Agriculture and Economic Reform in African Socialist Economies." In J. Paulson, *African Economies in Transition*, Vol. 2: *The Reform Experience*. New York: St. Martin's Press, 1999, 235–87.

Joseph, R. "Class, State and Prebendal Politics in Nigeria," *Journal of Commonwealth and Comparative Studies*, 21, 3 (November 1983), 21–38.

Kazancigil, A. "Governance and Science: Market-Like Modes of Managing Society and Producing Knowledge," *International Social Science Journal*, 155 (March 1998), 69–79.

Keyishan, H. "'We Bring Good Things to Life'/'We're Always There': The AdWorld of GE." In M. Cross, ed., *Advertising and Culture: Theoretical Perspectives*. Westport, CT: Praeger, 1996, 49–60.

Kohli, A., P. Evans, P. Katzenstein, A. Przeworski, S. Rudolph, J. Scott and T. Skocpol, "The Role of Theory in Comparative Politics," *World Politics*, 48 (October 1995), 1–49.

Lan, D. *Guns and Rain: Guerrillas and Spirit Mediums in Zimbabwe*. London: James Currey, 1985.

Landau, L. *Rebuilding the Mozambique Economy: Assessment of a Development Partnership*. Country Assistance Review. World Bank Operation Evaluations Department. Washington, DC: World Bank, 1998.

Leite, J. "Diáspora Indiana em Moçambique," *Economia Global e Gestão*, 2 (1996), 67–108.

Lewis, P. "Political Transition and the Dilemma of Civil Society in Africa." In P. Lewis, ed., *Africa: Dilemmas of Development and Change*. Boulder, CO: Westview, 1998, 137–58.

Lewis, P., ed. *Africa: Dilemmas of Development and Change*. Boulder, CO: Westview, 1998.

Leys, C. *The Rise and Fall of Development Theory*. Bloomington, IN: Indiana University Press, 1996.

Lonsdale, J. "Political Accountability in African History." In P. Chabal, ed., *Political Domination in Africa: Reflections on the limits of power*. Cambridge: Cambridge University Press, 1986, 126–57.

Lundin, I. "A pesquisa piloto sobre a Autoridade/Poder Tradicional em Moçambique-Uma somatório comentado e analisado." In I. Lundin and F. Machava, eds., *Autoridade e Poder Tradicional*, Vol. 1. Maputo: Ministério da Administração Estatal, Núcleo de desenvolvimento administrativo, 1995, 7–32.

Lundin, I. and F. Machava, eds., *Autoridade e Poder Tradicional*, Vol. 1. Maputo: Ministério da Administração Estatal, Núcleo de desenvolvimento administrativo, 1995.

MacGaffey, J. *Entrepreneurs and Parasites: The Struggle for Indigenous Capitalism in Zaire*. Cambridge: Cambridge University Press, 1987.

Mamdani, M. *Citizen and Subject: Contemporary Africa and the Legacy of Late Colonialism*. Princeton, NJ: Princeton University Press, 1996.

Manning, C. "Constructing Opposition in Mozambique: Renamo as Political Party," *Journal of Southern African Studies*, 24, 1 (March 1998), 161–89.

*The Politics of Peace in Mozambique*. Westport, CT: Praeger, forthcoming.

Marshall, J. *War, Debt and Structural Adjustment in Mozambique: The Social Impact*. Ottawa: The North-South Institute, 1992.

Martinez, F. *O povo macua e a sua cultura*. Lisbon: Ministério da Educação, Instituto de Investigação Científica Tropical, 1989.

Martz, J. "Review Essay: Economic Challenges and the Study of Democratization," *Studies in Comparative International Development*, 31, 1 (Spring 1996), 96–120.

Mazula, B., ed., *Mozambique: Elections, Democracy and Development*. Maputo: Inter-Africa Group, 1996.

McGregor, J. "Violence and Social Change in a Border Economy: War in the Maputo Hinterland, 1984–1992," *Journal of Southern African Studies*, 24, 1 (March 1998), 37–60.

Meyer, K. "International Production Networks and Enterprise Transformation in Central Europe," *Comparative Economic Studies*, 42, 1 (Spring 2000), 135–50.

Middlemas, K. *Cabora Bassa: Engineering and Politics in Southern Africa*. London: Weidenfeld and Nicolson, 1975.

"Twentieth-Century White Society in Mozambique," *Tarikh*, 6, 2 (1979), 30–45.

Migdal, J., A. Kohli, and V. Shue, eds. *State Power and Social Forces: Domination and Transformation in the Third World*. New York: Cambridge University Press, 1994, repr. 1996.

Minter, W. *Apartheid's Contras: An Inquiry into the Roots of War in Angola and Mozambique*. Atlantic Highlands, NJ: Zed Press, 1994.

Mittelman, J. *The Globalization Syndrome: Transformation and Resistance*. Princeton, NJ: Princeton University Press, 2000.

Moore, B. *The Social Origins of Dictatorship and Democracy: Lord and Peasant in the Making of the Modern World*. Boston, MA: Beacon Press, 1966.

Moore, D. "'Sail on, O Ship of State': Neo-Liberalism, Globalisation and the Governance of Africa," *Journal of Peasant Studies*, 27, 1 (October 1999), 61–96.

Morna, C. "Mozambique." *Institutional Investor*. Sponsored section.

Mosca, J. *A Experiencia Socialista em Moçambique (1975–1986)*. Lisbon: Instituto Piaget, 1999.

"Mozambique Country Report." Corporate Location. 1992.

Munro, W. "Power, Peasants and Political Development: Reconsidering State Construction in Africa," *Comparative Studies in Society and History*, 38, 1 (January 1996), 112–48.

Munslow, B., ed. *Samora Machel: An African Revolutionary*. London: Zed Books, 1985.

Murray, M. *South Africa: Time of Agony, Time of Destiny*. London: Verso Press, 1987.

Nee, V., D. Stark, with M. Selden, eds. *Remaking the Economic Institutions of Socialism: China and Eastern Europe*. Stanford, CA: Stanford University Press, 1989.

Negrão, J. "Repensando as modas do desenvolvimento rural". In D. Sogge, ed., *Moçambique: Perspectivas sobre a Ajuda e o Sector Civil*. Amsterdam: Gemeenschappelijk Overleg Medefinanciering, 1997, 117–33.

Nelson, P. *The World Bank and Non-Governmental Organizations: The Limits of Apolitical Development*. New York: St. Martin's Press, 1995.

Newitt, M. *A History of Mozambique*. Bloomington, IN: Indiana University Press, 1995.

Nordstrom, C. *A Different Kind of War Story*. Philadelphia, PA: University of Pennsylvania Press, 1997.

O'Laughlin, B. "Interpretations Matter: Evaluating the War in Mozambique," *Southern Africa Report*, 7, 3 (January 1992), 23–33.

"A Base Social da Guerra em Moçambique," *Estudos Moçambicanos*, 10 (1992), 107–42.

"Past and Present Options: Land Reform in Mozambique," *Review of African Political Economy*, 22, 63 (March 1995), 99–106.

"Through a Divided Glass: Dualism, Class and the Agrarian Question in Mozambique," *Journal of Peasant Studies*, 23, 4 (July 1996), 1–39.

Ostergaard, T. "The Role of the 'National' Bourgeoisie in National Development: The Case of the Textile and Clothing Industries in Zimbabwe." In B. Berman and C. Leys, eds., *African Capitalists in African Development*. Boulder, CO: Lynne Rienner, 1994, 115–37.

Ottaway, M. "Mozambique: From Symbolic Socialism to Symbolic Reform," *Journal of Modern African Studies*, 26, 2 (1988), 211–26.

Overseas Companies of Portugal. *Mozambique*. Lisbon: Overseas Companies of Portugal, 1961.

Parsons, T. *The Social System*. Glencoe, IL: The Free Press, 1951.

Paulson, J, ed. *African Economies in Transition*, vol. 1: *The Changing Role of the State* and vol. 2: *The Reform Experience*. New York: St. Martin's Press, 1999.

Penvenne, J. *African Workers and Colonial Racism: Mozambican Strategies and Struggles in Lourenço Marques, 1877–1962*. Portsmouth, NH: Heinemann, 1995.

    "Seeking the Factory for Women: Mozambican Urbanization in the Late Colonial Era," *Journal of Urban History*, 23, 3 (March 1997), 342–79.

Pereira da Silva, L. and A. Solimano. "The Transition and the Political Economy of African Socialist Countries at War (Angola and Mozambique)." In J. Paulson, ed. *African Economies in Transition*, Vol. 2. New York: St. Martin's Press, 1999, 9–67.

Petiteville, Franck. "Three Mythical Representations of the State in Development Theory," *International Social Science Journal*, 155 (March 1998), 115–24.

Pitcher, M. *Politics in the Portuguese Empire: The State, Industry and Cotton, 1926–1974*. Oxford: Oxford University Press, 1993.

    "Recreating Colonialism or Reconstructing the State? Privatisation and Politics in Mozambique," *Journal of Southern African Studies*, 22, 1 (March 1996), 49–74.

    "Conflict and Cooperation: Gendered Roles and Responsibilities Within Cotton Households in Northern Mozambique," *African Studies Review*, 39, 3 (December 1996), 81–112.

    "Disruption without Transformation: Agrarian Relations and Livelihoods in Nampula Province, Mozambique 1975–1995," *Journal of Southern African Studies*, 24, 1 (March 1998), 119–43.

    "What's Missing from 'What's Missing'? A Reply to C. Cramer and N. Pontara," *Journal of Modern African Studies*, 37, 4 (December 1999), 697–710.

Pitcher, M. with S. Kloeck-Jenson. "Homens, Mulheres, Memória e Direitos aos Recursos Naturais na Província da Zambézia". In R. Waterhouse, and C. Vijfhuizen, eds., *Estratégias das Mulheres, Proveito dos Homens: Género, terra e recursos naturais em diferentes contextos rurais em Moçambique*. Maputo: Universidade Eduardo Mondlane, 2001, 147–79.

Plank, D. "Aid, Debt and the End of Sovereignty: Mozambique and Its Donors," *The Journal of Modern African Studies*, 31, 3 (1993), 407–30.

Rapley, J. *Ivoirien Capitalism: African Entrepreneurs in Cote d'Ivoire*. Boulder, CO: Lynne Rienner, 1993.

    "The Ivorien Bourgeoisie." In B. Berman, and C. Leys, eds., *African Capitalists in African Development*. Boulder, CO: Lynne Rienner, 1994, 39–68.

Ribeiro-Torres, J. "Rural Development Schemes in Southern Moçambique," *South African Journal of African Affairs*, 3, 2 (1973), 60–69.

Riddell, J. "Things Fall Apart Again: Structural Adjustment Programmes in Sub-Saharan Africa," *Journal of Modern African Studies*, 30, 1 (1992), 53–68.

Roesch, O. "Rural Mozambique Since the Frelimo Party Fourth Congress: The Situation in the Baixo Limpopo," *Review of African Political Economy*, 41 (1988), 72–91.

"Renamo and the Peasantry in Southern Mozambique: A View from Gaza Province," *Canadian Journal of African Studies*, 26, 3 (1992), 462–85.

"Mozambique Unravels? The Retreat to Tradition," *Southern Africa Report* (May 1992), 27–30.

Rothchild, D. and N. Chazan, eds. *The Precarious Balance: State and Society in Africa.* Boulder, CO: Westview Press, 1988.

Róna-Tas, A. "The First Shall Be Last? Entrepreneurship and Communist Cadres in the Transition from Socialism," *American Journal of Sociology*, 100, 1 (July 1994), 40–69.

Rufino, J. dos Santos. *Albuns Fotográficos e Descritívos da Colónia de Moçambique,* Vols. 2, 10. n.p. Hamburgo, Broschek & CO. 1929.

Salstrom, B. and A. Sopa, *Catálogo dos Cartazes de Moçambique – Catalogue of Mozambican Posters.* Maputo: Arquivo Histórico de Moçambique, Universidade Eduardo Mondlane, 1988.

Saul, J. *Recolonization and Resistance in Southern Africa in the 1990s,* Trenton, NJ: Africa World Press, 1993.

Saul, J., ed. *A Difficult Road: The Transition to Socialism in Mozambique.* New York: Monthly Review Press, 1985.

Scott, C. "Socialism and the 'Soft State' in Africa: An Analysis of Angola and Mozambique," *Journal of Modern African Studies*, 26, 1 (1988), 23–36.

Scott, J. *Seeing Like a State: How Certain Schemes to Improve the Human Condition Have Failed.* New Haven, CT: Yale University Press, 1998.

Self, P. *Government by the Market? The Politics of Public Choice.* London: Macmillan, 1993.

Sheldon, K. "Sewing Clothes and Sorting Cashew Nuts: Factories, Families, and Women in Beira, Mozambique." *Women's Studies International Forum*, 14, 1/2 (1991), 27–35.

"Machambas in the City: Urban Women and Agricultural Work in Mozambique." *Lusotopie* (1999), 121–40.

Shoulberg, W. "Levi Stress." *Home Textiles Today* (8 March 1999).

Sidaway, J. and M. Power. "Sociospatial Transformations in the 'Postsocialist' Periphery: The Case of Maputo, Mozambique." *Environment and Planning A*, 27, 4 (1995), 1463–91.

Simpson, M. "Foreign and Domestic Factors in the Transformation of Frelimo." *Journal of Modern African Studies*, 31, 2 (1993), 309–37.

Sketchley, P. and F. Lappé. *Casting New Molds: First Steps Toward Worker Control in a Mozambique Steel Factory.* San Francisco, CA: Institute for Food and Development Policy, 1980.

Slater, R., B. Schutz, and S. Dorr, eds. *Global Transformation and the Third World.* Boulder, CO: Lynne Rienner, 1993.

So, A. *Social Change and Development: Modernization, Dependency and World-System Theories.* Newbury Park, CA: Sage, 1990.

Sogge, D., ed. *Moçambique: Perspectivas sobre a Ajuda e o Sector Civil.* Amsterdam: Gemeenschappelijk Overleg Medefinanciering, 1997.

Special Issue on Mozambique. *Journal of Southern African Studies*, 24, 1 (March 1998).

Spring, A. and B. McDade, eds. *African Entrepreneurship: Theory and Reality.* Gainesville, FL: University Press of Florida, 1998.

Stark, D. and L. Bruszt. *Postsocialist Pathways: Transforming Politics and Property in East Central Europe.* New York: Cambridge University Press, 1998, repr. 1999.

Streeten, P. "Markets and States: Against Minimalism." *World Development,* 21, 8 (1993), 1281–98.

Szelényi, I. *Privatizing the Land: Rural Political Economy in Post-Communist Societies.* London: Routledge, 1998.

Tangri, R. *The Politics of Patronage in Africa: Parastatals, Privatization and Private Enterprise.* Trenton, NJ: Africa World Press, 1999.

Tibana, R. "Structural Adjustment and the Manufacturing Industry in Mozambique." In J. Paulson, ed., *African Economies in Transition,* Vol. 2: *The Reform Experience.* New York: St. Martin's Press, 1999, 178–232.

Tickner, V. "Structural Adjustment and Agricultural Pricing in Mozambique." *Review of African Political Economy,* 53 (1992), 25–42.

Torp, J. *Industrial Planning and Development in Mozambique: Some Preliminary Considerations.* Scandinavian Institute of African Studies. Research Report no. 50. Uppsala: Scandinavian Institute of African Studies, 1979.

United Nations Development Program, Management Development and Governance Division, Bureau for Policy and Programme Support. *Reconceptualising Governance.* Discussion Paper 2. New York: United Nations Development Program, 1997.

Vail, L. and L. White. *Capitalism and Colonialism in Mozambique: A Study of Quelimane District.* Minneapolis: University of Minnesota Press, 1980.

Vail, L., ed. 1989. *The Creation of Tribalism in Southern Africa.* Berkeley, CA: University of California Press, 1989.

Vallely, P. "Mozambique: Will War Wreck Mozambique's IMF Recovery?" *Facts and Reports* (Amsterdam, 13 March 1987).

van de Walle, N. "The Politics of Nonreform in Cameroon." In T. Callaghy and J. Ravenhill, eds., *Hemmed In: Responses to Africa's Economic Decline.* New York: Columbia University Press, 1993, 357–97.

van den Berg, J. "A Peasant Form of Production: Wage-Dependent Agriculture in Southern Mozambique." *Canadian Journal of African Studies,* XXI, 3 (1987), 375–89.

van der Geest, W., ed. *Negotiating Structural Adjustment in Africa.* Portsmouth, NH: Heinemann, 1994.

van Nieuwaal, E. and R. van Dijk. *African Chieftaincy in a New Socio-Political Landscape.* New Brunswick, NJ: Transaction Publishers, 1999.

Verdery, K. *National Ideology Under Socialism: Identity and Cultural Politics in Ceausescu's Romania.* Berkeley, CA: University of California Press, 1991.

  *What Was Socialism and What Comes Next?* Princeton, NJ: Princeton University Press, 1996.

Verdier, I. *Mozambique – 100 Men in Power.* Paris: Indigo Publications, 1996.

Villalón, L. and P. Huxtable, eds. *The African State at a Critical Juncture: Between Disintegration and Reconfiguration.* Boulder, CO: Lynne Rienner, 1998.

Vines, A. *Renamo: Terrorism in Mozambique.* Bloomington, IN: Indiana University Press, 1991.

Vuylsteke, C. *Techniques of Privatization of State-Owned Enterprises,* Vol. I: *Methods and Implementation.* World Bank Technical Paper no. 88. Washington, DC: The World Bank, 1988.

Waterhouse, R. and C. Vijfhuizen, eds. *Estratégias das Mulheres, Proveito dos Homens: Género, Terra e Recursos Naturais em Diferentes Contextos Rurais em Moçambique*. Maputo: Universidade Eduardo Mondlane, 2001.

Weiss, L. *The Myth of the Powerless State*. Ithaca, NY: Cornell University Press, 1998.

West, H. "Creative Destruction and Sorcery of Construction." *Cahiers d'Etudes Africaines*, 147, XXXVII-3 (1997), 675–97.

"'This Neighbor is Not My Uncle!': Changing Relations of Power and Authority on the Mueda Plateau." *Journal of Southern African Studies*, 24, 1 (March 1998), 141–60.

White, O. and A. Bhatia. *Privatization in Africa*. Washington, DC: World Bank, 1998.

Widner, J. ed. *Economic Change and Political Liberalization in Sub-Saharan Africa*. Baltimore, MD: Johns Hopkins University Press, 1994.

Wield, D. "Mozambique – Late Colonialism and Early Problems of Transition." In G. White, R. Murray, and C. White, eds., *Revolutionary Socialist Development in the Third World*. Lexington, KY: University Press of Kentucky, 1983, 75–111.

Williams, G. "Taking the Part of Peasants: Rural Development in Nigeria and Tanzania." In P. Gutkind and I. Wallerstein, eds., *Political Economy of Contemporary Africa*. London: Sage, 1976, 131–54.

Wilson, K. "Cults of Violence and Counter-Violence in Mozambique." *Journal of Southern African Studies*, 18, 3 (1992), 527–82.

World Bank, *Sub-Saharan Africa: From Crisis to Sustainable Growth, A Long-Term Perspective Study*. Washington, DC: World Bank, 1989.

*Adjustment in Africa: Reforms, Results and the Road Ahead*. New York: Oxford University Press, 1994.

*World Development Report 1996: From Plan to Market*. New York: Oxford University Press, 1996.

*World Development Report, 1997: The State in a Changing World*. New York: Oxford University Press, 1997.

Regional Program on Enterprise Development, Africa Region. *Survey of Mozambican Manufacturing Firms*. Washington, DC: World Bank, 1998.

Wuyts, M. *Money and Planning for Socialist Transition: The Mozambican Experience*. Brookfield, VT: Gower Publishing, 1989.

Young, C. *Ideology and Development in Africa*. New Haven, CT: Yale University Press, 1982.

"The African Colonial State and its Political Legacy." In D. Rothchild and N. Chazan, eds., *The Precarious Balance: State and Society in Africa*. Boulder, CO: Westview Press, 1988, 3–21.

*The African Colonial State in Comparative Perspective*. New Haven, CT: Yale University Press, 1994.

Young, R. "Privatisation in Africa." *Review of African Political Economy*, 51 (July 1991), 50–62.

UNPUBLISHED THESES AND PAPERS

Abt Associates. "Structure, Conduct and Performance of the Cashew Subsector in Nampula Province." Draft. January 1998.

Alexander, J. "Land and Political Authority in Post-War Mozambique: A View from Manica Province." Land Tenure Center, University of Wisconsin-Madison. 1994.

Associação Algodoeira de Moçambique. "Preço de algodão anunciado pelo CNSP no dia 21.05.98." Letter to Minister of Agriculture and Fishing. Mimeo. 26 May 1998.

Associação Algodoeira de Moçambique. "Alternativas de compensação do diferencial entre os preços aprovados pelo governo e os propostos pelas empresas para o algodão, na campanha agricola 1997/98." 29 May 1998.

Bager, T., V. Tickner, and L. Sitoi. "Rehabilitation of the Retail Trading Network involved in Agricultural Marketing in the Five Northern Provinces of Mozambique." February 1989.

BCP. Home page. "Fusões por Incorporação." 30 November 2001. <http://www.bcp.pt>.

British-Portuguese Chamber of Commerce. "As maiores empresas de Moçambique." Mimeo. 1970.

Bruce, J. "Options for State Farm Divestiture and the Creation of Secure Tenure." Land Tenure Center, University of Wisconsin-Madison. 28 December 1989.

Carrilho, J. "Acesso e Uso de Terra para a Agricultura." 2o Seminário sobre o Estudo do Sector Agrário. Maputo. 16–20 April 1990.

Coelho, J. "Protected Villages and Communal Villages in the Mozambican Province of Tete (1968–1982)." Ph.D. dissertation, Department of Social and Economic Studies, University of Bradford. 1993.

Cooperação Suiça. "'Uma vida boa': perspectivas locais de desenvolvimento em Nametil, Mecubúri." MóZ-44. Mecubúri District, Nampula Province. April 1997.

Cravinho, J. "Modernizing Mozambique: Frelimo Ideology and the Frelimo State." Ph.D. dissertation, Oxford University. 1995.

de Brito, L. "Le Frelimo et la construction de L'etat national au Mozambique: le sens de la référence au marxisme (1962–1983)." Ph.D. dissertation, Université de Paris VIII-Vincennes. 1991.

de Vletter, F. "Privatization and Labour in Mozambique: Worker and Management Perceptions." Report prepared for the World Bank and UTRE. Mimeo (October 1996).

de Vletter, F. no title. Report prepared for the World Bank and UTRE. Mimeo. 1998.

Eichengreen, B. and R. Kohl. "The External Sector, the State and Development in Eastern Europe." Working Paper 125, Berkeley Roundtable on the International Economy. March 1998.

Forum de Concertação Social. "Desempenho da economia durante o ano de 1995: Posição do movimento sindical." Mimeo. 22 April 1996.

Gengenbach, H. "Where Women Make History: Pots, Stories, Tattoos, and Other Gendered Accounts of Community and Change in Magude District, Mozambique, C. 1800 to the Present." Ph.D. dissertation, University of Minnesota. 1999.

GIBB Africa (Pty) Ltd. "Draft Findings of the Environmental Impact Assessment for the Maputo Iron and Steel Project (MISP)." May 1998.

Guamba, J. "Reforma das orgãos locais." II Seminário sobre a reforma dos orgãos locais e o papel da autoridade tradicional. Ministério da Administração Estatal. Maputo. 19–23 April 1993.

Hibou, B. "The Political Economy of the World Bank's Discourse: From Economic Catechism to Missionary Deeds (and Misdeeds)." Les Etudes du CERI (Centre d'études et de recherches internationales), 39 (March 1998). English trans. (January 2000).

Hilmarsson, H. "Cashew Pricing and Marketing in Mozambique." World Bank Working Paper, second draft. n.d.

João Ferreira dos Santos. "Brief Presentation of João Ferreira dos Santos Group." Mimeo.

José de Mello. Home page. 30 November 2001. <http://www.josedemello.pt>.

Kloeck-Jenson, S. "Análise do Debate Parlamentar e da Nova Lei Nacional de Terras para Moçambique." Land Tenure Center-Mozambique. September 1997.

"A Brief Analysis of the Forestry Sector in Mozambique with a Focus on Zambezia Province." Land Tenure Center Project-Mozambique. Draft. 22 December, 1998.

Langa, C. "A actividade do Banco Nacional Ultramarino em Moçambique 1864–1974". Banco de Moçambique. Staff Paper no. 8. June 1997.

Leite, J. "A guerra do caju e as relações Moçambique-India na epoca pós-colonial," Documentos de Trabalho no. 57, CEsA (Lisbon, 1999).

Machado, P. "'Without Scales and Balances': Indian Merchant Capital in Mozambique, c. 1770–1830." 1997.

Manning, C. "Democratic Transition in Mozambique, 1992–1995: Beginning at the End?" Ph.D. dissertation, University of California, Berkeley. 1997.

"The Maputo Development Corridor." Mimeo. January 1998.

Metselaar, L., R. Gonçalves, O. Baloi and F. Maiopue, "Relatório da missão de levantamento de dados nos distritos de Malema, Lalaua, Ribaué e Murrupula na Província de Nampula." Maputo. March 1994.

Mole, P. "An Economic Analysis of Smallholder Cashew Development Opportunities and Linkages to Food Security in Mozambique's Northern Province of Nampula." Ph.D. dissertation, Michigan State University. 2000.

Myers, G. and H. West, "Land Tenure Security and State Farm Divestiture in Mozambique: Case Studies in Nhamatanda, Manica, and Montepuez Districts." Land Tenure Center (LTC) Research Paper 110, LTC, University of Wisconsin-Madison. January 1993.

Myers, G., H. West and J. Eliseu, "Appendices to Land Tenure Security and State Farm Divestiture in Mozambique: Case Studies in Nhamatanda, Manica and Montepuez Districts." LTC, University of Wisconsin-Madison. January 1993.

Myers, G., J. Eliseu, and E. Nhachungue, "Segurança e conflito em Moçambique: estudos de caso sobre acesso á terra no período do pós-guerra." LTC, University of Wisconsin and Ministry of Agriculture. December 1993.

"Principais grupos financeiros e industriais de Portugal." Mimeo., n.d.

Roesch, O. "Socialism and Rural Development in Mozambique: The Case of Aldeia Comunal 24 de Julho." Ph.D. dissertation, University of Toronto. 1986.

Sheldon, K. "Working Women in Beira, Mozambique." Ph.D. dissertation, University of California, Los Angeles. 1988.

Sociedade agrícola do Madal, SARL *Relatório*. 1979–1987.

SODAN. "Fomento Algodoeiro – Posição em 14.5.94." Mimeo.

"Plano Necessidade de sacaria, campanha 93/94." All agencies. Mimeos.

Tanner, C., G. Myers, R. Oad, J. Eliseu, and E. Macamo. "State Farm Divestiture in Mozambique: Property Disputes and Issues Affecting New Land Access Policy – The Case of Chokwe, Gaza Province." University of Wisconsin-Madison LTC report prepared for USAID-Maputo and the Government of the Republic of Mozambique, Ministry of Agriculture. May 1992.

Tarp, F. "Agrarian Transformation in Mozambique." n.d.

Taylor, M. "Spirits of Capitalism in Chokwe: Experiences of Work and Identity among Shangaan Peasants in Southern Mozambique." Ph.D. dissertation, Brandeis University. May 1998.

Telecomunicações de Moçambique. Annual Report. 1996, 1998–1999.

Texmoque-Textil de Moçambique, SARL *Relatório.* 1980.

Textáfrica. *Relatório.* 1980.

Universidade Eduardo Mondlane, (UEM) Centro de Estudos Africanos (CEA). "A actuação do estado ao nível do distrito: o caso de Lugela." Relatório 81/9. 1981.

"Plantações de Chá e Economia Camponesa." Projecto da Emochá: Relatório (A). 1982.

"O Papel Dinamizador da Emochá na Transformação Socialista da Alta Zambézia," Projecto da Emochá: Relatório (B). 1982.

"A Transformação da Agricultura Familiar na Província de Nampula." CEA Relatório no. 80/3, 1980. Reprint 1986.

Vines, A. " 'No democracy without money': the road to peace in Mozambique (1982–1992)." Catholic Institute for International Relations briefing paper. April 1994.

West, H. "Sorcery of Construction and Sorcery of Ruin: Power and Ambivalence on the Mueda Plateau, Mozambique (1882–1994)". Ph.D. dissertation, University of Wisconsin-Madison. 1997.

World Bank. "Mozambique." December 2000. <http://www.worldbank.org/afr/mz2.html>.

"Mozambique Country Economic Memorandum: Growth Prospects and Reform Agenda." Report no. 20601-MZ. 7 February 2001.

Southern Africa Department, Macro, Industry, and Finance Division. "Mozambique: Impediments to Industrial Sector Recovery." Mimeo. 15 February 1995.

World Bank and the Government of Mozambique. "Mozambique: Evaluating the Impact and Effectiveness of the Enterprise Restructuring Program." Confidential Preliminary Discussion Draft. Mimeo. 22 July 1996.

# Index

OTHER BOOKS IN THE SERIES

For EU product safety concerns, contact us at Calle de José Abascal, 56–1°,
28003 Madrid, Spain or eugpsr@cambridge.org.

www.ingramcontent.com/pod-product-compliance
Ingram Content Group UK Ltd.
Pitfield, Milton Keynes, MK11 3LW, UK
UKHW042152130625
459647UK00011B/1293